D1277461

Mike Meyers' CompTIA Network+® Guide to Managing and Troubleshooting Networks Lab Manual, Third Edition

(Exam N10-005)

About the Authors

Michael Meyers is the industry's leading authority on CompTIA Network+ certification. He is the president and founder of Total Seminars, LLC, a major provider of PC and network repair seminars for thousands of organizations throughout the world, and a member of CompTIA.

Mike has written numerous popular textbooks, including the best-selling *Mike Meyers' CompTIA A+® Guide to Managing and Troubleshooting PCs* and the *Mike Meyers' CompTIA Network+® Guide to Managing and Troubleshooting Networks*.

Dennis Haley (BSEET, MCSE, MCSA, MCTS, MCT, CompTIA Network+, CompTIA A+) is the administrator and teacher for the CompTIA Authorized Academy Partner program and the Microsoft IT Academy program at POLYTECH Technical High School in Woodside, Delaware. Dennis has worked in the Information Technology industry for more than 25 years (General Instrument Corporation, OKIDATA, and Computer Networking Technologies) and has spent more than half of that time as a technical instructor. Dennis has co-authored multiple CompTIA A+ and CompTIA Network+ Lab Manuals with Mike Meyers, all published by McGraw-Hill. When Dennis is not immersed in computer/networking technology, writing and developing curriculum, or teaching, he spends some downtime composing and performing electronic music and honing his skills as an audio engineer.

About the Technical Editor

Jonathan S. Weissman earned his master's degree in Computer and Information Science from Brooklyn College (CUNY), and holds nineteen industry certifications, including Cisco CCNA, CompTIA Security+, CompTIA i-Net+, CompTIA Network+, CompTIA A+, CompTIA Linux+, Novell CNE, Novell CNA, Microsoft Office Master, Microsoft MCAS Word, Microsoft MCAS PowerPoint, Microsoft MCAS Excel, Microsoft MCAS Access, Microsoft MCAS Outlook, and Microsoft MCAS Vista.

Jonathan is a tenured Assistant Professor of Computing Sciences at Finger Lakes Community College, in Canandaigua, New York, and also teaches graduate and undergraduate Computer Science courses at nearby Rochester Institute of Technology. In addition, Jonathan does computer, network, and security consulting for area businesses and individuals. Between FLCC and RIT, Jonathan has taught nearly two dozen different Computer Science courses, including networking, security, administration, forensics, programming, operating systems, hardware, and software.

Mike Meyers' CompTIA Network+® Guide to Managing and Troubleshooting Networks Lab Manual, Third Edition

(Exam N10-005)

Mike Meyers
Dennis Haley

New York   Chicago   San Francisco
Lisbon   London   Madrid   Mexico City
Milan   New Delhi   San Juan
Seoul   Singapore   Sydney   Toronto

The McGraw·Hill Companies

Library of Congress Cataloging-in-Publication Data

Meyers, Michael, 1961-
     Mike Meyers' CompTIA network+ guide to managing and troubleshooting networks lab manual /
Mike Meyers, Dennis Haley.
         p.   cm.
     ISBN 978-0-07-178883-0 (alk. paper)
     1. Computer networks—Examinations—Study guides.   2. Telecommunications engineers—Certification.
     3. Electronic data processing personnel—Certification.   I. Haley, Dennis.   II. Title.   III. Title: CompTIA
network+.
     TK5105.5.M4842   2012
     004.6076—dc23   2012006526

McGraw-Hill books are available at special quantity discounts to use as premiums and sales promotions, or for use in
corporate training programs. To contact a representative, please e-mail us at bulksales@mcgraw-hill.com.

**Mike Meyers' CompTIA Network+® Guide to Managing and
Troubleshooting Networks Lab Manual, Third Edition (Exam N10-005)**

Copyright © 2012 by The McGraw-Hill Companies. All rights reserved. Printed in the United States of America. Except
as permitted under the Copyright Act of 1976, no part of this publication may be reproduced or distributed in any form
or by any means, or stored in a database or retrieval system, without the prior written permission of publisher, with the
exception that the program listings may be entered, stored, and executed in a computer system, but they may not be
reproduced for publication.

All trademarks or copyrights mentioned herein are the possession of their respective owners and McGraw-Hill makes no
claim of ownership by the mention of products that contain these marks.

     34567890   QDB QDB   0198765432

ISBN   978-0-07-178883-0
MHID   0-07-178883-2

Sponsoring Editor
   Tim Green

Editorial Supervisor
   Jody McKenzie

Project Manager
   Sheena Uprety,
   Cenveo Publisher Services

Acquisitions Coordinator
   Stephanie Evans

Technical Editor
   Jonathan Weissman

Copy Editor
   Margaret Bersen

Proofreader
   Paul Tyler

Indexer
   Jack Lewis

Production Supervisor
   Jim Kussow

Composition
   Cenveo Publisher Services

Illustration
   Cenveo Publisher Services

Art Director, Cover
   Jeff Weeks

Information has been obtained by McGraw-Hill from sources believed to be reliable. However, because of the possibility of human or mechanical error by
our sources, McGraw-Hill, or others, McGraw-Hill does not guarantee the accuracy, adequacy, or completeness of any information and is not responsible
for any errors or omissions or the results obtained from the use of such information.

McGraw-Hill is an independent entity from CompTIA. This publication may be used in assisting students to prepare for the CompTIA Network+ exam
N10-005. Neither CompTIA nor McGraw-Hill warrants that use of this publication will ensure passing any exam. CompTIA and CompTIA Network+ are
registered trademarks of CompTIA in the United States and/or other countries.

This book is dedicated to Theresa for her support, tolerance, and love; to my family and friends for their understanding; and to my students, past, present, and future. You inspire me to do my best!

—Dennis Haley

Contents

Acknowledgements

Many great people worked together to make this book happen.

As our sponsoring editor at McGraw-Hill, Tim Green set the entire book in motion and stayed the helm as the guiding hand. Thanks, Tim!

At Total Seminars, Dudley Lehmer was a great CEO, creating an environment for getting projects done. Scott Jernigan performed his usual magic as Editor in Chief. Ford Pierson, Aaron Verber, and Michael Smyer assisted with photographs, illustrations, and as technical sounding boards. Thanks also with help on copy edits and page proofs.

Our technical editor, Jonathan Weissman, did a great job, catching anything not precisely accurate and holding our feet to the fire.

On the McGraw-Hill side, our acquisitions coordinator, Stephanie Evans, and our editorial supervisor, Jody McKenzie, helped us keep it all on track.

Sheena Uprety, our Project Manager, did an outstanding job managing this book through the many phases of development. It was great to work with you and your team at Cenveo Publisher Services. Thanks!

To the copy editor, Margaret Berson, and the proofreader, Paul Tyler—thank you for your excellent work!

Finally, Tim Basher, Jesse King, Max Kerkula, and Cathy Roselli provided excellent feedback on ideas and projects that work in the real world. You're the best! Thanks!

Additional Resources for Teachers

The answer keys to the lab manual activities in this book are provided along with resources for teachers using *Mike Meyers' CompTIA Network+ Guide to Managing and Troubleshooting Networks, Third Edition (Exam N10-005)*. The answer keys are available on the McGraw-Hill Connect Online Learning Center that supports the textbook and the lab manual. Please visit: www.meyersnetplus.com.

McGraw-Hill Connect, a Web-based learning platform, connects instructors with their support materials. The Connect Online Learning Center provides resources for teachers in a format that follows the organization of the textbook.

This site includes the following:

- Answer keys to the Mike Meyers' Lab Manual activities

Instructors who have adopted the *Mike Meyers' CompTIA Network+ Guide to Managing and Troubleshooting Networks, Third Edition (Exam N10-005)* textbook (available separately) can also access:

- Answer keys to the end-of-chapter activities in the textbook

- Instructor's Manual that contains learning objectives, classroom preparation notes, instructor tips, and a lecture outline for each chapter

- Access to test bank files and software that allows you to generate a wide array of paper- or network-based tests, and that features automatic grading. The test bank includes:

    - Hundreds of practice questions and a wide variety of question types categorized by exam objective, enabling you to customize each test to maximize student progress

    - Test bank files available on EZ Test Online and as downloads from the Online Learning Center in these formats: Blackboard, Web CT, EZ Test, and Word

- Engaging PowerPoint slides on the lecture topics that include full-color artwork from the book

Please contact your McGraw-Hill sales representative for details.

Chapter 1

CompTIA Network+ in a Nutshell

Lab Exercises

Congratulations! You have decided to tackle the prestigious CompTIA Network+ certification. Whether you are a seasoned network engineer pursuing certification to further your career, or a relative novice building your fundamental skills in networking, you're in the right place. The fact that you've got the *Mike Meyers' CompTIA Network+® Guide to Managing and Troubleshooting Networks* textbook and this Lab Manual in your hands shows that you're serious about earning that certification. That's a smart move!

As discussed in the textbook, the term *networking* describes a vast field of study, far too large for any single certification book, training course, or for that matter, lab manual to cover. However, armed with the textbook and this Lab Manual, you have the tools not only to pass the certification exam, but also to exercise the skills you will need to develop and grow as a networking professional. Ask any veteran network tech, and they will tell you that the key to being a good tech is working through the installation, configuration, management, and troubleshooting of network devices, cabling, protocols, and applications. That's where this lab manual is invaluable. It will take you through hands-on exercises with cabling, switches, routers, and servers. You'll configure protocols and services such as TCP/IP, DNS, DHCP, QoS, VPNs, and many more. If some of these abbreviations are new to you, don't worry; you will learn them all!

Another skill required by network techs is the ability to find information regarding network devices, protocols, and applications and their interoperability quickly and efficiently. Many times when you run into problems, it's not necessarily a failure of one specific device, protocol, or application but a combination of the configuration parameters and interaction between those devices, protocols, and applications. Many of the labs will have you practice the art of researching information on these devices, protocols, and services as if your job depended on it. It just might!

To help you grasp these networking concepts, the following scenario is used throughout this Lab Manual. You are a newly hired desktop support specialist in a mid-sized IT consulting firm, ITCF. ITCF has clients of all sizes scattered all over the country. Client networks can be as small as a single insurance office with 15 computers to a financial institution with 1500 computers and dozens of servers.

You are CompTIA A+ certified, but are immediately encouraged to pursue the CompTIA Network+ certification. Maggie, one of the network technicians in the department, offers to mentor you. She believes that achieving the CompTIA Network+ certification will strengthen your fundamental understanding of networking and will really help when communicating with both customers and your new boss, CJ. You respect her advice and dive right in to a CompTIA Network+ training course—this course!

This chapter will show you how to prepare for the Network+ exam, while the labs will take you through the steps needed to start studying for it. First, you'll make certain that you understand the important details of the certification itself. Next, you'll look at how Network+ applies toward other IT industry certifications. Then you'll formulate a study plan. Finally, you'll schedule your Network+ exam. Ladies and gentlemen, start your engines!

 45 MINUTES

Lab Exercise 1.01: Exploring the Network+ Requirements

The CompTIA Network+ certification is an industry-wide, vendor-neutral certification qualifying a tech's basic skills in supporting networks, and knowledge of networking concepts. Network+ is to network techs what A+ is to PC techs: a valuable credential assuring clients and employers that you possess the aptitude and specific technical skills to implement and maintain computer networks on a variety of hardware and software platforms. To achieve this certification, you must pass the Network+ exam at an approved exam administration center. The CompTIA Network+ certification requires just a single exam, unlike the CompTIA A+ certification, which requires you to pass two exams: the CompTIA A+ Essentials exam (currently 220–701) and the Practical Application exam (currently 220–702). The Network+ (N10-005) certification exam is defined by a documented list of exam objectives separated into domains. Each domain counts toward a percentage of the exam's total scoring. These domains are organized into five categories: Network Technologies, Network Installation and Configuration, Network Media and Topologies, Network Management, and Network Security.

The domains are divided fairly evenly with Network Technologies weighted at 21 percent; Network Installation and Configuration weighted at 23 percent (the highest percentage); Network Media and Topologies weighted at 17 percent; Network Management weighted at 20 percent; and Network Security comes in at 19 percent, to add up to 100 percent. It's important to understand what's required to pass the Network+ exam, so you should become familiar with the exam objectives. Detailed Network+ objectives may be downloaded from the CompTIA Web site.

Learning Objectives

In this lab, you will visit the CompTIA Web site to download the latest Network+ exam objectives. By the end of this lab, you will be able to

- Define the objectives being tested on the Network+ exam

Lab Materials and Setup

The only requirements for this lab are a PC, Internet access, a pencil or pen, and some paper.

Getting Down to Business

Many techs pursue certifications to validate their current skill set or to advance their careers. The Network+ certification not only meets these criteria; it also provides the candidate (you) with an excellent foundation in networking and serves as a stepping-stone to more specialized certifications.

To develop your understanding of the Network+ exam requirements, domains, and objectives, complete the following steps:

Step 1   Launch your Web browser and head over to the CompTIA Web site, www.comptia.org. Follow the links (currently Certifications & Exams | CompTIA Certifications | CompTIA Network+ | Training & Testing | Exam Objectives) to download the Network+ objectives as a PDF file. Web sites change often, so you may have to enter different information than at the time of this writing. Currently you must enter your name, e-mail address, and country before you can download the Network+ objectives.

Step 2   Summarize the Network+ exam objective domain 1.0, Network Technologies.

_____

_____

Step 3   Summarize the Network+ exam objective domain 2.0, Network Installation and Configuration.

_____

_____

Step 4   Summarize the Network+ exam objective domain 3.0, Network Media and Topologies.

_____

_____

Step 5   Summarize the Network+ exam objective domain 4.0, Network Management.

_____

_____

Step 6   Summarize the Network+ exam objective domain 5.0, Network Security.

_____

_____

_____

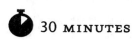 30 MINUTES

Lab Exercise 1.02: The Next Step: Related Certifications

In addition to the value of the Network+ certification itself, the IT industry recognizes that the skill sets defined by the Network+ objective domains provide an excellent foundation for the pursuit of other established IT certifications. The Network+ certification can be a great foundation, leading to some of the certifications offered by Microsoft and Cisco.

Because of the broad base of networking skills that it covers, the Network+ certification will also give you a leg up on other IT certifications in the areas of network administration, server management, and cyber security.

Learning Objectives

In this lab, you'll explore the benefits of Network+ certification as it applies toward further IT industry certifications.

At the end of this lab, you will

- List the IT certifications toward which CompTIA Network+ provides an excellent foundation.

- Map out your own certification path beyond Network+.

Lab Materials and Setup

The only requirements for this lab are a PC, Internet access, a pencil or pen, and some paper.

Getting Down to Business

The CompTIA Network+ certification is vendor-neutral. This means that the broad skill base encompassed by Network+ can be used to launch further, specialized certifications with IT vendors such as Microsoft and Cisco.

Step 1   Navigate over to the CompTIA certification roadmap and Career Pathways Web site at http://certification.comptia.org/certroadmap.aspx. CompTIA has done a nice job with the active controls on this tool, allowing you to display or hide the various CompTIA and vendor-specific certifications that fill in the roadmap. Which other IT certifications build off the CompTIA Network+ certification? What are some of the career directions you could apply the CompTIA Network+ certification toward?

_____

_____

Step 2   While at the CompTIA certification site, click on the **Get Certified** tab in the upper left-hand corner and explore some of the other certifications offered by CompTIA. Which of these do you think might build on some of the skills you develop while preparing for the CompTIA Network+ certification?

_____

_____

Step 3   Visit Microsoft's certification Web site at www.microsoft.com/learning/en/us/certification/cert-overview.aspx and explore the requirements for the various Microsoft certifications. How do you think the Network+ certification will benefit an IT tech pursuing these certifications?

_____

_____

Step 4   Now explore some of the organizations offering certifications on Linux at http://gocertify.com/faq/linuxfaq.shtml. How do you think the Network+ certification might benefit an IT tech pursuing these certifications?

_____

_____

Step 5   Next, surf over to Cisco certifications at www.cisco.com/web/learning/le3/learning_career_certifications_and_learning_paths_home.html and explore the various paths to become a Cisco certified professional. How do you think the Network+ certification might benefit an IT tech pursuing these certifications?

_____

_____

Step 6   Now that you've seen the more common certifications that relate to Network+, what do you think will be a natural certification progression for you?

_____

_____

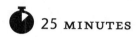 25 MINUTES

Lab Exercise 1.03: Study Preparation

If you take a look at the certification blogs, I'm sure you will find candidates claiming to have passed some certification exam or other with little or no preparation. Though everybody is different, even seasoned network techs have to spend some time on areas that they are less familiar with to be successful on the Network+ exam. The CompTIA Network+ exam is a thorough test of your understanding of a broad range of networking topics and concepts. As such, it can be very challenging. No matter how much networking experience and skill you possess, it is highly recommended that you develop a strong preparation plan to maximize your chance of passing the exam the first time.

With that in mind, your next step is to come up with a plan of attack for the Network+ exam. Preparation is the key, so start by identifying what you need to study and how to go about studying.

Learning Objectives

In this lab, you will develop your plan of action for preparing for the Network+ exam. To do this you need to deal with two issues: determining which topics you need to study the most and checking your study habits.

At the end of this lab, you will

- Identify the Network+ topics you need to spend the most time on
- Develop a study plan

Lab Materials and Setup

The only requirements needed for this lab are a PC, Internet access, a pencil or pen, and some paper.

Getting Down to Business

The instructors of Total Seminars have taught the Network+ certification for years and have helped thousands of techs achieve their CompTIA Network+ certification. Incorporating this experience, we have developed a handy template to give students some idea of what they need to study and how much time they need to devote to preparing for the Network+ exam. This template is essentially the same one that appears in the *Mike Meyers' CompTIA Network+® Guide to Managing and Troubleshooting Networks* textbook, except that here we have added an extra step to help you determine which topics you need to study.

Step 1   Look at each of the listed skills and circle the corresponding number of study hours for that skill based on the amount of experience you have. Either you have no experience with it, or you have performed that skill once or twice, a few times, or quite a bit.

Type of Experience	Amount of Experience			
	None	Once or Twice	A Few Times	Quite a Bit
Installing a SOHO wireless network	4	2	1	1
Installing an advanced wireless network (such as 802.1x, RADIUS)	2	2	1	1
Installing structured cabling	3	2	1	1
Configuring a home router	5	3	2	1
Configuring a Cisco router	4	2	1	1
Configuring a software firewall	3	2	1	1
Configuring a hardware firewall	2	2	1	1
Configuring an IPv4 client	8	4	2	1
Configuring an IPv6 client	3	3	2	1
Working with SOHO WAN connection (DSL, cable)	2	2	1	0
Working with advanced WAN connection (Tx, OCx, ATM)	3	3	2	2
Configuring a DNS server	2	2	2	1
Configuring a DHCP server	2	1	1	0
Configuring a Web application server (HTTP, FTP, SSH)	4	4	2	1
Configuring a VLAN	3	3	2	1
Configuring a VPN	3	3	2	1
Configuring a dynamic routing protocol	2	2	1	1

Now that you've got a feel for the topics that you need to concentrate on, determine your total study time. Add up all of the hours you circled in the previous table to get your base study time. Take that base time and use the following table to calculate the additional hours you'll need to study relative to your work experience.

Months of Direct, Professional Experience...	To Your Study Time...
0	Add 60 hrs
Up to 6	Add 30 hrs
6 to 9	Add 10 hrs
Over 9	Add 0 hrs

What is the estimate for the total number of hours you will need to study for the CompTIA Network+ certification exam?

_____

Step 2   Now that you know what topics are important to you and how much time they will take, you need to develop your study plan. First of all, take the amount of time you've set aside and determine how many days you will need to prepare. Consider work, holidays, weekends—anything that will affect your study time. (If you're in an instructor-led course, this is easy. Just use the duration of the course.) Then break down your textbook into manageable chunks. (Again, if you're in a course, your instructor will certainly already have done this for you.) You now have your deadline—the day that you will say you're ready to take the test!

What is your deadline for taking the Network+ exam?

_____

 15 MINUTES

Lab Exercise 1.04: Scheduling the Network+ Exam

Schedule your exam with one of the approved exam administration centers, Prometric or Pearson VUE. Don't put this off—do it now! Get it out of the way so that you'll feel you're working toward a deadline.

Learning Objectives

In this lab, you'll learn how to schedule your Network+ exam with an approved exam administration center.

At the end of this lab, you will be able to

- Schedule your Network+ exam with an approved test administration center

Lab Materials and Setup

The materials you need for this lab are

- A PC with Internet access, or a telephone
- Payment method (credit card or voucher number)

Getting Down to Business

There are a lot of very qualified, yet uncertified, techs out there in the IT world. Many of them have even gone through the training courses to get certified, only to postpone (sometimes permanently) taking the certification exam. To paraphrase Steve Jobs, real techs certify. Sure, some people scoff and say that certifications are just pieces of paper, but even competent, seasoned techs will tell you that certifications have only helped their careers.

Take the plunge! Schedule your exam for the CompTIA Network+ exam right now.

Step 1   You can register online for Prometric exams at www.register.prometric.com/menu.asp. Pearson VUE's online exam registration is at www.vue.com/comptia/. You can also register the old-fashioned way by calling them on the telephone. In the United States and Canada, call Prometric at (888) 895–6116 or Pearson VUE at (877) 551–7587 to locate the nearest testing center and schedule the exam. You'll also find toll-free numbers for test centers on the respective testing organizations' Web sites. Prometric's phone numbers are at www.prometric.com/CompTIA/default.htm. Pearson VUE's toll-free telephone numbers are at www.vue.com/contact/vuephone/. Make sure you have a method of payment (credit card or voucher number) and some form of identification (driver's license).

Here's some great news: You don't have to pay full price for your Network+ exam! Virtually every organization that provides Network+ training and testing also offers discount vouchers. In a nutshell, you pay a CompTIA member a discounted price, and in return you get a unique number that you provide instead of a credit card number when you schedule your exam. One provider of Network+ vouchers is Total Seminars. You can call Total Seminars toll-free from the United States or Canada at (800) 446-6004, or check the Web site: www.totalsem.com. If you don't buy your voucher from us, for goodness' sake, buy one from some other organization.

When are you scheduled to sit for the CompTIA Network+ exam?

✖ Cross-Reference

For details on taking the Network+ test, go to the CompTIA Web site (www.comptia.org).

Lab Analysis

1. You are interviewing for a network support position at a large business organization. The human resources officer isn't familiar with the CompTIA Network+ certification. Can you briefly summarize the value of the Network+ certification for her?

    _____

    _____

2. Preparing for and passing the Network+ certification exam demonstrates that you have built a strong foundation in networking concepts and technologies. What might you list as your next step in certification?

    _____

    _____

3. The TCP/IP suite has become the de facto standard for networking protocols. Joshua is studying with you and while exploring the CompTIA Network+ domain Network Technologies, he notices a long list of networking protocols. What are some of the protocols included in the TCP/IP suite?

    _____

    _____

4. Megan is also studying with you and has been reviewing the CompTIA Network+ Certification Exam Objectives. She recognizes some of the network topologies that were covered on the CompTIA A+ Certification Exam. What are some of the network topologies you should be familiar with?

    _____

    _____

5. Matthew notices that under the domain 4.0 Network Management, various network appliances are mentioned. What is a network appliance?

    _____

    _____

Key Term Quiz

Use the vocabulary terms from the list below to complete the sentences that follow. Not all of the terms will be used.

approved exam administration center	MCSE
CCENT	MCTS
Cisco	Microsoft
CompTIA	Network+
CompTIA Network+	objective domains
CompTIA Security+	Pearson VUE
MCP	Prometric
MCSA	

1. _____ is the organization that offers the Network+ certification.

2. The Network+ certification has a total of five _____, including Network Technologies, Network Installation and Configuration, Network Media and Topologies, Network Management, and Network Security.

3. After achieving the Network+ certification, you might consider working toward _____, _____ and _____ advanced certifications.

4. Your Network+ exam must be taken at a(n) _____.

5. _____ and _____ are the two organizations that administer the Network+ exam.

Chapter 2
Network Models

Lab Exercises

In the early 1970s the Department of Defense (DOD) developed a network model that the military, government agencies, and large educational organizations could use to enable their mainframe computers to communicate and share information. This model, then referred to as the *DOD model*, now refined and more commonly referred to as the *TCP/IP model*, is rising in popularity once again.

Around 1984, the International Organization for Standardization (ISO, derived from the Greek word *isos* meaning "equal") developed the Open Systems Interconnect model (OSI model). That's right, the ISO OSI model! This model provided a multiprotocol, prescriptive template for network hardware manufacturers and network software developers to use so that products from different manufacturers and developers would work together. This template, the OSI seven-layer model, is still in use today.

As you study to pass the CompTIA Network+ exam and work to be a better network tech, you should develop an understanding of both the TCP/IP model and the OSI model.

Delivering data across a network is a process both elegant in its simplicity and mind-boggling in its complexity. For one thing, data files don't move across the network intact. Instead, computers break any kind of data transfer into smaller chunks, and then package, address, and send those chunks across the network. This applies to any kind of data, whether you browse the Web, copy files to a co-worker's computer, or stream music across the Internet (legally, of course). Computers on the receiving end reassemble all the pieces upon receipt. Every computer network— regardless of the operating system, protocols, or network media—works this way.

To appreciate the process and define the process using the TCP/IP and OSI models, you have to understand a few important things. First, you should understand what kind of hardware and software a computer needs to connect to a network. You also need to know how a computer sends and retrieves data using a network. Finally, you need to understand the rules that govern the structure of Ethernet networks and how data moves across these networks. In this lab, I'll talk about these concepts, applying examples of the activity taking place at the various layers of the TCP/IP and OSI models, to help you develop a greater understanding of the big networking picture.

There's no time like the present to get started!

 15 MINUTES

Lab Exercise 2.01: Exploring Network Hardware

In the OSI model, the Physical, Data Link, and Network layers define the operation of network hardware. Cabling and hubs work at the Physical layer. The Data Link layer, split into the sublayers of Logical Link Control (LLC) and Media Access Control (MAC), is where the physical address comes into play. The various devices that utilize the physical address, such as network interface cards (NICs) and switches, function at this layer, Layer 2. *Ethernet* defines all Layer 1 and 2 aspects of wired networks today. The Network layer handles logical addressing and routing. Routers work at Layer 3.

The Link layer in the TCP/IP model encompasses the technologies at Layers 1 and 2 in the OSI model. (The Link layer is also called the *Network Interface* layer.) The Internet layer in the TCP/IP model compares to OSI Layer 3. Figure 2-1 maps the OSI model layers to the TCP/IP model layers.

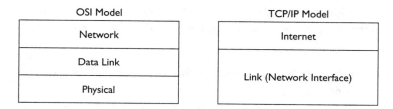

FIGURE 2-1 Mapping of OSI model layers 1, 2, 3 to TCP/IP model layers 1 and 2

Network connectivity starts with the network connection—the physical link between the PC and the network media. A good network tech can quickly locate and identify the network cabling and network hardware installed on a PC and determine the PC's state of connectivity. The tech should also be able to identify the protocols used by the PC to communicate on the network, as well as the PC's unique network identification and address. You're about to take a look at the steps accomplishing these goals.

Learning Objectives

In this lab exercise, you'll explore the hardware and software components of a networked PC. At the end of this exercise, you'll be able to

- Identify the network interface, network cabling, and network connectors
- Determine which protocols the PC uses
- Record the PC's MAC and network addresses

Lab Materials and Setup

The materials you need for this lab are

- A Windows XP, Windows Vista, or Windows 7 PC with a network interface card (NIC)
- A network cable
- A network hub (optional)
- A network switch (optional)
- A network router (optional)

Getting Down to Business

Your employer, ITCF, has three locations in the tri-state area. All of the offices have multiple computers, servers, and printers, all connected via the local area network (LAN) in each office. The offices can communicate with each other and the outside world via the Internet.

When you speak with Maggie, she recommends that you start your study by examining the home office's network connections, devices, and addressing. She asks if you have learned about the OSI or TCP/IP models yet and adds that you might want to define at which layers the various devices, protocols, and addresses belong.

Step 1   Locate the network interface of your computer. On newer machines, this interface will probably be integrated into the motherboard. Older machines may have a physical network interface card (NIC) installed in a PCI or PCI Express slot. What type of network interface does your PC have? At what layer of the OSI model does the NIC operate? At what layer of the TCP/IP model does the NIC operate?

_____

_____

Step 2   Identify the type of network cabling and network connector that plugs into the network interface. At what layer of the OSI model do cabling and connectors operate? At what layer of the TCP/IP model do cabling and connectors operate?

_____

_____

Step 3   Identify the network protocols installed on the PC. Open your **Local Area Connection Properties** dialog box. On a Windows 7 system, click the **network status** icon in the system tray (notification area), now click the **Open Network and Sharing Center**, and then click **Change Adapter Settings**. Lastly, right-click the **Local Area Connection** icon and select the **Properties** menu item. You should see a screen similar to Figure 2-2.

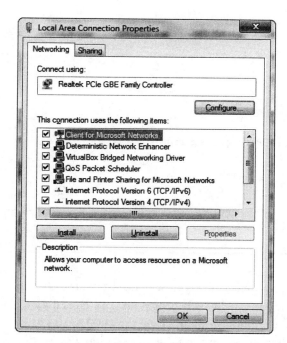

FIGURE 2-2 Windows 7 Local Area Connections properties sheet

What items are listed in the **This connection uses the following items:** section on the **General** properties sheet?

_____

_____

Step 4   Highlight the **Internet Protocol Version 4 (TCP/IPv4)** item and click the **Properties** button. See Figure 2-3.

FIGURE 2-3 Windows 7 Internet Protocol Version 4 (TCP/IPv4) properties sheet

How is the protocol assigned to receive an address?

_____

_____

Step 5   If the PC is configured to obtain an IP address automatically, you will need to determine the IP address using a different utility. Click **Start**, and then in the **Search programs and files** dialog box, type **CMD** and press the ENTER key. This will bring up a command prompt. Type the **IPCONFIG /ALL** command at the command prompt and press ENTER. Note the following: the Ethernet adapter Description, Physical Address (MAC address), and IPv4 Address. My system's information is shown in Figure 2-4.

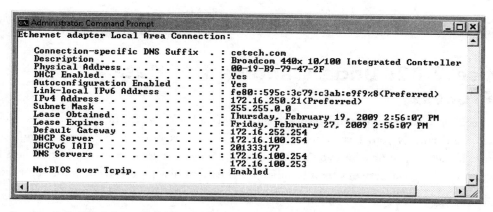

Figure 2-4 Partial results of running the IPCONFIG /ALL utility

What layers of the OSI model are these components associated with? How about the TCP/IP model?

_____

_____

Step 6   Optionally, determine how the PCs on your network connect to each other. If a hub is used, at what layer of the OSI model and the TCP/IP model does it operate?

_____

_____

If a switch is used, at what layer of the OSI model and the TCP/IP model does it operate?

_____

_____

Step 7   Optionally, how does your network connect to the outside world? If a router is used, at what layer of the OSI model and the TCP/IP model does it operate?

_____

_____

 30 MINUTES

Lab Exercise 2.02: Understanding the Data Delivery Process

Often the network tech's role as installer and administrator takes a back seat to the tech's role as educator. Many clients, and certainly your bosses, want to know what you're doing when they see you stringing cables from hither to yon or when you're gazing at some obscure-looking string of numbers in a command-line window. The good network tech is able to explain not just practical, nuts-and-bolts configuration tasks but also the "fuzzier" conceptual topics that describe the functions of a network.

Learning Objectives

In this lab, you'll examine the process of data delivery on a network. You will also identify the components involved in transferring data between two computers on a network. At the end of this lab, you will be able to

- Identify the parts of a frame
- Examine the process of packet delivery
- List the number of active sessions on a computer

Lab Materials and Setup

- Pencil and paper
- A Windows XP, Windows Vista, or Windows 7 PC with network access

Getting Down to Business

You've examined your office and determined that most of the PCs and physical offices are fairly up to date. Most of the devices are connected through 100BaseT or 1000BaseT interfaces over CAT 5e UTP cabling and 3Com 1000BaseT switches. The top-level manager of your IT department, CJ, noticing that you have spent most of your lunch hour inspecting the office connections, asks you to provide a quick explanation of how data moves from one PC to another on the network.

Step 1   List and define the parts of a generic data frame.

_____

_____

Step 2 Briefly describe the process of data delivery from one networked PC to another. Use the concept of data frames, the OSI model, and the NIC's functionality to formulate your answer. (See Figure 2-5.)

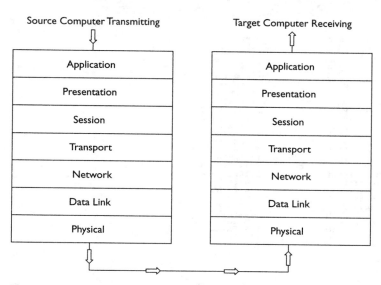

Figure 2-5 Diagram of a data frame traveling from one networked PC to another

_____

_____

Step 3 CJ is impressed with your response and introduces you to a utility that enables you to explore the connections between networked computers. To generate some network traffic, he has you launch your browser and access the CompTIA Web site. He then has you bring up a command prompt and type the following line:

```
netstat -a
```

The output should be similar to Figure 2-6.

```
Administrator: Command Prompt                                        _ □ ×
Active Connections

  Proto  Local Address            Foreign Address       State
  TCP    0.0.0.0:135              dennis-PC:0           LISTENING
  TCP    0.0.0.0:49152            dennis-PC:0           LISTENING
  TCP    0.0.0.0:49153            dennis-PC:0           LISTENING
  TCP    0.0.0.0:49154            dennis-PC:0           LISTENING
  TCP    0.0.0.0:49155            dennis-PC:0           LISTENING
  TCP    0.0.0.0:49156            dennis-PC:0           LISTENING
  TCP    0.0.0.0:49157            dennis-PC:0           LISTENING
  TCP    127.0.0.1:10080          dennis-PC:0           LISTENING
  TCP    127.0.0.1:10080          dennis-PC:51766       ESTABLISHED
  TCP    127.0.0.1:10080          dennis-PC:51768       ESTABLISHED
  TCP    127.0.0.1:13128          dennis-PC:0           LISTENING
  TCP    127.0.0.1:18080          dennis-PC:0           LISTENING
  TCP    127.0.0.1:51766          dennis-PC:10080       ESTABLISHED
  TCP    127.0.0.1:51768          dennis-PC:10080       ESTABLISHED
  TCP    172.16.250.21:139        dennis-PC:0           LISTENING
  TCP    172.16.250.21:51767      DATASERVER100:http    ESTABLISHED
  TCP    172.16.250.21:51769      DATASERVER100:http    ESTABLISHED
  TCP    [::]:135                 dennis-PC:0           LISTENING
  TCP    [::]:445                 dennis-PC:0           LISTENING
  TCP    [::]:5357                dennis-PC:0           LISTENING
  TCP    [::]:49152               dennis-PC:0           LISTENING
  TCP    [::]:49153               dennis-PC:0           LISTENING
  TCP    [::]:49154               dennis-PC:0           LISTENING
  TCP    [::]:49155               dennis-PC:0           LISTENING
  TCP    [::]:49156               dennis-PC:0           LISTENING
  TCP    [::]:49157               dennis-PC:0           LISTENING
  UDP    0.0.0.0:123              *:*
  UDP    0.0.0.0:500              *:*
  UDP    0.0.0.0:4500             *:*
  UDP    0.0.0.0:53760            *:*
  UDP    127.0.0.1:1900           *:*
  UDP    127.0.0.1:51756          *:*
  UDP    127.0.0.1:58165          *:*
  UDP    127.0.0.1:63328          *:*
  UDP    127.0.0.1:65265          *:*
  UDP    172.16.250.21:137        *:*
  UDP    172.16.250.21:138        *:*
  UDP    172.16.250.21:1900       *:*
  UDP    192.168.1.102:1900       *:*
  UDP    [::]:123                 *:*
  UDP    [::]:500                 *:*
  UDP    [::1]:1900               *:*
  UDP    [::1]:58164              *:*
  UDP    [fe80::ffff:ffff:fffe%10]:1900   *:*
  UDP    [fe80::595c:3c79:c3ab:e9f9%8]:1900   *:*
  UDP    [fe80::e81f:a27f:9952:deea%9]:1900   *:*
```

FIGURE 2-6 Output of running the netstat–a command

Don't worry about all of the data you see, but take notice of your computer name (host name) and the number of connections. How many connections are there?

_____

With which layer of the OSI model are these components associated? To what layer of the TCP/IP model do you think this corresponds?

_____

_____

 30 MINUTES

Lab Exercise 2.03: Examining the Layers of the OSI Seven-Layer Model vs. the TCP/IP Model

Given that the OSI seven-layer model's functions are largely hidden from our eyes, it's sometimes difficult to appreciate how each discrete level performs a necessary step of the data delivery process. Nonetheless, it's important for you to understand just how the OSI seven-layer model operates. Every modern network technology conforms to the OSI seven-layer model, so understanding OSI is one of the keys to understanding modern networking technology.

In addition to the OSI seven-layer model, there is the more compact TCP/IP model. This model handles the same technologies and defines the data delivery process, but maps perfectly to the TCP/IP suite of protocols.

Learning Objectives

In this lab, you'll examine the layers of the OSI seven-layer model and the TCP/IP model, and then diagram how the two models compare. When you've completed the lab, you will be able to

- Identify and define the seven layers of the OSI seven-layer model
- Identify and define the four layers of the TCP/IP model
- Recognize the functions of each layer in the OSI seven-layer model
- Recognize the functions of each layer in the TCP/IP model
- Map the layers of the OSI model to the TCP/IP model

Lab Materials and Setup

- The *Mike Meyers' CompTIA Network+® Guide to Managing and Troubleshooting Networks* textbook
- Pencil and paper

Getting Down to Business

Using the *Mike Meyers' CompTIA Network+® Guide to Managing and Troubleshooting Networks* textbook and the prior labs, work through the following steps to further examine the details of network data delivery using the OSI seven-layer model.

Step 1   Label the OSI network model layers listed here and arrange them in their proper order from top to bottom:

Data Link   _____

Application   _____

Physical   _____

Session   _____

Presentation   _____

Network   _____

Transport   _____

✔ **Hint**

Remember that the OSI model is usually diagrammed with the seventh layer at the top and the first layer at the bottom. As noted in the textbook, many students will develop mnemonics to remember the layers and their order. Two popular mnemonics are: From the top down, **all people seem to need data processing**. From the bottom up, **please do not throw sausage pizza away**.

Step 2   Unlike the OSI model, the TCP/IP model does not really number the layers. Rearrange the TCP/IP model layers listed here in their proper order from top to bottom:

Link   _____

Transport   _____

Application   _____

Internet   _____

Step 3   Read the following descriptions and fill in the appropriate OSI network model layer:

Description	OSI Network Model Layer
The topmost layer; in this layer, programs access network services.	
This layer enables computers to establish, use, and close connections.	
This layer breaks up data into individual containers (also referred to as segments or datagrams) and assigns each a sequence number.	
This layer determines the data format used for computers to exchange data.	
This layer is divided into two sublayers: the Logical Link Control layer and the Media Access Control layer.	

This layer converts the digital signal into a form compatible with the network media and sends it out.	
This layer adds routable addresses to segments or datagrams and creates packets.	

Step 4   Read the following descriptions and fill in the appropriate TCP/IP model layer:

Description	TCP/IP Model Layer
The topmost layer; this layer essentially correlates to the Application, Presentation, and Session layers of the OSI seven-layer model.	
This layer contains most of the physical devices associated with networking, cables, NICs, hubs and switches; even physical addresses reside here.	
This layer provides reliable, end-to-end, connection-oriented communication.	
This layer ensures that IP packets have a valid IP address and are routed to the proper destination.	

Step 5   Often it will be important to be able to compare where a function operates in both network models. For instance, you may know that the Hypertext Transfer Protocol with Secure Sockets layer (HTTPS) functions in the Application layer of the TCP/IP model. Since HTTPS establishes the secure connection and transmission of data from your Web browser, it actually functions in the Application, Presentation, and Session layers of the OSI model.

Based on your understanding of the two models, use the following space to sketch a quick diagram mapping out the correlation between the layers of the OSI seven-layer model and the TCP/IP model.

 1 HOUR

Lab Exercise 2.04: Preparing a Presentation of the OSI Seven-Layer Model

As discussed in Lab Exercise 2.02, sometimes the network tech's role as installer and administrator takes a back seat to the tech's role as educator. There is a second benefit to the latter role. One of the best ways to learn the concepts of networking is to teach the concepts of networking to others. This helps you review the concepts and reinforce them in your memory. CJ knows that you have just finished learning about the ISO OSI seven-layer model and asks you to prepare a brief presentation for the other desktop support technicians.

You should plan on preparing enough material for a 15- to 20-minute presentation and leave about 10 minutes for a question and answer session. If things keep going this well at work, you may have that new pay grade in conjunction with your CompTIA Network+ certification.

Learning Objectives

In this lab, you'll research the OSI model and develop a Microsoft PowerPoint presentation to teach the concepts and layers of the OSI model. Finally, you will teach this information to your peers. At the conclusion of this lab, you will be able to

- Introduce the ISO OSI model
- Define the layers of the OSI model
- Teach the concepts and functions of networking based on the OSI model
- Prepare and deliver a professional presentation

Lab Materials and Setup

- The *Mike Meyers' CompTIA Network+® Guide to Managing and Troubleshooting Networks* textbook
- A Windows PC with Microsoft PowerPoint (or similar presentation software)
- Optionally, an LCD projector or large display to facilitate the presentation

Getting Down to Business

A good presentation begins with an introduction of what you plan to present. The body of the presentation will cover the actual material, in this case, the OSI seven-layer model. For a strong finish, the conclusion to the presentation should include a review of what you just presented. The following lab steps will walk you through setting up an informative presentation on the OSI seven-layer model.

> **→ Note**
>
> If you are in an instructor-led class, you may be assigned to a group and instructed to focus on only one or two of the layers for your presentation. Given this situation, work with your team members to develop a comprehensive introduction and concise summary review of the entire OSI model. You may then spend the remaining time to develop the details of your assigned layers.

Step 1   Using the textbook and prior labs, review the OSI seven-layer model.

Step 2   Using Microsoft PowerPoint, or comparable presentation software, begin your presentation by developing an outline of the number of slides and subject of each slide. About 1 to 2 slides per component should be plenty, so plan on your presentation being 9 to 16 slides.

Step 3   Develop an introduction based on the overview of the OSI model.

Step 4   For each of the layers, include details on the function, protocols, and addressing, and where applicable, the hardware associated with the layer. Building the model from either the bottom up or the top down is acceptable as long as you remain consistent. You may want to integrate a block diagram of the model as it unfolds.

Step 5   Conclude the presentation with a summary review of the OSI seven-layer model.

Step 6   Deliver the presentation to an audience of your peers.

Lab Analysis

1.   Jonathan asks you why the function of the NIC is defined in the Data Link layer as opposed to the Physical layer of the OSI seven-layer model. How would you explain this?

_____

_____

2.   Seth keeps hearing the term "frames" when discussing networking with fellow techs. What are the basic components of a frame?

_____

_____

3.   Janelle and Dana are working on a small network with 10 PCs. Janelle's PC sends a frame to Dana's PC. Which PC's NIC on the network reads the frame? Which PC's NIC on the network processes the frame?

_____

_____

4.   Draw a block diagram of the OSI seven-layer model in the proper sequence and label the numbers of the layers. Can you add any sublayer information?

5.   Skyler is still trying to memorize the correlation between the OSI seven-layer model and the TCP/IP model. Draw a block diagram mapping the OSI model to the TCP/IP model. Can you add some of the TCP/IP protocols that are defined by each of the layers?

Key Term Quiz

Use the vocabulary terms from the list below to complete the sentences that follow. Not all of the terms will be used.

application program interface (API)	network interface card (NIC)
broadcast address	network protocol
frame	OSI seven-layer model
frame check sequence (FCS)	router
IPCONFIG /ALL	TCP/IP
MAC address	TCP/IP model

1. A(n) _____ is a container for data chunks moving across a network.

2. Running the command _____ on a Windows computer will display the MAC address of the computer's network interface card.

3. The _____ is the portion of a frame that a NIC uses to determine whether data in the received frame is valid.

4. A networked computer discovers another computer's MAC address by sending a request via the _____.

5. A physical address is another name for the _____ of a NIC.

Chapter 3
Cabling and Topology

Lab Exercises

Most of ITCF clients' users never give a moment's thought to the mechanics of how their particular workstation ties into their corporate network. They just want to know that their data gets where it's supposed to go when they click the Send button in their e-mail program or that they can get to important sites on the Internet. As a network technician, you're the one who has to make sure that your network users' data can get from here to there, and vice versa. In the last couple of lessons, you learned about the concepts and models that serve as a basis for modern networks. Now it's time to look at the base hardware that makes a network—a network.

First, you will explore the network's physical and logical layout—the topology. Next, you'll examine the needs of a new building project and recommend the different types of physical network media, or cabling. You'll then explore a number of the governing bodies that handle the management and configuration of the networking standards. You have already met the ISO organization; now meet ANSI, TIA/EIA, and IEEE. Lastly, you will further explore the IEEE specifications that define the different network standards.

 15 minutes

Lab Exercise 3.01: Identifying Network Topologies

A network's physical topology defines the physical layout of network cabling, hubs, switches, routers, patch panels, and other hardware that carries the network's data. Some network topologies define how wireless networking devices such as wireless network adapters and wireless access points transfer data between computers. In this lab, you'll explore network topologies.

If you're setting up a network from scratch, start with your topology design. You won't always have this luxury, of course. If you're walking into a situation where a network is already in place, for example, evaluating the topology design is a top priority. Identifying the current network topology is the key to determining the type of network cabling and hardware or wireless communication technology that you'll be using.

Good network techs document everything about their network, listing the location of every network cable (usually called a *cable run* or *drop*) and all wireless access points. They make sure to describe the type of cabling used, and give details about the associated network hardware (brand and model of each network hub, switch, router, and so on). Unfortunately, not all network techs take the time to create this documentation or update it when they make changes, so you may wind up having to gather this information on your own. This is where your knowledge of the different network topologies, network cabling, and network hardware pays off.

✖ Cross-Reference

When network techs or, more importantly, professional cable installers plan a new network installation or upgrade existing network installations, they will utilize much more formal techniques to organize and document the install. These techniques include a formal site survey in which the installer will identify and document the location of Demarcation points (Demarcs), Main Distribution Frames (MDFs), Intermediate Distribution Frames (IDFs), and punchdown blocks. You will further explore these components in Chapter 6 of the *Mike Meyers' CompTIA Network+ Guide to Managing and Troubleshooting Networks* textbook as well as the Lab Exercises in Chapter 6 of this manual.

Learning Objectives

In this lab, you'll examine several network topologies. When you've completed the lab, you will be able to

- Identify and describe the different standard network physical topologies

- Identify the advantages and disadvantages of selected topologies

- Suggest an appropriate topology solution

Lab Materials and Setup

The materials you'll need for this lab are

- The *Mike Meyers' CompTIA Network+ Guide to Managing and Troubleshooting Networks* textbook

- Pencil and paper

Getting Down to Business

You are studying network topologies at the end of the day, when your friend Maggie stops by. You explain to her that you have a handle on the old network topologies like bus and ring, but you are trying to better understand the more current network topologies such as hybrid star-bus, mesh, and point-to-multipoint. Making a little bit of time in her busy schedule (one of ITCF's clients is rolling out new Internet cafés at rest stops along the freeways), she offers to help.

Maggie comes up with the excellent idea of describing various network installations she has been involved with. She will detail cabling, hardware components, and where applicable, wireless components and technologies. Using this information, she asks you to define the network topology employed in the scenario.

✖ **Cross-Reference**

To review the various network topologies, refer to the "Topology" section of Chapter 3 of the *Mike Meyers' CompTIA Network+ Guide to Managing and Troubleshooting Networks* textbook.

Step 1   Maggie starts you off with a story of an after-work, impromptu LAN party at one of your co-worker's houses. Everybody brought their laptops, and rather than set up everybody on his wireless access point (he is using MAC address filtering), Brandon configures an ad-hoc SSID of CrisisLAN. The whole crew joins the network and the members start gaming against each other. When a number of computers are using an ad-hoc network, what type of network topology does this emulate?

_____

_____

Step 2   Maggie is really excited about this new project: equipping freeway rest stops with wireless Internet connectivity. Each location will have a high-speed Internet connection with a wireless access point. When travelers visit, they can sign on to the network using devices with wireless network adapters. What does this tell you?

_____

_____

Step 3   To finish up, Maggie recommends that you take a look at the network installation in your own office. You begin by examining the computer in your cubicle. A CAT 5e, unshielded twisted pair (UTP) cable runs from the back of your computer to a wall jack. It appears to use RJ-45 connectors. You then walk down the hall to the wiring closet, observing a mass of cables (also UTP) terminating in a number of patch panels. Patch cables are then connected from the patch panel to an equal number of gigabit switches. What topology do you think this depicts?

_____

_____

Step 4   When analyzing the various topologies, what conclusions can you draw concerning the most prevalent wired network topologies, and the most prevalent wireless network topologies?

_____

_____

Step 5 When discussing topologies, the concept of a logical topology versus a physical topology is often confusing. Using the hybrid star-bus topology as an example, define a logical topology versus a physical topology; see Figure 3-1.

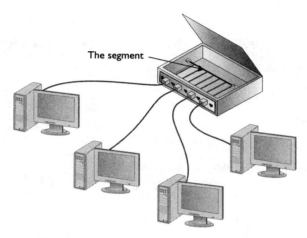

The segment

FIGURE 3-1 Diagram of the internal workings of a hybrid star-bus hub or switch

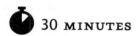 30 MINUTES

Lab Exercise 3.02: Determining Network Cabling Requirements

One of ITCF's larger clients, the Department of Transportation, is building a new regional Department of Motor Vehicles (DMV) complex consisting of two physical buildings. One building will house all of the administrative departments (licensing, title, tags, and registration). The other building, located approximately 900 feet away from the administrative building, will be a large, garage-like structure, where the physical inspection of the automobiles will be conducted. Along with designing the overall network infrastructure, ITCF has been asked to make recommendations regarding the physical cabling for the two buildings, as well as the connection between the two buildings. You have been invited to work with the team to make these cabling recommendations. Professional installers will be hired, so you may even get to review some of the proposals.

You have two choices when it comes to network cabling: glass-cored fiber optics or good old-fashioned copper wire. UTP copper cable is currently used in most network installations from small to gigantic. UTP cabling is differentiated by characteristics such as cost, bandwidth, and fire ratings. Fiber-optic cable provides high speed, the ability to travel long distances, and a high degree of security. To make informed decisions about what kind of network cabling best suits a given network installation, you have to examine the features, functions, and limitations of different network cabling media as applied to various networking applications.

Learning Objectives

In this lab, you'll practice researching the characteristics, typical application, and overall cost of network cables. When you've completed this lab, you will be able to

- Identify the various network cabling options
- Recommend specific cabling based on application
- Compare the function, speed, and maximum data transfer distance of each cable
- Suggest the cabling solutions with the best price/performance ratio

Lab Materials and Setup

The materials you'll need for this lab are

- The *Mike Meyers' CompTIA Network+ Guide to Managing and Troubleshooting Networks* textbook
- A computer with Internet access
- Pencil and paper

Getting Down to Business

When you're designing a new building plan, one of the major expenses can be the network infrastructure, and a portion of that is the physical cabling. It is imperative that the design implemented meet a price/performance balance along with future-proofing for technological improvements. The cabling installation can be broken down into two distinct applications. Cabling will need to be purchased for the two buildings, the main administrative building and the inspection garage, and the backbone between the two buildings.

Step 1 You'll start the cabling layout with the administrative building and the inspection garage. The team determines that approximately 11,500 feet of cabling will be required. The cabling will have to meet the strict fire codes for office buildings and should meet the specifications allowing for future technology improvements.

What grade of cable would you recommend to meet the city's building codes?

_____

What category cable would you recommend to future-proof this cable installation?

_____

Step 2   Now launch your browser and navigate to www.cablestogo.com. Select the **Bulk Cable** menu item and record the bulk cost of 1000 feet of the following categories and grades of cable.

Category 5e, Solid Core PVC cable: US$_____

Category 5e, Plenum-Grade cable: US$_____

Category 6, Solid Core PVC cable: US$_____

Category 6, Plenum-Grade cable: US$_____

Based on your recommendations, what are the final specifications and total cost for the 11,500 feet of internal cabling for the two buildings?

_____

_____

Step 3   The run between the two buildings, as stated previously, is approximately 900 feet. You'll want to select cabling that will handle the distance in one run, require the least amount of maintenance, and provide for future technological improvements. It will probably be buried, so it will be very difficult and expensive to upgrade in the future.

What type of cable would you recommend for the run between the two buildings?

_____

Step 4   Fire up your browser again and visit www.l-com.com. Select **Fiber Optic** from the menu items on the left, then navigate to bulk fiber-optic cables and locate the various types of cable. Use the information to calculate the bulk costs of 1000 feet of the following fiber-optic cabling:

Multimode duplex 2-fiber-optic cable: US$_____

Single-mode 6-fiber-optic cable: US$_____

Single-mode 12-fiber-optic cable: US$_____

Based on your recommendations, what are the final specifications and total cost of the cabling for the run between the two buildings? Remember, you want the cable to provide for improvements for years to come, so you'll want to select the highest-performance cable you can purchase today.

_____

_____

Step 5   In the following chart, list the currently recognized categories of UTP cabling. For each category, list the maximum frequency and the maximum bandwidth.

CAT Rating	Maximum Frequency	Maximum Bandwidth

Step 6   After working with the team on the prior cabling project, CJ informs you that a number of the remote offices of the Department of Transportation are scheduled for network upgrades. The offices are currently using CAT 5 UTP, and the office space is roughly 2000 square feet. There are approximately 15 computers and two servers at each office.

Based on this information, he asks what type of network cabling you would recommend for this network upgrade. List your reasons.

_____

_____

 20 MINUTES

Lab Exercise 3.03: The Governing Bodies

One of the amazing aspects of networking in general is that thousands of hardware manufacturers and software developers can create devices and applications that allow computers to communicate with each other, and it all works! Part of the reason that it works is that there are established organizations that set the standards for development and manufacturing of these components and devices. These organizations define the international standards so that when you try to access a Web site in Japan from a computer in the United States, you connect.

You have already encountered the International Organization for Standardization (ISO), but there are others that are just as important to the successful communication of digital data. You're going to research a little about each of these organizations, starting with the groups that work with cabling, devices, and technologies like Ethernet. In later labs, after you have traveled further up the OSI model, you'll explore some of the organizations that handle TCP/IP, the Internet, and the World Wide Web.

Learning Objectives

In this lab, you'll explore various organizations that are responsible for the development and management of international standards. By the end of this lab, you will be able to

- Describe the purpose and detail some of the features of the governing bodies, the organizations that define the standards for networking, and much more.

Lab Materials and Setup

The materials you need for this lab are

- A PC with Internet access
- Pencil and paper

Getting Down to Business

If you have ever been a member of a World of Warcraft guild, you have probably teamed up with people from all over the world. When your avatar and theirs are on the same quest, have you ever thought about the fact that their computer is connected to some hub, switch, or router in some distant country, yet here they are virtually, standing next to you. Thank goodness for standards!

Step 1   You're going to start with the granddaddy of all the organizations, the International Organization for Standardization (ISO). Launch your Web browser and enter this URL: www.iso.org/iso/about.htm. Now just take a few notes on who ISO is, where they are located, how long have they been around, and what is their general purpose.

_____

_____

Step 2   Next, navigate to this Web site, www.ansi.org/about_ansi/overview/overview.aspx?menuid=1. This is the American National Standards Institute (ANSI), who is both the official U.S. representative of ISO and a major international player. View the page and capture some of the information as you did in Step 1. ANSI checks the standards and accredits other groups, such as the Telecommunications Industry Association (TIA) and the Electronic Industries Alliance (EIA).

_____

_____

Step 3   ANSI also has the responsibility to check the standards and accredit other groups, such as the Telecommunications Industry Association (TIA) and the Electronic Industries Alliance (EIA). Check these two organizations out on the Web at www.tiaonline.org/about/ and www.ecaus.org/eia/site/index.html. What are their credentials?

_____

_____

Step 4   As a precursor to the last lab exercise, check out the Institute of Electrical and Electronics Engineers (IEEE), often pronounced as *I-triple-E*. The URL is www.ieee.org/about/index.html. What pertinent information can you find about the IEEE?

_____

_____

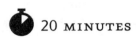 20 MINUTES

Lab Exercise 3.04: Industry Standards

You have just learned about various organizations that drive the standards for just about every technological industry. One of these organizations, the IEEE, formed a committee known as the 802 committee. The 802 committee sets the standards that all modern networking hardware must meet in order to function with other networking hardware. The 802 committee is divided into a number of subcommittees, each responsible for defining the standards and methods by which different networking devices are governed. Among these are the subcommittees that have established the 802.2, 802.3, and 802.11 networking standards.

Before wrapping up this chapter, you'll review these important IEEE standards and definitions.

Learning Objectives

In this lab, you'll identify the function of each of the important IEEE 802 subcommittees. By the end of this lab, you will be able to

- Describe the IEEE subcommittee responsible for defining the standards of the most popular network technology implementations

Lab Materials and Setup

The materials you need for this lab are

- The *Mike Meyers' CompTIA Network+ Guide to Managing and Troubleshooting Networks* textbook
- Pencil and paper

Getting Down to Business

Having studied network topologies and the physical cabling that is usually employed to realize them, you wonder how all of these components are designed to be compatible with each other. You'll soon determine that all modern networking equipment conforms to the same standards, and therefore compatibility is not an issue.

Step 1   Utilizing the textbook, fill in the function of each of the most common IEEE 802 subcommittees listed.

Subcommittee Designation	Description
802.1s	
802.1w	
802.1x	
802.3	
802.11	
802.15	
802.16	

Step 2   Explain why compliance with these IEEE standards is important.

_____

_____

Lab Analysis

1. Diagram a mesh topology configured with five computers. What is the total number of separate connections that are needed to complete the design? Eavan asks you, what is the formula?

    _____

    _____

    _____

    _____

2. Explain the physical design of a star-bus topology and the advantage of this topology.

    _____

    _____

3. When designing a cable installation, what is the primary grade of cabling that should be used for horizontal runs in the ceilings and walls? Why?

    _____

    _____

4. What are the most common categories and speeds of UTP cabling?

    _____

    _____

5. Which IEEE 802 subcommittee represents the Ethernet standard?

    _____

    _____

Key Term Quiz

Using the vocabulary terms from the list below, complete the sentences that follow. Not all of the terms will be used.

ANSI

bus topology

CAT 5e UTP

CAT 6 UTP

coaxial

Ethernet

fiber-optic

hybrid star-bus topology

hybrid star-ring topology

IEEE 802 committee

LC connector

mesh topology

plenum-grade

polyvinyl chloride (PVC)

ring topology

RJ-11 connector

RJ-45 connector

SC connector

star topology

ST connector

UTP (unshielded twisted pair)

1. When you're planning a new local area network infrastructure, the most common type of network cable implemented would be either _____ or _____ cable.

2. _____ describes a network in which all the computers connect to a central wiring point, or hub. The hub creates a logical bus topology.

3. The TIA, EIA, and IEEE are all standards organizations that are accredited by _____.

4. _____ cables transmit light for distances up to ten kilometers.

5. When you're working with fiber optic cabling, there are three prominent connector types used: the _____, the _____, and the _____.

Chapter 4
Ethernet Basics

Lab Exercises

Ethernet is, by far, the most widely used type of networking technology in the IT world today. For this reason, it's important for network techs to understand Ethernet's functions and features as defined by the IEEE 802.3 standard. These include such things as how Ethernet network nodes build data frames, how they access the network media, and how they send and receive data.

Even though Ethernet speeds have increased exponentially over the years—primarily by increasing the bandwidth of the media (cables) and hardware (NICs and switches)—the core technology remains the same. Network nodes identify each other by MAC address, data is transferred between machines using Ethernet frames, and devices negotiate when they can send data using the CSMA/CD access method. The basics you explore here still apply to the higher-speed implementations you will explore in later chapters.

In these labs, you'll examine the IEEE 802.3 (Ethernet) committee, review the bits and pieces of Ethernet data frame construction and media access methods, look at the physical characteristics of Ethernet networks using unshielded twisted pair cabling, talk about how you enhance the performance of Ethernet, and define the Spanning Tree Protocol.

On your marks, get set, GO!

 10 MINUTES

Lab Exercise 4.01: Meet the IEEE 802.3 (Ethernet) Committee

In the early 1970s, Xerox developed a set of standards to facilitate the exchange of data between computers. These standards, Ethernet, have gone on to become the dominant industry standard. Over the years, the control of these standards has changed hands a few times. In the late 1970s, Xerox joined forces with Digital Equipment Corporation (DEC) and Intel to propagate the standard. Today, the Institute of Electrical and Electronics Engineers (IEEE) has the responsibility of controlling and updating the Ethernet standards. The IEEE formed a special committee to manage these standards—the 802.3 (Ethernet) committee.

As a competent network technician, you should have a basic understanding of how Ethernet operates. Visiting the IEEE 802.3 (Ethernet) committee is a great place to start.

Learning Objectives

At the completion of this lab, you will be able to

- Utilize Internet resources for research

- Identify and record key components of the Ethernet standard

Lab Materials and Setup

The materials you'll need for this lab exercise are

- A working computer with Internet access

- The *Mike Meyers' CompTIA Network+ Guide to Managing and Troubleshooting Networks* textbook

- Pencil and paper

Getting Down to Business

The IEEE 802 committee defines and manages the standards for network communication and hardware. The IEEE 802.3 committee specifically manages the standards for Ethernet. You're going to visit the IEEE Web site, download specific Ethernet standards, and then answer some questions based on the information contained within these documents.

Step 1   Open your favorite browser and navigate over to www.ieee802.org. What are the stated objectives of the IEEE 802 committee?

_____

_____

Step 2   Select the hyperlink to the standards download page. Now click on the 802 committee you are interested in, currently the **IEEE 802.3™: CSMA/CD Access Method**. Follow the directions to download Section 1 of this document. What is the title of this standards document?

_____

_____

➔ Note

Due to the dynamic nature of the content available on the Internet, Web sites, pages, and hyperlinks change often. If one of the sites, pages, or links referenced in the lab steps is no longer available, with a little investigation, you should be able to find the appropriate information.

Step 3   Within the introduction, scroll down to the paragraphs defining the contents of each section. What are some of the key points covered in Section 1?

_____

_____

What are some of the key points covered in Section 3?

_____

_____

Step 4   Locate Clause 3.1.1 packet format. Note the diagram of the Ethernet frame. How does this diagram compare to the diagram of the Ethernet frame in Figure 4-2 of the textbook? List the main fields of the MAC Frame.

_____

_____

 20 MINUTES

Lab Exercise 4.02: Accessing Ethernet Networks

Pop quiz! How many PCs can transmit data on a given network segment at the same time? Is it four? Eight? Sixty-four? Or is it one? As amazing as it seems, only a single PC can access any given network segment at a time. This is true no matter how many network nodes populate the network segment. When two PCs try to send data on the network at the same time, the data frames collide, causing both frames to become corrupted.

Since it's only possible for one PC to tap out its data onto the wire at a time, the designers of Ethernet had to devise a method for the network nodes to access the network media without stepping on each other's frames. This network access method is called *Carrier Sense, Multiple Access/Collision Detection*, or CSMA/CD. The CSMA part of CSMA/CD defines the method by which network nodes monitor the network media to determine if any other nodes are currently transmitting data. The CD part defines how the network nodes deal with collisions when they occur. In this lab, you'll discuss how the CSMA/CD mechanism functions.

Learning Objectives

In this lab, you'll review the Carrier Sense, Multiple Access/Collision Detection function of Ethernet. At the end of this lab, you will be able to

- Define the function of CSMA/CD

Lab Materials and Setup

The materials you'll need for this lab exercise are

- The *Mike Meyers' CompTIA Network+ Guide to Managing and Troubleshooting Networks* textbook
- Pencil and paper
- An Ethernet hub (optional)

Getting Down to Business

It has been some time since Maggie has studied for (and passed) the CompTIA Network+ exam. She knows that it is pretty amazing how multiple PCs can be on the same network at the same time without interrupting each other's network sessions. She also knows it's important to understand this for the Network+ exam, and she asks you to explain how the method that Ethernet uses, CSMA/CD, functions to enable the sharing of network media.

Step 1   In the following space, describe how the Ethernet Carrier Sense function enables network nodes to determine if the network media is in use.

_____

_____

Step 2   Describe how the Ethernet Multiple Access rules govern which network node gets precedence with regard to network media access.

_____

_____

Step 3   Explain how Ethernet's Collision Detection function enables network nodes to recover from data collisions.

_____

_____

Step 4   Maggie asks if there is a way to configure the network so that no data collisions occur. What do you tell her?

_____

_____

Step 5   If you have access to an old Ethernet hub with a collision detection indicator, monitor and make note of the collision rate on your network for a short time period (ten minutes or so). What are your results?

_____

_____

 30–60 MINUTES

Lab Exercise 4.03: Building an Ethernet Patch Cable

In Chapter 3, you learned that CAT 5e and CAT 6 UTP cabling are now the dominant cabling media for wired networks. This is due to the fact that Ethernet has become the dominant networking technology, and Ethernet uses UTP cabling to electrically transmit the data frames. To ensure that these data frames are transmitted and received correctly requires that these UTP cables are wired to exacting specifications. The Telecommunications Industry Association/Electronics Industries Alliance (TIA/EIA) defines the industry standard for wiring Ethernet UTP cables.

Installing the cabling infrastructure when a facility is being built or upgrading the cabling infrastructure of an existing building is largely left to professional cable installers (though you will assemble a small structured cabling installation in the Lab Exercises for Chapter 6). However, when it comes to connecting devices, computers, and printers to the network jack in the wall, or patching the switches in a wiring closet, this job falls squarely on the shoulders (or in the hands) of the network tech. The common patch cable is a length of UTP cable with RJ-45 connectors on each end wired to the specifications of the TIA/EIA 568A or 568B standards.

Typical IT departments will have several lengths of premade patch cables on hand to be used as needed. Nonetheless, a well-versed network tech should have a good command of assembling and testing UTP patch cables. Some folks refer to building UTP patch cables as an "art." It requires stripping the insulation, arranging the wires to meet the TIA/EIA standards, and crimping RJ-45 connectors onto the ends of the wire.

Learning Objectives

In this lab, you'll assemble a TIA/EIA 568B patch cable. When you've completed this lab, you will be able to

- Identify proper orientation of RJ-45 connectors

- Identify the wire pairs of a UTP patch cable according to the specification of the TIA/EIA 568A and 568B standards

- Successfully crimp an RJ-45 connector to the end of a UTP cable

- Verify proper wiring of a completed patch cable using a commercial cable tester

Lab Materials and Setup

The materials you'll need for this lab exercise are

- A working computer with Internet access

- A length of CAT 5, CAT 5e, or CAT 6 UTP cable

→ **Note**

Though CAT 6 UTP cable is the current choice for high performance, it can prove much more difficult to use when making cables. CAT 6 cable has a plastic spine that must be trimmed before inserting it into the RJ-45 connectors. There are many variations on the RJ-45 connectors for CAT 6 cable, and special crimping tools may be required.

- RJ-45 connectors

- Wire strippers

- Wire snips

- Crimping tool

- TIA/EIA 568B color codes

- Cable tester

Getting Down to Business

The TIA/EIA 568A and 568B standards define the arrangement of 4-pair UTP cabling into RJ-45 connectors. In purchasing commercial, premade cables, the emerging default standard is the TIA/EIA 568B. For the purposes of this lab, you will adhere to the default industry standard of TIA/EIA 568B.

You'll find that once you develop some technique, you will enjoy making patch cables. As mentioned earlier, in the eyes of some, this is an "art," and any skill that you become better at with practice holds an attractive quality for many. I want to caution you against spending too much time making cables, and therefore, spending too much time completing this lab exercise. The skill you develop will not be tested on the CompTIA Network+ examination, and even in the field, making cables will not be the prime example of your skills as a network tech.

That said, you will want to spend enough time to know the basics so that you will not look like a novice when it comes to whipping up a few patch cables.

Step 1   You'll begin with a cut length of UTP cable. Your instructor may define the lengths based on actual implementation. Shorter, 2- to 5-foot cables may be made to patch in a new switch or router, and medium lengths of 14 to 25 feet may be used to connect computers and printers to wall jacks. What lengths of cable will you be using?

_____

_____

Step 2   Using the Internet, conduct a search for TIA/EIA 568A and 568B wiring diagrams. There are many sites that offer color-coded diagrams of the standards for wiring both straight-through and cross-over patch cables. I found a nice diagram on the Alberta, Canada Internet provider Web site "The Internet Centre" at www.incentre.net/content/view/75/2/. I have also included the wiring diagram from the *Mike Meyers' CompTIA Network+ Guide to Managing and Troubleshooting Networks* textbook (see Figure 4-1).

✖ Cross-Reference

The textbook is now in **FULL COLOR**! Take a look at Figures 4.8 through 4.12 in the "Early Ethernet Networks" section of Chapter 4 of *Mike Meyers' CompTIA Network+ Guide to Managing and Troubleshooting Networks*.

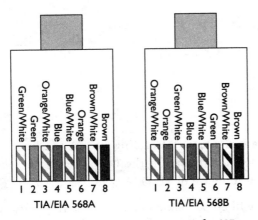

FIGURE 4-1   The TIA/EIA 568A and 568B standards

Using either the previous diagram, or one of the diagrams you have found, record the proper color wire for each of the pins of the RJ-45 modular connector when assembled using the TIA/EIA 568B standard.

PIN 1:   _____

PIN 2:   _____

PIN 3:   _____

PIN 4:   _____

PIN 5:   _____

PIN 6:   _____

PIN 7:   _____

PIN 8:   _____

Step 3   Using wire strippers (often the crimping tool has wire strippers and snips built in), carefully remove approximately 0.5 inches of the outer insulating jacket of each end of the UTP cable.

➜ **Note**

After removing the outer insulating sheathing, look for any damaged or cut wires. This is a very delicate procedure, so finesse is required. If any of the eight wires have been damaged, use the wire snips to cut off the entire end (all eight wires and insulation) and repeat Step 3.

Step 4   Separate each pair of wires and align them in the correct sequence according to the TIA/EIA 568B standards defined in Step 2. The next step where you insert the wires into the RJ-45 connector will go more smoothly if you take your time during this procedure. Once the sequence is correct, grasp the wires firmly between your thumb and forefinger, and carefully snip the edges of the wires to make them even as in Figure 4-2.

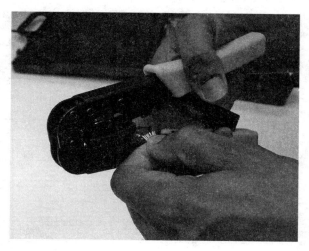

FIGURE 4-2 Aligning the wires and evening the ends

Step 5   With the pins of the RJ-45 connector facing up and away from you, slide the wires all the way into the connector. The outer insulating sheath should be just past the first crimping point in the connector, and you should be able to see the copper of all eight wires if you look at the head of the RJ-45 connector.

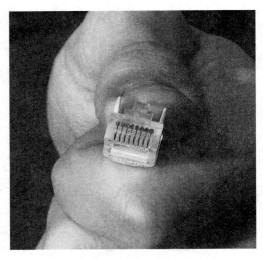

Figure 4-3 Head of an RJ-45 connector showing all eight wires firmly inserted

Step 6   Place the RJ-45 connector into the crimping tool. Firmly squeeze the handle of the tool until the wires are crimped into place. The crimp should bind each of the wires tightly, and the connector should bind the outer jacket. If any of the wires can be pulled from the connector with a gentle tug, the connection is incorrect. Snip the RJ-45 connector off and return to Step 3.

Step 7   To complete the assembly of the patch cable, repeat Steps 3–6 to add a connector to the other end of the cable.

Step 8   Now you will verify the construction of the UTP patch cable using a commercial cable tester. Most testers come with a remote end and a master module. Plug each of the RJ-45 plugs into the jacks on the cable tester. Following the directions provided with the cable tester, verify the performance of the UTP patch cable. Record your results in the following table:

TIA/EIA 568 Pair	Connection	Results (Good/Bad)
Wire Pair 1	Pin 5 to Pin 5	
	Pin 4 to Pin 4	
Wire Pair 2	Pin 1 to Pin 1	
	Pin 2 to Pin 2	
Wire Pair 3	Pin 3 to Pin 3	
	Pin 6 to Pin 6	
Wire Pair 4	Pin 7 to Pin 7	
	Pin 8 to Pin 8	

Lab Exercise 4.03a: Alternate Ending: Building an Ethernet Crossover Cable

Sometimes when troubleshooting a networking problem, it is a timesaver to be able to just connect two computers directly together. This bypasses any complications from the horizontal cabling or hubs/switches of the structured network. To accomplish this, all you need to do is construct a crossover cable to connect directly between the two machines.

To build a crossover cable, simply follow the instructions in Lab Exercise 4.03: Building an Ethernet Patch Cable above. Perform Steps 1–6 just as instructed, discarding and re-performing steps if you make mistakes.

In Step 7, instead of completing the cable with a TIA/EIA 568B termination, substitute a TIA/EIA 568A termination. This will create a cable with a 568B termination on one end of the cable and a 568A termination on the other end of the cable. From one end of the cable to the other, the White-Orange/Orange and White-Green/Green pairs will swap, creating the Ethernet crossover cable.

When you perform Step 8 and test the crossover cable, depending on your cable tester, you should be able to confirm that all of the four pairs are properly connected. Most cable testers will indicate that there are crossed connections, though some may not indicate that the proper pairs are crossed. Use the following table to verify the crossover cable.

TIA/EIA 568 Pair	Connection	Results (Good/Bad)
Wire Pair 1	Pin 5 to Pin 5	
	Pin 4 to Pin 4	
Wire Pair 2	Pin 1 to Pin 3	
	Pin 2 to Pin 6	
Wire Pair 3	Pin 3 to Pin 1	
	Pin 6 to Pin 2	
Wire Pair 4	Pin 7 to Pin 7	
	Pin 8 to Pin 8	

You can perform a quick check of the crossover cable simply by inserting it directly between the NICs of two working, networked computers. You may have to alter some of the network configuration settings to allow the machines to communicate with each other, but you should be able to share a folder or copy a file.

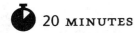 20 MINUTES

Lab Exercise 4.04: Enhancing the Performance of Ethernet Networks

The specifications for Ethernet, such as the number of supported network nodes and the length of network cable runs, require some thought on the part of the network tech when physically designing the network. How can you stretch the network cabling beyond the stated distance limits? How do you configure a network to support more network nodes? How do you achieve bandwidth at close to rated speeds as the number of network nodes grows?

As you learned in Chapter 3, the dominant network topology is the hybrid star-bus topology. Even the early 10-Mbps networks implemented this topology using UTP cable and a central device to facilitate communication between network nodes. Originally, multiport repeaters known as Ethernet hubs were the primary central devices. Later, Ethernet switches were incorporated to improve bandwidth utilization.

In this lab, you'll explore the basic functions of hubs and switches. You'll configure a simple multihub-based network and a multiswitch-based network, and then compare how hubs and switches affect the performance capabilities of Ethernet networks.

Learning Objectives

Upon the completion of this lab, you will be able to

- Define the configuration and characteristics of a multihub Ethernet network
- Define the configuration and characteristics of a multiswitch Ethernet network
- Recommend a hardware solution to achieve optimal bandwidth performance

Lab Materials and Setup

The materials you'll need for this lab exercise are

- The *Mike Meyers' CompTIA Network+ Guide to Managing and Troubleshooting Networks* textbook
- Pencil and paper
- Three Ethernet hubs
- Three Ethernet switches
- Two working computers with Ethernet NICs
- Five UTP patch cables
- Two UTP crossover cables

Getting Down to Business

Using the lab materials, you will build a simple multihub-based network and a simple multiswitch-based network. You will then review the characteristics of hubs and switches, summarizing the basic features and limitations of each, and recommend the solution that will provide the highest performance.

✖ Cross-Reference

To refresh your understanding of the function of Ethernet hubs and switches, refer to the "Extending and Enhancing Ethernet Networks" section of Chapter 4 of *Mike Meyers' CompTIA Network+ Guide to Managing and Troubleshooting Networks.*

Step 1 Using either the uplink ports or crossover cables, daisy-chain the three hubs together. Connect one of the computers to the hub at one end of the chain. Then connect the second computer to the hub at the other end of the chain and establish connectivity between the two machines. Document your configuration.

_____

_____

Step 2 In the space that follows, describe the function of a hub.

_____

_____

Step 3 Disassemble the hub-based network, and locate the Ethernet switches. Using the switches, configure a switched network with a central switch and two subswitches. Connect one of the computers to one of the subswitches, and the other to the other subswitch. Confirm connectivity between the two machines. Document your configuration.

_____

_____

Step 4 In the space that follows, describe the function of a switch.

_____

_____

Step 5 You have been asked to design a simple 30-node Ethernet network for a classroom. Describe how you would configure this network. Would you use Ethernet hubs or Ethernet switches in your design? Why?

_____

_____

 10 MINUTES

Lab Exercise 4.05: Exploring the Spanning Tree Protocol

As you finish up your study of Ethernet switches (at least for now), it would be a good time to discuss a situation that sometimes happens when you are interconnecting multiple switches. Whether by design or by accident, if you connect a number of switches so that one or more can connect back into themselves, you will create what is known as a _bridging loop_. Left unchecked, this can cause a packet storm, basically flooding the network with damaged packets and bringing the network to a crawl.

Enter the Spanning Tree Protocol (STP), designed to detect and blocok bridging loops. This protocol was developed in the early 1980s by DEC but is now defined by the IEEE 802.1D standards.

Learning Objectives

At the completion of this lab, you will be able to

- Utilize Internet resources for research
- Summarize the Spanning Tree Protocol

Lab Materials and Setup

The materials you'll need for this lab exercise are

- A working computer with Internet access
- Pencil and paper

Getting Down to Business

As you have already learned, the IEEE 802 committee defines and manages the standards for network communication and hardware. The IEEE 802.1D committee specifically manages the standards for MAC bridges. An independent vendor, Cisco, is renowned for its implementation of switches and routers. You're going to visit both the IEEE 802 Web site and the Cisco Web site to gather some information and summarize the Spanning Tree Protocol.

Step 1   Open your favorite browser and navigate over to standards.ieee.org/about/get. Now click on the 802 committee you are interested in, currently **IEEE 802.1™: Bridging and Management**. Follow the directions to download the IEEE 802.1D-2004 standards. Navigate to clause 17 of this document. What is the title of this clause?

_____

_____

→ **Note**

Due to the dynamic nature of the content available on the Internet, Web sites, pages, and hyperlinks change often. If one of the sites, pages, or links referenced in the lab steps is no longer available, with a little investigation, you should be able to find the appropriate information.

Step 2   Now pop over to the Cisco Web site and search for information on the Spanning Tree Protocol. Your instructor can help with the search if you get stuck. Document one or two of the URLs that the search directs you toward.

_____

_____

Step 3   Given the information from the textbook, the IEEE 802 standards, and the Cisco implementation, write a short summary of the Spanning Tree Protocol.

_____

_____

Lab Analysis

1. How does an Ethernet switch improve the overall performance of a network?

    _____

    _____

2. What is the basic function of the Frame Check Sequence (FCS) in an Ethernet frame? How does the FCS compare to the Cyclic Redundancy Check (CRC) used by other technologies?

    _____

    _____

3. Brittney creates an Ethernet crossover cable. What pins are connected to each other on the RJ-45 connector? How does this facilitate communication between two PCs without a hub or a switch as a central interface?

    _____

    _____

4. What is the purpose of including the destination address and source address fields in an Ethernet frame? What is the common name for these addresses?

    _____

    _____

5. Mitchell is throwing a LAN party this weekend and needs to whip up a few extra Ethernet patch cables for his guests. He already has the cable and the connectors. What tools would you recommend he use to build and test the cables?

    _____

    _____

Key Term Quiz

Use the vocabulary terms from the list below to complete the sentences that follow. Not all of the terms will be used.

attenuation

baseband

BNC connector

bridge

broadband

crossover cable

CSMA/CD

DIX connector

Ethernet hub

Ethernet switch

frame

IEEE 802.1D

IEEE 802.3 committee

packet

reflection

repeater

RJ-45

Spanning Tree Protocol (STP)

TIA/EIA 568A

TIA/EIA 568B

1. The symptom of a signal losing strength as it travels over a cable is known as _____.

2. The _____ prevents switches that have been mistakenly connected back into themselves, forming a bridge loop, from flooding the network with damaged packets.

3. A(n) _____ is created when you construct a UTP cable using the _____ standard for one end of the cable, and the _____ standard for the other end of the cable.

4. The Ethernet standard developed by Xerox was eventually handed over to the _____, who continue to manage the standard today.

5. Ethernet uses a method called _____ to determine which computers can use a shared cable at any given time to send data.

Chapter 5
Modern Ethernet

Lab Exercises

Ethernet has gone through a number of evolutionary changes to bring us to where we are today. Modern Ethernet networks are based on the same technologies and standards that you learned about in the previous chapter. The newer versions continue to improve the bandwidth, but use the same frame types, access methods, and so on—even the connectors, NICs, and switches have relatively the same form factor. Modern Ethernet enables network techs to build larger, faster, more reliable networks!

In this lab, you'll examine the specifications and hardware that make up 1000BaseT, 1000BaseSX, and 1000BaseLX Ethernet; look at design aspects to keep in mind when planning a modern switched Ethernet network; and then explore the Ethernet developments that take us beyond Gigabit Ethernet.

 30 MINUTES

Lab Exercise 5.01: Modern Ethernet: 1000BaseT, 1000BaseSX, and 1000BaseLX

Ethernet networks have evolved over the last 20 years or so from the early 10-Mbps implementations to today's speeds of 100 Mbps, 1 Gbps, and even 10 Gbps. Wired networks utilize either copper wire or fiber-optic cabling to physically transmit the Ethernet frames from device to device. You explored the basics of Ethernet in Chapter 4, "Ethernet," learning that no matter what speed Ethernet performs at, the fundamentals of the technology remain the same.

100BaseTX (copper wire) and 100BaseFX (fiber-optic cabling) Ethernet provide 100-Mbps performance. Both technologies have a large installed base, utilizing hybrid star-bus topology with central hubs or switches. You'll still need to familiarize yourself with their characteristics to provide quality network support for existing installations. However, the current trend when installing or upgrading wired networks is 1000BaseT utilizing CAT 5e or better UTP copper cabling and gigabit NICs and switches. In addition, many backbones are implementing either 1000BaseSX multimode fiber or 1000BaseLX single-mode fiber, depending on distance.

With this in mind, you're going to spend some time exploring the characteristics of Gigabit Ethernet and gather some information on Gigabit Ethernet NICs. In the next lab exercise, you will examine Gigabit Ethernet switches.

Learning Objectives

In this lab, you'll examine the standards and technology of 1000BaseT, 1000BaseSX, and 1000BaseLX Ethernet. When you have completed this lab, you will be able to

- Define the 1000BaseT Ethernet specifications, requirements, and limitations

- Define the 1000BaseSX and 1000BaseLX Ethernet specifications, requirements, and limitations

- Recommend Gigabit Ethernet NICs

- Determine appropriate use of fiber-optic Ethernet based on application

Lab Materials and Setup

The materials you'll need for this lab are

- The *Mike Meyers' CompTIA Network+ Guide to Managing and Troubleshooting Networks* textbook

- A computer with Internet access

- Pencil and paper

Getting Down to Business

Recalling the cabling scenario from Chapter 3, your client, the Department of Transportation, is building a new regional Department of Motor Vehicles (DMV) complex consisting of two physical buildings. One building will house all of the administrative departments (licensing, title, tags, and registration). The other building, located approximately 900 feet away from the administrative building, will be a large, garage-like structure where the physical inspection of the automobiles will be conducted. The professional installers have submitted a proposal that has been accepted, outlining the following parameters:

- The proposed cabling for the internal office space of the administrative building is Category 6 UTP. The administrative network will need to support 75 to 100 devices (servers, computers, and printers).

- The proposed cabling for the internal area of the inspection building is Category 6 UTP. The network in the inspection building will need to support 25 to 40 devices (computers and printers).

- For the backbone between the two buildings, the proposal is single-mode 12-fiber optic cabling.

Using this general information, follow Steps 1 through 4 to develop an implementation plan for the new site. The design should take advantage of the Gigabit Ethernet technology.

Step 1 Utilizing the textbook and online resources, research and document the following information for 1000BaseT Ethernet:

Speed: _____

Distance: _____

Cabling: _____

Connectors: _____

Step 2   Utilizing online resources, research and document the following information for 1000BaseTX Ethernet:

Speed: _____

Distance: _____

Cabling: _____

Connectors: _____

Step 3   Utilizing the textbook and online resources, research and document the following information for 1000BaseSX Ethernet:

Speed: _____

Distance: _____

Cabling: _____

Connectors: _____

Step 4   Utilizing the textbook and online resources, research and document the following information for 1000BaseLX Ethernet:

Speed: _____

Distance: _____

Cabling: _____

Connectors: _____

Step 5   Utilizing online resources, research and document the following information for 1000BaseZX Ethernet:

Speed: _____

Distance: _____

Cabling: _____

Connectors: _____

Step 6   As discussed in the scenario, the new facility will have approximately 100 to 140 network devices (computers and printers). In order to implement Gigabit Ethernet throughout the organization, each device will need a gigabit NIC. Launch your browser and research the current pricing for Gigabit Ethernet NICs. Document your findings in the following space:

→ **Note**

Most commercial computer vendors (Dell, Gateway, Hewlett-Packard, and so on) will provide Gigabit Ethernet NICs on the ATX motherboards of new machines. For the purposes of this lab step, assume that you are purchasing network interface cards for 100 new computers.

Step 7 Ethernet networks using 1000BaseSX and 1000BaseLX fiber-optic hardware and cabling share most of the qualities of 1000BaseT networks, but are considerably more expensive to implement. What are the circumstances under which 1000BaseSX or 1000BaseLX would be preferable to 1000BaseT?

Which technology would you recommend for the 900-foot backbone run between the administrative building and the inspection building?

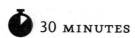 30 MINUTES

Lab Exercise 5.02: Ethernet Network Design: Implementing Switches

Continuing with the installation of the Department of Transportation regional DMV complex, you have determined that the administrative building will need to support 75 to 100 network devices, and the inspection building will need to support 25 to 40 network devices. The professional cable installers will calculate the horizontal runs and cable drops needed from the telecommunications room(s) to each node.

Now it is your turn! You will need to research Gigabit Ethernet switching technology to provide recommendations regarding make and model, quantity, and specific solutions based on application.

Learning Objectives

In this lab, you'll explore Ethernet switch technology.

By the end of this lab, you will be able to

- Research and recommend Ethernet switches to meet specific applications
- Define solutions to implement high-speed backbone ports
- Design a simple network using Gigabit Ethernet switches
- Define full-duplex operation

Lab Materials and Setup

The materials you'll need for this lab are

- The *Mike Meyers' CompTIA Network+ Guide to Managing and Troubleshooting Networks* textbook
- A computer with Internet access
- Pencil and paper

Getting Down to Business

The physical layout of the buildings and proposed location of telecommunications rooms, cubicles, computers, and printers is complete. The cable installers have provided 100 drops in the correct locations throughout the administrative building, and 40 drops in the inspection garage. The design of the network will have to meet the following criteria:

- A total of 82 network devices will be installed in Phase 1 of the administrative building.
- A total of 30 network devices will be installed during Phase 1 in the inspection garage.
- In the administrative building, there are two areas where clusters of computers will outnumber the wall jacks in close physical proximity. It has been recommended that desktop switches be employed in these two areas.
- The cable installers have qualified the single-mode fiber-optic backbone and have terminated a pair of the cables with LC connectors on each end. Each termination is fed into the telecommunications room of both the administrative building and the inspection garage.

In the following steps, you will research and select the switches to meet the design specifications of the campus and define the quantity and location of each switch. You'll also explore some of the modular interface options to connect local area network and wide area network backbones. Better get to work!

Step 1 With the current layout of the facilities and total number of network nodes (devices), you will need to provide anywhere from 100 to 140 network connections throughout the two physical buildings. Each NIC ultimately connects to a port on a switch.

Depending on the application of the switch, you may have to make some decisions, such as whether to install economical, desktop switches or enterprise, fully-managed switches, and whether you will provide power to downstream devices through the Ethernet cabling known as Power over Ethernet (PoE). You'll also want to plan on having one switch in each physical building that will provide fiber-optic ports to tie in the backbone between the two buildings.

✖ **Cross-Reference**

You will study and perform other exercises with Ethernet switches later in Chapter 6, "Structured Cabling," and Chapter 12, "Advanced Networking Devices." If you would like to familiarize yourself with managed and unmanaged switches or multilayer switches, you can jump ahead and read the sections "VLAN" and "Multilayer Switches" in Chapter 12. You do not need detailed understanding of these switching technologies to complete this lab exercise step, but you will want to understand these technologies before taking the CompTIA Network+ Certification Exam.

Using the Internet, explore the various gigabit switches available today, and price out a configuration to meet the needs of this facility. You should document the following varieties at various price points:

✔ **Hint**

You can learn a lot about switches and switching technology from the manufacturers' product descriptions. Take some time while you are researching the following models to explore the various applications and options presented in the online documentation. You will also find that you may have to visit multiple Web sites of manufacturers and resellers to uncover aspects of specifications, options, and pricing.

Here are some keywords to help you in your search: Gigabit Ethernet switch, Cisco, 3Com, D-Link, NETGEAR, Linksys, SFP LC, GBIC, and 1000BaseLX SFP transceivers.

a. Economical, desktop switches:

_____

_____

b. Managed switch supporting PoE:

_____

c. To implement the fiber-optic backbone, almost every mid- to high-end switch offers some type of Small Form Factor (SFF) port. Most manufacturers are offering a modular design with either Small Form-factor Pluggable (SFP) or gigabit interface converter (GBIC) transceivers to support multiple technologies and connections without replacing the switch. Explore the offerings for 1000BaseLX SFP transceivers to enable these switches for the single-mode fiber-optic backbone connection between the buildings:

_____

_____

Step 2   Now it is time to configure the telecommunications rooms and workgroups to enable the network. Using the information you have gathered in Step 1, describe the switch configuration you will be using to support the regional DMV.

a. The administrative building will initially implement 82 of the 100 cable drops available throughout the building. Remember that you will need to configure the interface for the fiber-optic connection between the two buildings. What quantity and configuration of switches do you recommend to meet the requirements of the network design?

_____

_____

b. There will be two workgroups located in areas that will not support the total number of network devices that the workgroups will be using (only one or two drops in these areas). What is your recommendation to accommodate the additional network devices?

_____

_____

c. The inspection garage will initially implement 30 of the 40 cable drops available throughout the building. Remember that you will need to configure the interface for the fiber-optic connection between the two buildings. What quantity and configuration of switches do you recommend to meet the requirements of the network design?

_____

_____

Step 3   Describe the advantages and requirements of using full-duplex Ethernet over half-duplex Ethernet.

✖ **Cross-Reference**

To refresh your understanding of half-duplex versus full-duplex, refer to the "Full Duplex Ethernet" section of Chapter 5 in the *Mike Meyers' CompTIA Network+ Guide to Managing and Troubleshooting Networks* textbook.

_____

_____

_____

_____

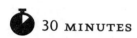 30 MINUTES

Lab Exercise 5.03: Beyond Gigabit: 10 Gigabit Ethernet

Gigabit Ethernet is becoming the standard for new installs right to the desktop! In other words, 1000-Mbps NICs and switches are reaching a price point where they can be implemented cost-effectively throughout an organization. As you learned in previous labs, many gigabit NICs and switches are available to complement the design of modern organizational networks.

10 Gigabit Ethernet (10 GbE) is currently the reigning champion of speed for computer networks providing 10 gigabits of data per second over copper or fiber-optic connections. 10 GbE is still comparatively pricy and therefore relegated to high-demand, high-speed applications: high-demand servers, campus backbones, and WAN communications. In this lab, you'll explore some of the aspects of 10 GbE.

Learning Objectives

In this lab, you will examine 10 GbE options for modern network environments. When you've completed this lab, you will be able to

- Describe the 10GBaseT, 10GBaseSR/SW, 10GBaseLR/LW, and 10GBaseER/EW Ethernet specifications, requirements, and limitations

- Examine 10 GbE NICs

- Determine appropriate switching interfaces to implement 10 GbE backbones

Lab Materials and Setup

The materials you'll need for this lab are

- The *Mike Meyers' CompTIA Network+ Guide to Managing and Troubleshooting Networks* textbook

- A computer with Internet access

- Pencil and paper

Getting Down to Business

One of the benefits of the network design the team has implemented for the regional DMV is known as *future-proofing*. Throughout the design and install, the highest-performance cabling has been used (Category 6 UTP, 10 GbE single-mode fiber-optic), and switches in the telecommunications room utilize modular SFP interfaces that can be upgraded as well. Running 10 GbE to the desktop is still cost-prohibitive, but implementing 10 GbE for the communication on the high-traffic servers and the backbone between the administrative building and the inspection garage may be feasible.

CJ asks Maggie to research 10 GbE solutions and to prepare a presentation of her findings, including interfaces and pricing, to the network design team. Maggie asks if it would be okay to have you assist, so the two of you set off to prepare your report.

Step 1   10 GbE is still in its infancy stages, so the specifications of the various media and interfaces are still in development. Using various resources such as the textbook and the Internet, research and document the following implementations of 10 GbE:

a. 10GBaseT

   Cabling: _____

   Cable Details: _____

   Connectors: _____

   Length: _____

b. 10GBaseSR/SW

   Cabling: _____

   Cable Details: _____

   Connectors: _____

   Length: _____

c. 10GBaseLR/LW

   Cabling: _____

   Cable Details: _____

   Connectors: _____

   Length: _____

d. 10GBaseER/EW

Cabling: _____

Cable Details: _____

Connectors: _____

Length: _____

Step 2   The high-traffic servers are located in the telecommunications room, so copper or fiber-optic solutions are feasible. Research the current availability of network interface cards supporting 10 GbE technology. Document some of the makes and models, characteristics, and pricing:

_____

_____

What do you recommend: copper or fiber-optic technology? Why?

_____

_____

Step 3   Using online manufacturers' and resellers' Web sites, explore the various SFF 10 GbE interfaces available. Document the make, model, characteristics, and pricing as if you are shopping for the modular transceivers for the switches to implement the link between the administrative building and the inspection garage:

→ **Note**

In keeping with the scenario presented, the fiber-optic cabling you chose between the administrative building and the inspection garage may be specified to support 10 gigabit multimode fiber (MMF) (10GBase-SR). However, the total distance recommended for 10GBase-SR is only 26–300 meters (about 85–980 feet), so the distance of 900 feet could push the specifications for 10 GbE performance. In this case, higher-performance single-mode cable would be the better choice to implement 10 GbE. For the purposes of this lab exercise, provide the results of both 10GBase-SR and 10GBase-LR.

You will also have to be careful when physically implementing 10 GbE transceivers due to the various form factors of both the modular interfaces and the cable interfaces. Currently there are SFP+, XENPAK, X2, and XFP modules available, utilizing SC, LC, and various other fiber-optic cable terminations.

✔ **Hint**

Here is a cool Cisco page that covers all of the versions of modular transceiver they currently support. Cisco 10 Gigabit Ethernet Transceiver Modules Compatibility Matrix: www.cisco.com/en/US/docs/interfaces_modules/transceiver_modules/compatibility/matrix/OL_6974.html

_____

_____

Lab Analysis

1. Zilong has decided to install CAT 6 UTP cabling in a small office so that they may upgrade to 10GBaseT in the future without having to "pull" cable again. Are there any concerns you would voice with Zilong before he installs the CAT 6 cable?

_____

_____

2. Jeremy has been studying the requirements to implement 10 GbE and has discovered that the technology requires all interfaces to operate in full-duplex mode. What are the operational differences between half-duplex and full-duplex communication?

_____

_____

3. Katelyn is going to implement Gigabit Ethernet for a small office, home office (SOHO) campus. What kind of network cabling is necessary to implement Gigabit Ethernet?

_____

_____

4. Nate is studying fiber-optic technology and asks what the major differences are between 10GBaseSR and 10GBaseLR. Can you explain the difference?

_____

_____

5. Howard understands that high data-throughput speeds and longer throughput distances are two advantages of fiber-optic cabling over copper cabling. He doesn't understand why the cable installers are recommending the use of fiber-optic cable for the machine shop of a local high school. Can you describe two other advantages that fiber-optic cabling offers over copper wire that would help him understand?

_____

_____

Key Term Quiz

Use the vocabulary terms from the list below to complete the sentences that follow. Not all of the terms will be used.

100BaseT

100BaseFX

1000BaseT

1000BaseCX

1000BaseSX

1000BaseLX

10GBaseSR/SW

10GBaseLR/LW

10GBaseER/EW

auto-sensing

Fast Ethernet

full-duplex

Gigabit Ethernet

Gigabit Interface Converter (GBIC)

half-duplex

modular transceivers

Small Form-factor Pluggable (SFP)

SFP+

X2

XENPAK

XFP

1. The specification for 10-gigabit technology that uses 850 nm lasers over 50 and 62.5 multimode fiber (MMF) cable is _____.

2. The IEEE 802.3ae committee developed a multisource agreement (MSA) to define the 10 GbE modular transceiver. These specs are now incorporated into the revisions of the IEEE 802.3-2008. There are four versions of 10 GbE modular transceivers. The _____, _____, _____, and the _____ are all vying for market share.

3. A(n) _____ device is one that can send and receive data simultaneously.

4. To implement _____, CAT 5e or higher UTP cabling must be installed.

5. Many Gigabit Ethernet switches support _____ to allow support of the ever-increasing speeds. The two dominant forms of these switches are _____ and _____.

Chapter 6
Installing a Physical Network

Lab Exercises

Now that you're familiar with the major network types, topologies, and technologies that network techs have at their disposal, it's time to dive into the physical aspects of network implementation. These include installing the network media and network hardware that tie your network together, installing the switches that form the central communication point of the physical network, configuring the network adapters that connect your network nodes (PC workstations, servers, printers, and so on) to the network, testing network connections, and troubleshooting any ensuing network errors.

As discussed in the textbook and defined in the CompTIA Network+ Certification Exam Objectives, you are not expected to be as knowledgeable as a professional network designer or cable installer when it comes to the actual implementation of the physical network. However, you will need to be familiar with the concepts! Working with the cable, hardware, devices, installation tools, and troubleshooting tools is a great way to learn the concepts, so this is a good place to start practicing.

 20 MINUTES

Lab Exercise 6.01: Examining Structured Network Cabling

One of the proposals that your client received for the installation of the Department of Motor Vehicles (DMV) complex was from an inexperienced firm. The professional cable installers calculated the horizontal runs and cable drops needed from the telecommunications room to each node, the methods to install the cable runs in the inspection garage, the type of UTP cabling to implement, and the outfitting of the telecommunications room. CJ asks for your assistance to double-check the proposal.

Learning Objectives

In this lab, you will examine the principles that lead to a successful structured network cabling installation. When you have completed this lab, you will be able to

- Understand the proper planning issues that go into a network deployment
- Make informed recommendations for a network installation

Lab Materials and Setup

The materials you'll need for this lab are

- The *Mike Meyers' CompTIA Network+ Guide to Managing and Troubleshooting Networks* textbook

- A small length of CAT 5e or CAT 6 plenum grade, solid-core cable

- A small length of CAT 5e or CAT 6 stranded copper patch cable

- Pencil and paper

Getting Down to Business

When planning a building project these days, almost all designs will take into account the design of the network infrastructure. The professional network designers will work hand in hand with the architects to include telecommunications room(s) right from the initial design. If it is a new build, as the DMV project is, network cable will be strung along with electrical and telephone cabling during the building process, saving the cable installers from the tedious task of "pulling cable" after the building is in place.

Examine the following steps as if they were components of the proposal from the professional cable installers and network infrastructure design team.

✖ Cross-Reference

You may want to review the "Understanding Structured Cabling" section of Chapter 6 in the *Mike Meyers' CompTIA Network+ Guide to Managing and Troubleshooting Networks* textbook. Also review the specifics of CompTIA Network+ Exam Objectives, Domain 3.6—Given a scenario, troubleshoot common physical connectivity problems, and Domain 4.2—Given a scenario, use appropriate hardware tools to troubleshoot connectivity issues.

Step 1   The administration building will have 100 cable runs. You are examining the network cabling installation proposal that was submitted by the inexperienced professional cable installers. The following is a sample of some of the runs, shortest to longest, that the proposal calls out:

Location	Distance
MDF Telecommunications Room Patch Panel to Network Node A	48 meters (157 feet)
MDF Telecommunications Room Patch Panel to Network Node B	55 meters (180 feet)
MDF Telecommunications Room Patch Panel to Network Node C	60 meters (197 feet)
MDF Telecommunications Room Patch Panel to Network Node D	68 meters (223 feet)
MDF Telecommunications Room Patch Panel to Network Node E	75 meters (246 feet)
MDF Telecommunications Room Patch Panel to Network Node F	84 meters (275 feet)

Location	Distance	
MDF Telecommunications Room Patch Panel to Network Node G	91 meters (300 feet)	
MDF Telecommunications Room Patch Panel to Network Node H	102 meters (334 feet)	
MDF Telecommunications Room Patch Panel to Network Node I	113 meters (371 feet)	
MDF Telecommunications Room Patch Panel to Network Node J	122 meters (400 feet)	
MDF Telecommunications Room Patch Panel to Network Node K	125 meters (410 feet)	

The proposal calls for using CAT 6 UTP network cabling. Which, if any, of the network cabling runs are outside the limits for that type of cabling? Does your answer change if you are running 10 GbE equipment? What solutions can you offer to overcome any limit violations?

_____

_____

Step 2   Many of the runs in the inspection garage will be terminated at inspection stations right on the garage floor. These stations will be unfinished areas of the garage (no office walls or cubicles). The walls of this area are concrete. What is the best way to install the network cable drops in this area?

_____

_____

Step 3   As you have learned, the horizontal cable runs will most likely be snaking through walls and ceilings of public offices. As such, the proper type of cabling should be used for the horizontal runs. Closely examine a small length of UTP cable recommended for horizontal use. Look for information printed right on the outer insulation of the cable and then strip a length off one end and examine the copper wires. Document some of the features of the cable.

_____

_____

There will also be patch cables between the wall jack and the network devices as well as the patch panels and switches. Closely examine a small length of UTP patch cable. Look for information printed right on the outer insulation of the cable and then strip a length off one end and examine the copper wires. Document some of the features of the cable.

_____

_____

Step 4   List at least four requirements for the telecommunications room(s) that will house rack-mounted patch panels, a stack of switches, and at least one file server.

_____

_____

 1 HOUR

Lab Exercise 6.02: Implementing a Small Network Infrastructure

Installing the cabling that carries data frames from one network node to another (affectionately called "pulling cable") is the most physically demanding task in a network installation and is typically left to professional cable installers. Believe me, once you've got your network cabling installed, you don't want to have to go back into the walls and pull it out again! Tasks include planning the installation, pulling the cabling, connecting network access jacks, and finally testing the connections to ensure that your installation is successful.

Though full-blown corporate cable installs are left to the professionals, many network techs have been called upon to wire a room, upgrade a floor, or punch down a new patch panel. You'll want to be familiar with the basic skills of pulling cable through a ceiling, punching down a patch panel, and connecting the wall jack (also known as a *keystone*). This will not only help you in the field; it will also clarify key concepts you will see on the CompTIA Network+ exam.

Learning Objectives

In this lab, you'll practice the art of installing network cabling, hardware, and devices.

When you have completed this lab, you will be able to

- Pull a length of cable through a ceiling (or raceway)
- Use a punchdown tool and terminate UTP cabling into a rackmounted patch panel
- Drop a cable through a wall and terminate the cable drop with an RJ-45 keystone
- Mount a wall plate
- Verify the run using a cable tester

Lab Materials and Setup

> **→ Note**
>
> It would really help to have an actual wall and equipment rack to perform this lab. There are commercial practice walls that are sold just for this purpose. However, over the years I have actually built my own practice wall with a handful of drywall screws, a number of 2×4 studs, and a couple of sheets of drywall (see Figure 6-1). It doesn't have to be pretty, just functional. You can even get some cable trays to form a false ceiling for the cables to run over. Worst case, just get the cable, hardware, and devices and complete all of the punchdowns on a lab bench. You should still be able to demonstrate connectivity.

Figure 6-1 Do-it-yourself wall

The materials you'll need for this lab are

- Bulk UTP cabling (CAT 5e or better)
- Nylon pull rope
- 24- to 48-port rackmount patch panel
- RJ-45 wall jack keystone (quantity 2 to 4)
- Low-voltage mounting bracket and faceplate (quantity 2 to 4)
- Drywall saw
- Wire snips
- 110-punchdown tool
- Cable tester
- Label maker

Getting Down to Business

Installing structured network cabling begins with planning. You should physically survey the site and examine the site's floor plan for any hazards that you may not be able to spot visually. Then you can examine the logistics of your planned installation, such as the methods that you will use to deploy and install the horizontal cabling, network outlet drop locations, and so on. You also need to select the most appropriate type of cabling for the job, making sure to comply with any applicable codes and regulations. Then you should document your plans and note any discrepancies during installation. Remember to label your runs and outlets while you're at it. Finally, you need to test your network cabling for continuity and troubleshoot any problems that arise. These are the basic steps that apply to any network cabling installation, from the small office/home office (SOHO) environment with only a few workstations to the large enterprise with thousands of clients.

In the following steps, you will "pull cable," drop it through a small practice wall, punch down one end to a rackmount patch panel, punch down the other end to an RJ-45 keystone, and then fix the RJ-45 keystone into a wall-mounted faceplate. You will repeat this a second time, providing two cable drops. Later, in Lab Exercise 6.03, you will install and verify the configuration of a couple of NICs, add a switch, connect the two computers, and then voilà, you have a small network! You have a lot of work to do, so get going!

Step 1 Start with the placement of the wall jack. Using a pencil and tape measure, choose the location along the wall for the wall jack and mark the wall 18 inches off the floor. Depending on the style of low-voltage mounting bracket you are using, use the drywall saw to cut an appropriate size hole to mount the bracket. See Figures 6-2 and 6-3 for an example of cutting the drywall and mounting a bracket.

FIGURE 6-2 Cutting a hole

FIGURE 6-3 Installing a low-voltage mounting bracket

✖ **Cross-Reference**

Consult the "Installing Structured Cabling" section of Chapter 6 in the *Mike Meyers' CompTIA Network+ Guide to Managing and Troubleshooting Networks* **textbook**.

Step 2   Now using the tape measure, measure the lateral distance between the proposed cable drop and the telecommunications room. This will be the basis for the length of cable you will need for this run. Remember, you will typically be "pulling" this cable through the drop ceiling and either using cable hangers or trays to keep it suspended off the ceiling tiles. You will want to include the distance for the height of the ceiling and the cable hangers or trays to the wall outlet and the patch panel to the total length of cable that you will cut.

➜ **Note**

Professional cable installers will typically pull one or more cables at a time from the telecommunications room through the walls and ceilings to the cable drop location. They will leave the cable on the spool as they pull it through the ceiling and walls, rolling out the amount needed plus some slack before snipping the cable from the spool. Since you are most likely using a smaller practice wall, you may not follow this exact technique.

What is the total length of cable that you have calculated?

_____

_____

Step 3   Starting at the telecommunications room (where you have located your equipment rack and patch panel), attach a nylon pull rope to the UTP cable and begin to pull the cable through the cable hangers or cable trays until you reach the cable drop location. Be careful to ease the cable through any snags or twists as you do not want to break the internal cables, rendering the run useless.

At the point of the cable drop, fasten a small weight to the end of the nylon pull rope, and using some finesse, drop the pull rope through the wall to the hole created for the wall jack (see Figure 6-4). The cable should be long enough that you have six inches to a foot of spare cable at each end. One end will be terminated to the patch panel; the other will be terminated to the RJ-45 keystone.

Figure 6-4 Dropping the cable

Step 4 While located at the equipment rack, strip approximately one inch of the outer insulation from the UTP cable, and slightly untwist the four pairs. Following the labeling or color code guide on the patch panel, use the 110-punchdown tool to fasten the cables to the block for port 1 of the patch panel (see Figure 6-5).

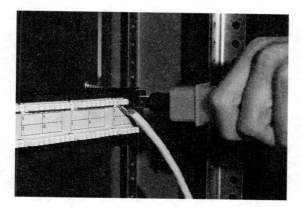

Figure 6-5 Punching down the patch panel

Step 5 While you're at the wall jack, feed the cable through the low-voltage mounting bracket and fasten the bracket to the wall. Strip approximately one inch of the outer insulation from the UTP cable and slightly untwist the 4-pairs. Following the labeling or color code guide on the RJ-45 keystone, use the 110-punchdown tool to fasten the cables to the block (see Figure 6-6).

➜ **Note**

RJ-45 keystones come in many styles, incorporating different methods to connect the wires to the pins of the RJ-45 jack. Most use a small 110-punchdown block to facilitate this connection. Follow the instructions for the style of RJ-45 keystone you are working with.

Figure 6-6 Punching down the RJ-45 keystone

Step 6   Insert the keystone into the faceplate, and fasten the faceplate to the low-voltage mounting bracket (see Figure 6-7).

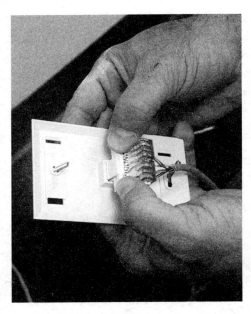

Figure 6-7 Fitting the keystone into the faceplate

Step 7   Verify the cable run using a commercial cable tester.

➜ **Note**

Professional cable installers will use much more complex, and expensive, cable certifiers to verify not only connectivity but attenuation, near-end crosstalk (NEXT), and far-end crosstalk (FEXT) of the cable run. For the purposes of this lab exercise, only the connectivity of the cable run will be verified. If you have access to a high-end cable certifier, by all means, examine the attenuation, NEXT, and FEXT.

Most testers come with a remote end and a master module. Using a known-good patch cable, connect the master module to port 1 of the patch panel. Using a second known-good patch cable, connect the remote end to the RJ-45 connector in the wall jack. Following the directions provided with the cable tester, verify the connectivity of the cable run. Record your results in the following table:

TIA/EIA 568 Pair	Connection	Results (Good/Bad)
Wire Pair 1	Pin 5 to Pin 5	
	Pin 4 to Pin 4	
Wire Pair 2	Pin 1 to Pin 1	
	Pin 2 to Pin 2	
Wire Pair 3	Pin 3 to Pin 3	
	Pin 6 to Pin 6	
Wire Pair 4	Pin 7 to Pin 7	
	Pin 8 to Pin 8	

Step 8   Don't forget to label both the patch panel and the wall jack (see Figures 6-8 and 6-9). After all of the runs are in place, you will save hours of troubleshooting time with properly labeled patch panels and wall jacks!

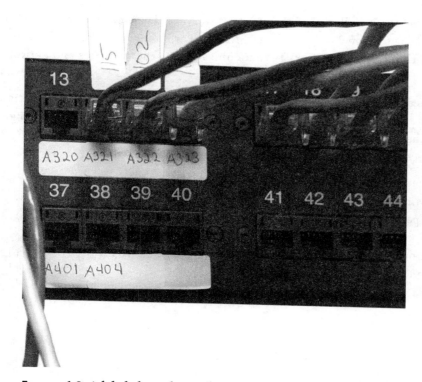

FIGURE 6-8 A labeled patch panel

Figure 6-9 Properly labeled wall jack

Step 9   Create a second run and drop, following Steps 1 through 8. In Step 4, use the second port of the patch panel.

 30 MINUTES

Lab Exercise 6.03: Installing Switches, Network Adapters, and PCs

In the prior exercise, you completed the installation of the physical wiring of the network, and verified that you had connectivity from the patch panel to the wall jack. Now you are going to explore and install the devices that allow PCs to use that physical network to communicate: Ethernet switches and network interface cards.

Switches form the central meeting point for all of the cable runs and provide smooth communication between all of the devices attached to those cable runs. The telecommunications room is the gathering place for patch panels and switches. Each run that is terminated at the patch panel will be "patched" into the switch to provide connectivity to all the other devices on the network.

Your PC's physical link to the network is the network adapter. You're probably used to hearing this piece of equipment referred to simply as a network interface card (NIC), because historically, this device was only available as an add-on peripheral card. With the worldwide application of networking, most notably the Internet, modern PC manufacturers have adopted the practice of integrating the network adapter (electronics and connector) right on the motherboard. Newer machines are incorporating 1- to 2-Gbps Ethernet interfaces using RJ-45 jacks.

→ **Note**

NICs haven't gone away; they are just utilized slightly differently these days. Often, an older machine can be upgraded with higher-speed copper, fiber-optic, or wireless adapters. Sometimes USB adapters are used to facilitate connectivity (especially for wireless and Bluetooth). You will still see PC Card (PCMCIA) network adapters being used on laptops, but even laptop manufactures are incorporating wired and wireless interfaces into the onboard electronics. Installing and configuring switches, network adapters, and PCs is a task that many network techs do so often it becomes second nature. In later chapters you will study more complex configuration components and practices for both switches and network interfaces. Currently, I want you to focus on the physical aspects of the installation and configuration; that is, connecting and communicating from one PC to another over your physical installation.

Learning Objectives

You'll begin this lab by installing and patching the Ethernet switch into the rack. You will then install and/or configure a network interface. This may include an integrated network interface, or an add-on device such as an internal NIC or USB network adapter, on your PC. You'll finish up by verifying proper operation through the device and configuration tools included with the operating system and establishing connectivity between two machines. By the end of this lab, you will be able to

- Install a rackmount switch and correctly cable it to a patch panel
- Properly install and configure a network interface
- Verify connectivity between two PCs

Lab Materials and Setup

The materials you'll need for this lab are

- A rackmount Ethernet switch
- Minimum four (4) CAT 5 or better straight-through patch cables
- Two PCs with either integrated network interfaces or expansion card NICs (PCI, PCIe, and the like)
- Windows XP, Vista, or Windows 7 operating systems installed
- A Phillips-head screwdriver

Getting Down to Business

With the fine art of pulling cable, terminating connections, and verifying continuity of the structured cabling complete, it's time to get the telecommunications room and the work area up to par. This is where the network tech is responsible for the connectivity! The network tech must be able to connect and verify switches, servers, and wide area network devices in the telecommunications room, and guarantee that all of the PCs can communicate with the servers and the outside world.

Using the mock wall from the previous exercise, you are now going to install a rackmount switch, and two PCs (with network interfaces) to complete a small working office network.

Step 1   Starting in the telecommunications room (the equipment rack between your two mock walls), mount the Ethernet switch.

Step 2   Using two of the straight-through patch cables, connect ports one and two of the patch panel to two of the open ports on the switch.

Step 3   Now moving to the work area (the two PCs you are going to use near the two wall jacks), examine the physical PCs and determine if there are integrated network interfaces. If the systems are equipped with on-board interfaces, you may skip to Step 8. If a NIC needs to be installed in either of the machines, use the following guidelines (Steps 4 through 7) to install the NIC.

Step 4   To install a network interface card in a Windows XP–based machine, choose **Start | Shut Down**, and then select **Shut down** and click the **OK** button to turn the PC off. Once the PC is completely powered down, unplug all cables, including the power cable, from the power supply.

→ Note

As recommended by CompTIA A+ certified techs the world over, be sure to follow all proper anti-static procedures when working inside your PC case. Use an anti-static mat and anti-static wrist strap if you have them. If you lack these components, the next best thing is to discharge any static electricity in your body by touching a grounded metal component on the PC case (such as the power supply casing). Before you start poking around inside the PC case, remove any rings, bracelets, watches, or any other items that may snag on exposed components.

Step 5   Place the PC case on an anti-static mat and attach your anti-static wrist strap (a.k.a. nerd bracelet), and then remove the PC case cover to expose the interior.

Step 6   Using the NICs provided by your instructor (PCI, PCIe), locate an available expansion bus slot. Remove the slot cover, and then insert the NIC into the slot. Be sure to handle the NIC only by its edges, and firmly press the card straight down into the slot. Once the NIC is properly seated in the slot, make sure it is secure by applying whichever locking mechanism the expansion card uses.

Step 7   Replace the PC case cover and reattach all cables to the PC, including the power cable, then start the PC and log on when the desktop appears. Windows XP, Vista, and Windows 7 have built-in support for many NICs, so assuming you're running Windows XP, Vista, or Windows 7, Plug-and-Play kicks in, detects the card, installs Windows' built-in drivers, and alerts you that the NIC is ready to use, as shown in Figure 6-10. In most cases, the Windows NIC driver works fine, but it's usually a good idea to use the latest driver provided by the NIC manufacturer.

FIGURE 6-10 The Windows XP Professional New Network Device Installed alert

Step 8   Open the Windows Device Manager and expand the list of installed NICs. Double-click the NIC's icon to open its **Properties** dialog box, as shown in Figure 6-11. Record the make and model of the NIC. Is the NIC functional? What are the details of the driver that is installed?

FIGURE 6-11 The NIC Properties dialog box

Step 9   Once the systems have been verified to have working network interfaces, place each system in proximity of each wall jack. Using the patch cables, connect each machine to the respective wall jack.

✔ **Hint**

At this point in your studies, you are not expected to perform the configuration of the network operating system and protocols. The next two steps will go much more smoothly if the computers have been preconfigured for network connectivity. If any of the results seem incorrect, please consult with your instructor to troubleshoot and diagnose the connectivity issues.

Step 10   Power up the Ethernet switch and the two PCs. With a little effort, you should be able to determine if the network has basic connectivity. Are there any visual indicators that the systems are connected to the switch?

_____

Step 11   Log on to the systems and experiment with Explorer to see if you can see each system from the other. Can you share or copy files from machine to machine? Are there any additional visual clues that the systems are communicating over the network?

_____

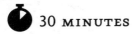 30 MINUTES

Lab Exercise 6.04: Diagnostics and Troubleshooting

Network connectivity issues come in many shapes and sizes. Just like networks themselves, these issues can range from the simple to the complex. In this exercise, you'll walk through some simple diagnostic and troubleshooting steps to ensure that the physical network is in tip-top shape. Network adapter hardware is fairly foolproof, assuming that it has been installed and configured correctly. A couple of quick tests confirm whether a lack of network connectivity lies with the network adapter hardware or somewhere else.

Once installed, network cabling doesn't suffer from a lot of wear and tear—after all, there are no moving parts, and the voltage carried is very low. Nonetheless, network cabling is subject to physical damage and interference, so it's important for you to be able to diagnose and repair this type of failure. Locating breaks in the cable is particularly frustrating, so having a time domain reflectometer (TDR) really comes in handy.

Even well-meaning, organized network techs can have a telecommunications room become a nightmare of snaked, unlabeled patch cables and runs. A toner is invaluable in this situation and will allow the network tech to get organized!

Basic Ethernet switches are fairly robust and normally provide for auto-sensing multispeed communications. It is not uncommon to have legacy devices on a gigabit network operating at 100 Mbps or even 10 Mbps. It is important that you be able to quickly verify that the switch is indeed communicating with legacy devices.

Learning Objectives

In this lab, you will go through some basic network connectivity troubleshooting scenarios, so by the time you complete this lab, you'll be able to

- Troubleshoot simple, physical network connectivity issues

Lab Materials and Setup

The materials you'll need for this lab are

- The two networked Windows PCs from the previous exercise

- A length of patch cable that can be cut in half

- A 10/100/1000 Ethernet switch

- A time domain reflectometer (TDR)

- A toner unit

- Access to the telecommunications room and patch panel from the previous exercise

Getting Down to Business

The first symptom of a network connectivity issue usually manifests itself as a loud screeching noise! Oddly enough, the noise is not coming from the network hardware or fancy test equipment, but from the frustrated user. Typically, this noise will be accompanied by a vocal error message, such as "I can't get on the Internet!" or "I can't get my e-mail!" "Great, the network is down!" is also pretty common. In most cases, network connectivity problems are simple in nature. Accordingly, you should begin your diagnosis and troubleshooting with simple solutions.

Assume for a moment that one of your network users is unable to access network resources. In the following steps, you'll go through a simple diagnostic and troubleshooting scenario.

✖ Cross-Reference

Additional information may be found in the "Testing the Cable Runs," "Link Lights," and "Diagnostics and Repair of Physical Cabling" sections of Chapter 6 in the *Mike Meyers' CompTIA Network+ Guide to Managing and Troubleshooting Networks* textbook.

Step 1 Your first step is to determine whether or not the PC has a network connection, and then determine the state of the connection. The obvious place to start is with the physical connection. Locate the PC's network adapter. Is the RJ-45 connector of the Ethernet cable plugged into the network adapter?

If so, check the status lights. What is the result?

_____

_____

Step 2 If you have physical connectivity, your next step is to determine if the operating system recognizes the connection. Windows provides a couple of methods to determine the network connection state quickly.

First, look in the System Tray/Notification area of the taskbar. Is there a **Local Area Connection Status** icon? If so, click **Open Network and Sharing Center**. (See Figure 6-12.) Now click on Connections: **Local Area Connection** to bring up the **Local Area Connection Status** dialog box as shown in Figure 6-13.

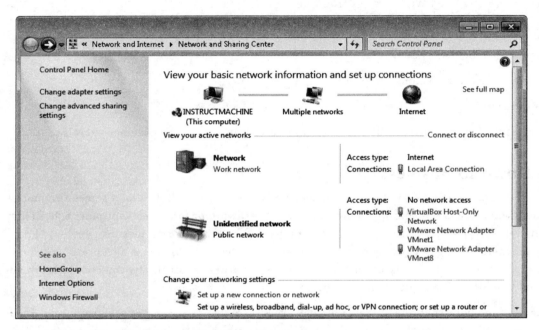

FIGURE 6-12 Windows 7 Network and Sharing Center

FIGURE 6-13 Windows 7 Local Area Connection Status

Fill in the following information. If no icon is visible, skip to Step 3.

IPv4 Connectivity: _____

IPv6 Connectivity: _____

Media State: _____

Duration: _____

Speed: _____

Step 3 An alternate path to the Status window in Windows 7 is as follows: Choose **Start | Control Panel**, select the **Network and Sharing Center** icon (if you're in the icon view), and then click **Change adapter settings** on the side menu.

Right-click the **Local Area Connection** icon and select **Status** from the pop-up menu to bring up the network connection's status dialog box. Are the reported results for the IPv4 Connectivity, IPv6 Connectivity, Media State, Duration, and Speed the same as in the previous Status report?

_____

_____

✔ Hint

Within Windows 7, it is possible to configure the **Local Area Connection Status** icon so that it is visible or hidden in the System Tray/Notification area. Open Control Panel, select **Notification Area Icons** (in the icon view), then select **Network Icon Behaviors** and choose to show or hide icons and notifications as shown in Figure 6-14.

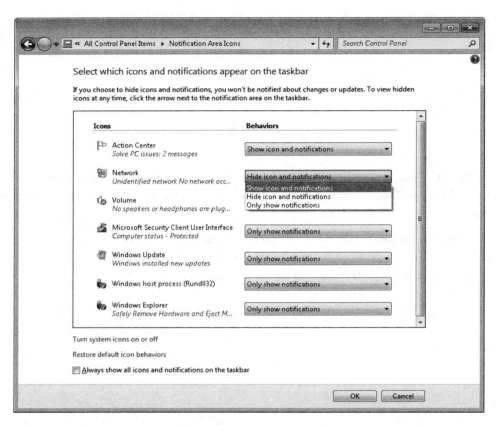

FIGURE 6-14 Windows 7 Notification Area Icons

Step 4 Disconnect the PC's network cable from the network adapter. What are the results?

_____

_____

Step 5 Using a loose patch cable, possibly with a partial slice or a missing RJ-45 connector, connect the cable to a TDR. What are the results?

_____

_____

Step 6 Using the mock wall with the equipment rack and the patch panel, attach the tone generator unit from a network toner to an active network drop wall outlet. Then go to the patch panel and use the tone probe unit to locate the patch panel cable that corresponds to the network outlet. What are the results?

_____

_____

Step 7   Most gigabit switches support auto-sensing, multispeed performance enabling 10-Mbps, 100-Mbps, and 1000-Mbps devices to connect and communicate through the same switch. Often, these switches will even have status lights (LEDs) that indicate the operating speed of the attached device.

Using a 10/100/1000 Ethernet switch, configure a small network with devices using a mixture of 100BaseT NICs and 1000BaseT NICs. Include a device with a 10BaseT NIC, if one is available, just to see what happens. Document the results of the status lights on the switch. Can all of the devices communicate with each other?

_____

_____

→ Note

A simple five-port or eight-port workgroup 10/100/1000 Ethernet switch will work fine for this exercise. Different switches may or may not support status indicator lights for multispeed operation, so the only confirmation of the operation of the switch with different speed NICs will be successful communication.

You may also need to work with the network configuration of the devices (computers or printers) to implement network communication. Please consult with your instructor for further directions.

 Open

Lab Exercise 6.05: Field Trip: A Visit with the IT Department

You have spent the first third of this class studying the physical components of computer networking. Classroom exercises involving topologies, technologies, the OSI model, Ethernet, and devices have strengthened your understanding of these components. Now it is time to go see these components in a real-world environment!

Just about every organization has some collection of information technology, and often, the IT department is more than happy to show off their implementation of the technology to meet their users' needs. If you are attending a CompTIA Network+ class, the facility or the school where you are taking the class is a great place to request a tour of the IT department and the telecommunications room(s). Talk with your instructor, make a few inquiries, and set up a visit with the IT department of an organization in your community.

Learning Objectives

This lab is actually more of a recommended activity. When you have completed this lab, you will be able to

- Explore the real-world implementation of the physical network

- Establish communication with local IT department personnel

Lab Materials and Setup

The materials you'll need for this lab are

- Pencil and paper

- An invite to tour an organization's facilities and telecommunications room(s)

Getting Down to Business

It is important to establish a rapport with the personnel that you will be spending time with. Obviously, it is not their primary responsibility to be ushering around a small class of students through their facilities and discussing their physical network with you. However, you will find that if you are courteous, many network techs enjoy talking about their network infrastructure solutions.

If you are in an instructor-led class, you will most likely be invited to visit a location of the instructor's choosing. This can be very informative as the instructor usually will have established a rapport with the techs prior to your visit, which means they will probably be very agreeable to entertaining your questions. Plan on asking a bunch!

Step 1   When visiting a physical location, it would be beneficial if you could examine a copy of the floor plans. However, with the need for heightened security at every level, viewing the floor plans will probably not be an option. Work through the following scenario even if your answers do not pertain to an actual physical location. The steps will still reinforce your understanding of the physical layout of a network.

The blueprints will offer a visual indication of all of the important areas of the facility including the Main Distribution Frame (MDF), any Intermediate Distribution Frames (IDFs), the Demarc, and all of the cable drops to wall outlets. Study the floor plan and prepare a detailed description of the facility, including the following points:

a.   Identify and note the approximate location of the MDF.

_____

b.   Identify the IDF(s). How many are implemented in this facility? What is the approximate location of each compared to the MDF?

_____

c.   Is the Demarc identified in the floor plans? Is it located in the MDF or is it located in a completely isolated part of the building?

_____

d. What is the approximate total number of drops (wall outlets) for this facility? The network administrator may be able to help you with this one, as opposed to your counting all of the cable drops in the floor plan!

_____

Step 2   Ask if it is possible to get a tour of the facilities. One area of interest would be the MDF telecommunications room. Most likely this is where the foundation of the network infrastructure has been established. You might use some of the following questions as openers for further discussion about the facilities:

a. Are there any special conditions that have been set up in the telecommunications room (that is, air conditioning, electrical service, and so on)?

_____

b. Is most of the equipment (UPSes, switches, patch panels, and servers) rackmounted? What are the approximate quantities of equipment (racks, patch panels, switches, servers, and so on)?

_____

c. Note the labeling technique. Are most of the important components and runs labeled?

_____

d. What category of cable is used throughout the facility?

_____

e. What are the common speeds of switches and NICs?

_____

f. Are there any fiber-optic technologies implemented in this facility?

_____

Step 3   What complement of test equipment do the network techs employ to verify the connectivity of the network?

cable tester   _____

time domain reflectometer   _____

cable certifier   _____

toner   _____

Lab Analysis

1. James complains that he cannot get on your corporate network. You discover that he moved his desk and PC to another part of his office, and in doing so forcibly pulled the CAT 5e patch cable out of its wall outlet. A quick visual inspection doesn't reveal any obvious damage to the patch cable. How do you determine if the patch cable is damaged?

2. Nick has been asked to patch in a new install. What specialized equipment will he use to connect the endpoint of a cable run to a patch panel?

3. The cable installers have been working all day and have now completed the internal wiring for 48 wall outlets. Mitch asks if he can use the leftover cabling to create the patch cables for some of the workstations. You explain to Mitch that this would not be a good idea. Why?

4. Cynthia was talking with Maggie, and asked why you would always defer to professional cable installers to guarantee cable runs, and why the higher-bandwidth cabling and connections needed more precise placement and termination when installed. How do you think Maggie responded to these questions?

5. Joseph has upgraded a small 25-node network with cabling and switches to operate at 1000Base-T. He has a few old HP LaserJet 4100n printers with 100Base-T JetDirect cards. He is concerned that they will have to be upgraded as well. What do you recommend he do?

Key Term Quiz

Use the vocabulary terms from the list below to complete the sentences that follow. Not all of the terms will be used.

110-punchdown	network interface card (NIC)
activity light	patch cable
ANSI/TIA	patch panel
auto-sensing	plenum
building entrance	punchdown tool
cable certifier	PVC (polyvinyl chloride)
cable drop	run
cable tester	solid core
Demarc	stranded core
horizontal cabling	structured cable
Intermediate Distribution Frame (IDF)	telecommunications room
link light	time domain reflectometer (TDR)
Main Distribution Frame (MDF)	tone generator
mounting rack	tone probe
multispeed	units (U)
network	work area

1. Chase has determined that his connectivity problem is between the patch panel and the wall outlet. He uses a(n) _____ to pinpoint the exact location of the cable break.

2. Use a(n) _____ and _____ to trace network cabling between a wall outlet and a patch panel.

3. In a facility, the point where responsibility of the physical cabling shifts from the ISP to the organization is known as the _____.

4. Practically all modern Ethernet switches and NICs are _____ and _____.

5. The simplest test of network connectivity is to check the NIC's _____.

Chapter 7
TCP/IP Basics

Lab Exercises

The Transmission Control Protocol/Internet Protocol (TCP/IP) suite can trace its beginnings all the way back to the late 1960s, when the first four network nodes were connected to the Advanced Research Project Agency Network (ARPANET). This enabled communication between host computers at UCLA, Stanford Research Center, UC Santa Barbara, and the University of Utah. Over the next decade, a group of scholars and engineers contributed specifications for the initial protocols that make up the TCP/IP suite, which was officially "launched" on January 1, 1983.

While other networking protocols have come and gone, TCP/IP has stood the test of time, and is the most popular protocol in use today. Many factors have contributed to this popularity, including the fact that TCP/IP is the protocol suite of the Internet. If you send or receive an e-mail, research information, or play an online role-playing game with thousands of people from around the world, you're using the TCP/IP suite to communicate! Also, the TCP/IP suite was placed in the public domain, ensuring that companies could design network software using the protocol suite. All of the major operating systems—Windows, Linux, UNIX, and OS X—provide network communication via TCP/IP. Another important contribution to TCP/IP's popularity is that it is built on a set of dynamic specifications that are constantly modified and updated through a process known as *Request for Comments (RFCs)*. RFCs ensure that TCP/IP is relevant to the networking technologies and methodologies now and in the future. You may peruse the thousands of RFCs at www.ietf.org/rfc.html.

In this chapter, you'll explore and configure the basics of IPv4 addressing and subnet masks. You'll examine how a network node—or, as they're usually called when discussing TCP/IP, a network host—determines whether an IP address is local or remote, and you'll set up the parameters that will enable your system to communicate with hosts on remote networks. This chapter will focus on IPv4. Later, in Chapter 13, you will dive into IPv6.

Wireshark, a freeware network protocol analyzer, will enable you to view the contents of Ethernet frames. You'll use this to examine how IP addresses (the logical addresses) are resolved to MAC addresses (the physical addresses). Remember, Ethernet ultimately uses the MAC addresses to get the frames from machine to machine. You'll configure both static and dynamic IP addressing, then finish with a review of Automatic Private IP Addressing (APIPA).

As you develop the skill sets required of a network technician, and study to pass the CompTIA Network+ certification exam, it is imperative that you comprehend the finer details of the TCP/IP suite. There is a lot to cover in this chapter, and at times it will be pretty intense, but I know you have what it takes to see it through. Mike suggests taking a break midway through with World of Warcraft or Counter-Strike. Me; I think I'll just go rock some Aerosmith in Guitar Hero!

 45 MINUTES

Lab Exercise 7.01: Diagramming the IP Address and Subnet Mask

There are two key components to all IP addresses: the IP address itself and the corresponding subnet mask. The IP host addresses follow defined rules that specify whether they are valid IP addresses, which network they belong to, and their unique computer address on that network. These are configured using the IP address and the subnet mask. You should appreciate that a network host's IP address and subnet mask, both displayed in dotted decimal notation, are simply numeric representations of the binary values. It's these binary values that identify each node on the TCP/IP network. Finally, you should recognize that there are defined IP address classes, and that each of those classes comes with its own default subnet mask.

Valid IP addresses must follow a specific format. Knowing the rules for valid IP addresses is particularly important when you must manually configure a network node's IP address. Configuring an IP address in the wrong format means that your PC won't communicate on the network.

There's a T-shirt available from thinkgeek.com that reads, "There are only 10 types of people in the world: Those who understand binary, and those who don't." It's good for a laugh to anyone who understands the basics of IP addressing. You don't have to speak binary as fluently as Sheldon from *The Big Bang Theory* to be a good network tech, but you should be able to perform simple decimal-to-binary and binary-to-decimal conversions without much trouble.

You also need to understand the default IP address class ranges specified by the Internet Assigned Numbers Authority (IANA), and the corresponding subnet masks that define them.

Learning Objectives

In this lab, you will review the basic rules of IP addressing. When you've completed this lab, you will be able to

- Convert IP addresses and subnet masks from dotted decimal notation to binary values
- Identify IP address class ranges

- Name default subnet masks

- Define network IDs and host IDs

- Validate IP addresses and subnet masks for a given network

Lab Materials and Setup

The materials you will need for this lab are

- Pencil and paper

- A working, networked computer with Windows

- Calculator with scientific or programmer view (the Windows calculator will do just fine!)

Getting Down to Business

CJ has appropriated some funds to set up a small networking lab in one of the spare offices at ITCF. It will consist of six Windows machines (Windows 7), four Linux machines (Ubuntu), and a server running Windows Server 2008. For the time being, he has provided a couple of simple eight-port workgroup switches and a Linksys router.

Maggie recommends that you head up the group to assemble and configure the network. Before working with the hardware, you'll work through the basic configuration of IP addressing. Follow these steps to strengthen your prowess in IP addressing.

Step 1   Maggie explains that every TCP/IP network must have a valid network ID and that each device (host) on the network must have a unique host ID on that network. She starts you off with a Class C network and provides the following network ID and subnet mask.

| Network ID | 192. | 168. | 5. | 0 |
| Subnet Mask | 255. | 255. | 255. | 0 |

You'll start this exercise by converting the network ID and subnet mask to their binary equivalents. The built-in Windows calculator is an invaluable tool for configuring and converting network IDs, IP addressess, and subnet masks into their rudimentary binary format. As with many of the Windows tools, there are a number of ways to launch the Windows calculator. In Windows 7, click the Start button, type **calc** in the **Start | Search programs and files** dialog box, and press ENTER. Once the calculator is up and running, select **View** from the menu bar and click **Programmer** to change the view to programmer mode, as shown in Figure 7-1.

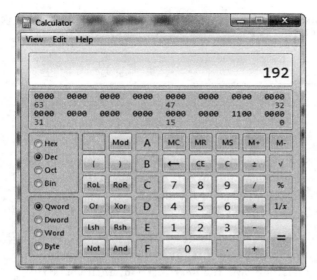

FIGURE 7-1 The Windows 7 calculator in programmer view mode

Note the radio buttons that enable you to convert between hexadecimal, decimal, octal, and binary values. By default, the decimal number system is selected. To convert a value from decimal to binary, simply enter the value and then select the binary (Bin) radio button. For example, the decimal value for the IP address of the Microsoft Web site, 207.46.131.43, converts to 11001111.00101110.10000011.00011111 in binary. In the following Lab Exercise, use the Windows calculator to convert the provided network ID and subnet mask into their binary values.

✔ Hint

For accurate results, convert each decimal value one octet at a time rather than entering the entire string of the IP address's digits all at once. Note also that smaller decimal values will generate fewer than eight digits when converted to binary. This is simply the Windows calculator leaving off the leading zeroes of the binary octet. When this happens, simply "pad" the binary value with enough leading zeroes to bring the total number of digits to eight. For example, the decimal value 46, converted to binary in the Windows calculator, displays a six-digit binary value of 101110. To bring this value "up to code," add two zeroes at the beginning for a result of 00101110.

Network ID	Dotted Decimal Notation	192.	168.	5.	0
	Binary Equivalent				
Subnet Mask	Dotted Decimal Notation	255.	255.	255.	0
	Binary Equivalent				

Step 2   Now close the Windows calculator and use the following chart to convert the following network IDs and subnet masks into binary values the "old-fashioned" way.

2^7	2^6	2^5	2^4	2^3	2^2	2^1	2^0
128	64	32	16	8	4	2	1

✔ **Hint**

The binary system, also referred to as the "base 2 numbering system," is based on powers of two, just as the decimal system is based on powers of 10. Each digit in this conversion table can be turned "on," represented by a value of 1, or "off," represented by a value of 0, to complete the eight digits contained in a binary octet.

To convert a decimal value to binary using this table, start with 128 and work your way to the right, marking a 1 in each position where your decimal value "fits" and subtracting that value from the decimal total. Then move to the next position, and the next position, until you arrive at 0. For example, take the decimal value 155 and match it to the chart. Can 128 fit into 155? Yes, so mark a 1 in that position. That leaves 27. Can 64 fit into 27? No, it cannot, so mark a 0 in that position. Same for 32, it does not fit into 27, so mark a 0 in that position. Since 16 fits into 27, mark a 1 in that position. This leaves 11. And 8 fits into 11, so mark a 1 in that position. You now have a 3 left. The 4 position gets a 0 since it's too large to fit into 3. However, 2 does fit into 3, so mark a 1 in that position. This leaves you with 1, which can be subtracted from 1. This finalizes the conversion with a 1 in the last position and a remainder of 0.

128	64	32	16	8	4	2	1
1	0	0	1	1	0	1	1

Network ID	Dotted Decimal Notation	10.	0.	0.	0
	Binary Equivalent				
Subnet Mask	Dotted Decimal Notation	255.	0.	0.	0
	Binary Equivalent				
Network ID	Dotted Decimal Notation	172.	16.	0.	0
	Binary Equivalent				
Subnet Mask	Dotted Decimal Notation	255.	255.	0.	0
	Binary Equivalent				

Step 3   Maggie wants you to define the different IP address classes. Using your favorite search engine, research the IP address ranges defined by each of the default address classes. In the following table, fill in the appropriate address ranges for each IP address class and identify the private address reserved for that class.

✱ **Cross-Reference**

Additional information may be found in the "IP Addresses" and "Class IDs" sections of Chapter 7 in the *Mike Meyers' CompTIA Network+ Guide to Managing and Troubleshooting Networks* textbook.

IP Address Class	Beginning IP Address	Ending IP Address	Private IP Address
Class A			
Class B			
Class C			
Class D			
Class E			

Step 4   The IP address classes skip the entire 127.0.0.1 – 127.255.255.254 range. This is a special range reserved for testing the configuration of TCP/IP on the local machine. It is referred to as the loopback address. Open a command prompt and type ping 127.0.0.1. What are the results?

_____

_____

Step 5   Before closing the command prompt, type **ipconfig /all**. What is your PC's IP address and subnet mask? What IP address class is it?

_____

_____

Step 6   Define the function of an IP address's subnet mask.

_____

_____

Step 7   In the following table, fill in the appropriate default subnet mask for each IP address class:

IP Address Class	Default Subnet Mask
Class A	
Class B	
Class C	

Step 8   Based on the default subnet masks for the preceding classes, identify the class, network IDs, and host IDs for the following IP address examples:

IP Address	IP Address Class	Network ID	Host ID
131.194.192.3			
45.200.49.201			
194.39.110.183			
208.154.191.9			
126.9.54.172			

Step 9   Explain what is meant by using the Classless Inter-Domain Routing (CIDR) notation (for example, /24) following an IP address. For example, what does the value 201.23.45.123/24 represent?

_____

_____

Step 10   Now that you have explored IP addresses and subnet masks, Maggie asks you to take a look at some of the network IDs she has configured for the lab network.

The network ID is 192.168.5.0/24.

She asks you to determine if they are valid addresses, and if not, to explain why.

IP Address	Valid/Invalid
192.168.5.10/24	
192.168.6.10/24	
192.168.5.10/24	
192.168.5.11/26	
192.168.7.12/24	
192.168.5.13/24	
192.168.5.255/24	
172.16.5.15/16	
10.168.5.16/8	
192.168.5.0/24	

 30 MINUTES

Lab Exercise 7.02: Configuring IP Addresses and Subnet Masks

Having now spent some time working through the concepts of IP addresses and subnet masks, it is time to build and configure the lab network. The addressing scheme will vary from one network administrator to another, but all will have some logic to the class range and assignment that they use. Maggie has already provided the Class C network ID of 192.168.5.0/24. Now it is up to you to choose how to assign individual host addresses. You will work through planning the address scheme, connecting the hardware, and then configuring each machine's TCP/IP properties to communicate on the network.

Learning Objectives

In this lab, you will configure the IP addresses and subnet masks for a small lab network. When you've completed this lab, you will be able to

- Assemble the hardware (computers, cabling, and switches) in a small network environment

- Determine an addressing scheme for the 192.168.5.0/24 network you have been provided

- Configure the static IP addresses and subnet masks on both Windows-based machines and Linux-based machines

- Confirm connectivity between machines on the specified network

Lab Materials and Setup

The materials you will need for this lab are

- Pencil and paper

- Calculator with scientific or programmer view (the Windows calculator will do just fine!)

- An Ethernet switch and eight UTP patch cables

- Two or more Windows PCs

- Optionally, at least one computer configured with Linux

→ **Note**

For the purposes of this Lab Exercise, students may build a lab setup similar to the lab setup described in the ITCF scenario or apply the steps to the classroom lab setup as directed by the instructor. The speed of the switches and NICs as well as the category of UTP cabling is not critical as long as connectivity can be established. 10-Mbps, 100-Mbps, and 1000-Mbps switches and NICs along with CAT 5, 5e, or 6 cabling are all acceptable. The Lab Exercise steps were performed on Windows XP, Vista, and Windows 7 machines as well as Ubuntu and Knoppix Linux machines.

Getting Down to Business

You will begin this exercise with the assembly of a small lab network using a switch, four Windows computers, and two Linux computers. You will then calculate the range of host addresses that you will assign to the computers.

When network administrators plan out their network addressing scheme, they always work to have expansion planned into the design. Typically, a range of addresses will be set aside for network routers, servers, and network printers. Over the years, depending on the overall population of the network, I have used a methodology in which the first 10 addresses are reserved for routers, the last 20 to 50 addresses for servers, and 10 to 20 addresses below the servers for network printers.

For example, the Class C network of 192.168.1.0/24 might be distributed as follows:

Routers: 192.168.1.1 – 192.168.1.10

Clients: 192.168.1.11 – 192.168.1.212

Printers: 192.168.1.213 – 192.168.1.232

Servers: 192.168.1.233 – 192.168.1.254

After planning the network addressing scheme, you'll configure each machine with an appropriate static address and subnet mask, and then test the connectivity between the computers.

Step 1 Utilizing the lab hardware provided by your instructor, assemble the computers into a small network connected via UTP patch cables to the Ethernet switch. Ideally, you would work with four Windows machines and two Linux machines; however, one of each will suffice. Alternatively, the instructor may have students utilize the existing classroom computers and network to facilitate the Lab Exercises.

Step 2 Now calculate the IP addresses and subnet masks for each of the host computers on this network. The lead network administrator has reserved the addresses from 192.168.5.1/24 through 192.168.5.10/24 for network routers, 192.168.5.220/24 through 192.168.5.229/24 for network printers, and 192.168.5.230/24 through 192.168.5.254/24 for servers.

Pay careful attention to these reserved addresses, and avoid assigning duplicate addresses as they will create TCP/IP conflicts on the network.

Host Computer	IP Address	Subnet Mask
Windows Computer A		
Windows Computer B		
Windows Computer C		
Windows Computer D		
Linux Computer A		
Linux Computer B		

Step 3 With your documentation in hand, log on to Windows Computer A and open the Network and Sharing Center. On the left-hand side of the window, click on **Change adapter settings** to open the Network Connections applet. Right-click the **Local Area Connection** icon and select **Properties**. Scroll down to the **Internet Protocol Version 4 (TCP/IPv4)** menu item and select **Properties**. Select the **Use the following IP address** radio button and enter the IP address and subnet mask for Windows Computer A (see Figure 7-2).

Figure 7-2 The Windows Internet Protocol version 4 (TCP/IPv4) Properties window

Step 4 Repeat the configuration steps with each of the Windows computers (B–D).

Step 5 Now log on to Linux Computer A and open the Network Configuration utility. Just as in Windows, there are a number of ways that you can navigate to the Network Configuration utility in Ubuntu Linux. One of the more formal methods begins by clicking the power icon and selecting **System Settings** from the drop-down menu. This opens the **Control Center** where you can select **Network Connections**. Select the wired adapter (Auto eth1) and click the **Edit** button.

Select the **IPv4 Settings** tab. Click on **Method:** and then click on **Manual** from the drop-down menu. Click the **Add** button and enter the IP address and Netmask (as the number of masked bits; for example, a Class C address has a Netmask of 24) for Linux Computer A (see Figure 7-3).

Figure 7-3 Ubuntu's Network Configuration utility

Step 6   Repeat the configuration steps with Linux Computer B.

Step 7   Your small six-node network should now be configured for communication. Test to see if you can view other machines on the network. This is an excellent opportunity to reintroduce you to the ping command-line utility. Open a command prompt on one of the newly configured machines and type the following command: **ping 127.0.0.1**, and then press ENTER. What are the results?

_____

_____

Ping the IP address of the current machine you are working on. What are the results?

_____

_____

Now ping the IP address of one of the other machines on the network. What are the results?

_____

_____

✔ **Tech Tip**

The `ping` utility uses a built-in function of the TCP/IP protocol to send a series of small "echo" data packets (using TCP/IP's Internet Control Message Protocol, or ICMP, which you will explore further in Chapter 9) to a named network PC. When you're troubleshooting network connectivity issues, `ping` is a network tech's best friend!

To finish up this exercise, try sharing some Word files between the Windows and Linux computers. After all, when you are testing the connectivity of machines, what better way than using the network to share resources?

 45 MINUTES

Lab Exercise 7.03: Configuring Subnetting

As you learned in Lab Exercise 7.01, when it comes to IP addressing, the IP address is only half the story. The other component is the subnet mask. Network hosts need both an IP address and a matching subnet mask in order to communicate on a network.

Up to now, you have only explored IP addresses and subnet masks that conform to standard configurations for each major IP address class. Network techs can also use custom configurations that extend the network ID portion of the subnet mask into the host ID portion of the subnet mask, creating what are affectionately known as *subnets*. Classless Inter-Domain Routing (CIDR) is the method of further subnetting a Class A, B, or C address to provide multiple network IDs from one assigned address.

Depending on your particular IP network needs, especially if you're working with an Internet service provider (ISP), you will need to become familiar with the task of identifying and configuring CIDR addresses and subnet masks. To develop a deeper understanding of CIDR, you'll practice configuring CIDR addresses and subnet masks, creating additional networks from one Class A, B, or C address.

Learning Objectives

In this lab, you will explore CIDR. When you've completed this lab, you will be able to

- Define a custom subnet mask

- Calculate variable-length subnet masks and the total number of network IDs and host IDs they define for each IP address class

- Define a CIDR address to provide a specific number of networks for future lab exercises

Lab Materials and Setup

The materials you will need for this lab are

- Pencil and paper

- Calculator with scientific or programmer view

Getting Down to Business

While working on the configuration of the lab machines in the previous exercise, you may have noticed that all of the addresses are on the same network. You know that in the near future, you would like to expand to additional networks, separated by routers, but Maggie has provided only the Class C network ID of 192.168.5.0/24.

She would like you to explore using CIDR to create multiple networks from the one Class C address, dividing the lab network into several subnets.

✖ Cross-Reference

To prepare for the following lab steps, review the "CIDR and Subnetting" section of the *Mike Meyers' Network+ Guide to Managing and Troubleshooting Networks* textbook. This will further strengthen your understanding of the concepts and calculations involved when configuring the subnets and hosts defined using Classless Inter-Domain Routing.

Step 1 What is the motivation behind using a custom subnet mask versus a default subnet mask?

_____

Step 2 To get you started with some calculations, Maggie presents you with the Class B network ID of 165.1.0.0/16. How many hosts can this network support?

_____

_____

✔ Hint

To determine the number of hosts supported by a network (or subnet), convert the 32-bit subnet value to binary, and separate the network portion from the host portion. Count the number of bits in the 0 ("off") position in the host portion of the subnet mask. Then use the formula $2^x - 2$, with x being the number of bits. Using a default Class C subnet mask as an example, note that there are 8 bits in the 0 position in the host portion, so $2^8 - 2 = 254$ possible hosts.

Step 3 Using the same address of 165.1.0.0/16, subdivide the network into at least five subnets. You need to configure the subnet mask to create an extension of the network ID, allowing for additional subnets. How many bits of the host portion of the subnet mask do you need to "borrow"? What will the resultant subnet mask be in decimal value? How many hosts will each subnet support?

_____

_____

✔ **Hint**

To determine the number of bits to borrow from the host portion of the subnet mask, first convert the subnet mask into binary. Then separate the network portion from the host portion. Using the formula 2^y = number of subnets, calculate the number of bits you will have to borrow from the host portion in order to support the number of subnets that are needed.

For example, to define at least 12 subnets for a Class C network using the default subnet mask of 255.255.255.0, convert the subnet mask to binary: 11111111.11111111.11111111.00000000. Separate the network portion (11111111.11111111.11111111) from the host portion (00000000). Now calculate the number of bits to borrow. Using the formula 2^y, plug in successive number of bits until you arrive at the number that provides 12 or more subnets. Using 2^4, you will arrive at 16 subnets.

The host portion of the subnet mask is now 11110000 in binary. To determine the decimal value of the subnet mask, add together the numeric value of each borrowed binary bit. With the first four bits of the host portion of the subnet mask borrowed, add 128 + 64 + 32 + 16 for a decimal value of 240. Append the default subnet mask with this value (that is, 255.255.255.240).

Step 4 Using the techniques practiced in the preceding steps, create a table of the variable-length subnet masks. Include the appropriate values for both the binary and decimal representations, number of subnets, and the number of Class A, Class B, and Class C hosts for each subnet mask. Maggie has calculated the first two subnets as an example:

Subnet Mask Host Portion with:	Binary and Decimal Value of Subnet	# Subnets	# Class A Hosts	# Class B Hosts	# Class C Hosts
No bits borrowed	.0 (00000000)	1 (2^0)	16,777,214 ($2^{24}-2$)	65,534 ($2^{16}-2$)	254 (2^8-2)
One bit borrowed	.128 (10000000)	2 (2^1)	8,388,606 ($2^{23}-2$)	32,766 ($2^{15}-2$)	126 (2^7-2)
Two bits borrowed					

Subnet Mask Host Portion with:	Binary and Decimal Value of Subnet	# Subnets	# Class A Hosts	# Class B Hosts	# Class C Hosts
Three bits borrowed					
Four bits borrowed					
Five bits borrowed					
Six bits borrowed					
Seven bits borrowed					
Eight bits borrowed					

Step 5 Take the original network ID of 192.168.5.0/24 and calculate the variable-length subnet mask to produce at least five subnets for the lab network.

Document the total number of bits "masked" for the network ID and record the subnet mask for this variable-length subnet mask.

_____

_____

✔ **Hint**

To define the network ID, host address range, and broadcast address for each subnet, you first must determine the "multiplier" (interval of the furthermost right one bit). This defines the spacing between each subnet. Begin with the original network ID (for this example, 192.168.1.0/26) and convert the subnet mask into binary as follows:

Dotted Decimal Notation	255.	255.	255.	192
Binary Equivalent	11111111.	11111111.	11111111.	11000000000

Now identify the furthermost right one bit and convert it to its decimal equivalent, in this case 64. This is the number you will use to increment each network. Including the subnet zero and the all-ones subnet produces the following table of subnets:

Subnet	Beginning Address	Ending Address	Broadcast Address
192.168.1.0/27	192.168.1.1	192.168.1.62	192.168.1.63
192.168.1.64/27	192.168.1.65	192.168.1.126	192.168.1.127
192.168.1.128/27	192.168.1.129	192.168.1.190	192.168.1.191
192.168.1.192/27	192.168.1.193	192.168.1.254	192.168.1.255

Now take the network ID you defined above to produce at least five subnets. Using the method just described, define the subnet, host address range, and broadcast address of each subnet and record it in the following table:

Subnet	Beginning Address	Ending Address	Broadcast Address
1.			
2.			
3.			
4.			
5.			
6.			
7.			
8.			

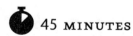 45 MINUTES

Lab Exercise 7.04: Local vs. Remote IP Addresses: The Function of the Default Gateway

So far, so good! You just finished configuring six computers in a small LAN and validated that all of the machines can at least communicate using IP addresses. Now it is time to expand your horizons, so to speak, and facilitate communication beyond the LAN. Wise network techs, after plowing through the "bits" and pieces of configuring IP addresses and subnet masks, inevitably ask themselves, "Why am I doing this again?" It's a valid question, because when your brain is overheating from converting decimal to binary and calculating subnet network IDs and host IDs, it's easy to lose sight of the real purpose behind all of these mathematical gymnastics. The answer is deceptively simple: to distinguish between local and remote network addresses!

That's right. The whole point of all the previous ciphering and decimal-to-binary flip-flopping is to tell the network host how to distinguish between data packets meant for the LAN and those meant to go beyond the LAN. In the following exercises, you'll review how a network host uses the IP address and subnet mask to determine if a data packet is meant for the local or remote network, and how data packets that are meant for remote networks get there. Then, with the help of your instructor, you'll add a router to your lab network and configure PCs on both sides to enable communication between the network segments.

Learning Objectives

In this lab, you will examine how computers communicate beyond the local area network and configure a router to implement that communication. When you've completed this lab, you will be able to

- Define how a network host distinguishes between local and remote addresses

- Describe the function of a default gateway

- Configure PCs on different networks to communicate through a router

Lab Materials and Setup

The materials you will need for this lab are

- Pencil and paper

- Calculator with scientific or programmer view

- A router such as Linksys WRT54GL

- A second Ethernet switch and six UTP patch cables

- Two or more additional Windows PCs

- Optionally, at least one additional computer configured with Linux

✖ Cross-Reference

To complete the steps contained in this lab, students may expand on the lab setup from Lab Exercise 7.02 or apply the steps to the classroom lab setup as directed by the instructor. The router can be a simple wireless router from Linksys or NETGEAR (currently, you'll only be using the wired interfaces on the router), or a full-function Cisco Systems or Juniper Networks router. The router may be configured by the instructor, or you may want to jump ahead to Lab Exercise 8.01, where you will practice the configuration of routers.

Getting Down to Business

It's time to expand your lab's local area network beyond one local area network with the introduction of a router and a remote network. Before you assemble the hardware, cabling, and additional machines, you'll calculate how computers on one network know whether data is for them or for a different network.

You will then explore how computers on different networks send data to each other. Finally, you'll set up CIDR IP addresses for both the local and remote networks, install the router and machines, then configure the default gateways and confirm data delivery.

Step 1 Describe the process that a network host uses to determine whether a data packet is local or remote. Provide an example using the following IP addresses:

- Host IP address 188.254.200.13/28

- Data packet destination IP address 188.254.157.9/28

_____

_____

_____

✔ **Hint**

To determine if an IP address is local or remote, you must first convert the IP addresses and subnet masks to their binary values. You then perform the Boolean logic operation of AND on the IP addresses and subnet masks for each of the nodes and compare the results. If the results are the same (all 1s and 0s match), the hosts are on the same network. If the results do not match, the hosts are on different networks.

The actual ANDing operation to determine if a destination host is local or remote is performed internally in the sending host. It is a complex process involving ANDing the destination host's IP address against entries in the sending host's routing table. This example is a extremely simplified method and is included for educational purposes only.

In Boolean logic, 0 AND 0 = 0, 1 AND 0 = 0, 0 AND 1 = 0, and 1 AND 1 = 1. For example:

Host IP Address (192.168.5.98)	11000000.10101000.00000101.01100010
Host Subnet Mask (255.255.255.224)	11111111.11111111.11111111.11100000
ANDed Result	11000000.10101000.00000101.01100000

Data Packet Destination IP Address (192.168.5.131)	11000000.10101000.00000101.10000011
Host Subnet Mask (255.255.255.224)	11111111.11111111.11111111.11100000
ANDed Result	11000000.10101000.00000101.10000000

Host ANDed Result	11000000.10101000.00000101.01100000
Destination ANDed Result	11000000.10101000.00000101.10000000
Result	Results do not match = remote address

Step 2   Compare the following IP addresses and determine whether they are local or remote:

Host IP Address	Host Subnet Mask	Destination IP Address	Local or Remote?
a) 210.145.149.123	255.255.255.0	210.145.253.199	
b) 192.168.4.189	255.255.255.224	192.168.1.107	
c) 10.154.187.89	255.192.0.0	10.152.179.88	
d) 132.100.45.5	255.255.252.0	132.100.45.45	
e) 151.251.100.101	255.255.0.0	166.200.110.10	

✔ **Hint**

A good online subnet calculator is available here:
www.subnetonline.com/pages/subnet-calculators/ip-subnet-calculator.php

Step 3   When a network host determines that a data packet is intended for a remote network, what does it do with the packet?

_____

_____

Step 4   Name two ways that a network host determines the IP address of its default gateway.

_____

_____

Step 5   What is the function of the default gateway?

_____

_____

Step 6   Now, using the additional lab hardware provided by your instructor, assemble the computers into Network 2 connected via the UTP patch cables to the second Ethernet switch. Ideally, you will install two Windows machines and two Linux machines; however, one of each will suffice. Using the router, connect one port of the switch on Network 1 to one of the LAN ports on the router. Then connect one of the ports of the switch on Network 2 to the WAN port of the router.

Step 7 Maggie has established the following IP network IDs for each network:

Network 1 (LAN):   192.168.5.32/27
Network 2 (WAN):   192.168.5.96/27

She has also reserved the first address in each range for the IP address of each interface. The Network 1 (LAN) interface is 192.168.5.33/27, and the Network 2 (WAN) interface is 192.168.5.97/27. Now she would like you to configure each of the machines on both networks with appropriate IP addresses, subnet masks, and default gateways.

As in Lab Exercise 7.02, pay careful attention to reserved addresses (such as the router interfaces) and avoid assigning duplicate addresses, as they will create TCP/IP conflicts on the network.

Step 8 The two-subnet, 10-node network should now be configured for communication. Ping various IP addresses of the other machines on the network. Ping both of the IP addresses for the router. Ping between machines from Network 1 to machines on Network 2 and vice versa. What are the results?

_____

_____

Test to see if you can view other machines on the network. What are the results?

_____

_____

Step 9 On one of the Windows machines, open a command prompt and type **ipconfig /all**. What is the IP address of your PC's default gateway? Do the same on one of the Linux machines by opening Terminal and typing the command **route -n**. The Gateway of Last Resort (0.0.0.0) should display the default gateway.

_____

_____

 30 MINUTES

Lab Exercise 7.05: IP Addressing, MAC Addressing, and Ethernet: Working Together

The most basic unit of data transmission on an Ethernet network is the frame. Back in Chapter 2, you learned how data travels down through the OSI model. Transmission Control Protocol (TCP) segments or User Datagram Protocol (UDP) datagrams come down from the Transport layer and are encapsulated with a header and trailer. The header, data, and trailer comprise an IP packet. The IP packets come down from the Network layer and are encapsulated with another header and trailer. The header, data (packet), and trailer comprise the frame.

Data frames include the MAC address of both the sending and receiving computer, an error-checking value called the *frame check sequence (FCS)*, and, of course, the data itself. When the TCP/IP protocol is utilized, other important values that are included are IP addresses, TCP and UDP ports, and protocols from the TCP/IP suite.

Because the data frame process is hidden from us, it's sometimes hard to get a real grasp of the mechanics involved. Luckily, network techs have tools available to help make these concepts a bit more tangible. The tool of choice for this purpose is a protocol analyzer, usually called a *packet sniffer*. This isn't just a clever moniker; packet sniffers "sniff" network traffic and Sniffer Technologies was the real name of a company that made protocol analyzer devices. The name is apropos for the whole category of tools.

Packet sniffers are available as hardware-based devices and as software applications, but they all enable you to do the same thing: pull data frames off the network and cache them for offline analysis. Using a packet sniffer, you can view each of the components that make up the data segments, datagrams, packets, and frames.

Beyond the "because it's cool" factor, are there practical reasons for examining data frames? Plenty of them! Packet sniffers are some of the best tools for optimizing network performance. Using packet sniffers, you can determine the type of network traffic that is tying up a busy network. A network switch that is connected to itself or a malfunctioning NIC, for example, will send excessive (and usually incomplete) data frames—network techs call this *jabbering*. Either of these conditions (and others) can be detected using a packet sniffer.

In this lab, you'll use a packet sniffer application to capture data frames from your network and view the captured data to explore the Address Resolution Protocol (ARP), which resolves IP addresses to MAC addresses.

✔ **Tech Tip**

The terms data *frame* and data *packet* are often used interchangeably. However, this is incorrect. The most common frames are Ethernet frames and the most common packets are IP packets. You should try to use the proper terms!

Learning Objectives

In this lab, you'll install and run the Wireshark packet sniffer application, use it to capture data from your network, and examine the captured data. When you've completed this lab, you will be able to

- Perform a data frame capture from a network

- Examine the captured data to view each data frame's contents specifically focusing on ARP frames

Lab Materials and Setup

The materials you'll need for this lab are

- Setup file for the Wireshark packet sniffer application

- Two or more networked Windows PCs

Getting Down to Business

In the previous chapters, you learned that Ethernet is the dominant networking technology using the hybrid star-bus topology. When devices communicate over Ethernet, they use a unique, 48-bit hexadecimal media access control (MAC) address to identify each machine on the network. You are now studying TCP/IP and have learned that each device on a TCP/IP network must have a unique IP address. Each IP address uses a subnet mask to establish both the network ID and the host ID from the 32-bit address, both of which are displayed in dotted decimal notation. TCP/IP is the most prominent network protocol primarily running over the most prominent technology, Ethernet.

When one computer wants to establish communication with another computer, it will send a message out to the network to determine who has the IP address to which the computer would like to send the data. As mentioned, Ethernet uses MAC addressing, so inevitably, the IP address will need to be resolved to the MAC address for communication to take place. The Address Resolution Protocol (ARP) is used to resolve IP addresses to MAC addresses, allowing devices to communicate over TCP/IP–Ethernet networks. In this Lab Exercise, you will explore the mechanics of the ARP and dissect individual frames to clarify further the relationship between IP addresses and MAC addresses.

To make a detailed analysis of network traffic, you must install Wireshark on one of the networked PCs and confirm that it operates satisfactorily.

Step 1   The steps for this exercise and other exercises in this chapter and subsequent chapters call for using a packet sniffer to capture segments, datagrams, packets, and frames from your network. Wireshark is an excellent software-based packet sniffer that runs on just about any platform. Wireshark has many compelling features that put it on par with other packet sniffer applications, and best of all, it is free and open source. Follow these steps to download and install Wireshark:

1. Go to www.wireshark.org and click on the **Download Wireshark Get Started Now** button.

2. On the Get Wireshark page, click the link for the **Windows Installer** (32-bit or 64-bit depending on your machine).

3. Download the Wireshark executable installation file (the current version at the time of this writing is 1.6.1) to your Windows desktop or downloaded files folder.

4. Double-click the Wireshark installation file to start the installation wizard, and follow the prompts to complete the installation.

Step 2   Start the Wireshark packet sniffer, shown in Figure 7-4, by clicking **Start | All Programs | Wireshark** and selecting the **Wireshark** program icon.

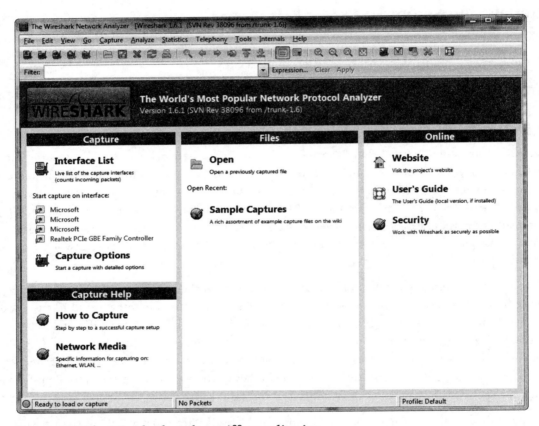

Figure 7-4 The Wireshark packet sniffer application

Wireshark has a nice splash page giving you options to start a capture, open an existing file, or get further information online right from the opening page.

Step 3   You can now start a data frame capture by selecting **Capture Options** right from the welcome screen menu. This brings up the **Wireshark: Capture Options** dialog box, shown in Figure 7-5.

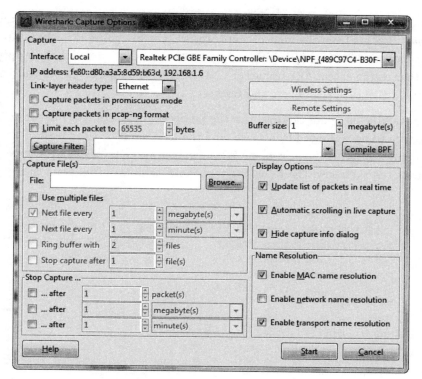

FIGURE 7-5 The Wireshark: Capture Options dialog box

List some of the default settings here:

_____

_____

Step 4 Start by selecting the interface from the drop-down menu. Deselect the **Capture packets in promiscuous mode** check box to reduce some of the traffic that will be "picked up" by the network interface. Start capturing data frames that are sent or received by this machine by clicking the **Start** button at the bottom right of the window. Depending on the network you are attached to, you may or may not observe any capture activity until you generate network communication.

Notice the Wireshark display is divided into three panes. The top section is the Packet List pane, which lists a summary of each frame captured. The middle section is the Tree View pane, which displays details of each captured frame. The bottom section is the Data View pane, which shows hexadecimal values of captured data. The right side of the bottom section will show the ASCII values for the hex values, even if it's not meant to be translated into ASCII. When you see a dot, it means that there is no ASCII equivalent. Other times you'll see ASCII translations that make no sense, because they weren't meant to be translated.

Step 5   Computers and devices generate a large amount of network traffic just establishing communications. To clear away some of these packets from the view of your capture, you are going to apply a filter. In the **Filter:** dialog box on the toolbar, enter the following string: **ARP or ICMP** and click the **Apply** button. This will filter out all other traffic except ARP frames or ICMP packets from the displayed traffic, although Wireshark will continue to capture all packets and frames.

Step 6   Now, to see a concrete example of a data capture, run the ping command on your network. Open a command-line window, type **ping**, followed by a space, and the host name or IP address of a remote PC on your network. To ping a PC with the host name **WindowsComputerB**, for example, type **ping windowscomputerb** and press the ENTER key. The following text shows sample output from the ping command.

```
C:\>ping windowscomputerb
Pinging windowscomputerb [192.168.5.13] wcith 32 bytes of data:
Reply from 192.168.5.13: bytes=32 time=110ms TTL=48
Reply from 192.168.5.13: bytes=32 time=115ms TTL=48
Reply from 192.168.5.13: bytes=32 time=107ms TTL=48
Reply from 192.168.5.13: bytes=32 time=111ms TTL=48
Ping statistics for 192.168.5.13:
      Packets: Sent = 4, Received = 4, Lost = 0 (0% loss)
Approximate round trip times in milli-seconds:
      Minimum = 107ms, Maximum = 115ms, Average = 110ms
```

What are the results of your ping operation?

_____

_____

Step 7   Close the command-line window by typing **exit** at the prompt. In Wireshark, click the **Stop** button to stop the data capture. Now it's time to analyze the captured data for the ping operation you just ran. Again, depending on the traffic on your network, you should have 10 to 12 frames of data displayed in the Wireshark viewer.

Step 8   Packet sniffers can capture hundreds of data frames in just a matter of seconds, especially if left in promiscuous mode, so applying the ARP or ICMP filter should help you to easily identify the 10 to 12 packets of data you want to analyze. The important information you are interested in for this Lab Exercise are the frames concerning the address resolution protocol (ARP). There should be two lines of ARP frames displaying IP addresses and the MAC addresses to which they resolve, followed by eight lines of ICMP packets showing the results of the ping (see Figure 7-6). What are the results?

_____

_____

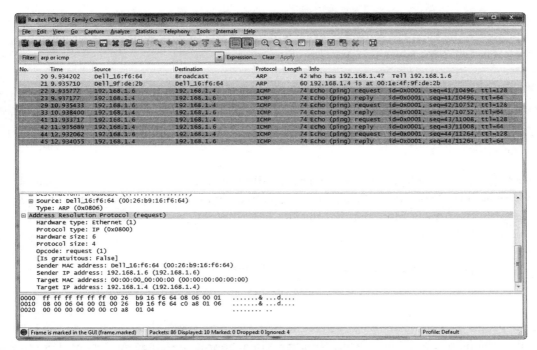

FIGURE 7-6   Two lines of ARP frames and eight lines of ICMP packets

✔ Hint

If, when you display the capture information, there are no ARP frames displayed, it may be caused by one of two situations. First, if you have used the ping command, or have been sharing files back and forth with the target computer prior to collecting the capture data, there may be entries in the ARP cache. Open a command prompt and run the following command:

```
C:\>arp -a
```

If the following information (or similar with the IP address of your target machine) is displayed, you have an entry in the ARP cache.

```
Interface: 192.168.5.12 --- 0x3
Internet Address        Physical Address
192.168.5.12            00-0e-28-92-ac-b7
```

Once two machines have communicated, they will place entries into the ARP cache to avoid generating broadcast traffic. The entries can remain anywhere from 2 to 20 minutes depending on the operating system. In this Lab Exercise, you want to create ARP broadcast traffic to capture, so you'll want to clear the ARP cache. To clear the ARP cache entries, use the following command. You may need to run the command prompt in elevated mode (as administrator). When opening the command prompt, right-click **cmd.exe** and select **Run as administrator** from the drop-down menu.

```
C:\>netsh interface ip delete arpcache
```

The above routine to clear the ARP cache is somewhat overkill when you could use the command `arp -d`. However, the CompTIA Network+ exam will expect you to have some experience using the `netsh` command, so consider this practice.

To verify the ARP cache is cleared, type **arp -a** once again. Your results should match the following output:

```
C:\>arp -a
No ARP Entries Found
```

The second situation could be an incorrectly entered filter setting in Wireshark. Open Wireshark and examine both the Capture and Display filters. Confirm that the "ARP or ICMP" filters have been selected in the Display filter and that the "No ARP" filter has not been selected in either the Capture or Display filters.

Now perform Steps 3 through 7 again to capture ARP frames in Wireshark.

Step 9   In the **Packet List** summary pane, select the first ARP data frame listed and fill in the information displayed in the following column fields: **Number**, **Time**, **Source**, **Destination**, **Protocol**, and **Info**.

_____

_____

Step 10   In the **Tree View** pane, you'll see a wealth of information relating to the data frame, including frame information, Ethernet information, protocol information, and data payload information. Clicking the small plus sign (+) at the beginning of each line expands it into a tree view showing details. Expand the **Frame**, **Ethernet II**, and **Address Resolution Protocol** (request) tree listings to determine the answers to the following questions:

- What is the total size in bytes of the data frame?
- What is the sender MAC address?
- What is the sender IP address listed in the frame?
- What is the target MAC address?
- What is the target IP address listed in the frame?

_____

_____

Step 11   In the **Packet List** summary pane, select the very next ARP data frame listed (this should be a reply to the ARP request) and fill in the information displayed in the following column fields: **Number, Time, Source, Destination, Protocol,** and **Info.**

_____

_____

Step 12   In the **Tree View** pane, expand the **Frame, Ethernet II,** and **Address Resolution Protocol** (reply) tree listings to determine the answers to the following questions:

- What is the total size in bytes of the data frame?

- What is the sender MAC address?

- What is the sender IP address listed in the frame?

- What is the target MAC address?

- What is the target IP address listed in the frame?

_____

_____

Step 13   Now you are going to repeat Steps 3 through 11; however, this time you will use the address of a computer on the remote network. Record your results and compare them to the data you captured for the machine on the local network. What are the results?

_____

_____

➜ **Note**

If your network is not currently set up to resolve host names to IP addresses using DNS, the ping of a computer on the remote network may fail. To complete the Lab Exercise, just ping the IP address of the remote computer. You will study DNS in Chapter 10.

✖ **Cross-Reference**

To clarify the relationship between IP addresses and MAC addresses and ARP, reread the "Subnet Masks" section of Chapter 7 in the _Mike Meyers' CompTIA Network+ Guide to Managing and Troubleshooting Networks_ textbook.

Step 14 Before you wrap up this dissection of data frames, take a minute to examine the information displayed in the **Data View** pane of Wireshark. The pairs of alphanumeric characters you see listed in the **Data View** pane represent the hexadecimal values of each byte of the captured data frame. You may recall from working with MAC addresses (which are displayed in hexadecimal) that the hexadecimal numbering system is a shorthand way of representing binary. Each hexadecimal digit represents four bits, so a byte can be represented with two hexadecimal digits. For example:

```
AF hex = 10101111 bin
```

You explored the details of the binary numbering system in Lab Exercise 7.01, but for now, concentrate on knowing how to find the hexadecimal value for each piece of the captured data frame information. Wireshark automatically highlights the hexadecimal portion shown in the **Data View** pane of any data selected in the **Tree View** pane. As an example, while the **Target IP** address line is selected in the **Tree View** pane, note that the hexadecimal value of that IP address is now highlighted in the **Data View** pane.

What is the hexadecimal value for the selected IP address?

_____

_____

Wireshark is a fantastic tool for displaying the actual nuts-and-bolts data that you have examined conceptually. You'll see more of this tool as you complete steps in the next lab exercise and later exercises in this book. Move on to the next lab to examine the sequence of events involved in obtaining an IP address automatically.

> **→ Note**
>
> Hexadecimal is a numbering system commonly used to represent binary values. Remember that everything is binary to a computer, so hexadecimal is simply a method to display long strings of binary numbers in a shorter format. Each hexadecimal digit represents four binary digits, so a MAC address of 1a:2b:3c:4d:5e:6f is a bit easier for people to understand than the binary equivalent of 00011010:00101011:00111100:01001101:01011110:01101111. You will be working with the hexadecimal number system again in Chapter 13.

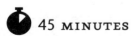 45 MINUTES

Lab Exercise 7.06: Static IP Addressing vs. Dynamic IP Addressing

One of the reasons that TCP/IP is so widely adopted is that it's extremely flexible. The TCP/IP protocol suite not only works on any number of computer platforms and applications, but it also interfaces with a variety of advanced network services. One of these important services is the Dynamic Host Configuration

Protocol (DHCP) IP addressing service. DHCP provides valuable functions that make your job as a network tech easier. In this Lab Exercise, you will take a look at what DHCP does, how you configure your host to use DHCP, and how DHCP actually works. You will then examine what happens if the DHCP server goes down or becomes unavailable.

Learning Objectives

In this lab, you will explore and configure the various components of the DHCP client. When you have completed this lab, you will be able to

- Describe the functions of the DHCP service

- Configure PCs to use DHCP

- Diagram how DHCP requests work between a DHCP client and DHCP server

- Customize a Windows client to use DHCP and static IP information for unique situations

- Recognize some typical DHCP problems and know how to deal with them

Lab Materials and Setup

The materials you will need for this lab are

- Pencil and paper

- A DHCP server (either the service on the router or a Windows or Linux server).

✖ Cross-Reference

These steps again utilize the lab setup from Lab Exercise 7.02. As before, you may perform these steps on the classroom network as directed by the instructor. The DHCP server services may be enabled on the router or a server may be added to the network (for example, Windows Server 2003 or Windows Server 2008 supports DHCP server services). For the purposes of this lab, DHCP need only be enabled on the LAN network. The instructor should configure the DHCP server for proper operation.

Getting Down to Business

Up to now, you have configured all of the IP addresses, subnet masks, and default gateways manually. This is known as *static IP addressing*. Imagine though, if instead of ten computers on a two-subnet network, you were responsible for managing thousands of devices (computers, servers, printers, and so on) on hundreds of networks. The documentation alone would be staggering! DHCP to the rescue!

CJ stops by to see how the network lab is shaping up just as you are setting up for some DHCP exercises. He conveys to you that the inspection facilities are actually experiencing problems that seem to be related to DHCP. Some of the systems are intermittently receiving Automatic Private IP Addressing (APIPA) addresses, signifying no connection to a DHCP server. He also states that some of the systems are being assigned IP addresses with the wrong network ID! CJ compliments you on the progress with the network lab and asks you to run a few tests to see if you can re-create the problems over at the inspection facilities.

Step 1   Describe the function of the DHCP service on a TCP/IP network.

_____

_____

Step 2   With the assistance of your instructor, enable the DHCP server on the router. Optionally, you may add a Windows or Linux server and enable the DHCP services on the physical server. If both are available, you can have the instructor configure an improper scope on one of the DHCP servers and actually see the results discussed in Step 14.

Step 3   Log on to one of the Windows computers on network 1. Open the **Network Connections** applet. Right-click the **Local Area Connection** icon and select **Properties**. Scroll down to the **Internet Protocol version 4 (TCP/IPv4)** menu item and select **Properties**. Select the **Obtain an IP address automatically** radio button and the **Obtain DNS server address automatically** radio button, and then click the **OK** button. Click the **Close** button to save your changes and exit the Local Area Connection Properties. Repeat these configuration steps with the other Windows computers.

Step 4   Now log on to one of the Linux computers and open the Network Configuration utility. Select the **IPv4** tab, then select the **DHCP** option from the drop-down menu. Perform this configuration on the second Linux machine.

Step 5   To view your PC's TCP/IP configuration, including advanced settings such as the DHCP information, type `ipconfig /all` at the command prompt. What are the results?

→ **Note**

Don't concern yourself with the IPv6 information at this time. You will be exploring the characteristics and configuration of IPv6 in the Lab Exercises for Chapter 13.

_____

_____

Step 6   Network techs sometimes must manually refresh a network host's DHCP lease, such as when a major change has been made to the network's configuration. To release and renew a network host's DHCP lease manually, you must execute two commands. The first of these commands is `ipconfig /release`, which, when typed at the command prompt, releases the IP address back into the pool of addresses. The second command is `ipconfig /renew`. When you type this at the command prompt, it causes the host to obtain a new DHCP lease. You will now use Wireshark to capture data frames while you obtain an IP address from a DHCP server.

Step 7 Run Wireshark on one of the DHCP client systems, but do not start capturing frames. Open a command prompt and run **ipconfig /release**. Go back to Wireshark and start capturing frames. As in the previous Lab Exercise, you are going to use a filter to isolate DHCP traffic. In the **Filter: Toolbar** dialog box, type **bootp** and click the **Apply** button. Return to your command prompt and run **ipconfig /renew**. When the renewal is successful, stop capturing frames.

✔ Tech Tip

In the preceding step, you added a filter by the name of *bootp*. The bootstrap protocol (bootp) was the predecessor to DHCP. You may explore the original RFC 951 at www.ietf.org/rfc/rfc951.txt.

Step 8 You should find four frames labeled as DHCP under the **Protocol** column, as shown in Figure 7-7. Note that there are four distinct UDP frames: DHCP Discover, DHCP Offer, DHCP Request, and DHCP ACK.

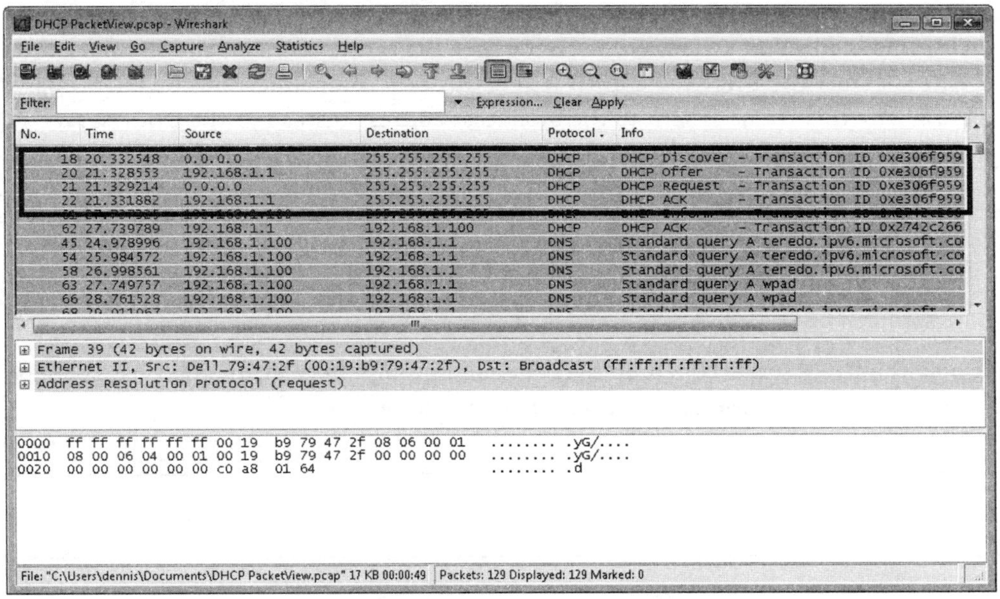

FIGURE 7-7 Wireshark capture of a DHCP request

Step 9 Examine the first frame of the exchange, the DHCP Discover. What is the Source Address? Is the Destination Address 255.255.255.255? What do you think is the significance of this destination address? Go into the bootstrap protocol details of this frame. Did your system request a particular IP address? If so, why do you think it did so?

Step 10   The second frame is DHCP Offer. What IP address did this come from? Go into the frame's details. What is the IP address the DHCP server is offering? What other IP information is being offered by the DHCP server?

_____

_____

Step 11   The third frame is DHCP Request. This frame is almost identical to DHCP Discover. This step is not intuitive. Why should the DHCP client make a second request if the DHCP server has already responded with all the information it needs?

_____

_____

Step 12   The final frame is DHCP ACK. This is the step where the client confirms the IP information. The DHCP server will not start the DHCP lease until it gets this ACK command from the client. Based on this fact, speculate why this frame is sent to the broadcast address instead of the DHCP server's IP address.

_____

_____

Step 13   Now disable the DHCP server. Open up the command prompt once again and type **ipconfig /release**. After a moment, type **ipconfig /renew**. What are the results?

_____

_____

Step 14   Going back to the situation with the inspection facilities, why do you think that some of the systems have completely different IP addresses than the ones the DHCP server is designed to lease to clients? The different addresses do not start with 169.254. What could be the problem? How could you use Wireshark to test your conclusions?

_____

_____

Lab Analysis

1. Tegan works for an ISP and has been asked to set up the IP addressing scheme for a new region of the city they are providing with Internet service. She is provided the Class B address of 141.27.0.0/16 as a starting point and needs at least 25 subnets. What is the CIDR subnet mask, how many networks does this allow for, and how many hosts will be available on each subnet?

_____

_____

2. Describe the function of private IP addresses, and list the private IP address ranges for Class A, B, and C TCP/IP networks.

_____

_____

3. Alexis has arrived at work this morning, logged on to her Windows 7 machine, and found that she has no Internet access. You respond to her network support call. All of the obvious hardware and configuration settings check out, so you run `ipconfig /all`. The IP address is 169.254.113.97/16. What do you think the problem could be? What might you check next?

_____

_____

4. Ian is troubleshooting a network connectivity problem. He tries pinging 127.0.0.1, but the command is unsuccessful. What might this indicate?

_____

_____

5. Matthew is trying to determine if he needs an Ethernet switch or a router to connect Workstation A to Workstation B. Workstation A has an IP address of 172.16.33.1/20 and Workstation B has an IP address of 172.16.45.254/20. Which device should he choose?

_____

_____

Key Term Quiz

Use the IP addresses and vocabulary terms from the list below to complete the sentences that follow. Not all of the terms will be used.

10.0.0.0/8	host ID
169.254.0.0/16	Internet Assigned Numbers Authority (IANA)
172.16.0.0/16	Internet Protocol version 4 (IPv4)
192.168.0.0/24	ifconfig
Address Resolution Protocol (ARP)	ipconfig
arp -a	ipconfig /all
Automatic Private IP Addressing (APIPA)	ipconfig /release
Classless Inter-Domain Routing (CIDR)	ipconfig /renew
default gateway	network ID
DHCP ACK	packet sniffer
DHCP Discover	ping
DHCP Offer	subnet mask
DHCP Request	Wireshark
Dynamic Host Configuration Protocol (DHCP)	

1. There are many utilities available, both software-based and hardware-based, that enable you to capture data frames and analyze the contents. The generic name for these utilities is a(n) _____, and an excellent free and open source version is _____.

2. When a PC communicates with another PC over a TCP/IP network, the IP address must be resolved to the MAC address in order for the communication to take place. After the communication is established, the system stores the resolved address in cache. The command to view this cache is _____.

3. To determine the IP address, subnet mask, and default gateway on a Windows XP, Vista, or Windows 7 PC, type _____ at a command prompt. To display even more information, such as Physical Address, DHCP Server, and DHCP Lease information, type _____.

4. The _____ is the IP address of a router that passes data packets outside of your LAN.

5. When a client is negotiating with a DHCP server to obtain an address, the sequence of transmissions is as follows: The client will broadcast a(n) _____ to all of the DHCP servers. All of the DHCP servers will respond with a(n) _____. The client will select one DHCP server and then send a formal _____ informing all of the DHCP servers that an address has been obtained. Finally, The DHCP server selected will send a(n) _____ confirming the address to the client.

Chapter 8
The Wonderful World of Routing

Lab Exercises

As you learned in the last chapter, TCP/IP is built on a set of dynamic specifications that are constantly modified and updated through a process known as Request for Comments (RFCs). There is an RFC for every component of the TCP/IP protocol suite, so you can imagine how many are associated with routing. As a precursor to working with routers, you will explore the organizations that deal with the TCP/IP protocol suite, including RFCs.

Taking communications off the LAN and moving them out to other networks and ultimately the Internet requires a re-examination of a number of concepts, components, and software you have already worked with. For example, you've configured client computers to communicate with other computers on the local network as well as computers on remote networks using the default gateway. Now you need to look at routing from the perspective of the router itself to learn how to configure the routers to make those connections beyond the local network possible.

In addition, you will work with some important components that really enhance IP routing, in particular Network Address Translation (NAT) and dynamic routing. These two technologies are critical for communication over the Internet and the protection of any private network you want to connect to the Internet. In this chapter, you'll explore some additional organizations and then you'll install and configure routers, NAT, and dynamic routing protocols to see how they work in the real world.

 20 MINUTES

Lab Exercise 8.01: Governing Bodies, Part 2

The TCP/IP suite is so important to modern networking that both the textbook and Lab Manual devote multiple chapters to the various components of TCP/IP. These chapters cover in detail IPv4 and IPv6 addressing, IP routing, DNS and DHCP, VPNs, and VLANs. In almost every chapter, you will work with various TCP/IP utilities.

Just as there are organizations that handle the specifications and management of Ethernet and cabling, so too are there organizations that handle the specifications and management of the TCP/IP protocol suite. Before starting your journey through the wonderful world of routing, it is a good time to introduce you to some of these organizations.

Learning Objectives

In this lab, you'll explore various organizations that are responsible for the development and management of standards for TCP/IP, the Internet, and the World Wide Web. By the end of this lab, you will be able to

- Describe the purpose and detail some of the features of the organizations responsible for the TCP/IP standards, Internet addressing, and domain naming

- Research and report on some of the paramount RFCs

Lab Materials and Setup

The materials you need for this lab are

- A PC with Internet access

- Pencil and paper

Getting Down to Business

Imagine for a moment you are working for a large company that wants to have their own pool of public IP addresses. Or you have decided to launch your own Web site discussing, trading, and selling vintage guitars, and you want a great domain name like www.vintageguitars.com, also known as a Uniform Resource Locator (URL). Who knows, you might decide to write the next all-encompassing dynamic routing protocol. All of these situations are administered by official organizations that help to manage the TCP/IP protocol suite. In the next few steps you will explore these organizations and document some of the information you uncover.

Step 1   Similar to the International Organization for Standardization (ISO), the Internet Corporation for Assigned Names and Numbers (ICANN) owns and operates some of the other key organizations responsible for TCP/IP and the Internet. Open your Web browser and enter this URL: **www.icann.org/ en/about**. Record who ICANN is, how long they have been around, and their mission statement.

_____

_____

Step 2   Navigate to this Web site, www.iana.org/about/. This is the Internet Assigned Numbers Authority (IANA). Write a short summary of who they are, when they were founded, and what their main responsibilities are.

_____

_____

Step 3   The IANA works closely with the Internet Society (ISOC). Record some of the facts you learn about ISOC at www.isoc.org/isoc.

_____

_____

Step 4   There are numerous organizations responsible for steering the Internet. Yet another of these organizations is the Internet Engineering Task Force (IETF). What are some of the characteristics of the IETF? Check them out at www.ietf.org/about.

_____

_____

Step 5   One of the most important contributions of the IETF is the stewardship of the Request for Comment (RFC) database. The RFCs are the open-source recommendations and standards for the Internet (more specifically, TCP/IP is defined by RFCs). The main repository for the RFCs is the RFC Editor at www.rfc-editor.org. Once there, click on **Search for an RFC and its meta-data**, and then search for the following RFCs and document some of the information pertaining to the standard.

RFC 2131   _____

RFC 792   _____

RFC 826   _____

RFC 2616   _____

RFC 2460   _____

RFC 2453   _____

As you progress through the rest of the Lab Exercises in this Lab Manual, you may find it interesting and beneficial to consult the RFCs as you learn about the application of the protocols of the TCP/IP protocol suite. For example, in the next chapter you will be working with the Simple Mail Transfer Protocol (SMTP), Post Office Protocol, version 3 (POP3), and Internet Message Access Protocol version 4 (IMAP4). Can you find the RFCs that define these protocols?

_____

_____

 45 MINUTES

Lab Exercise 8.02: Installing and Configuring Routers

In the previous chapter, you learned that in order to move TCP/IP packets from a machine on the local network (LAN) to a machine on a remote network, like the Internet (WAN), you needed to use a router. Until now, you have only been responsible for configuring a PC to use the default gateway to send packets destined for remote networks to the near port of the router. The router then handles the delivery of these packets from the local network to the remote network.

Now it is time to explore the fine details of installing and configuring routers. You will begin with this Lab Exercise, where you will install and configure one router, creating two networks. In Lab Exercise 8.03, you will add additional routers (creating additional networks) emulating the router configuration and management that an enterprise network technician would be responsible for.

✔ Tech Tip

The following routing labs were designed to utilize the excellent capabilities of inexpensive Linksys wireless routers. Linksys, a division of Cisco Systems, Inc., offers many models such as the WRT54G, WRT54GL, WRT160N, E2000, E3000, and others. For the lab exercises in this chapter, I used the WRT54GL wireless router, although other Linksys models—in fact, other manufacturers' wireless routers—can be used with similar results. Using just the wired interfaces, the WRT54GL will route packets between two networks, enable the configuration of NAT and Port Forwarding, and create dynamic routing tables via the Routing Information Protocol (RIP).

Interested students (and instructors) may even expand the capabilities of the WRT series (as well as other manufacturers' routers) by upgrading to third-party firmware provided by DD-WRT or Sveasoft. You may explore these upgrades at www.dd-wrt.com and www.sveasoft.com, and will even have the opportunity to upgrade using dd-wrt in Chapter 12, "Advanced Networking Devices." Please understand that flashing the routers with third-party firmware can sometimes damage the router and voids all warranties from Linksys. This procedure should not be performed on critical routers.

If you have access to Cisco or Juniper routers such as the Cisco 2600 series routers, or the Juniper J-series routers, they will obviously meet the requirements of the following labs. The full configuration of these routers is beyond the scope of these Lab Exercises (as well as the objectives for the CompTIA Network+ exam).

Learning Objectives

When you have completed this lab exercise, you will be able to

- Design and implement a routed, two-network, network infrastructure
- Physically install router hardware
- Configure multiple interfaces on Ethernet routers
- Implement static routes in routers

Lab Materials and Setup

Preferably, you will have access to the small "Network Lab" you assembled in the previous chapter's exercises. The materials you'll need for this lab are

- Pencil and paper
- Two or more PCs
- One router (Linksys WRT54GL or similar wireless routers will work fine)
- Two eight-port Ethernet switches (Simple NETGEAR or Linksys Workgroup switches are acceptable)
- Appropriate UTP cabling

Getting Down to Business

Maggie stops by the Networking Lab to see how you are progressing to find that not only do you have the small network up and running, but you have configured both static and dynamic IP addressing. You demonstrate the communication between the two networks over the router using the ping utility. Packets are successfully sent to one of the machines on the remote network, which successfully replies to one of the machines on the local network.

She is duly impressed and asks if you are up for experimenting with the configuration of the router. You respond with "You bet!" and begin to disassemble the network lab. Maggie stops you and says you won't need to disassemble the physical setup, but she is going to give you new network IDs that you'll need to configure.

Network 1 (LAN):   192.168.10.0/24

Network 2 (WAN):   192.168.20.0/24

Step 1   Based on these network IDs for the two networks, complete the following table, filling in the appropriate IP addresses for each router interface and each computer. Remember, as you learned in the last chapter, to plan out your network addressing scheme. Typically, a range of addresses will be set aside for network routers, servers, and network printers.

Network 1	IP Address	Subnet Mask	Default Gateway
Router Interface (LAN)			
Computer A			
Computer B			

Network 2	IP Address	Subnet Mask	Default Gateway
Router Interface (WAN)			
Computer A			
Computer B			

Step 2   Verify the configuration of the physical setup as follows using Figure 8-1.

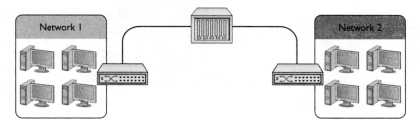

FIGURE 8-1 Physical layout of the network for Lab Exercise 8.01

Step 3   Armed with your addresses for the LAN and WAN interfaces, launch your browser and open the router configuration utility. On the Linksys WRT54GL routers used in our lab, the default address is 192.168.1.1 with a default user name "admin" and default password "admin." Consult the user's manual or the Internet to determine the correct information for the specific model you are using. You should arrive at the main setup screen, similar to Figure 8-2.

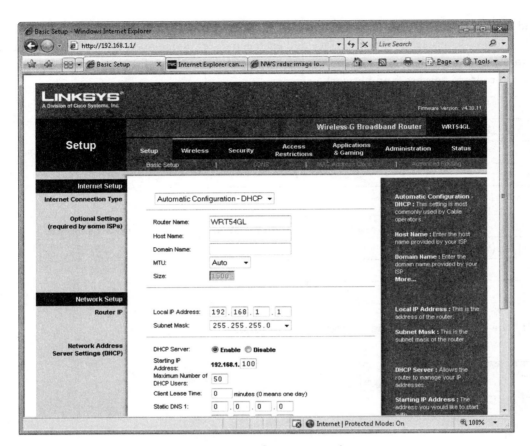

FIGURE 8-2 Title page of the WRT54GL configuration utility

Step 4   You will begin by configuring the IP addresses of the WAN interface and the LAN interface. Start with the WAN interface and select **Static IP** from the drop-down menu. Configure the **IP Address**, **Subnet Mask**, and **Default Gateway** for the WAN interface. For the default gateway, enter an IP address for the second router interface on the same network (in our Network Lab, this is 192.168.20.2). Next, configure the LAN interface **IP Address** and **Subnet Mask**. Disable **DHCP**. Select **Save Settings** at the bottom of the page to commit all of the configuration changes that you made.

✔ **Hint**

Since you have just changed the IP address of the router's WAN and LAN interfaces, you have effectively changed the IP address for the Setup Web page. In order to re-enter the router setup utility, you will need to configure the computer from which you are accessing it to be on the correct network and use the new IP address for the router. If the IP addresses were improperly configured, you would have to reset the router. There is a small recessed button on the back of most Linksys routers. Pressing the reset button for 20 seconds or so will reset the router to default values. Use the default values to once again enter the setup page and reconfigure the Lab Exercise settings.

Step 5   Next, select the **Advanced Routing** tab and select **Router** instead of **Gateway** from the drop-down menu. This procedure disables Network Address Translation (NAT) and allows properly routed packets to travel freely between the two networks. Select **Save Settings** at the bottom of the page to commit all of the configuration changes that you made.

While you are working in the **Advanced Routing** tab, select **Show Routing Table**. This is a simple static routing table that is created when you configure the LAN and WAN interfaces. Note the destination network, subnet mask, gateway, hop count (metric), and interfaces for each entry. See Figure 8-3.

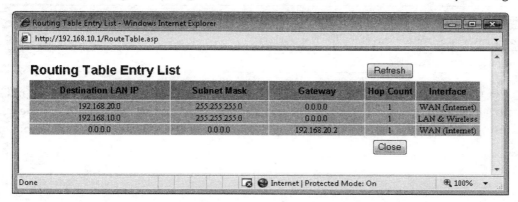

FIGURE 8-3 Routing table for the router in the Network Lab

Destination LAN IP	Subnet Mask	Gateway	Hop Count	Interface

✖ Cross-Reference

Review the "Routing Tables" section of Chapter 8 in the *Mike Meyers' CompTIA Network+ Guide to Managing and Troubleshooting Networks* textbook. This will help you better understand the details of the specific entries in the preceding table.

Step 6   Select the **Security** tab and disable the firewall. You would probably not do this if you were using the router to access the Internet, but these two segments are private LANs and will be isolated from the Internet. Select **Save Settings** at the bottom of the page to commit all of the configuration changes that you made.

Step 7   Now configure each of the computers on both Network 1 and Network 2. Remember to use the router's IP address for the network you are configuring as the default gateway for each of the systems on that network. You will also want to disable the Windows firewall on each machine in the Security Configuration applet.

Step 8 On one of the computers on Network 2 (WAN), open a command prompt, and using the `ping` utility, record the results of testing the communication with the following interfaces:

Interface	IP Address	Result
Loopback address		
This computer		
Another computer on Network 2		
The "Near" router interface (router interface for Network 2)		
The "Far" router interface (router interface for Network 1)		
One of the computers on Network 1		

If any or all of the prior communication tests fail, try to isolate the problem (individual computer, router, or switch). Depending on your findings, check the cabling, review the configurations of the PCs, or review the configuration of the router. If everything checks out, congratulations! You have a routed internetwork.

 45 MINUTES

Lab Exercise 8.03: Exploring NAT

Network Address Translation (NAT) is a powerful technology that enables many network clients on a TCP/IP network to share a single Internet connection. This provides an extremely important function: the conservation of the increasingly scarce, public IPv4 addresses distributed by the IANA. Most popular Internet gateway routers and home network routers on the market have built-in NAT functionality.

Since, by design, NAT blocks access from computers on the public network to computers on the private network, nobody can connect to and use any services on your computer. Normally, this is a good thing; it is difficult for a malicious program to attack your computer based solely on IP address. But what if you want to host a game or a Web site? Nobody would be able to access your computer with NAT enabled. NAT uses logical ports to translate the packets from the private IP address to the public IP address and vice versa, so you can authorize packets to be forwarded through logical ports for specific applications to the specific computer hosting that application.

The competent network tech (you) should be well versed with the concepts of NAT. You should be able to identify the various versions of NAT and provide their functional definitions. You need to practice enabling NAT on both "Small Office, Home Office" (SOHO) routers and commercial routers until mastered. Lastly, to ensure unhindered communication when necessary, you will configure port forwarding. When machines on the private network must be accessed from the outside world (such as Web servers, mail servers, terminal servers), port forwarding is the way to go!

In this lab, you will explore Network Address Translation.

Learning Objectives

In this lab, you will explain the function of NAT. When you have completed this lab, you will be able to

- Define the versions of NAT

- Implement NAT on a SOHO router

- Configure port forwarding to allow applications to pass through the router from the outside world

Lab Materials and Setup

The materials you need for this lab are

- Pencil and paper

- The *Mike Meyers' CompTIA Network+ Guide to Managing and Troubleshooting Networks* textbook

- A computer with Internet access

- The basic one-router, two-switch, four-computer lab network from the prior Lab Exercise

Getting Down to Business

Network techs, administrators, and engineers often find themselves working beyond the traditional workday of 9:00 A.M. to 5:00 P.M. that other business professionals enjoy. Often they continue to work utilizing personal computers in the privacy of their own homes, only to find when they return to the office the following day that they could really use an item of information that they left on their home computer. There are many tools that allow you to connect to a remote computer to share files and folders or even run programs as if you were on the actual machine. Windows provides one such tool in the Remote Desktop utility.

Until now, you have been treating the routers you are working with as internal-only routers, so they are "wide open" to communication from both the local segment and the remote segment. Since it is not unusual for IT personnel at ITCF to access their home computers from the office using Remote Desktop, Maggie asks you to research how to configure the home systems to allow this communication. She reminds you that the SOHO routers will inevitably have NAT enabled to allow one external IP address to service multiple internal computers, as well as to protect those computers from unwanted access from the Internet.

You'll need to explore the types of NAT, configure the computers on your lab network for Remote Desktop, and then enable routers to simulate the SOHO routers utilizing NAT. You'll want to try Remote Desktop after NAT is enabled, and then configure port forwarding to allow Remote Desktop to access machines on the local segment from machines on the remote segment.

Step 1   Using the section on "NAT" from Chapter 8 in the *Mike Meyers' CompTIA Network+ Guide to Managing and Troubleshooting Networks* textbook, and resources from the Internet, complete the following table outlining the various flavors of NAT.

Acronym	Description	Function
NAT		
SNAT		
DNAT		
PAT		

Step 2   Now using the Network Lab setup, log on to one of the machines on Network 2 (WAN) and use the Remote Desktop Connection to connect to one of the machines on Network 1 (LAN).

✔ **Tech Tip**

A quick refresher on Remote Desktop:

1. First, make sure that both systems have been enabled to use the Remote Desktop Connection. In Windows 7, click **Start | Control Panel | System and Security | System | Remote settings**. Under the Remote Desktop settings, enable **Allow connections from computers running any version of Remote Desktop (less secure)** as in Figure 8-4.

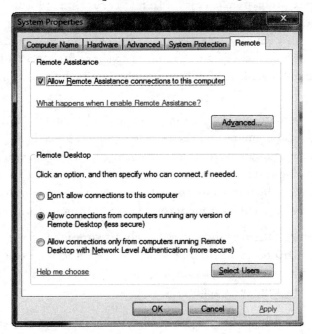

FIGURE 8-4 Windows 7 Professional System Properties Remote tab

2. Next, click **Start | All Programs | Accessories | Remote Desktop Connection.**

3. Enter the IP address of the remote machine.

4. You will then be prompted for a User name and Password.

5. If you entered the proper credentials, you should now have control of the remote computer.

You will explore the Remote Desktop utility in much greater detail in Chapter 14, "Remote Connections," Lab Exercise 14.03 Using Remote Desktop Connection (RDC).

What are the results?

_____

_____

Step 3 Now enter the router configuration utility (remember to use the new IP address since the router no longer has the default settings). Select the **Advanced Routing** tab and select **Gateway** from the drop-down menu. This procedure enables Network Address Translation (NAT), hiding all of the addresses on Network 1 from systems on Network 2. Select **Save Settings** at the bottom of the page to commit all of the configuration changes that you made.

Step 4 Log on to one of the machines on Network 2 (WAN) and use the Remote Desktop Connection to connect to one of the machines on Network 1 (LAN). What are the results? Can you ping any of the computers on Network 1 from the computers on Network 2? How about the opposite direction, Network 2 from Network 1? Why can or can't you communicate anymore?

_____

_____

_____

Step 5 Once again, enter the router configuration utility and select the **Applications and Gaming** tab (Figure 8-5). You are going to configure the router to pass the Remote Desktop Protocol (RDP) by enabling the proper port that the RDP uses, 3389, and link it with the specific IP address of the machine that you want to establish a Remote Desktop Connection with. This procedure enables port forwarding from systems on Network 2 that want to establish Remote Desktop connections with the specific machine on Network 1. Select **Save Settings** at the bottom of the page to commit all of the configuration changes that you made.

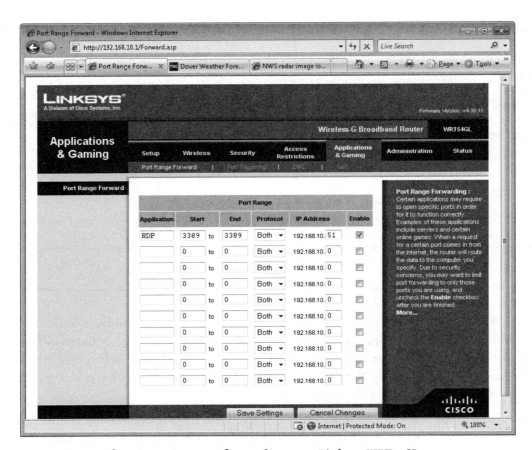

Figure 8-5 Configuring port range forwarding on a Linksys WRT54GL

✔ **Hint**

Although you have been working from the same initial network IDs that are shown in the figure, you may be using a different computer with a different IP address for the Remote Desktop connection. Make sure that you include your address when configuring and enabling port forwarding.

Step 6   Once again, log on to one of the machines on Network 2 (WAN) and launch the Remote Desktop Connection applet. To connect to the computer on Network 1 (LAN), you will have to use the IP address of the router. Your request will then be forwarded to the computer matching the IP address you configured to receive packets through the port number for the RDP. What are the results? Can you ping any of the computers on Network 1 from the computers on Network 2? How about the opposite direction, Network 2 from Network 1? Why can or can't you communicate anymore?

_____

_____

_____

_____

✖ Cross-Reference

Overloaded NAT (Port Address Translation) uses the logical ports assigned to services to transmit the packets destined for that service on a specific computer. You will be working with logical ports in the Lab Exercises in Chapter 9, "TCP/IP Applications." If you would like to review ports, check out the "Adding Ports to the Mix" section of Chapter 8 in the *Mike Meyers' CompTIA Network+ Guide to Managing and Troubleshooting Networks* textbook.

 1 HOUR

Lab Exercise 8.04: Configuring Multiple Routers and Implementing Dynamic Routing

Routing tables provide TCP/IP nodes and routers with the ability to move data successfully from one node or network to another as efficiently as possible. Every TCP/IP host system has some form of routing table. Client systems have relatively simple routing tables, while routers may or may not have complex routing tables. Whatever the size of the tables, being comfortable reading and understanding routing tables is the key to understanding exactly how IP packets move around large networks, including the Internet.

In this exercise, you'll explore the various dynamic routing protocols, configure a small, routed, four-network network, enable the Router Information Protocol (RIP), confirm connectivity, and document your findings. From this information, you'll develop an understanding of how routing tables and dynamic routing protocols operate from the simplest to the most complex networks.

Learning Objectives

In this lab, you will examine the basic characteristics of routing tables and dynamic routing protocols. When you have completed this lab, you will be able to

- Define the individual components of a generic routing table

- Implement a dynamic routing protocol

- Diagnose and correct routing issues

Lab Materials and Setup

Preferably, you will have access to the small "Network Lab" you assembled in the previous chapter's exercises. The materials you'll need for this lab are

- Pencil and paper

- The *Mike Meyers' CompTIA Network+ Guide to Managing and Troubleshooting Networks* textbook

- A computer with Internet access

- Four or more PCs

- Three routers (Linksys WRT54GL or similar wireless routers will work fine)

- Four eight-port Ethernet switches (Simple NETGEAR or Linksys Workgroup switches are acceptable)

- Appropriate UTP cabling

Getting Down to Business

Maggie has one last set of experiments she would like you to conduct with the routing lab. Maggie leaves the room and returns with a few more switches and two additional routers. She requests that you configure a four-network network using the multiple switches and routers that are now available to you. As before, she provides you with the network IDs for each of the networks, but leaves the addressing scheme up to you. The diagram in Figure 8-6 defines the basic setup.

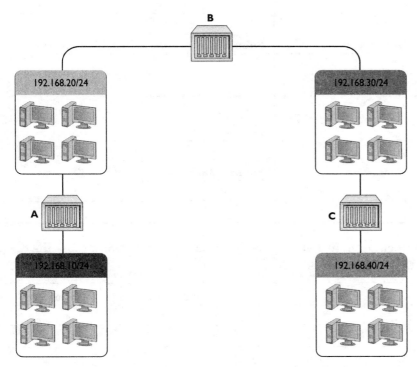

Figure 8-6 Four networks interconnected by three routers

Step 1 Using the assembled hardware, build and configure the physical network based on the network diagram in Figure 8-6. Document the IP address configuration for the computers and router interfaces on each network:

✔ Hint

On each of the three routers, remember to disable DHCP, NAT, and the firewall to allow packets to move freely from both the LAN interface to the WAN interface and vice versa.

Network 1 192.168.10.0/24	IP Address	Subnet Mask	Default Gateway
Router A interface (LAN)			
Windows Computer A			

Network 2 192.168.20.0/24	IP Address	Subnet Mask	Default Gateway
Router A interface (WAN)			
Router B interface (LAN)			
Windows Computer B			

Network 3 192.168.30.0/24	IP Address	Subnet Mask	Default Gateway
Router B interface (WAN)			
Router C interface (LAN)			
Windows Computer C			

Network 4 192.168.40.0/24	IP Address	Subnet Mask	Default Gateway
Router C interface (WAN)			
Windows Computer D			

Step 2 After completing the configuration in Step 1, log on to a computer on Network 1. Use the `ping` utility to verify connectivity with the following addresses:

Interface	IP Address	Result
Loopback address		
Computer A		
The "Near" interface for Router A on Network 1 (192.168.10.0/24)		
The "Far" interface for Router A on Network 2 (192.168.20.0/24)		
Computer B		
The "Near" interface for Router B on Network 2 (192.168.20.0/24)		
The "Far" interface for Router B on Network 3 (192.168.30.0/24)		
Computer C		
The "Near" interface for Router C on Network 3 (192.168.30.0/24)		
The "Far" interface for Router C on Network 4 (192.168.40.0/24)		
Computer D		

→ **Try This!**

Since you may be using Linksys SOHO wireless routers for the Lab Exercise, the Internet (WAN) interface actually has an entry that configures the gateway address for that segment. If your configuration uses the preceding table where each LAN interface is the "Near" interface and each WAN interface is the "Far" interface, this effectively creates a routing table entry for this interface. When you ping from a computer on Network 1, the partial routing table on each of the routers may allow packets to complete additional hops.

To fully test connectivity, log on to a computer on Network 4 (maybe Computer D), open a command prompt, and ping Computer A. What are the results?

Step 3   In Step 2, what do you think contributed to some of the connections not being able to communicate?

_____

_____

Step 4   In the following steps you will enable one of the dynamic routing protocols (RIP) to automatically configure the routing tables on each router. This will facilitate the communication of computers on all four networks. First, you should familiarize yourself with the various dynamic routing protocols, types, and features, completing the following table:

✖ **Cross-Reference**

To further study dynamic routing protocols, launch your favorite Web browser, and conduct a search on any of the protocols in the following table. You will find a wealth of information, much of it beyond the scope of the CompTIA Network+ requirements, but good to know for a competent network tech.

Excellent additional information regarding the various dynamic routing protocols may also be found in the "Dynamic Routing" section in Chapter 8 of the _Mike Meyers' CompTIA Network+ Guide to Managing and Troubleshooting Networks_ textbook.

Dynamic Routing Protocol	Description	Type	IGP/BGP	Features
RIPv1				
RIPv2				
BGP4				
OSPF				
IS-IS				
EIGRP				

Step 5   Starting with Router A, launch the setup utility and tab over to the **Advanced Routing** tab. Before you change any of the settings, click the **Show Routing Table** button. Refer back to Figure 8-3 in Lab Exercise 8.02 for an example of a default static routing table. Record the results in the following table:

Destination LAN IP	Subnet Mask	Gateway	Hop Count	Interface

You may notice that the table has only information on networks 1 and 2. There is no information on how packets travel to network 3 or 4. How can this situation be remedied?

_____

_____

Step 6 Now close the Routing Table information and enable **Dynamic Routing (RIP)**. Select **Save Settings** at the bottom of the page to commit all of the configuration changes that you made. Repeat this step on both Router B and Router C.

Wait a minute or so to allow convergence of the routing tables, and then on Router A, launch the setup utility once again. Tab over to the **Advanced Routing** tab and click the **Show Routing Table** button. See Figure 8-7.

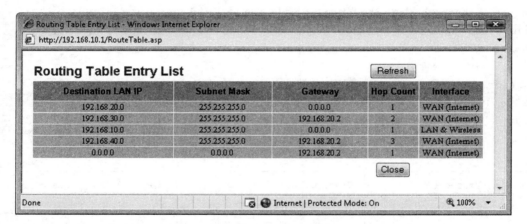

FIGURE 8-7 Routing table for Router A after implementing RIP

Record the results in the following table:

Destination LAN IP	Subnet Mask	Gateway	Hop Count	Interface

Step 7   Log on to Computer A on Network 1. Use the ping utility to verify connectivity with the following addresses:

Interface	IP Address	Result
Loopback Address		
Computer A		
The "Near" interface for Router A on Network 1 (192.168.10.0/24)		
The "Far" interface for Router A on Network 2 (192.168.20.0/24)		
Computer B		
The "Near" interface for Router B on Network 2 (192.168.20.0/24)		
The "Far" interface for Router B on Network 3 (192.168.30.0/24)		
Computer C		
The "Near" interface for Router C on Network 3 (192.168.30.0/24)		
The "Far" interface for Router C on Network 4 (192.168.40.0/24)		
Computer D		

To fully test connectivity, log on to a computer on Network 4 (maybe Computer D), open a command prompt, and ping Computer A. What are the results?

_____

_____

Step 8   You're going to finish up this Lab Exercise with another TCP/IP utility known as traceroute (tracert). Tracert will allow you to record the number of "hops" or routers a packet has to pass through to get from a source computer to a destination computer (usually on a far-removed remote network).

Log on to Computer A and open a command prompt. At the command prompt, type **tracert 192.168.40.XX** where XX is the address of your computer on Network 4. See Figure 8-8. Record the results in the following space:

_____

_____

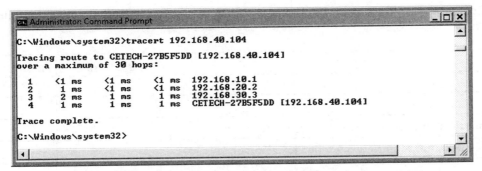

FIGURE 8-8 Trace Route (`tracert`) command from Computer A to Computer D

Lab Analysis

1. Trevor has just manually edited the routing table on an internal Cisco 2610 router. He knows that these routes will remain fairly constant but wants to understand how you would configure routers on the Internet where routes change all the time. Explain to Trevor the concept of dynamic routing and why it is so important for the Internet.

_____

_____

_____

_____

2. Theresa has been working with some routers and she keeps hearing the term "overloaded NAT." She is concerned that this may be something that could restrict network bandwidth or even damage the router. What can you tell Theresa about overloaded NAT that will ease her concerns?

_____

_____

_____

_____

3. Bryan has just installed two new internal routers to configure separate networks for the marketing department and the sales department of his organization. Now the sales team is having trouble reaching the Internet. Using ping, what troubleshooting sequence should Bryan follow to determine where the connectivity issues are located?

_____

_____

_____

_____

4. Max would like to see an example of a routing table but currently does not have access to a router. Show Max how to use the route print command on any Windows computer and record some of the entries listed in the routing table.

_____

_____

_____

_____

5. Sandra has heard you mention the terms "distance vector" and "link state" when you were discussing dynamic routing protocols. She would like you to explain the difference between these two types of dynamic routing protocols in more detail.

_____

_____

_____

_____

Key Term Quiz

Use the vocabulary terms from the list below to complete the sentences that follow. Not all of the terms will be used.

Border Gateway Protocol version 4 (BGP4)

convergence

Dynamic Network Address Translation (DNAT)

dynamic routing

Enhanced Interior Gateway Routing Protocol (EIGRP)

Network Address Translation (NAT)

Open Shortest Path First (OSPF)

Port Address Translation (PAT) Router

Router Information Protocol version 1 (RIPv1)

Router Information Protocol version 2 (RIPv2)

routing table

Static Network Address Translation (SNAT)

static route

tracert

1. _____ enables the use of one public address for a network of private addresses that connect to the Internet. This version is often referred to as overloaded NAT.

2. The version of RIP that added support for VLSM, authentication, and random update intervals is _____.

3. The _____ dynamic routing protocol uses "Hello" messages.

4. The command-line utility that allows you to follow the path that a packet takes as it travels over networks and through routers is _____.

5. _____ is the point when all of the routers have used a dynamic protocol and all of the routing tables on all of the routers are up to date.

Chapter 9
TCP/IP Applications

Lab Exercises

Obviously, one of the reasons you are spending all of this time and effort studying the minute details of the network infrastructure is to better provide networking services to users. The most popular applications—World Wide Web, e-mail, streaming audio and video, file transfers, Voice over IP, and so on—all require the configuration of specific components of the TCP/IP suite of protocols.

The two important protocols that operate at the Transport layer of the OSI model and the TCP/IP model are the Transmission Control Protocol (TCP) and User Datagram Protocol (UDP). There are also uncomplicated, specialized protocols that are associated with the Network layer of the OSI model and the Internet layer of the TCP/IP model, the Internet Control Message Protocol (ICMP), and the Internet Group Management Protocol (IGMP). TCP/IP applications use either a unique service port number or a combination of specific service port numbers over one of the Transport layer protocols. For instance, when you open your browser and navigate over to your favorite Web site, you are using some random registered port to connect with a Web server listening on TCP port 80 to transfer packets between the correct applications, for example, Internet Information Services (IIS) or an Apache Web server, and your browser.

To effectively perform the management of even the smallest network, administrators must develop a strong command of the network applications and the mechanisms they use to communicate over TCP/IP.

 30 MINUTES

Lab Exercise 9.01: Transport Layer and Network Layer Protocols

All of the upper-layer data communications that take place over the TCP/IP protocol suite (HTTP, FTP, SMTP, and so on) will be segmented at the Transport layer into either TCP segments or UDP datagrams. At the Network layer, two specialized protocols, ICMP and IGMP, provide for low-level messaging and management communication. In this Lab Exercise, you will explore the TCP, UDP, ICMP, and IGMP protocols.

Learning Objectives

In this lab, you will research and define the important characteristics of the Transport and Network layer protocols. By the end of this lab, you will be able to

- Define the Transmission Control Protocol
- Define the User Datagram Protocol
- Define the Internet Control Message Protocol
- Define the Internet Group Management Protocol

Lab Materials and Setup

The materials you will need for this lab are

- Pencil and paper
- The *Mike Meyers' CompTIA Network+ Guide to Managing and Troubleshooting Networks* textbook
- Internet access

Getting Down to Business

Maggie notices that you have been aggressively studying the configuration of IP addressing and routing. After some discussion, she agrees that you are really getting a handle on the IP component of the TCP/IP protocol suite. She thinks it would be an excellent time to delve into the other protocols that enable the TCP/IP protocol suite to successfully deliver packets between hosts.

You agree, fire up your favorite browser, and dive into some research on the protocols that work hand in hand with IP to communicate information from one machine to another over the network.

✖ Cross-Reference

For further information on TCP, UDP, ICMP, and IGMP, review the "TCP," "UDP," "ICMP," and "IGMP" sections in Chapter 9 of the *Mike Meyers' CompTIA Network+ Guide to Managing and Troubleshooting Networks* textbook.

Step 1 Research the Transmission Control Protocol (TCP) and provide a short summary of its features. Make sure to include discussion regarding the OSI model and TCP/IP model layer or layers it occupies.

Define the communication method used (such as connection-oriented or connectionless, reliable or unreliable), and some of the Application layer protocols that require it for their functionality.

_____

_____

_____

_____

Step 2   Research the User Datagram Protocol (UDP) and provide a short summary of its features. Make sure to include discussion regarding the OSI model and TCP/IP model layer or layers it occupies. Define the communication method used (such as connection-oriented or connectionless, reliable or unreliable), and some of the Application layer protocols that require it for their functionality.

_____

_____

_____

_____

Step 3   Research the Internet Control Message Protocol (ICMP) and provide a short summary of its features. Make sure to include discussion regarding the OSI model and TCP/IP model layer or layers it occupies. Define the communication method used (such as connection-oriented or connectionless, reliable or unreliable), and some of the applications that take advantage of its functionality.

✔ **Hint**

Refer to Chapter 7, "TCP/IP Basics," and review Lab Exercise 7.02: Configuring IP Addresses and Subnet Masks, and Lab Exercise 7.05: IP Addressing, MAC Addressing, and Ethernet: Working Together, to see ICMP in action. Pay special attention to the Tech Tips and the output of the Wireshark utility.

_____

_____

_____

_____

Step 4   Research the Internet Group Management Protocol (IGMP) and provide a short summary of its features. Make sure to include discussion regarding the OSI model and TCP/IP model layer or layers it occupies. Define the communication method used (such as connection-oriented or connectionless, reliable or unreliable), and some of the applications that take advantage of its functionality.

_____

_____

_____

_____

 30 MINUTES

Lab Exercise 9.02: Analyzing TCP/IP Ports and Associations

By this point, you should appreciate the complexity of the TCP/IP suite's many network functions. To the novice technician, it might seem as if these many capabilities could spill over into one another, but TCP/IP does a great job of keeping its different functions separate. It does this by using port associations.

Learning Objectives

In this lab, you will define the function of TCP/IP port associations and review the common port number assignments. You'll also use several utilities that will allow you to explore and analyze protocols, ports, and processes. When you have completed this lab, you will be able to

- Define the function of TCP/IP port associations

- List some of the well-known port number assignments

- Explore the various protocols, ports, and processes employed in a typical network communication

Lab Materials and Setup

The materials you will need for this lab are

- Pencil and paper
- PC running Windows XP, Windows Vista, or Windows 7
- Internet access

Getting Down to Business

After exploring the higher-layer transport protocols, you would like to know how TCP/IP keeps track of all the different sessions on a typical networked PC. You decide to examine the protocols, ports, and processes involved in the typical browsing of a Web site.

Step 1   Start with a description of the function of a TCP or UDP port.

_____

_____

Step 2   Match the following port numbers to the appropriate protocols.

Port 20	Port 21	Port 22	Port 23	Port 25	Port 69
Port 80	Port 110	Port 137	Port 138	Port 143	Port 443

➜ **Note**

Some protocols use more than one port number.

Application	Port
SMTP	
TFTP	
FTP	
HTTP	
HTTPS	
POP3	
IMAP4	
SSH	
Telnet	

Windows lists all of the well-known ports and protocol services that are associated with them in a document named "services." Access this list in Windows 7 by opening Notepad (**Start | All Programs | Accessories | Notepad**) and navigating to c:\windows\system32\drivers\etc. Change the view from "Text Documents (*.txt)" to "All Documents (*.*)" to view and open the services document. Other network operating systems maintain an equivalent document of port-to-service mappings. Linux, for example, also uses a file named "services" located in the /etc directory.

Step 3 The services document is a static list of well-known ports on a Windows PC. You will seldom if ever see all of these endpoint ports open or active at one time. You can view a static listing of the active ports using the netstat command-line utility. netstat has a number of switches to customize the output of the list. Run the netstat /? command and provide a description of the following switches:

netstat -a

_____

netstat -b

_____

netstat -n

_____

netstat -o

_____

➔ Note

You'll be making heavy use of the help functions of commands throughout the rest of the Lab Manual in order to use some of these more advanced functions! When in doubt, type the command and add a space and **/?** to the end of the command! For example: ping /?

✖ Cross-Reference

For further information on the configuration and usage of the netstat, TCPView, and Process Explorer utilities, consult the "Connection Status" section in Chapter 9 of the *Mike Meyers' CompTIA Network+ Guide to Managing and Troubleshooting Networks* textbook. You will also find excellent figures of netstat, TCPView, and Process Explorer in action!

Step 4   Maggie calls you over to see a system that she suspects may have a Trojan horse. Before running your company's standard antivirus program, she wants you to run netstat. Why would she want you to do this?

_____

_____

On your lab system, run netstat without any switches. Are there any established connections? See Figure 9-1.

_____

FIGURE 9-1 Output of the **netstat** utility with no established connections

Now launch a Web browser, navigate to www.microsoft.com, then run netstat with the -ano switches. Record some of the connections in the following space:

_____

_____

Step 5 While running netstat with the -n switch, you see connections to foreign systems using these ports. Use the Internet (check out www.iana.org/assignments/port-numbers) to determine what program is using these port numbers, and fill in the following table.

Port Number	Application Using This Port Number
80	
123	
445	
1214	
1863	
3389	
3689	

Step 6 After waiting for a few moments, if you run netstat -ano once again, you will find that the status of some of the connections will change and/or disappear. netstat is a static utility; however, a gentleman named Mark Russinovich has written a number of wonderful Microsoft utilities that are available for free. One of these, TCPView, is a dynamic, graphical endpoint tool.

Launch your browser and search for TCPView (the current version, v3.05, is available at http://technet .microsoft.com/en-us/sysinternals/bb897437.aspx). Download the ZIP file and extract the TCPView executable. Close all Internet connections and launch TCPView. In the **Options** menu, select **Always On Top**.

Now open your browser and load www.microsoft.com, observing the activity in TCPView. Record some of the features of TCPView.

_____

_____

Step 7 When you ran netstat with the -o switch, it added a column that displayed the process ID of each of the applications that were using the endpoint connections to communicate. Another of Mark Russinovich's tools, Process Explorer, is an excellent, dynamic process ID tool.

Fire up your Internet browser one more time and search for Process Explorer (the current version, v15.03, is available at http://technet.microsoft.com/en-us/sysinternals/bb896653.aspx). Download the ZIP file and extract the procexp.exe executable file. Close all Internet connections and launch Process Explorer.

You should see a number of running processes, many of which are local programs that are running. Launch a Web site, such as www.microsoft.com, and observe if any new processes launch. Record the results in the following space.

_____

_____

1 HOUR

Lab Exercise 9.03: Installing and Configuring a Web Server

In essence, most people mistakenly equate the World Wide Web with the Internet! In reality, the Internet is the infrastructure, while the World Wide Web is the multimedia content with hyperlinks. They probably make this mistake because the World Wide Web, using the Hypertext Transfer Protocol (HTTP), is the most widely used TCP/IP application. That said, one of the best ways to develop and practice the skills needed to support TCP/IP applications is to install and configure a server to support an Internet or intranet Web server.

There are really two important components associated with hosting a Web site. The first, and the one that you will be concerned with the most as a network support technician, is the installation, configuration, and management of the Web server itself. A close second would be the development and layout of the actual content (the actual Web pages), as a Web designer. To configure the Web server, you will probably work with one of the two most popular Web server engines, Microsoft Internet Information Services (IIS) or the UNIX/Linux Apache HTTP Server.

Learning Objectives

In this lab, you will install and configure Internet Information Services (IIS). When you have completed this lab, you will be able to

- Install and configure server-side and client-side networking applications

- Configure TCP/IP addressing and service ports

- Troubleshoot TCP/IP applications

Lab Materials and Setup

The materials you will need for this lab are

- Pencil and paper

- Microsoft Windows Server 2008 including Internet Information Services version seven (IIS7)

- Microsoft Windows XP, Windows Vista, or Windows 7 client computer

- The Linksys WRT54GL (or similar) router that was configured in Lab Exercise 8.01 and appropriate cabling to connect the small network

Getting Down to Business

CJ has decided to upgrade the Helpdesk and Desktop Support trouble-reporting system to a new intranet Web-based application. ITCF has already been using a Web-based program, but this new application has some really nice features that will help streamline the trouble-ticket process.

Before launching the new system, CJ asks you to use the resources in the Networking Lab to set up the Microsoft Windows Server 2008 machine with Internet Information Services version seven (IIS7) and load and run the Helpdesk application. You will run the application through its paces for a few weeks before going "live."

✔ Tech Tip

For the purpose of this Lab Exercise (and subsequent Lab Exercises in Chapters 10 and 11), it is recommended that you standardize the network configuration as follows:

1. Use Router # 1 that was previously configured in Lab Exercise 8.01. Confirm that the LAN configuration of the Linksys WRT54GL router (or similar) has an IP address of 192.168.10.1/24 and that DHCP is disabled. Use the LAN side of the wireless router as the switch for the server and client machines.

2. The Windows Server 2008 machine should be configured minimally prior to installing IIS. Disable IPv6 and configure the server with the host name netlabserver, an IP address 192.168.10.254/24, and a default gateway of 192.168.10.1. The server should not perform as a domain controller or be part of a domain. Dynamic Host Configuration Protocol (DHCP) should not be installed or enabled. Domain Name Services (DNS) should not be installed or enabled. You will install and configure DNS in the Lab Exercises in Chapter 10, "Network Naming."

3. On the client machine, disable IPv6 and configure an IP address of 192.168.10.11/24 with a default gateway of 192.168.10.1.

4. After configuring the simple Lab Network, verify that the Server 2008 network type is **Private Network** in the **Network and Sharing Center** applet. If using a Windows Vista or Windows 7 machine as the client system, verify that the network type is **Work Network** in the **Network and Sharing Center**.

Step 1   Starting with a basic installation of Windows Server 2008, install IIS by selecting **Start | Administrative Tools | Server Manager**. Select **Roles** from the left-hand pane and then click **Add roles**. Check the box next to **Web Server (ISS)** and click **Next**. Choose all of the default role services and features and click **Next**. Review the **Confirm Installation Selections** window, as shown in Figure 9-2, and click **Install**. Click **Close** to finalize the installation and exit the wizard. Close the **Server Manager** window.

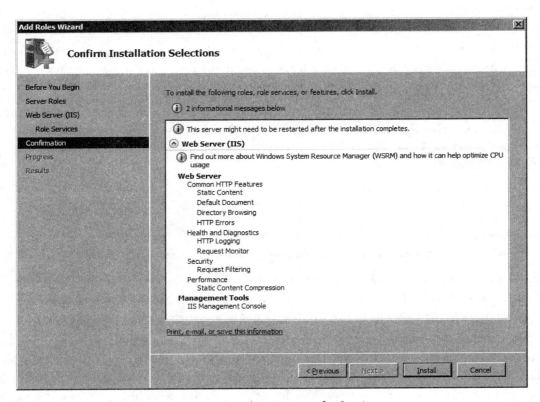

FIGURE 9-2 Configure Your Server Wizard summary of selections

Step 2 Now select **Start | Administrative Tools | Internet Information Services (IIS) Manager** and configure the following components:

a.   Expand **Local Computer | Sites | Default Web Site**. Right-click **Default Web Site** and select **Edit Bindings** from the drop-down menu.

b.   Highlight the first line, **Type HTTP**, and notice the default port 80 for HTTP. Click **Edit** and change the TCP port to 8080 for the intranet site and click **OK**. TCP port 8080 is HTTP-Alternate and is common to use as an alternate to well-known port 80 for intranet sites and proxy servers. It was adopted for this use since it is outside the range of the restricted well-known service ports (1–1023).

c.   Click **Basic Settings** and verify that the Physical path is %SystemDrive%\inetpub\wwwroot where %SystemDrive% is the variable for the primary hard drive, usually **C:**.

d.   Double-click the **Default Document** in the **Default Web Site Home** and verify that the file default.htm is at the top of the list.

e.   Click the **Black X** in the upper right-hand corner to close **Internet Information Services (IIS) Manager**.

You have now confirmed that the Web site will use a default Web page, which you will create in the next step. You have also configured your Web site to use the alternate registered TCP port of 8080 (HTTP – Alternate) instead of the well-known TCP port of 80 (HTTP).

Step 3   To create a default Web page, use Microsoft Word to create a simple document such as "Trouble-Ticket ITCF" and click **Save as Web Page** to create a Hypertext Markup Language (HTML) document. Save the document to the C:\inetpub\wwwroot folder with the name default.htm. This is a very simple Web page, but it will allow you to test the TCP/IP application and TCP port assignments.

✔ **Hint**

Obviously, you could easily spend an entire course studying HTML and Web design. However, the focus of this lab is to learn about the TCP/IP application and the installation, configuration, and management of a Web server. If you would like to explore Web design further, there are many applications such as Microsoft Expression Studio 4 Web Professional and Active Server Pages, Adobe Dreamweaver and Flash, PHP, or just good old HTML coding. Many IT professionals have some experience with Web design.

Step 4   Log on to your client machine and open your Internet browser (I'm using a Windows 7 machine with Internet Explorer 8). Enter the IP address of your Web server and press ENTER. What are the results? Are they similar to Figure 9-3? Why do you think this happened?

_____

_____

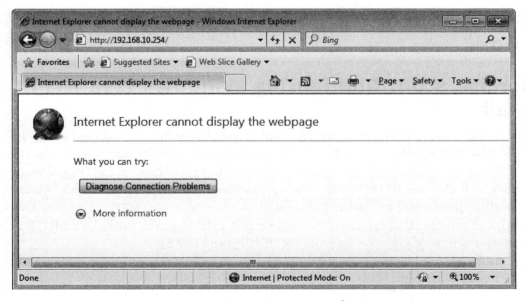

FIGURE 9-3 Entering the IP address for the Web server in Internet Explorer 8

Step 5   Now enter the IP address for the Web server; however, this time use the alternate TCP port 8080. For example, enter **http://192.168.10.254:8080** as shown in Figure 9-4, substituting your own Web server's IP address. What are the results?

_____

_____

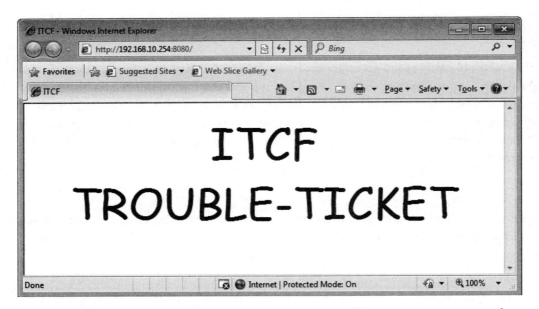

FIGURE 9-4   Entering the IP address and TCP port for the Web server in Internet Explorer 8

 30 MINUTES

Lab Exercise 9.04: Configuring Windows Live Mail and Gmail

When it comes to TCP/IP applications, you would be hard pressed to choose which of the two applications, the World Wide Web or e-mail, is the most important for communication and information sharing. The World Wide Web is primarily reliant on the Hypertext Transport Protocol (HTTP) and Gmail is a Web application, so it also uses HTTP. E-mail client applications such as Microsoft Outlook, Windows Live Mail, or Mozilla Thunderbird utilize the Simple Mail Transfer Protocol (SMTP), Post Office Protocol version 3 (POP3), and Internet Message Access Protocol version 4 (IMAP4). You worked with HTTP in Lab Exercise 9.03. Now it is time to explore e-mail and SMTP, POP3, and IMAP4.

Gmail, Google's Internet e-mail application, has gained considerable market share in the arena of free e-mail hosts. Gmail offers considerable storage space and a good Web interface to send, receive, and manage e-mail. With the introduction of Microsoft Windows Vista and continuing with Windows 7, Microsoft has discontinued the support for Outlook Express. However, you can use Windows Live Mail, a free program that is part of Windows Live Essentials.

These days, users often have more than one e-mail address, so it would be convenient if you could access multiple e-mail servers from one program, say Microsoft Windows Live Mail, to send, receive, and manage all of your e-mail accounts. With the simple configuration of a few of the TCP/IP applications, you'll be managing multiple e-mail accounts from one comprehensive e-mail client application.

Learning Objectives

In this lab, you will configure Windows Live Mail as your e-mail interface. When you have completed this lab, you will be able to

- Configure Windows Live Mail as your e-mail client for Internet e-mail accounts
- Discuss various TCP port associations associated with e-mail
- Send, receive, and manage e-mail

Lab Materials and Setup

The materials you need for this lab are

- A computer running Windows Vista or Windows 7
- Microsoft Windows Live Mail (included with the install of Windows 7)
- A valid Internet e-mail account
- Internet access

Getting Down to Business

Many of the clients of ITCF use multiple e-mail addresses for both work and personal communication. Brandon, one of your long-term clients, comes to you asking if there is any way to configure his personal e-mail (on his home system) so that he can send, receive, and manage messages the same way he does at work. In other words, he wants to use an e-mail client application to manage his e-mail.

You recommend using Windows Live Mail since it is already included with Windows 7, and agree to set it up as Brandon's e-mail client (after work hours as a favor to a good customer).

Step 1 First and foremost, you need to have a valid e-mail address. Many organizations, such as MSN Hotmail, Yahoo!, and AOL, offer free e-mail addresses. I chose to use Google's Gmail for the steps in this exercise. With a little research, you should be able to use the steps in this lab to configure Windows Live Mail as your e-mail client with any e-mail service provider. Alternatively, create a Gmail account to follow the steps exactly.

Step 2   Using Internet Explorer or Mozilla Firefox, log on to your e-mail account and view your messages. Notice the interface provided by the browser service. Each e-mail service offers a different look and feel and you have to log on to each of them individually.

✔ **Hint**

While on the e-mail service provider's Web site, you should be able to find detailed instructions on configuring an e-mail client to send, receive, and manage your messages. If you are using an e-mail service other than Gmail, download the specific instructions for your e-mail service provider. You can then follow along with the lab steps and substitute your e-mail service provider's instructions at the appropriate points in the lab.

Step 3   Begin by logging on to your Gmail account and clicking the **gear icon** in the upper-right corner and select the **Mail Settings** hyperlink. Select **Forwarding and POP/IMAP** from the **Settings** tab. Configure both **POP Download** and **IMAP Access** to be **enabled** as shown in Figure 9-5. Sign out and close your Web browser.

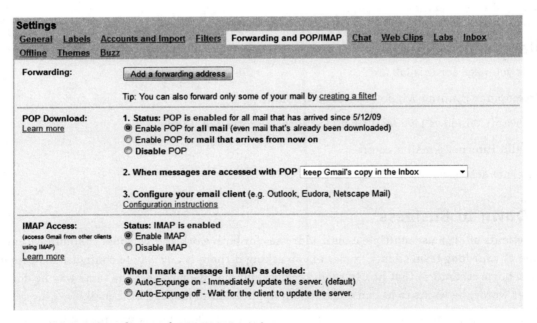

FIGURE 9-5 Forwarding and POP/IMAP settings

Step 4   Use the following steps to configure Microsoft's Windows Live Mail as the Gmail client:

   a.   Click **Start** and type **Windows Live Mail** in the **Search programs and files** dialog box.

   b.   Open **Windows Live Mail** and select the **Accounts** tab.

c. Click the **@+Email** icon to add a new e-mail account.

d. Configure the **Email Address, Password,** and **Display name** for the new e-mail account. See Figure 9-6.

e. Click **Next** and then **Finish** to complete the process.

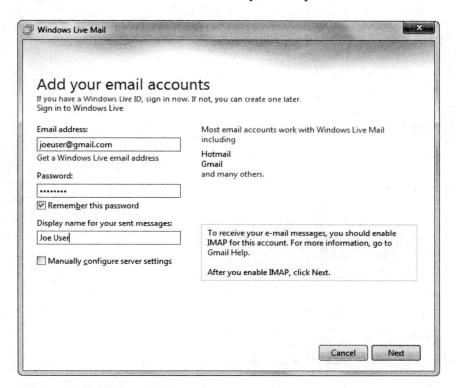

Figure 9-6 Add your email accounts

The configuration of Windows Live Mail as your e-mail client/server is so automated that you should now see your entire Gmail inbox. In order to explore "under the hood," you will now open the properties and record some of the TCP/IP components that you observe.

Step 5 To examine some of the details of the configuration, select the **@√Properties** icon and use the following steps to view and record the additional settings:

a. In the **General** tab of the **Properties** window, what is the name for the **Mail Account** that you have configured?

_____

b. In the **Servers** tab, record the configuration settings for **My incoming mail server is a** _____ **server, Incoming mail**, and **Outgoing mail**.

_____

c. Lastly, in the **Advanced** tab, observe and record the settings for **This server requires a secure connection (SSL)** and the **Server Port Numbers** for both the **Outgoing mail (SMTP)** and the **Incoming mail server (IMAP)** servers. Your settings should be similar to those shown in Figure 9-7.

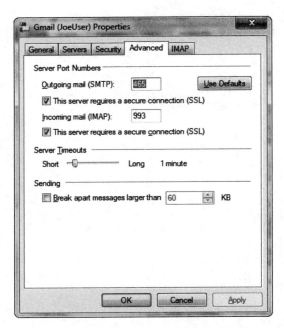

FIGURE 9-7 Gmail (JoeUser) Properties, Advanced tab settings

Since the e-mail client and server are using a secured connection, the TCP ports are not the standard for IMAP4 or SMTP. What are the default well-known port numbers for IMAP4 and SMTP?

✖ Cross-Reference

You will explore secure communications in much greater detail when working through the Lab Exercises in Chapter 11, "Securing TCP/IP."

Step 6 At this point you should be able to use Windows Live Mail to manage your e-mail accounts.

Lab Analysis

1. One of your co-workers, Shannon, asks you to explain the main operational difference between TCP and UDP. How does this difference affect which services use TCP or UDP?

   _____

   _____

2. Theresa has configured Microsoft Internet Information Services (IIS) to host an equipment sign-out application. Students who use the university video cameras and accessories to complete assignments in their film class will complete the online form. She has configured the server to use the alternate port of 8080 as opposed to the well-known port of 80 for the HTTP service. Why would Theresa choose to configure the application in this manner?

   _____

   _____

3. Noah notices that while setting up e-mail, he is instructed to use TCP port 995 for POP3, port 993 for IMAP4, and port 465 or port 587 for SMTP. Why would you use these port numbers instead of the well-known port numbers of 110 for POP3, 143 for IMAP4, and 25 for SMTP?

   _____

   _____

4. While Brianna is configuring Windows Live Mail to be the e-mail client for her Yahoo! account, she notices that the Internet Message Access Protocol v4 (IMAP4) is configured automatically instead of the Post Office Protocol v3 (POP3). What are the similarities and differences between POP3 protocol and IMAP4 protocol? Why do you think IMAP4 would be the preferred protocol?

   _____

   _____

5. Tymere is working with the Wireshark utility, and while capturing packets, she pings one of the other computers on her network. She examines the output of the capture and finds the section relating to the ping activity. What is the underlying protocol you would expect Tymere to observe?

   _____

   _____

Key Term Quiz

Use the vocabulary terms from the following list to complete the sentences that follow. Not all of the terms will be used.

Apache HTTP server

File Transfer Protocol (FTP)

Hypertext Transfer Protocol (HTTP)

Internet Control Message Protocol (ICMP)

Internet Explorer 8 (IE8)

Internet Group Management Protocol (IGMP)

Internet Information Services (IIS)

Internet Message Access Protocol v4 (IMAP4)

Mozilla Firefox

netstat -a

netstat -b

netstat -n

netstat -o

Post Office Protocol v3 (POP3)

Process Explorer

Simple Mail Transfer Protocol (SMTP)

Simple Network Management Protocol (SNMP)

TCPView

Telnet

Transmission Control Protocol (TCP)

Trivial File Transfer Protocol (TFTP)

User Datagram Protocol (UDP)

1. A command-line utility that will allow you to explore all of the current connections and the associated program executable is _____.

2. The _____ and the _____ are defined in the Transport layer of the OSI model, whereas the _____ and the _____ are defined in the Network layer of the OSI model.

3. When working with e-mail, the _____ is associated with sending e-mail and the _____ and the _____ are associated with receiving e-mail.

4. The UNIX/Linux-based _____ and the Microsoft product _____ are two of the most popular Web servers in use today.

5. When working with the _____, the most common well-known port used is 80. However, when implementing an intranet, many administrators will use the alternate port of 8080.

Chapter 10

Network Naming

Lab Exercises

As demonstrated in the last few chapters, you can cable some systems together and manually configure their IP addresses, subnet masks, and default gateways to create a very basic TCP/IP network. Over this network, users can send information to, and receive information from, each other. You can even add a Web server to this small network and host some information for the clients to access. However, without the addition of some sort of naming convention and resolution, you'll soon find that the use and management of this network becomes fairly tedious.

If you use only the basic configuration, you'll be stuck using IP addresses for everything. Instead of typing something like www.totalsem.com into your Web browser, you'll need to enter the IP address of the totalsem.com Web server. The answer to resolving this issue is the powerful TCP/IP application, Domain Name System (DNS). Microsoft fully adopted host names and DNS, instead of their proprietary NetBIOS names and Windows Internet Name Service (WINS), as the default naming convention with the introduction of Windows 2000. You will still work with NetBIOS names from time to time, and you should be aware that WINS existed, though it is seldom used today. DNS resolves fully qualified domain names (FQDNs) to IP addresses and WINS resolves NetBIOS names to IP addresses.

Several of the following labs build on the Web server you created in the Chapter 9 Lab Exercises, and deal with the real-world situations that involve DNS. You will configure, diagnose, and repair typical problems relating to name resolution.

This chapter also presents a great opportunity to introduce you to the server side of the Dynamic Host Configuration Protocol (DHCP). In the last Lab Exercise of this chapter, you will download a free DHCP server. You will then install and configure the server, scopes, and additional information allowing clients to obtain their addresses automatically.

✔ Tech Tip

In order to simplify the troubleshooting labs and overall DNS structure, where noted in the **Lab Materials and Setup** sections, it is recommended that you continue to use the Network Lab setup (one Microsoft Server 2008 system, and multiple clients in a closed local area network). This will allow you to keep the entire configuration to a basic level, which will be more demonstrative when conducting the lab exercises.

Currently, the Server 2008 system is configured as a stand-alone server and is hosting the Trouble Ticket Web server. DHCP should not be configured on the Network Lab systems to force manual configuration of all servers and clients. This will help reinforce the underlying process of DNS configuration on client machines. As mentioned earlier, you will explore DHCP in Lab Exercise 10.08.

 30 MINUTES

Lab Exercise 10.01: TCP/IP Network Naming Services: DNS and WINS

To begin your journey in the study of network naming, you will explore two of the advanced TCP/IP services: the dominant Domain Name System (DNS) and the retired Microsoft Windows Internet Naming Service (WINS). Each of these services enables the user to enter a much easier-to-remember, human-readable name, such as www.microsoft.com or netlabserver, as opposed to an IP address such as 192.168.10.254.

As a network tech, and in subsequent Lab Exercises, you will utilize and configure DNS to resolve host names to IP addresses. You will also briefly examine WINS to support legacy Windows systems. For now, you'll take a look at what these services do, and explore the settings that enable your TCP/IP network hosts to use them.

Learning Objectives

In this lab, you will define the DNS and WINS network services and explore the configuration settings a TCP/IP host needs to use them. When you have completed this lab, you will be able to

- Describe the functions of the DNS and WINS advanced network services

- Detail the common client configuration settings of DNS and WINS

Lab Materials and Setup

The materials you will need for this lab are

- Pencil and paper

- Windows XP, Windows Vista, or Windows 7 system with Internet access

- The *Mike Meyers' CompTIA Network+ Guide to Managing and Troubleshooting Networks* textbook

Getting Down to Business

Having just finished the chapter on network naming in the *Mike Meyers' CompTIA Network+ Guide to Managing and Troubleshooting Networks* textbook, you know that you are going to have to implement DNS on the network lab's systems. You want to get a jump on the setup, so you set out to define DNS and WINS and examine how they are configured on the client machines in use at the home office of ITCF.

Step 1   Describe the function of the DNS service on a TCP/IP network.

_____

_____

Step 2   Local PCs cache any addresses resolved by DNS on the hard disk. To view a display of resolved addresses cached on your PC, you will use the command-line utility ipconfig /displaydns. Open a command prompt and type **ipconfig /displaydns**. You should see a list of results similar to what's shown in Figure 10-1. What are your results?

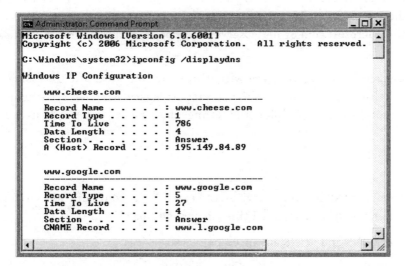

FIGURE 10-1 Section of output from the command **ipconfig /displaydns**

✔ **Hint**

Many anti-malware programs such as Spybot Search & Destroy utilize the hosts file to map malicious Web site redirections to the loopback address of 127.0.0.1. When your browser is instructed to go to www.antivirus-2009-pro.com, a known malware site, it resolves to the local machine and never gets off the ground.

If you are using a system with anti-malware programs running, you may receive an extremely full output when you run ipconfig /displaydns because the hosts file is copied into the DNS cache automatically. To narrow down the content of the DNS cache, temporarily disable the hosts file by navigating to c:\windows\system32\drivers\etc\hosts and renaming the hosts file to hosts.lab. (See Lab Exercise 10.02 for additional information on working with the hosts file.)

_____

_____

Step 3   Describe the function of the WINS service on a TCP/IP network.

_____

_____

Step 4   WINS is pretty much a legacy service, so there is a good chance that your network is not running a WINS server. However, NetBIOS names are still fairly common, so you can explore NetBIOS names with the nbtstat utility. Start by opening a command-line window, and then run nbtstat -A [IP Address] where the IP address is a valid address of a Windows machine on your network. This will return a list of the system's NetBIOS name table and generate a cache entry of the system's NetBIOS name (in the example shown in Figure 10-2, the NetBIOS name of the system is LANDMARQ).

→ **Note**

Like other command-line utilities you have explored, the nbtstat command has a number of switches allowing you to modify the output of the command. As with the other commands, you can type **nbtstat /?** to return a list of valid switches. Note the switch in the preceding Lab Step is a capital –A, displaying output based on the IP address of the remote machine, rather than a lowercase –a, which would display output based on the name of the remote machine.

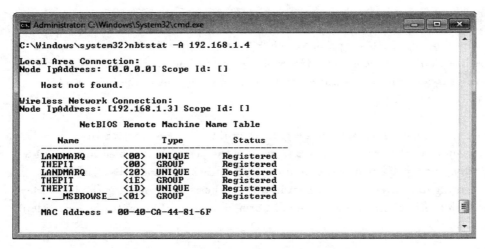

FIGURE 10-2 Result of the **nbtstat -A** [IP Address] command

Windows machines cache any addresses resolved by WINS (or by broadcast) on the hard disk. To view a display of resolved addresses cached on your PC, type **nbtstat -c** in the command-line window. You should see an entry for the machine you just connected with, as shown in Figure 10-3. What are your results?

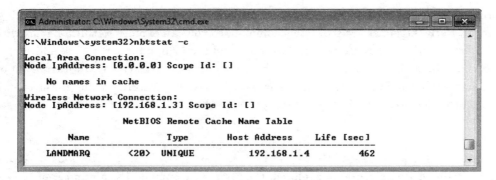

FIGURE 10-3 Result of the **nbtstat -c** command

Step 5 To view your PC's TCP/IP configuration, including advanced settings such as the DNS, WINS, or DHCP servers, type **ipconfig /all** at a command prompt. What are your results?

Step 6   To further explore the DNS process, run the Wireshark program on your client system and start to capture frames. Open your Web browser and access a Uniform Resource Locator (URL) for a Web site you've never visited—for example, go to the www.cheese.com Web site. After the Web page appears, stop the capture. Look for two lines in the capture file (they should look similar to Figure 10-4). The first line is the initial query from your system, while the second line is the response. You'll have plenty of other lines in your capture file—look for the ones labeled DNS under the **Protocol** column.

✖ Cross-Reference

As you learned while using Wireshark in Lab Exercise 7.05, you may apply a filter to limit the frames that the Wireshark capture displays. In this case, apply a DNS filter after capturing the frames.

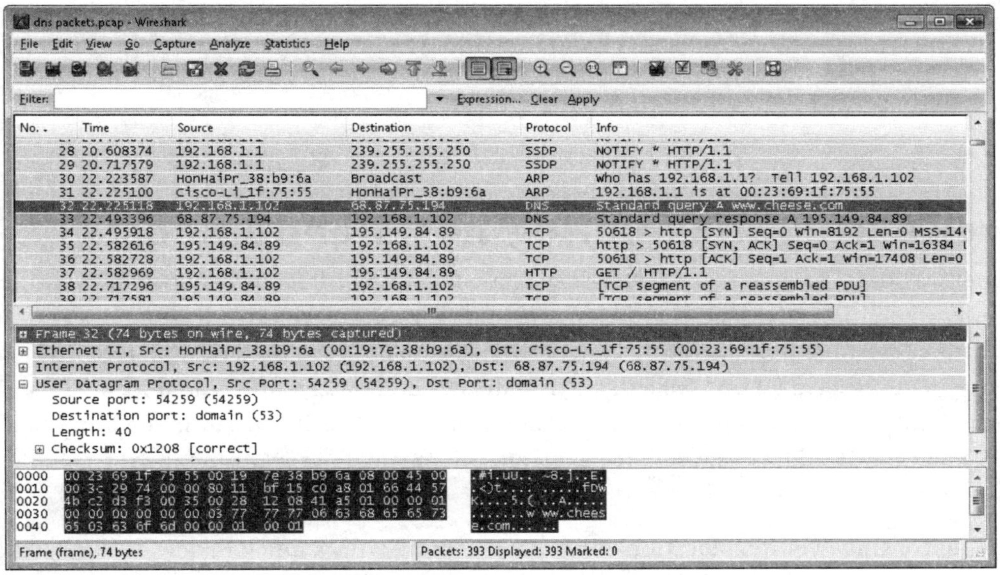

FIGURE 10-4 Wireshark capture showing a DNS query and response

Click the initial query line in Wireshark and look in the lower pane. This is a detailed breakdown of the frame. Expand the User Datagram Protocol in the details pane of the Wireshark utility. Referring back to the OSI model, DNS is in the UDP datagram at Layer 4. The data is then encapsulated by a Layer 3 IP packet. Finally, the IP packet is encapsulated by a Layer 2 frame. Why would the designers of DNS use UDP instead of TCP?

Step 7 Go through both the query and response frames in detail and answer the following questions. What port does DNS use? What port will the response to the DNS query use? What is the IP address for www.cheese.com? What are the IP addresses for the name servers?

_____

_____

Step 8 Close Wireshark and run the **ipconfig /displaydns** command. Can you find the listing for www.cheese.com? Record some of the information that is displayed.

_____

_____

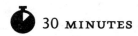 30 MINUTES

Lab Exercise 10.02: Exploring hosts and lmhosts

When the Internet was in its early stages, the engineers created a text file named _hosts_. This text file had a listing of every valid IP address on the Internet along with a corresponding host name. The hosts file is still included on most modern operating systems and is actually consulted first (before DNS) when a system is attempting to resolve a host name to an IP address. Later, Microsoft created its own naming convention called NetBIOS and developed their own resolution text file called _lmhosts_. The lmhosts file resolves NetBIOS names to IP addresses, used, for example, when you don't want to take the trouble to set up a WINS server.

You are going to continue your exploration of network naming with a quick review of the hosts and lmhosts files. Normally, you would be working with a network that already has a configured DNS server and these files would not be necessary; however, you will want to be aware of them for the CompTIA Network+ exam.

In an actual production network, you would almost always be using DHCP to fill in all of the critical TCP/IP settings. However, in your network lab, the TCP/IP configuration is manual, to encourage you to explore the critical settings that are often automated.

Learning Objectives

In this lab, you will explore the early name resolution process of hosts and lmhosts files. When you have completed this lab, you'll be able to

- Examine and configure entries in a hosts file
- Identify entries in an lmhosts file

Lab Materials and Setup

The materials you'll need for this lab are

- Pencil and paper

- Windows XP, Windows Vista, or Windows 7 client system

- Windows Server 2008 that was configured in the previous chapter's Lab Exercises

- The Linksys WRT54GL (or similar) router that was configured in Lab Exercise 10.03 and appropriate cabling to connect the small network

---

✔ Hint

For this and subsequent Lab Exercises in this chapter, it will make the labs run much smoother if you configure the client machines and server as follows:

1. Standardize the IP addressing scheme for the network. I used the network ID of 192.168.10.0/24 for all of the systems and used the "best practice" of placing the router in the lower ranges of the available network addresses (192.168.10.1), the server in the upper ranges of the available network addresses (192.168.10.254), and the clients starting at 192.168.10.11. It will also keep the output from some of the command-line utilities less cluttered if you disable IPv6. In Windows Server 2008 and Windows 7, disable IPv6 by selecting **Start | Control Panel | Network and Sharing Center | Change adapter settings**. Right-click **Local Area Connection** and select **Properties**. Uncheck the box for **Internet Protocol Version 6 (TCP/IPv6)**, and click **OK**.

2. To remove some of the complexity while performing the following Lab Exercises, open the IIS Manager by selecting **Start | Administrative Tools | Internet Information Services (IIS) Manager**. Expand **Local Computer | Sites | Default Web Site**, right-click **Default Web Site**, and select **Edit Bindings** from the drop-down menu. Highlight the first line **Type HTTP** and configure the **Port** as **80** instead of TCP port 8080 as configured for the previous chapter's labs.

3. In Windows Vista and Windows 7, the process of editing the hosts and lmhosts files will require you to utilize User Account Control (UAC) to open Notepad as administrator of the client system. To launch Notepad with administrative privileges, click **Start | All Programs | Accessories.** Right-click **Notepad** and select **Run as Administrator** from the drop-down menu.

4. You will also want to enable the viewing of hidden files, file extensions (*.txt), and protected operating system files. In Windows Vista or Windows 7, select **Start | Control Panel | Appearance and Personalization | Folder Options** and then the **View** tab. Select **Show hidden files, folders, and drives**; uncheck **Hide extensions for known file types**; and uncheck **Hide protected operating system files** as shown in Figure 10-5.

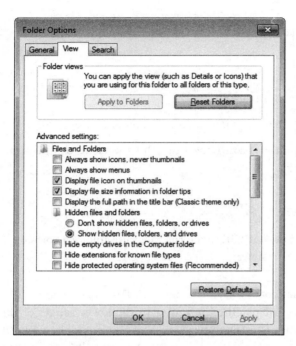

Figure 10-5 Folder Options window

Getting Down to Business

Having just finished the configuration of the intranet Web site www.troubleticket.local on the Network Lab setup, you are pleased with the results of the test communications. CJ stops by to see how the project is progressing and, after hearing that you are very happy with the results, attempts to access the Trouble Ticket application by typing in the fully qualified domain name (FQDN). To his surprise, it returns an error message: "The address is not valid."

CJ recommends that you study and implement name resolution on the Network Lab network and contact him when you have resolved (no pun intended) the issue. You set out on your quest and delve into hosts and lmhosts as a precursor to implementing DNS.

➜ **Note**

If you can re-create this scenario in class—great! If not, go through the exercise anyway. Use the differences between your classroom setup and the one described here to compare and contrast results!

Step 1   Log on to one of the client machines, open a browser, and type the URL **www.troubleticket.local** to see what happens. What are the results?

_____

_____

What test could you run to determine whether this is a DNS problem? What are the results?

_____

_____

Step 2   To verify the results, you open a command prompt and type **ipconfig /displaydns**. What is the initial output from running this command?

_____

_____

Step 3   Now you are going to use the hosts file to create an entry to allow you to use the fully qualified domain name (FQDN) of www.troubleticket.local to access the intranet Web site. To open the hosts file, open **Notepad** with elevated privileges, navigate to c:\windows\system32\drivers\etc, and open the **hosts** file. Enter the following line of text:

```
192.168.10.254        www.troubleticket.local
```

where www.troubleticket.local is the FQDN of your intranet Web site and 192.168.10.254 is the IP address of your Web server. Now select **File | Save As** and select **All Files (*.*)** from the drop-down menu. Highlight the hosts file in the file pane and select **Yes** when prompted if you would like to replace this file.

Step 4   Open your Web browser and enter **www.troubleticket.local**. What are the results?

_____

_____

Step 5   Once again, open your command prompt and type **ipconfig /displaydns**. You should see a response similar to the one in Figure 10-6.

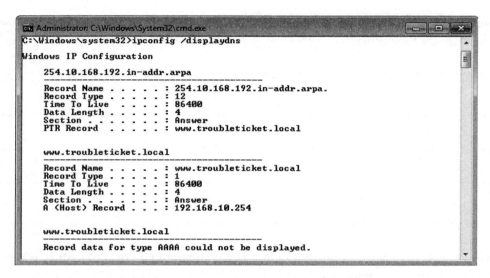

FIGURE 10-6 Output of the **ipconfig /displaydns** command

Record the results in the following space.

_____

_____

Step 6 Now navigate back to the c:\windows\system32\drivers\etc folder and open the hosts file with Notepad. Remove the entry for www.troubleticket.local. This will return the hosts file to its default status.

Step 7 Navigate to the c:\windows\system32\drivers\etc folder and open the lmhosts.sam file with Notepad. This is a sample lmhosts file. Examine the contents and define the following components:

    #PRE

_____

    #DOM: <domain>

_____

Write the line you would include, adding the netlabserver to an lmhosts file and preloading the Net-BIOS name into the name cache.

_____

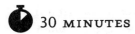 30 MINUTES

Lab Exercise 10.03: Installing and Configuring a DNS Server

If it ended up being your job to configure and maintain a hosts file on every computer that needed to access Web sites by their URLs, just the sheer number of entries would be astounding! DNS to the rescue! DNS allows a distributed database of host name–to-IP-address mappings (called *zones*) to be stored on dedicated DNS servers and be accessed by clients to resolve those host names to IP addresses.

From the Internet DNS root servers to simple intranet DNS servers, the goal is to make the access to Web sites as transparent to the end user as possible while keeping administrative overhead to a minimum. Even entry-level network techs are expected to have some understanding of DNS server configuration and maintenance.

Learning Objectives

In this lab, you will install a DNS server. When you have completed this lab, you'll be able to

- Install and configure a DNS server on a Microsoft Windows Server 2008 system

- Configure DNS server entries to resolve host names to IP addresses

Lab Materials and Setup

The materials you'll need for this lab are

- Pencil and paper

- Windows XP, Windows Vista, or Windows 7 client machine

- Windows Server 2008 that was configured in the previous chapter's Lab Exercises

- The Linksys WRT54GL (or similar) router that was configured in Lab Exercise 9.03 and appropriate cabling to connect the small network

Getting Down to Business

Having played with the hosts file, you realize that even for the intranet Web site, you will not want a network tech or administrator tied up with configuring hosts files on all of the client systems. You have to learn about DNS servers anyway, so you dive in and begin configuring the Server 2008 machine to provide DNS Services. You hope to have this up and running before CJ returns to check on your progress!

Step 1   Log on to your Windows Server 2008 machine as administrator and launch the Manage Your Server Wizard by clicking **Start | Administrative Tools | Server Manager**. Select **Roles** from the left-hand pane and then click **Add roles**. Check the box for **DNS Server** and then click **Next>**. Click **Next**

again to arrive at the **Confirm Installation Selection** window. Verify the DNS Server in the list of roles that will be installed and click **Install**. The installation will go through its paces and then tell you if it was successful. Verify that the installation was successful, and then select **Close**.

Once the DNS server is installed, open the DNS management tool by clicking **Start | Administrative Tools | DNS**. Launch the New Zone Wizard by clicking **Action | New Zone**. Follow the steps to configure the DNS server to provide resolution for the Network Lab network:

    a.   Click **Next**.

    b.   Select **Primary zone** (click Next).

    c.   Enter the Zone name: **troubleticket.local** (click Next).

    d.   Select **Create a new file with this file name** (click Next).

    e.   Select **Do not allow dynamic updates** (click Next).

    f.   Verify the settings in the Completing the New Zone Wizard screen as shown in Figure 10-7, and click Finish.

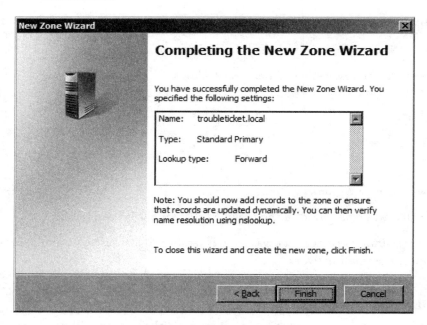

Figure 10-7 Completing the New Zone Wizard

→ **Note**

During the configuration of the DNS server, the wizard will attempt to find "root hints" for this DNS server. You may receive an error message stating, "The Configure a DNS Server Wizard could not configure root hints. To configure the root hints manually or copy them from another server, in the server properties, select the Root Hints tab."

Click **Finish** to complete the installation of the DNS Zone.

Step 2   Expand the netlabserver and expand the **Forward Lookup Zones**. Select the **troubleticket.local forward lookup zone** and record the records that appear in the **Contents** pane:

_____

_____

Step 3   Right-click **troubleticket.local** and select **New Host (A or AAAA)** from the drop-down menu. This will open the New Host applet. Enter the name of your Network Lab server (such as netlabserver) in the **Name** field, and your Network Lab server's IP address (such as 192.168.10.254) into the **IP address** field. Do not check the box **Create associated pointer (PTR) record** at this time. What is the FQDN of the new record?

_____

Click **Add Host** to add the new record and then **Done** to close the New Host applet.

Step 4   Lastly, right-click troubleticket.local and select **New Alias (CNAME)** from the drop-down menu. This will open the New Resource Record applet. Enter the name of your Network Lab Web site (www) in the **Name** field and your FQDN for the target host (**netlabserver.troubleticket.local**). What is the FQDN of the new record?

_____

Click **OK** to add the new record. The fully configured forward lookup zone should be similar to that shown in Figure 10-8.

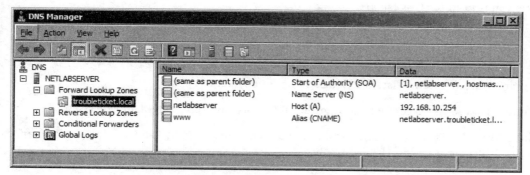

Figure 10-8 DNS management screen with records for netlabserver and www.troubleticket.local

Close the DNS Management Utility and log off the Windows Server 2008 machine.

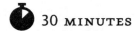 30 MINUTES

Lab Exercise 10.04: Troubleshooting Network Naming Services

The hierarchical structure of DNS makes it a robust, tolerant, and fast way to resolve fully qualified domain names (FQDNs) to IP addresses. When DNS problems take place, however, you'll want to remember that the secret to solving DNS issues is twofold. First, remember that DNS is robust and not prone to error. Many errors that might point to DNS issues are actually something else, such as the configuration of TCP/IP settings (both manual and automatic). Second, remember how DNS works. Many times the best way to diagnose and fix a DNS issue is to think through the process of DNS resolution and then test potential problem areas. Knowing how DNS works will also give you the ability to get around problems you can't immediately fix—like a downed DNS server.

In this Lab Exercise, you'll explore some of the core troubleshooting tools that will help resolve issues with DNS (you have already seen some of these, like `ping` and `ipconfig /displaydns`).

Learning Objectives

In this lab, you will review the DNS name resolution process. When you have completed this lab, you'll be able to

- Define the tools to test DNS settings and servers

- Use these tools properly in different troubleshooting scenarios

Lab Materials and Setup

The materials you'll need for this lab are

- Pencil and paper

- A system with Internet connectivity to facilitate downloading utilities

- Windows XP, Windows Vista, or Windows 7 client system

- Windows Server 2008 that was configured in the previous chapter's Lab Exercises

- The Linksys WRT54GL (or similar) router that was configured in Lab Exercise 9.03 and appropriate cabling to connect the small network

Getting Down to Business

After configuring the Web server in the last chapter and the DNS server in this chapter, you invite a few of your co-workers in to test the connectivity to the Trouble Ticket intranet Web site **www.troubleticket.local**. All complain that they cannot access the Web site. You have an idea what the problem is (the client machines have not been configured at this point), and you decide to run a few diagnostic tests to see if they will provide answers to this riddle and get the network running at optimum performance!

Step 1   To set this Lab Exercise up, log on to one of the client machines and open the Local Area Connection properties. Select **Internet Protocol Version 4 (TCP/IPv4)** and confirm that there are no entries for the **Preferred DNS Server** or the **Alternate DNS Server**. Select **OK** to save settings.

Now open a command prompt. At the command prompt, enter **ipconfig /displaydns**. What are the results?

_____

_____

If there are any listings in the DNS cache, enter **ipconfig /flushdns**. What are the results if you run **ipconfig /displaydns** again?

_____

_____

Step 2   You now look at the system of one user who has complained that she cannot access the Trouble Ticket Web site in her Web browser, even though she can access other computers on the local network. What test could you run to determine whether this is a DNS problem?

_____

_____

✔ **Tech Tip**

To successfully perform the next few steps from the client machine, you will prepare the DNS Server by enabling "Allow Zone Transfers to Any Server" using the DNS management tool. It must be stressed that you would **NEVER** enable "Allow zone transfers to any server" on a production DNS server! This would compromise the entire organization by allowing unscrupulous persons to transfer the entire DNS database. You will enable "Allow zone transfers to any server" in Step 3 to demonstrate the power of the nslookup and dig commands in Steps 4, 5, 6, and 7. You will then disable "Allow zone transfers to any server" in Step 8.

Step 3   Log on to your DNS server (possibly netlabserver) and perform the following sub-steps to enable "Allow zone transfers to any server":

  a.   Open the DNS management tool by clicking **Start | Administrative Tools | DNS.**

  b.   Expand **netlabserver, Forward Lookup Zones**, right-click **troubleticket.local**, and select **Properties** from the drop-down menu. Click the **Zone Transfers** tab and select **Allow zone transfers** and **To any server.**

  c.   Click **Apply** or **OK** to save your settings and close the **troubleticket.local Properties** window.

Step 4   You now are certain enough you have a DNS problem that you want to check the DNS server from the client system. On the client machine, launch a command prompt and type **ping www .troubleticket.local** and then press ENTER. Next, type **ping 192.168.10.254** and press ENTER (substitute the IP address of your Web server if it's different from the one in the example). What are the results? Are they what you expected?

Now type **nslookup** to enter the nslookup shell. Once in the nslookup shell, enter the IP address of the DNS server you want to query, that is, 192.168.10.254, by typing the following line at the nslookup prompt:

```
>Server 192.168.10.254
```

You can now verify the records you configured earlier by typing the following line:

```
>ls -d troubleticket.local
```

See Figure 10-9 for examples of these commands and their responses. Using the results from your own output, or the information in Figure 10-9, write a short description/definition for each of the important records in the following list:

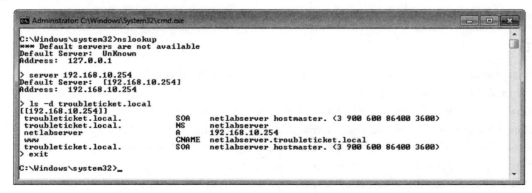

Figure 10-9 The **nslookup** commands and their output

SOA   _____

NS   _____

A   _____

CNAME _____

✖ Cross-Reference

To further explore DNS record entries, consult the "DNS Servers" section in Chapter 10 of the *Mike Meyers' CompTIA Network+ Guide to Managing and Troubleshooting Networks* textbook.

Why would you run the nslookup command to confirm that the DNS server is working? Why is ping a less than optimal choice?

_____

_____

Step 5 If the results of your **nslookup** were satisfactory, what two items would you want to check on the client system to make sure the client itself wasn't giving incorrect DNS data? How would you confirm that the problem wasn't with the IP configuration?

_____

_____

Step 6 When you're working in a Microsoft Active Directory Domain environment, one of the features that has been added to DNS is the dynamic registration of clients in the domain. This service is known as Dynamic Domain Name Systems (DDNS). One of the typical configuration errors that an administrator can make is to change DNS server information on a client machine but then forget to reboot the system. In this instance, the command ipconfig /registerdns can be used to force a dynamic update of the new DNS server.

Open a command prompt and type **ipconfig /?** as shown in Figure 10-10. Record the various switches that can be used to troubleshoot and manage name resolution components.

_____

_____

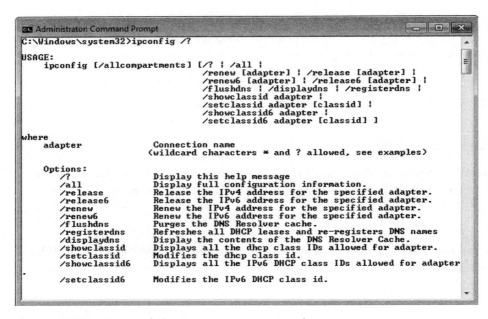

FIGURE 10-10 Output of the **ipconfig /?** command

Step 7 One last tool you will want to have some experience with is the dig utility. Dig stands for **domain Internet groper** and is native in Linux/UNIX systems. The Internet Systems Consortium provides a number of Linux/UNIX utilities that have been ported to the Windows operating system. You're going to download and install dig from a site maintained by Nicholas Fong: http://members.shaw. ca.nicholas.fong/dig/.

a. Download **dig-files3.zip** and save it to c:\dig

b. Extract all the files inside **dig-files3.zip** to c:\dig

c. You will need to add the c:\dig folder to your **PATH**. Click **Start** and type **environment variables** in the **Search programs and files** dialog box. Select **Edit environment variables for your account** and choose to edit or add the **PATH** in the **User variables** pane.

d. When you are done, open a command prompt and type **c:\path**. Your **PATH** should look similar to that shown in Figure 10-11.

```
Administrator: Command Prompt
Microsoft Windows [Version 6.1.7600]
Copyright (c) 2009 Microsoft Corporation.  All rights reserved.

C:\Windows\system32>path
PATH=C:\Windows\system32;C:\Windows;C:\Windows\System32\Wbem;C:\Windows\System32
\WindowsPowerShell\v1.0\;C:\dig

C:\Windows\system32>_
```

FIGURE 10-11 Output of the **PATH** command in a Windows 7 command prompt

The `dig` utility is a powerful command-line tool, and similar to `nslookup`, allows you to explore and troubleshoot DNS extensively. You are going to use two queries to explore the information about your DNS server that you explored with `nslookup`.

a. Open a command prompt as administrator and type the following command:

   `c:\dig\dig @192.168.10.254 troubleticket.local any`

b. Now type the second command as follows:

   `c:\dig\dig @192.168.10.254 www.troubleticket.local any`

c. See Figures 10-12 and 10-13 for examples of these queries and their responses. Using the results from your own output, or the information from Figures 10-12 and 10-13, capture some of the details for each of the important records in the following list:

```
Administrator: C:\Windows\System32\cmd.exe

C:\Windows\system32>c:\dig\dig @192.168.10.254 troubleticket.local any

; <<>> DiG 9.3.2 <<>> @192.168.10.254 troubleticket.local any
; (1 server found)
;; global options:  printcmd
;; Got answer:
;; ->>HEADER<<- opcode: QUERY, status: NOERROR, id: 353
;; flags: qr aa rd ra; QUERY: 1, ANSWER: 2, AUTHORITY: 0, ADDITIONAL: 0

;; QUESTION SECTION:
;troubleticket.local.            IN      ANY

;; ANSWER SECTION:
troubleticket.local.    3600    IN      NS      netlabserver.
troubleticket.local.    3600    IN      SOA     netlabserver. hostmaster. 3 900 600 86400 3600

;; Query time: 2761 msec
;; SERVER: 192.168.10.254#53(192.168.10.254)
;; WHEN: Mon Sep 12 14:09:53 2011
;; MSG SIZE  rcvd: 109
```

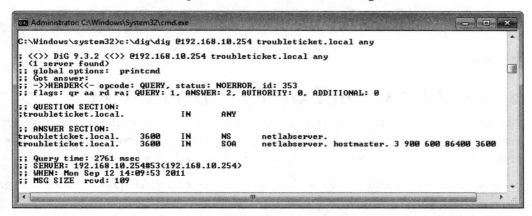

FIGURE 10-12 The responses to running dig on troubleticket.local

SOA ____

NS ____

```
Administrator: C:\Windows\System32\cmd.exe

C:\Windows\system32>c:\dig\dig @192.168.10.254 www.troubleticket.local any

; <<>> DiG 9.3.2 <<>> @192.168.10.254 www.troubleticket.local any
; (1 server found)
;; global options:  printcmd
;; Got answer:
;; ->>HEADER<<- opcode: QUERY, status: NOERROR, id: 1516
;; flags: qr aa rd ra; QUERY: 1, ANSWER: 1, AUTHORITY: 0, ADDITIONAL: 1

;; QUESTION SECTION:
;www.troubleticket.local.        IN      ANY

;; ANSWER SECTION:
www.troubleticket.local. 3600    IN      CNAME   netlabserver.troubleticket.local.

;; ADDITIONAL SECTION:
netlabserver.troubleticket.local. 3600 IN A      192.168.10.254

;; Query time: 0 msec
;; SERVER: 192.168.10.254#53(192.168.10.254)
;; WHEN: Mon Sep 12 15:03:17 2011
;; MSG SIZE  rcvd: 84
```

FIGURE 10-13 The responses to running dig on www.troubleticket.local

A   _____

CNAME   _____

Step 8 To disable the **Allow zone transfers to any server** setting, log on to your DNS server and perform the following sub-steps:

a. Open the DNS management tool by clicking **Start | Administrative Tools | DNS**.

b. Expand **netlabserver, Forward Lookup Zones**, right-click **troubleticket.local**, and select **Properties** from the drop-down menu. Click the **Zone Transfers** tab and uncheck **Allow zone transfers**.

c. Click **Apply** or **OK** to save your settings and close the **troubleticket.local Properties** window.

 30 Minutes

Lab Exercise 10.05: Configuring a DNS Client

DNS servers make Web surfers' lives much easier since they will not have to enter the IP address of every Web site they would like to visit. There is one important component to using the service, though; the client machine must be configured to query the DNS server for the host name–to–IP-address resolution.

Most often, advanced TCP/IP configuration settings such as DNS servers, WINS servers, and routers (default gateways) are configured by the DHCP server. However, for the purposes of this lab, you will manually configure the DNS server address to better understand the workings of name resolution.

Learning Objectives

In this lab, you'll configure a client machine to use DNS. When you have completed this lab, you will be able to

- Configure the TCP/IP properties with the address of the DNS server

- Connect to a Web site using the Uniform Resource Locator (URL)

Lab Materials and Setup

The materials you will need for this lab are

- Pencil and paper

- Windows XP, Windows Vista, or Windows 7 client system

- Windows Server 2008 that was configured in the previous chapter's Lab Exercises

- The Linksys WRT54GL (or similar) router that was configured in Lab Exercise 9.03 and appropriate cabling to connect the small network

Getting Down to Business

So now you have configured a DNS server for your Network Lab network! All that needs to be done to take advantage of it is to make sure each client machine points to the DNS server to retrieve the mapping and connect with the Web server requested. Remember, the next time CJ stops in (unlike the situation with your co-workers in the last Lab Exercise), you want him to be able to get to the Trouble Ticket Web application with no hassles.

Step 1 Before you change the configuration of any of the TCP/IP settings, make sure that you can still access the intranet Web site using the IP address (192.168.10.254). Record the results in the following space:

Now try to access the Web site using the URL: **www.troubleticket.local.** What are the results?

Step 2 In Windows 7, open the TCP/IPv4 properties by clicking **Start | Control Panel | Network and Sharing Center**. Select **Change adapter settings** from the side menu, right-click **Local Area Connection**, and select **Properties** from the drop-down menu. Highlight **Internet Protocol Version 4 (TCP/IPv4)** and click **Properties**.

Under the **Use the following DNS server addresses** radio button, in the **Preferred DNS server** box, enter the IP address of your DNS server (192.168.10.254) as shown in Figure 10-14.

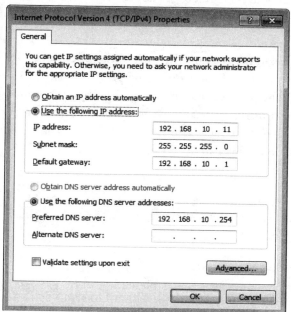

FIGURE 10-14 Internet Protocol Version 4 (TCP/IPv4) properties

Step 3   Now try to access the Web site once again using the URL: **www.troubleticket.local**. What are the results?

_____

Step 4   Can you access the Web site using the NetBIOS name netlabserver? What are the results?

_____

 30 Minutes

Lab Exercise 10.06: Exploring Dynamic DNS on the Web

You briefly interacted with Microsoft's DDNS in Lab Exercise 10.04 when you explored `ipconfig / registerdns` to force an update of Active Directory clients in DNS. There is another form of DDNS, Dynamic DNS on the Web. When a home user or small office sets up an Internet connection, they will probably use a consumer Internet Service Provider (ISP) to provide the connectivity. This is a completely acceptable solution for Internet access, but what happens if the user or business would like to host their own Web site? Even if the user or business has secured their own domain name, it can be tricky to host the site on an internal server because the external IP address is likely to change often. Since these ISPs are providing services to hundreds of thousands of people, they will charge a fairly stiff premium for a static address for the SOHO.

DDNS on the Web will track the external IP address and dynamically update the DNS service to resolve the FQDN to the new IP address. There are a number of companies who provide various levels of DDNS service. It is somewhat beyond the scope of this Lab Manual to have you configure an internal Web server, obtain a domain name, and host it using a DDNS service. However, you can gain a better understanding of DDNS by visiting the Web sites of these providers and exploring some of the services they provide. And that is just what you are going to do in this Lab Exercise!

Learning Objectives

In this lab, you'll explore the Web sites of various DDNS providers. When you have completed this lab, you will be able to

- Define DDNS on the Web services

- Detail some of the characteristics and components needed to implement a DDNS

Lab Materials and Setup

The materials you will need for this lab are

- Pencil and paper

- A PC with Internet access

Getting Down to Business

ITCF has a number of clients that are operating SOHO businesses. One of these clients would like to develop a better Web presence, and they feel that hosting their Web site on their own in-house server would allow them to be more responsive to customer's needs. They currently utilize a consumer ISP for their Internet connection, and they ask you to prepare a proposal for providing a solution using DDNS.

Step 1   To begin your exploration of DDNS on the Web, launch a browser and navigate to www.tzo.com. What are the three types of dynamic DNS services they offer? What are the options for establishing a domain name? Record the results in the following space:

_____

_____

Step 2   Next, open the home page of Dyn at dyn.com. They offer both dynamic DNS and e-mail services. To check out one of their products, a service called DynDNS Free, click on **Get started with DNS** and then navigate to the **Additional Products** section at the bottom of the page. What are some of the features of DynDNS Free?

_____

_____

Step 3   A company called no-ip provides yet another managed DDNS service. Visit them at www.no-ip .com. What are some of the packages/services they offer?

_____

_____

Step 4   Lastly, check out **FreeDNS – Free DNS – Dynamic DNS – Static DNS subdomain and domain hosting** at the URL **freedns.afraid.org**. What are some of the features offered by this DDNS service provider?

_____

_____

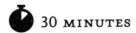 30 MINUTES

Lab Exercise 10.07: Utilizing NetBIOS to Access Resources

For years, back when Windows NT 4.0 Workstation and Server were kings, Microsoft used the NetBIOS naming convention exclusively. The NetBIOS name of the Network Lab server that you have configured is netlabserver. With the introduction of Windows 2000 Active Directory domains, the dominance of TCP/IP, and the Internet, Microsoft has adopted the DNS naming convention, such as netlabserver.troubleticket.local. Where host names are usually displayed as FQDNs or URLs, NetBIOS names are often used in the familiar Universal Naming Convention (UNC) names, that is, \\servername\sharename. NetBIOS names, along with some NetBIOS command-line utilities, are still used extensively by network administrators and techs.

The CompTIA Network+ exam expects you to be able to identify and use NetBIOS names, UNCs, and NetBIOS utilities. In this exercise, you'll explore the methods to access resources using NetBIOS.

Learning Objectives

In this lab, you will demonstrate how to access network resources from the local PC using Microsoft's NetBIOS naming convention. When you have completed this lab, you'll be able to

- Explain and demonstrate the various methods that enable network techs to view and access resources shared on a Windows network from a local PC

- Describe the different NetBIOS tools provided in Windows XP, Windows Vista, and Windows 7

Lab Materials and Setup

The materials you'll need for this lab are

- Pencil and paper

- Windows XP, Windows Vista, or Windows 7 client system

- Windows Server 2008 that was configured in the previous chapter's Lab Exercises

- The Linksys WRT54GL (or similar) router that was configured in Lab Exercise 9.03 and appropriate cabling to connect the small network

Getting Down to Business

CJ is very pleased that you had so much success with the Trouble Ticket intranet Web server and that you can now access the site utilizing the URL www.troubleticket.local. While you're concentrating on accessing network resources, and since ITCF is basically a Microsoft "house," he recommends that you explore the methods to view and access shared resources on a Microsoft network.

Step 1 To begin the examination of NetBIOS names, Universal Naming Convention (UNC) names, and the net command, you are going to set up a folder and share it out on the netlabserver.

Follow these steps to add a user, create a folder, and share it using the Sharing and Security applet:

a. Log on to **netlabserver** as administrator and click **Start | Administrative Tools | Server Manager**.

b. Expand **Configuration** and then expand **Local Users and Groups**.

c. Right-click **Users** and select **New User**.

d. Create a user account with the username **netlabuser** and **$3cr3+** as the password.

e. Uncheck **User must change password at next logon** and check **Password never expires**.

f. Click **Create** and then **Close** to add a user that you can use to connect from your client machine. This will ensure easy access to shared folders and printers.

g. Create a folder on the C:\ drive named netlabshare.

h. Right-click the folder and select **Share** from the drop-down menu.

i. Add netlabuser as one of the **people to share with** and select **Contributor** from the drop-down menu.

j. Click **Share**, then **Done**.

k. Add a text file named shareddoc.txt to the netlabshare folder and log off netlabserver.

Step 2 Log on to one of the client machines and create a user account that matches the account that you just created on the netlabserver. Add netlabuser as a member of the Administrators group to ease any problems with Windows 7 security. Log on as netlabuser and execute Steps 3, 4, 5, and 6 from the client machine to explore the various net commands.

Step 3 The net utility enables you to view shared network resources and configure network mappings the old-fashioned way. Open a command-line window and type **net view** at the prompt. What are the results?

_____

_____

→ **Note**

To view the valid parameters for the net view command, type **net view /?**.

Step 4 To view a list of network resources available on a specific system, type **net view \\computername** at the command prompt. For example, to view a list of resources shared on netlabserver, type **net view \\netlabserver**. What are the results?

_____

_____

Step 5 Using the list of available network resources displayed from the net view command earlier, create a network mapping via net use by typing **net use devicename \\computername\resourcename**. For example, to make a network mapping that uses the local drive L: to map to the shared resource netlabshare on the netlabserver, type **net use 1: \\netlabserver\netlabshare**. Optionally, add the **/persistent:yes** parameter to make the network mapping available every time you log on. What are the results?

_____

_____

Step 6 Now use the **net use** command without any switches to view the mapping you just configured on netlabserver. See Figure 10-15. What are the results?

_____

_____

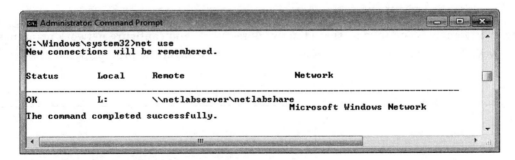

Figure 10-15 Output of the **net use** command

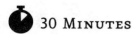 30 Minutes

Lab Exercise 10.08: Installing and Configuring a DHCP Server

As you have progressed through the Lab Exercises, it has been recommended that you disable any DHCP servers and manually configure all IP addresses, subnet masks, default gateways, and DNS servers (unless you were using a production system to gain Internet access). The primary objective is that if you manually configured these settings time and time again, you would gain a mastery of IP addressing and configuration.

As mentioned in Lab Exercise 10.05, IP addresses and subnet masks along with the advanced TCP/IP configuration settings such as DNS servers, WINS servers, and routers (default gateways) are normally configured by the DHCP server. Now it's time to install and configure a DHCP server to provide this invaluable IP information to client machines automatically.

Learning Objectives

In this lab, you'll install and configure a basic free DHCP server on a Windows 7 machine. When you have completed this lab, you will be able to

- Install and configure a DHCP server including scopes and advanced components (default gateway and DNS)
- Configure a client machine to obtain IP addressing and configurations automatically
- Test for network connectivity

Lab Materials and Setup

The materials you will need for this lab are

- Pencil and paper
- A client computer connected to the Internet to download source files
- Two Windows 7 client systems
- Ethernet switch and appropriate cabling to connect the small network

Getting Down to Business

Since you have access to plenty of machines in the ITCF Network Lab, Maggie recommends that you download a simple but elegant DHCP server known as "DHCP Server for Windows." She suggests you use two of your Windows 7 machines (one as the server, one as the client) to run through some of the DHCP configuration settings.

→ **Note**

In the last few Lab Exercises you have used Microsoft Server 2008 to host your Trouble Ticket intranet Web site and to implement a DNS server to resolve host names to IP addresses on the internal network. In this Lab Exercise you will explore a free third-party DHCP server that can be fully integrated into the Network Lab. If you would like to use the Server 2008 machine to implement the DHCP server, you may follow these steps, although the exact sequence and syntax will differ.

✔ **Hint**

In the following steps you will configure a small network (two machines) with fictitious default gateway and DNS server addresses. If you are performing these Lab Exercise steps in a classroom with an established network, your instructor may provide different scopes, and actual addresses for the default gateway, DNS server, and DHCP server.

Step 1   Using the system connected to the Internet, launch your Web browser and navigate to the following site: www.dhcpserver.de. Follow the instructions on the Web site to download **Newest Version V2.2 (dhcpsrv2.2.zip).**

Configure two of your Windows 7 machines and the switch in a small network. Copy and extract the dhcpsrv2.2.zip folder on the machine that will be used as the DHCP server. On the Windows 7 DHCP server, disable IPv6 and configure IPv4 settings as shown in Figure 10-16.

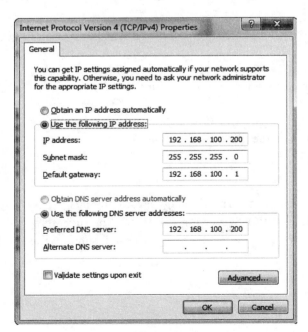

Figure 10-16 IPv4 settings for Windows DHCP Server

Step 2   On the Windows 7 client machine, disable IPv6 and configure IPv4 to **Obtain an IP address automatically.** Allow a few moments for the settings to take effect. Open a command prompt and type **ipconfig /all**. Record the results here:

_____

_____

Step 3   You'll now configure the DHCP server to provide addresses automatically.

a.   Open the folder where you extracted the files in dhcpsrv2.2.zip and launch dhcpwiz.exe. This will launch the configuration wizard.

b.   Click **Next** and select the network interface you want to install DHCP on.

c.   Click **Next**. The window will show supported protocols (HTTP, TFTP, and DNS). You will not add any additional supported protocols at this time.

d.   Click **Next** to advance to the next window. This window is where the key settings are configured. Configure the IP-Pool with a scope of 192.168.100.11 through 192.168.100.191 as shown in Figure 10-17.

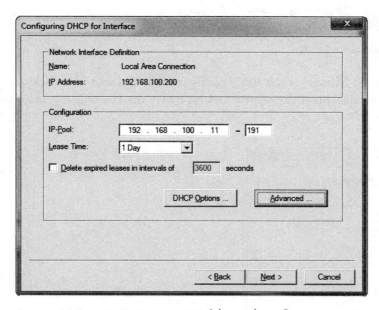

FIGURE 10-17   DHCP Server IP-Pool (Scope) configuration

e.   Now click the **Advanced** button to enter the Advanced Configuration window. Check the entries for both the DNS Servers and Gateways. What are these addresses?

_____

f. Close the Advanced Configuration window and click **Next**. Now you will write the .ini file as shown in Figure 10-18. DHCP Server for Windows runs as a service, which this .ini file configures. Click the **Write INI file** button.

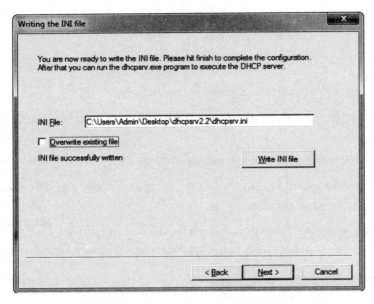

FIGURE 10-18 INI file creation routine and path

g. Click **Next** to advance to the last window of the DHCP configuration. You will now click the **Admin** button to install the service. Start the service and configure the Firewall exceptions as shown in Figure 10-19.

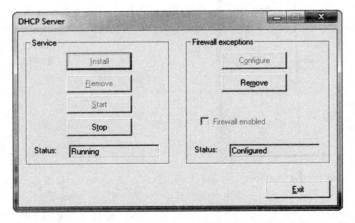

FIGURE 10-19 DHCP Service Install and Start and Firewall exceptions configuration window

h. Click **Exit** and then **Finish** to complete the installation and configuration of the DHCP Server and start running the service in the background.

Step 4 Now log on to the Windows 7 Client machine. Open a command prompt and type **ipconfig /all**. What are your results? Are they similar to those shown in Figure 10-20?

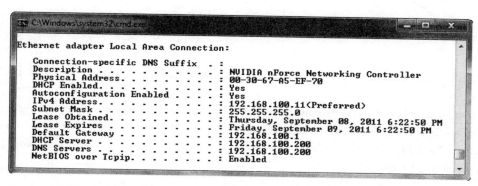

FIGURE 10-20 Output of **ipconfig /all** on Windows 7 client machine

Lab Analysis

1. Nathan is attempting to access a Web site, but he keeps receiving an error message. Someone told him that there may be a file on his computer that is keeping him from loading the site. He asks you to explain the relationship between the hosts file and DNS, and give an example of how they might conflict.

2. Chris is setting up a small Windows domain environment and notices that the Domain Controller (DC) needs a DNS server installed to operate properly. Explain the concept of DNS root servers, and discuss how a Windows domain environment not connected to the Internet might still need a DNS root server.

3. While installing and configuring a DNS server, Jesse observes various identifiers for the DNS record entries such as Host (A or AAAA), Alias (CNAME), and Mail Exchanger (MX). What are these identifiers?

    _____

    _____

4. After finally getting a number of systems configured in his SOHO, Willy discovers that one system cannot access the address www.ibm.com. It was able to access this Web site earlier, but now it just returns a message, "The address is not valid." What commands should Willy run, and why would he run them to diagnose the problem?

    _____

    _____

5. Now that Ian has finished working through half the Lab Exercises, especially Chapters 2, 7, and this chapter, Chapter 10, he realizes that he has explored many of the network addressing formats. To help you study, he asks you to name four popular addressing formats referenced on the Network+ exam.

    _____

    _____

6. Tim complains that he doesn't understand why Kerry insists on using manually configured static IP addresses on the corporate network. He asks for your assistance to explain to Kerry how using DHCP simplifies client administration for network techs.

    _____

    _____

Key Term Quiz

Use the technical terms from the list below to complete the sentences that follow. Not all of the terms will be used.

cache

DNS server

Domain Name System (DNS)

Dynamic Domain Name System (DDNS)

forward lookup zone

fully qualified domain name (FQDN)

host name

hosts

ipconfig /displaydns

ipconfig /flushdns

ipconfig /registerdns

lmhosts

name resolution

nbtstat

NetBIOS

NetBIOS name

netstat

net use

net view

nslookup

ping

reverse lookup zone

Uniform Resource Locator (URL)

Universal Naming Convention (UNC)

Windows Internet Naming Service (WINS)

WINS server

1. When troubleshooting DNS, you could use the _____ command to query the DNS server.

2. One of the legacy methods to access resources on a Windows network utilizes the _____ command along with the _____ to map a drive to a remote resource.

3. You can run the _____ command with the _____ to test if DNS is configured correctly. If this task returns an error, you can run the command with the IP address to further clarify if there is a problem with DNS.

4. There are two legacy files that are still included on every Windows machine. The _____ file resolves host name–to–IP address, whereas the _____ file resolves NetBIOS name–to–IP address.

5. When working on a system that is a member of a Windows Active Directory domain, you may have to run the _____ to reestablish a dynamic entry on a DDNS server.

Chapter 11
Securing TCP/IP

Lab Exercises

There are a number of mechanisms, utilities, and tools that make using the Internet safer for sharing private data and conducting business transactions. In broad terms, this is accomplished by securing the TCP/IP suite of protocols following the guidelines of four key components. First, the encryption of data, guaranteeing that only the intended parties will be able to view the data. Second, nonrepudiation, the process that guarantees that the data is the same as originally sent and that it came from the source you think it should have come from. The third component pertains to authentication; providing credentials such as username and password to gain access to the secure areas of information. The fourth component is authorization, the level of access you are granted to the area or the information you are dealing with.

In the following Lab Exercises you will work to secure communications with TCP/IP technologies that address all of these issues. You'll explore, install, and configure the components that handle encryption, nonrepudiation, authentication, and authorization.

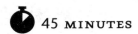 45 MINUTES

Lab Exercise 11.01: Evaluating Digital Signatures

Creating and implementing a Public Key Infrastructure (PKI) to secure the transfer of data can be achieved using various inexpensive encryption and authentication applications (you will actually experiment with these in Lab Exercises 11.02 and 11.03). This is all well and good, but are you going to trust sending private information such as credit card numbers or Social Security numbers to an organization that hasn't verified its integrity? Even if a Web site has implemented security using PKI, you still want verification that the organization is a valid, respectable outfit, and that this is really their Web site.

A number of organizations (VeriSign, Thawte, DigiCert, GoDaddy, or Entrust, to name a few), have established themselves as reputable providers of digitally signed certificates. A company that wants to do business over the Internet will apply with one of these organizations for a PKI key-pair, and after passing a background check, will receive a valid key-pair from the organization. This key-pair not only provides secure communications (encryption and authentication) but also validates the company's integrity by providing a digital signature from a reputable Certificate Authority (CA).

Learning Objectives

In this lab, you will examine the solutions provided by various certificate vendors. When you have completed this lab, you will be able to

- Confirm at least three certificate vendors

- Analyze various product offerings from these vendors

- Recommend a specific product based on needs

Lab Materials and Setup

The materials you'll need for this lab are

- Pencil and paper

- A Windows computer with Internet access

Getting Down to Business

ITCF's client, the Department of Transportation, has decided to add a customer response Web page to its Web site, where commuters can report traffic concerns road hazards/damage, or make suggestions for improvements. To keep the spam and prank comments to a minimum, they are going to implement a members-only site and require commuters to provide some personal data and create a username and password. To ensure the security of the commuter's personal data, Maggie is going to secure the site and assign a PKI certificate to the site.

Maggie would like you to research at least three certificate providers and put together a report on the costs and benefits of the various products. Due to the public nature of the client, Maggie recommends that you narrow your research to mid-level and top-of-the-line products.

Step 1 Log on to your Windows machine (I'm using a Windows 7 machine with Internet Explorer 9), and launch Internet Explorer. To view the default listing of trusted certificate authorities, select the **Gear icon (Tools)** and click **Internet Options** from the drop-down menu. Once in the **Internet Options** window, select **Content | Certificates | Trusted Root Certification Authorities**. This will provide a list similar to the one shown in Figure 11-1.

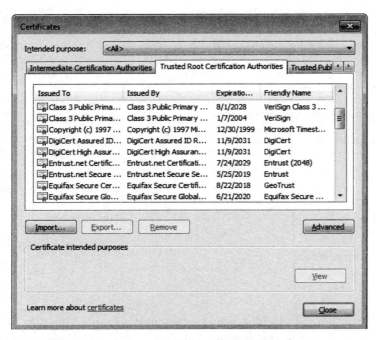

Figure 11-1 Trusted root certification authorities

Expand the columns and record the specific information for three of the trusted authorities. Include the information of the certificate's intended purposes located in the lower portion of the window.

_____

_____

_____

Step 2 Close the **Certificates** windows and cancel the configuration of the Internet options. Highlight the address box and enter the URL for VeriSign: **www.verisign.com/ssl/buy-ssl-certificates/secure-site-services/index.html**. Record some of the information such as certificate type, price, encryption strength, extended validation, and Green Address Bar for the mid-level product and the top-of-the-line product.

_____

_____

➜ **Note**

As discussed throughout this Lab Manual, Web site addresses change from time to time. If any of the listed Web sites are not valid, enter the home address for the company, and then navigate to the appropriate Web page for Secure Sockets Layer (SSL) certificates.

Step 3 Next, highlight the address box and enter the URL for DigiCert: **http://www.digicert.com/ssl-certificate-comparison.htm**. Record some of the information such as certificate type, price, encryption strength, extended validation, and Green Address Bar for the mid-level product and the top-of-the-line product.

Step 4 Highlight the address box and enter the URL for GoDaddy: **http://www.godaddy.com/ssl/ssl-certificates.aspx?ci=9039**. Record some of the information such as certificate type, price, encryption strength, extended validation, and Green Address Bar for the mid-level product and the top-of-the-line product.

Step 5 Using the information gathered in the research of the three Certificate Authority (CA) vendors, prepare a brief report on your findings. Compare your findings with those of other students and then work with your instructor to develop your recommendations to Maggie for the Department of Transportation customer response site.

---

 1 HOUR

Lab Exercise 11.02: Secure File Transfers with SSH and SFTP

One of the most efficient ways to transfer large files is to utilize the File Transfer Protocol (FTP). In the early days of remote connectivity, wide area connections were often direct, point-to-point connections, so there was less demand for secure connections. Telnet and FTP were used extensively to connect remotely to a distribution server, and transfer large files to the remote machine.

With the advent of the Internet, and the heightened need for security when accessing distribution servers and transferring files, the need for tools to provide authentication and encryption mechanisms became imperative! Secure Shell (SSH) and Secure File Transfer Protocol (SFTP) are the tools that have supplanted the use of Telnet and FTP to guarantee the secure access and delivery of files over the Internet.

Learning Objectives

In this lab, you will install and configure a secure SFTP server and appropriate secure client application to take advantage of the secure SFTP server. When you have completed this lab, you will be able to

- Install server-side and client-side secure networking applications
- Configure SSH and SFTP applications
- Securely transfer files from a server to a client

Lab Materials and Setup

The materials you will need for this lab are

- Pencil and paper
- A computer with Internet access or copies of the installation files for freeSSHd and PuTTY
- Microsoft Windows XP, Windows Vista, or Windows 7 client computer
- Windows Server 2008 that you configured and expanded on in the Chapter 10 Lab Exercises
- The Linksys WRT54GL (or similar) router that was configured in Lab Exercise 9.03 and appropriate cabling to connect the small network

Getting Down to Business

The main focus of this Lab Exercise is to provide secure TCP/IP communications between both server-side and client-side endpoints. You'll work with freeSSHd to install and configure a secure FTP server using SSH for the encryption. You will then implement PuTTY as the client-side application to successfully connect to the secure FTP server and transfer files.

You will also be working with local security on the Windows Server 2008 machine to integrate authentication (the FTP user will be a local server account). Before transferring files from the server, the FTP user will have to be assigned the proper access permissions (authorization) to the FTP source folders. There are a number of sub-steps to this Lab Exercise, so take your time and pay attention to each of the security components you are configuring in the steps.

Step 1   In the following sub-steps, you are going to create an FTP user account, an FTP distribution folder, and verify permissions for the FTP user in the distribution folder on the netlabserver.

   a.   Log on to the netlabserver as Administrator and launch the Local Users and Groups MMC. One method on Windows Server 2008 systems would be to select **Start | Administrative Tools | Server Manager**. Expand **Configuration** in the left-hand pane, then expand **Local Users and Groups**.

   b.   Right-click **Users** and select **New User** from the drop-down menu.

   c.   Create a user with the name **ftpuser01** and an easy-to-remember, complex password such as 1LoveBabyl0n5!.

   d.   Select the check box for **Password never expires**.

e. Select **Create** and close the New User utility.

f. Highlight **Users** and right-click on **ftpuser01** in the right-hand pane. Click on **Properties** and when the **ftpuser01 Properties** window opens, click on the **Member of** tab.

g. Verify that ftpuser01 is a member of the Users group.

h. Now navigate to the C:\ drive and create a subfolder named FTPDIST.

i. Verify that the Users group has **Read and Execute**, **List Folder Contents**, and **Read** permissions to the FTPDIST folder.

j. Copy some text or image files into the directory (such as c:\windows\web\wallpaper\server.jpg or c:\inetpub\wwwroot\welcome.png).

Step 2 Using the system connected to the Internet, navigate to the Web site www.freesshd.com, download the freeSSHd executable, and copy it to the Windows Server 2008 machine. Complete the following sub-steps to configure the freeSSHd SFTP Server:

a. Launch freeSSHd and follow the instructions provided by the Setup Wizard.

   i. Accept the default destination location.

   ii. Select **Full Installation**.

   iii. Accept the default Start menu folder.

   iv. Choose to create a desktop icon.

   v. Review the selections and click **Install**, then **Close**.

   vi. Create the private keys when prompted.

   vii. Run freeSSHd as a system service and click **Finish**.

→ **Note**

If the Windows Server 2008 system is not connected to the Internet, an error message may display stating "Error connecting to freeSSHd.com." Click **OK** to close the error message. The error should not affect the proper operation of the freeSSHd SSH/SFTP application.

b. Now right-click the freeSSHd system tray icon and select settings. Complete the following steps to configure the SFTP server:

   i. Click the **Server status** tab and verify that the SSH server is running.

   ii. Click the **SSH** tab and review the default settings. Are the RSA and DSA private keys configured? How many bits are the keys?

→ **Note**

RSA encryption is named after the developers' initials: Rivest, Shamir, and Adelman. DSA stands for Digital Signature Algorithm.

   iii.   Select the **Authentication** tab and verify that **Password authentication** and **Public key authentication** are **Allowed**. What is the default Public key folder?

---

   iv.   Select the **Encryption** tab and verify that **Any** ciphers are allowed.

   v.   Select the **SFTP** tab and browse to the FTPDIST folder you created earlier. See Figure 11-2.

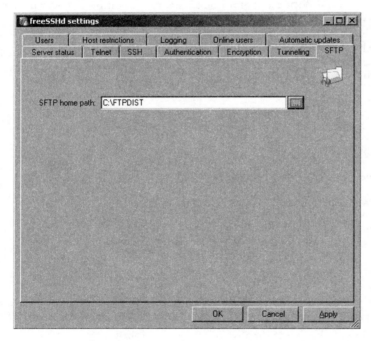

FIGURE 11-2 freeSSHd settings with the SFTP home path displayed

   vi.   Now select the **Users** tab and click **Add**. Add the user **ftpuser01**, select **NT authentication** from the drop-down menu, and select the **User can use SFTP** checkbox as shown in Figure 11-3. Click **OK** to add the user.

   vii.   Click the **Apply** button to save the freeSSHd settings.

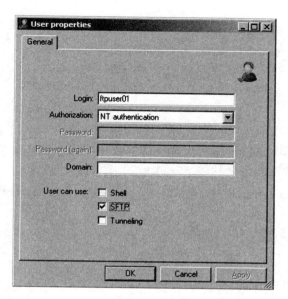

FIGURE 11-3 User properties configuration

    c.   You have now completed the configuration of the freeSSHd SFTP server. You can now select the **Online users** tab to monitor the activity of the user once the client system is configured and you connect to the SFTP server.

Step 3   Now log on to the system connected to the Internet again and navigate to the Web site www .putty.org. Follow the link to download the putty-o.6i-installer.exe file and copy the file to the client machine. Complete the following sub-steps to install and launch the PSFTP client:

    a.   Launch putty-0.6i-installer.exe and follow the instructions provided by the Setup Wizard.

        i.   Accept the default destination location.

       ii.   Accept the default Start menu folder.

     iii.   Do not select the check box to create a desktop icon.

      iv.   Review the selections and click **Install**.

       v.   Select the check box to view the README.txt file.

      vi.   Click **Finish**.

→ **Note**

Notice the line in the README file explaining that if you just want to use PSFTP to transfer files, you should be able to run it from the Start menu.

✖ **Cross-Reference**

For additional information on Secure Shell (SSH), PuTTY, and FTP through an SSH Tunnel [also known as a Secure File Transfer Protocol (SFTP)], review the "Encryption Standards" section in Chapter 11 of the *Mike Meyers' CompTIA Network+ Guide to Managing and Troubleshooting Networks* textbook.

Step 4   You will now create a folder on the client's C:\ drive to use as the working directory for the PSFTP client. When you download files, this is the folder where they will be deposited.

  a.   On a Windows 7 machine, log on with an administrative account and click **Start | Computer | Local Disk (C:)** to open the C:\ drive.

  b.   Click **New Folder** in the menu bar and enter the name **FTPREC** to create the working directory for the PSFTP application.

  c.   Click the **X** (in the red box) to close the window.

Step 5   Launch PSFTP by clicking **Start | All Programs | PuTTY | PSFTP** (on a Windows 7 system) and then follow the sub-steps to retrieve a file from the FTP server.

  a.   At the PSFTP> prompt, type **help** and press ENTER. This will provide a list of commands and their functions. You will be using a number of these commands in the next few steps.

  b.   Type **open <hostname>** where *<hostname>* is the name of your server, such as netlabserver, and press ENTER. You may choose to store the key in cache if you connect successfully to the SFTP server.

  c.   Login as **ftpuser01** and press ENTER.

  d.   Now enter the password **1LoveBaby10n5!** or whatever password you created on the Windows Server 2008 machine. Press ENTER. If the SFTP connection is successful, you will receive confirmation that the "Remote working directory is /" as shown in Figure 11-4.

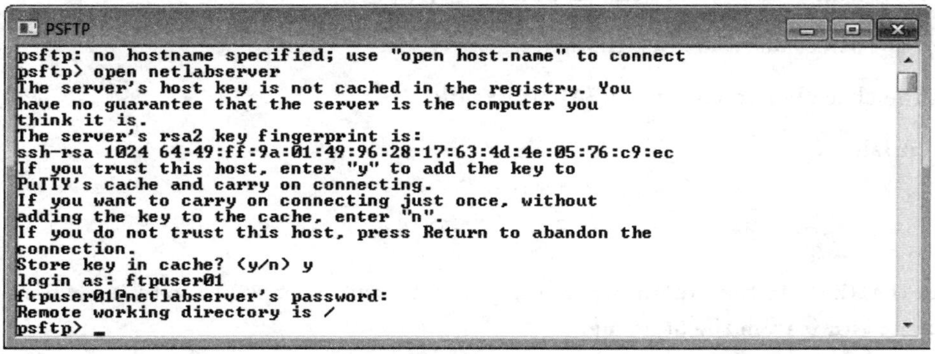

FIGURE 11-4   Successful login to SFTP server using PSFTP

e. You can view the current local working directory by entering the command **lpwd** and pressing ENTER. What is your current working directory?

---

f. Change your local working directory to the C:\FTPREC folder by typing **lcd C:\FTPREC**, and press ENTER.

g. Type **dir** and press ENTER. This will provide a list of the files available on the SFTP site.

h. To retrieve a file from the SFTP distribution site, type **get <filename.ext>** where *filename.ext* is one of the files available on the distribution site as listed by the dir command in Step 5e. On my server, I retrieved the file welcome.png, as shown in Figure 11-5. This file will be placed in the working directory, currently the C:\FTPREC folder.

```
PSFTP
psftp> dir
Listing directory /
drw-rw-rw   1     root      root         0 Sep 12 19:29 .
drw-rw-rw   1     root      root         0 Sep 12 19:29 ..
-rw-rw-rw   1     root      root    111952 Jan 19 03:23 server.jpg
-rw-rw-rw   1     root      root    184946 Sep 10 22:14 welcome.png
psftp> get welcome.png
remote:/welcome.png => local:welcome.png
psftp>
```

FIGURE 11-5 Securely transferring a file with the PSFTP utility

i. Navigate to the C:\FTPREC folder and verify that the file has been transferred.

j. In the PSFTP application, type **exit** to close the application.

 1 HOUR

Lab Exercise 11.03: Configuring Secure Transactions over HTTPS

In Lab Exercise 9.03, you configured a Web server to host the intranet Web site www.troubleticket.local. One of the popular uses of Internet and intranet Web sites is hosting specific material that requires secure connections between the client and the Web site. This secure connection is implemented through the Hypertext Transfer Protocol Secure (HTTPS) protocol utilizing Secure Sockets Layer (SSL) encryption. Through the use of certificates, the data transferred between the Web client's browser and the target Web site is encrypted and is only viewable by the two parties. This method is used extensively with business transactions where usernames, passwords, Social Security numbers, credit card information, or bank account information is being shared.

There are a number of additional steps required to implement a secure Web site, starting with obtaining a certificate from a valid provider. As you learned in Lab Exercise 11.01, there are a number of agencies, such as VeriSign, that provide commercial, valid certificates. You then have to install the certificate on the Web site, and associate the Web pages that you want to be secured. To facilitate this Lab Exercise, you will be using the Self-Signed Certificate generation tool included in Microsoft Internet Information Services (IIS 7) Manager (this is also a common practice to secure intranet Web sites). This would not provide a verified certificate for commercial use but provides a private certificate that you can trust because you created it, to implement a secure intranet Web site.

Learning Objectives

In this lab, you will install and configure a secure Web site. When you have completed this lab, you will be able to

- Install and configure an SSL certificate

- Associate the certificate with a specific Web page

- Access a secure Web page from a Web client browser

Lab Materials and Setup

The materials you will need for this lab are

- Pencil and paper

- Microsoft Windows XP, Windows Vista, or Windows 7 client computer

- Windows Server 2008 that you configured and expanded on in the Chapter 10 Lab Exercises (it will really help if IIS and DNS are already installed and operational and still hosting the www.troubleticket.local Web site)

- The Linksys WRT54GL (or similar) router that was configured in Lab Exercise 9.03 and appropriate cabling to connect the small network

Getting Down to Business

Since CJ is having you burn in the Trouble Ticket intranet application in the networking lab, and because it will need to have security implemented prior to the launch, he asks you to explore the implementation and configuration of a secure Web site.

You will utilize the Self-Signed Certificate tool that is included with IIS7. You'll then design a second Web page, add it to the Web site, and create a hyperlink to the page from the default Web page. Lastly, you will perform the steps to implement the successful access of the second Web page through a secure connection.

→ **Note**

To keep consistency, it is recommended that you continue to use the netlabserver and the Trouble Ticket intranet Web site for the following exercises. If you need to re-create the Network Lab setup, using a Windows Server 2008 system, perform the steps in Lab Exercise 9.03: Installing and Configuring a Web Server, and Lab Exercise 10.03: Installing and Configuring a DNS Server.

Step 1 Select **Start | Administrative Tools | Internet Information Services (IIS) Manager.** Highlight **netlabserver** and double-click **Server Certificates** in the feature pane. In the right-hand pane, click **Create Self-Signed Certificate** and complete the following sub-steps:

a. Type **netlabcert** in the **Specify Friendly Name** dialog box and click **OK.**

b. Now highlight **Default Web Site** in the left-hand pane. Click on **Bindings** in the right-hand pane under **Edit Site.**

c. In **Site Bindings** click the **Add** button and add the site binding of **HTTPS** as shown in Figure 11-6.

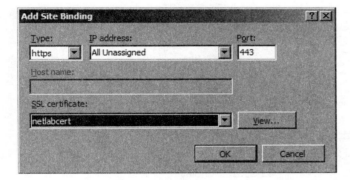

FIGURE 11-6 Adding the site binding of HTTPS (port 443) and netlabcert certificate

d. Click **OK** and then **Close.**

You have now successfully assigned a Self-Signed Certificate to **Default Web Site** (ID 1). In the next step you will create a second Web page on which you will assign security.

Step 2 To create a second Web page for the Web site, log on to the Windows Server 2008 machine and open Word. Use Microsoft Word to create a simple document such as "MY SECURE WEB PAGE" and click **Save as Web Page** to create a Hypertext Markup Language (HTML) document. Save the document to the C:\Inetpub\wwwroot folder with the name **secure.htm**. This is a very simple Web page, but it will allow you to test the SSL application and hyperlink assignments.

Step 3 To modify the default Web page with a hyperlink, you will once again use Microsoft Word to edit the simple document "ITCF TROUBLE TICKET" that was created in Lab Exercise 9.03.

   a. On the Server 2008 machine, open Word and open the c:\Inetpub\wwwroot\default.htm file to edit the original Web page.

   b. Type a second line such as "MY SECURE WEB PAGE." Highlight the text, right-click the selection, and select **Hyperlink** from the drop-down menu. This should launch the **Insert Hyperlink** window.

   c. In the address box, type the following URL: **https://www.troubleticket.local/secure.htm** as shown in Figure 11-7 and click **OK**. This will create the hyperlink to the second Web page, secure.htm (the text in Word should change to blue and underlined to denote the hyperlink).

   d. Select **File | Save**.

   e. Close the Word application.

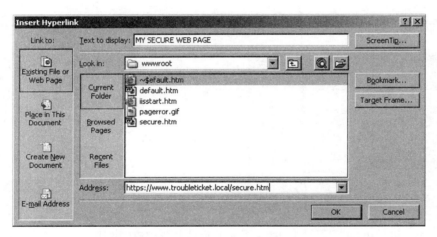

FIGURE 11-7 The Insert Hyperlink window in Microsoft Word

Step 4 Now select **Start | Administrative Tools | Internet Information Services (IIS) Manager** and configure the following components:

   a. Expand **Local Computer | Sites | Default Web Site**. Right-click **Default Web Site** and click **Switch to Content View**. Right-click **secure.htm** and select **Switch to Features View** from the drop-down menu.

b. Double-click the **SSL Settings** icon, select the **Require SSL** check box, and click **Apply** in the right-hand pane. See Figure 11-8.

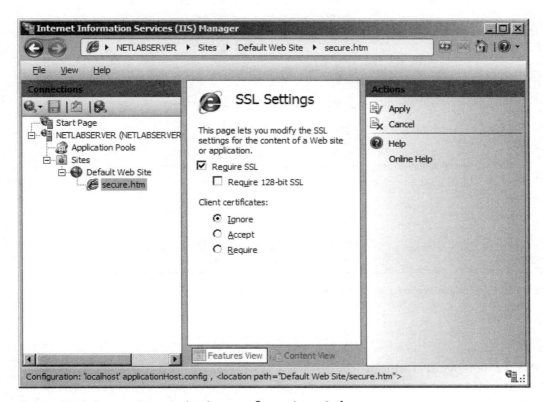

FIGURE 11-8 Secure Communications configuration window

You have now configured the Web site to use the SSL certificate on the new Web page (secure.htm). At this point, you should be able to access the Web site from your client browser; however, you may receive some error messages based on the certificate's validity. Try it! How do your results compare to the results in Figure 11-9?

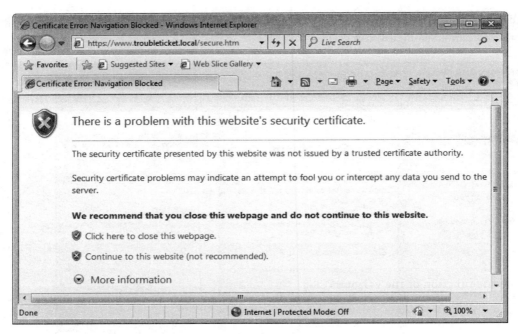

FIGURE 11-9 Certificate error in Microsoft's Internet Explorer 8

✔ **Tech Tip**

Since this is a Self-Signed Certificate, the certificate issuer (you) is not a trusted authority. In addition, the Self-Signed Certificate has been issued to your server name netlabserver as opposed to your FQDN of www.troubleticket.local, causing an address mismatch error. These are the limitations of the Self-Signed Certificate, and therefore, you will not be able to display the Extended Validation Green Bar.

Step 5   Click the icon that is a white X in a red shield with the text **Continue to this website (not recommended)** to continue on to the secure Web page. What are the results?

_____

_____

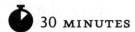 30 MINUTES

Lab Exercise 11.04: Analyzing Secure TCP/IP Ports and Associations

In Chapter 9 you examined the TCP and UDP ports of various TCP/IP applications such as HTTP and FTP. Now that you have been working with secure TCP/IP applications, you will spend some time analyzing the connection between secure applications, their port numbers, and the associated function the secure application provides.

Learning Objectives

In this lab, you will work with various TCP/IP security components. When you have completed this lab, you will be able to

- Define the function of the various TCP/IP security components

- List some of the well-known port number assignments for TCP/IP security protocols

- Explore the results of utilizing some of the secure protocols used in typical network communications

Lab Materials and Setup

The materials you will need for this lab are

- Pencil and paper

- A computer with Internet access

- Microsoft Windows XP, Windows Vista, or Windows 7 client computer

- Windows Server 2008 that you configured and expanded on in the Chapter 10 Lab Exercises

- The Linksys WRT54GL (or similar) router that was configured in Lab Exercise 9.03 and appropriate cabling to connect the small network

Getting Down to Business

Now that you have completed the implementation of both a secure FTP site and a secure Web site, you want to explore some of the inner workings of the secure protocols that were instrumental in creating the secure connection. While you're at it, go ahead and examine some of the other components that help keep TCP/IP secure, their function, port numbers, and associations.

Step 1 Start by redefining the four primary security concepts addressed when securing TCP/IP.

_____

_____

_____

_____

✖ Cross-Reference

To refresh your understanding of the four primary functions implemented when securing TCP/IP, consult the "Making TCP/IP Secure" section in Chapter 11 of the *Mike Meyers' CompTIA Network+ Guide to Managing and Troubleshooting Networks* textbook.

Step 2 Match the following port numbers to the appropriate protocols.

Port 22	Port 49	Port 88	Port 123	Port 143	Port 161
Port 162	Port 443	Port 1812	Port 1813	Port 3389	Port 5190

➜ Note

Some of the port numbers will be used more than once as some of the protocols use the same ports. Also, some of the protocols require more than one port.

Application	Port
Kerberos	
SFTP	
RADIUS	
NTP	
SSL	
SNMP	
SCP	
SSH	
TACACS+	

✔ **Hint**

Log on to your machine with Internet access and open a Web browser. Search for the associated port that each of the protocols use. You may find that more than one port is recognized for the same protocol; many of these are old and have been replaced with updated ports. The listed ports are the most recent for the protocol.

Step 3 Log on to your Network Lab client system and launch the Web browser. Navigate to the Trouble Ticket Web site www.troubleticket.local, and then access the secure Web page using the hyperlink. Run **netstat** with the **-ano** switches. You should see results similar to those shown in Figure 11-10. Record the connections related to the Web pages in the following space:

_____

_____

```
Administrator: C:\Windows\System32\cmd.exe
TCP    0.0.0.0:49156          0.0.0.0:0              LISTENING       1912
TCP    0.0.0.0:49157          0.0.0.0:0              LISTENING       524
TCP    192.168.10.11:139      0.0.0.0:0              LISTENING       4
TCP    192.168.10.11:49370    192.168.10.254:80      ESTABLISHED     3228
TCP    192.168.10.11:49374    192.168.10.254:443     ESTABLISHED     3228
TCP    [::]:135               [::]:0                 LISTENING       724
TCP    [::]:445               [::]:0                 LISTENING       4
```

FIGURE 11-10 Output of **netstat -ano** following the navigation to www.troubleticket .local/secure.htm

Step 4 Run the Wireshark packet analyzer on the client system, but do not start capturing frames until instructed in the next step. On the Server 2008 system, launch the freeSSHd secure SSH server. On the client system, open the PuTTY PSFTP application and log on to the netlabserver with the username **ftpuser01** and the password **1LoveBaby10n5!**. Change the focus of the local working directory by running the following command:

```
lcd c:\ftprec
```

Now view a listing of the files available for transfer by running the following command:

```
dir
```

Step 5 Go back to Wireshark and start capturing frames. Return to the PuTTY PSFTP application and transfer one of the listed files, for example:

```
get welcome.jpg
```

When the file transfer is successful, stop capturing frames.

Step 6   You should find a number of frames labeled as SSH under the **Protocol** column, as shown in Figure 11-11. Note that there are two distinct frames: encrypted request packets and encrypted response packets.

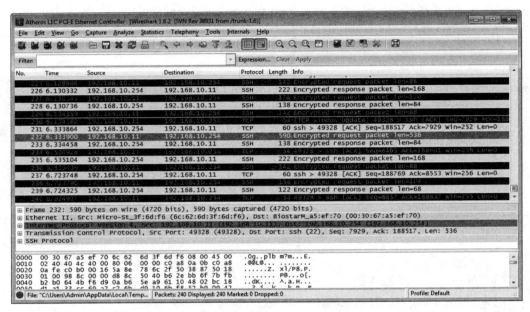

Figure 11-11   Wireshark capture of SSH packets during an SFTP file transfer

Step 7   Examine the first instance of an SSH encrypted request packet. What is the source port? What is the destination port? Why? Expand the **SSH Protocol** in the center pane of Wireshark. What is displayed?

_____

_____

Step 8   Now scroll down to the first instance of the SSH encrypted response packet. What is the source port? What is the destination port? Why? Expand the **SSH Protocol** in the center pane of Wireshark. What is displayed?

_____

_____

Step 9 Now scroll further down until you see clusters of SSH encrypted response packets. What do you think these clusters represent?

_____

_____

Step 10 To finish up the study of secure TCP/IP applications, you will once again use Mark Russinovich's TCPView. Close PSFTP by typing **exit** at the command prompt and launch TCPView. In the **Options** menu, select **Always On Top**.

Now open PSFTP and open your freeSSHd server (netlabserver in the example shown in Figure 11-12), observing the activity in TCPView. Record the entry for the process in TCPView.

_____

_____

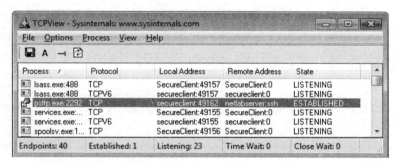

Figure 11-12 TCPView showing the established connection between the secureclient and netlabserver using PSFTP

Lab Analysis

1. While conducting the research to recommend a Certificate Authority to your client, Cathy notices that most of the providers are now offering Extended Validation and Green Address Bar. Do a little further investigation and provide a short description of these features.

_____

_____

2. Theresa is setting up an intranet site with security. She is using the Microsoft self-signed certificate generator and has completed all of the server-side installation tasks. When she attempts to access the Web site, she receives the following error message:
   "The security certificate presented by this website was not issued by a trusted certificate authority."
   What step does Theresa need to perform to eliminate this error message?

   _____

   _____

3. Your co-worker, Michael, has been using Wireshark to explore packets while running Secure Shell (SSH), Secure File Transfer Protocol (SFTP), and Secure Copy Protocol (SCP) applications. He notices that all of the packets destination ports are 22. What explanation can you provide to Michael regarding this finding?

   _____

   _____

4. Martin has heard the term "encryption" used throughout the entire lab session and is still not completely sure he understands the meaning or methodology behind the term. Write a short definition of the term "encryption."

   _____

   _____

5. Briana has decided to purchase a book from amazon.com. She is going to create an account so that she can use her credit card to make the purchase. Internet Explorer informs her that she is entering a secure page, but she is concerned about entering her credit card number. How can Briana be confident that the amazon.com Web site is the real one, and that she is indeed on a secure channel?

   _____

   _____

Key Term Quiz

Use the vocabulary terms from the list below to complete the sentences that follow. Not all of the terms will be used.

authentication

authorization

Certificate Authority (CA)

digital certificate

digital signature

encryption

Hypertext Transfer Protocol Secure (HTTPS)

Kerberos

key-pair

Network Time Protocol (NTP)

nonrepudiation

private key

public key

Public Key Infrastructure (PKI)

Remote Authentication Dial-In User Service (RADIUS)

Secure Copy Protocol (SCP)

Secure File Transfer Protocol (SFTP)

Secure Shell (SSH)

Secure Sockets Layer (SSL)

Simple Network Management Protocol (SNMP)

Terminal Access Controller Access-Control System Plus (TACACS+)

1. When an organization provides secure services over the Internet, they will obtain a certificate from a(n) _____ such as VeriSign that verifies the public key is legitimate.

2. Many of the secure TCP/IP applications that you have worked with use the _____ to provide the actual security mechanism. This method uses both a(n) _____ and a(n) _____ to form the key-pair.

3. Though not directly related to encryption or authentication, the _____ is used to provide a valid timestamp on data.

4. When you are required to enter valid credentials such as username and password, this is known as _____.

5. Both SCP and SFTP utilize _____ to provide the encryption algorithm.

Chapter 12

Advanced Networking Devices

Lab Exercises

Working with networks today, you will encounter a number of advanced and specialized network devices. You will still be responsible for troubleshooting clients, servers, and cables, but you will also deal with the detailed configuration of switches and routers.

In this chapter you will explore basic network terms, configure and work with VPNs and VLANs, play with QoS, and examine the properties of intrusion detection systems, intrusion prevention systems, and proxy servers.

 10 MINUTES

Lab Exercise 12.01: Exploring Network Terms

As with any discipline, developing an understanding of the terminology of the discipline is almost as important as being able to work with the technology. Network technicians must be very comfortable with their terminology so that they can talk properly with peers, management, and customers about network-related problems and solutions.

In this Lab Exercise you will develop clear definitions of popular network terms and network technologies.

Learning Objectives

At the completion of this lab, you will be able to

- Identify advanced networking terms

Lab Materials and Setup

The materials you'll need for this lab are

- The *Mike Meyers' CompTIA Network+ Guide to Managing and Troubleshooting Networks* textbook
- Pencil and paper

Getting Down to Business

Now that you have been with the company for some time, there actually are some techs who have less experience than you do. One of the junior network technicians is having some trouble understanding terms such as VLANs, VPNs, and collision domains, to name a few. He asks if you would sit with him and help him identify the purpose of each of the mentioned technologies. You decide to help out by creating definitions of each and ask him to associate the terms with the definitions.

Match the following terms to the appropriate definitions:

A. Layer 3 switch   _____ An encrypted tunnel across an unsecured network

B. Broadcast domain   _____ A piece of software or a device that detects suspicious activity and logs the action or sends an alert

C. Collision domain   _____ A switch that operates at Layer 2 and Layer 3 of the OSI model

D. Client/server   _____ A group of computers that receive each other's broadcast messages

E. Peer-to-peer   _____ A VPN protocol that uses IPSec for authentication and encryption

F. VPN   _____ A virtual network that allows hosts to belong to the same network ID even if they are not located on the same network switch

G. PPTP   _____ A network that has a dedicated server sharing resources and clients that connect to that server to access those resources

H. L2TP   _____ A piece of software or a device that detects suspicious activity and then takes corrective action

I. VLAN   _____ Controlling the flow of packets into or out from the network according to the type of packet

J. Traffic shaping   _____ A VPN protocol that uses Microsoft Point-to-Point Encryption (MPPE) to encrypt data

K. IDS   _____ A network in which all systems act as client and server

L. IPS   _____ A group of computers that have the potential to have their data collide

 30 MINUTES

Lab Exercise 12.02: Configuring VPN Connections

One of ITCF's new clients is a small insurance firm with a number of agents who work from their homes. CJ and Maggie ask you to use the machines in the Network Lab to configure and test a virtual private network (VPN) solution using the built-in Routing and Remote Access Services (RRAS) role in Windows Server 2008. You will first create the VPN server, and then you will configure the client systems to access that server using VPN.

Good luck!

✖ **Cross-Reference**

For additional information on VPN technologies, check out the "VPN" section in Chapter 12 of the *Mike Meyers' CompTIA Network+ Guide to Managing and Troubleshooting Networks* textbook.

Learning Objectives

In this lab, you'll configure a Windows VPN server and a Windows VPN client. At the end of this lab, you will be able to

- Configure the Routing and Remote Access Services (RRAS) virtual private network (VPN) on a Windows Server 2008 system

- Implement and test a Windows VPN

Lab Materials and Setup

The materials you'll need for this lab are

- Pencil and paper

- Windows XP, Windows Vista, or Windows 7 client machine

- Windows Server 2008 machine

- A second NIC installed in the Server 2008 machine to facilitate the installation of RRAS and VPN server

- A desktop switch or the Linksys WRT54GL (or similar) router that was configured in prior Lab Exercises and appropriate cabling to connect the small network

Getting Down to Business

You have really become quite efficient at managing the resources in the Network Lab and are very skilled at reconfiguring the machines and the network to test different scenarios. Maggie explains that you will need to install a second NIC in the Windows Server 2008 machine (and you might want to rename it NETLABRRAS) to install and configure the RRAS role on the Server 2008 machine.

Every time you configure these Lab Exercises, you learn a little more about networking technologies and reinforce the concepts you have been studying. In this Lab Exercise you will actually build an RRAS server to host your VPN server.

✔ **Tech Tip**

Microsoft allows you to create a VPN server with Windows Server 2008 using the Routing and Remote Access Services (RRAS). The RRAS role is installed from the Network Policy and Access Services under Server Roles. Due to the complexities of creating a VPN in a lab environment (valid DNS servers, DHCP servers, multiple networks, and Local Remote Access Security policies), you may or may not be able to access any resources once the VPN is established.

Step 1 To configure the hardware and network for this Lab Exercise, complete the following sub-steps:

    a.   Install a second NIC in a Windows Server 2008 system.

    b.   On the Server 2008 machine, configure the first NIC (LAN) with the IP address of 192.168.10.253/24. Leave the default gateway and DNS server addresses blank.

    c.   On the Server 2008 machine, configure the second NIC (WAN) with the IP address of 192.168.20.253/24. Leave the default gateway and DNS server addresses blank.

    d.   On the Windows 7 client machine, configure the IP address of 192.168.20.11/24.

    e.   Using the switch (or the 4-port switch on the WRT54GL), connect the client machine and the Server 2008 machine to form the 192.168.20/24 (WAN) network.

    f.   On all interfaces, disable IPv6 and firewalls.

Step 2 Now follow the sub-steps to install and configure RRAS and the VPN server.

    a.   On the Windows Server 2008 system, go to **Start | Administrative Tools | Server Manager | Roles** and choose **Add** to open the **Server Roles**. Click **Network Policy and Access Services** and click **Next** as shown in Figure 12-1. Click **Next** and select **Routing and Remote Access Services** and click **Next** one last time. Review the **Confirm Installation Selections** screen and click **Install**. Click **Close** to close the wizard. Exit Server Manager.

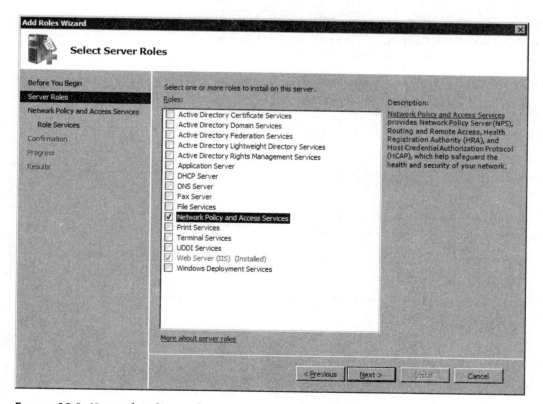

FIGURE 12-1 Network Policy and Access Services Server Role

b.   Click **Start | Administrative Tools | Routing and Remote Access**. On the left side of the console, right-click on your server and choose **Configure and Enable Routing and Remote Acceses** from the drop-down menu. When the wizard launches, click **Next**.

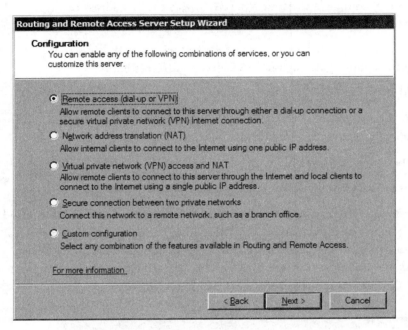

FIGURE 12-2 Possible configurations of the Routing and Remote Access Server on a Windows Server 2008 machine

c.   Using the **Configuration** window (see Figure 12-2), record the types of configurations listed and a short description of each service.

_____

_____

_____

_____

_____

d. Choose **Remote Access (dial-up or VPN)** and then choose **Next**.

e. Choose **VPN** to create a VPN server and then choose **Next**.

f. Now select the interface that is connected to the "Internet." This is the WAN interface (and IP address 192.168.20.253) that remote clients will connect to in order to access the network using VPN. Choose the appropriate network card and then disable the **Enable Security** option. Choose **Next**.

g. In **IP Address Assignment**, choose that you want the IP addresses to be assigned **Automatically** to remote clients, and click **Next**. If you are not using a DHCP server to assign addresses, this server will generate APIPA addresses for the VPN connection.

h. You are not using RADIUS, so choose **Next** and then **Finish**.

i. Click **OK** when a message appears asking you about DHCP Relay. In the **Routing and Remote Access** window, the server (as shown in Figure 12-3, the name is NETLABRRAS) should show a green arrow indicating that it is up and running. Highlight **Remote Access Clients**. You will view this window after the last step to verify the client is connected.

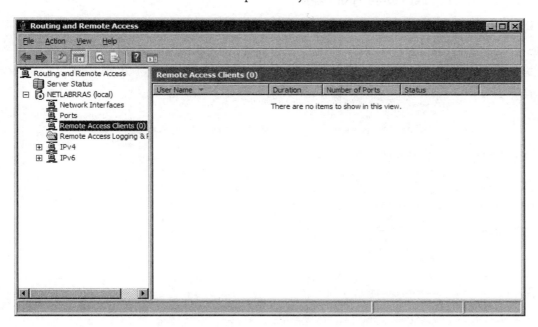

FIGURE 12-3 Routing and Remote Access configured as a VPN server

Step 3 In these sub-steps, you will create a simple share to be used when testing the VPN.

    a.   Navigate to the C:\ drive and create a folder named **VPNShare**.

    b.   Verify that the Administrators group has **Full Control** permissions to the VPNShare folder.

    c.   Copy some text or image files into the directory (such as c:\windows\web\wallpaper\server.jpg or c:\inetpub\wwwroot\welcome.png).

Step 4 Now that you have the VPN server installed, you can configure the VPN client to connect to the server. Go to your client machine and perform the following sub-steps:

    a.   On a Windows 7 machine, select the **Network icon** in the System Tray and select **Open Network and Sharing Center**.

    b.   Choose **Setup a new connection or network** in the **Change your network** settings on the bottom half of the screen.

    c.   Choose **Connect to a workplace to create a VPN connection** and then click **Next**.

    d.   Click **Use my Internet connection (VPN)**.

    e.   Click **I'll set up an Internet connection later**.

    f.   Enter the **Internet address** to connect to and the **Destination name** then click **next**. (See Figure 12-4.)

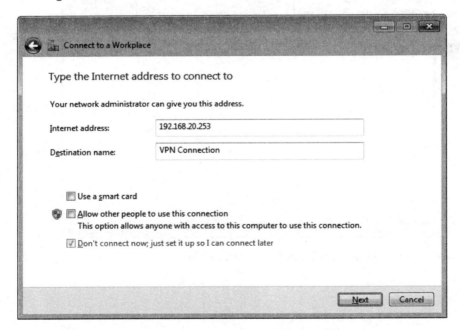

FIGURE 12-4 Configuring a VPN to connect to a workplace

    g.   Now type your **User name** and **Password** and click **Create** and **Close**.

Step 5 Test your connection by clicking the **Network icon** in the **System Tray**, selecting the **VPN Connection** you just created and clicking **Connect**. Type the administrator user name and password in the connection logon screen (see Figure 12-5) and then choose **Connect**.

FIGURE 12-5 Testing the VPN connection

Step 6 Click **Start** and in the **Search files and programs** dialog box, type **\\192.168.20.253** and then press ENTER. Enter the password for the administrator account on **NETLABRRAS** and press ENTER. What are the results?

_____

_____

Step 7 On the Server 2008 machine (NETLABRRAS), open **Start | Administrative Tools | Routing and Remote Access** and observe the **Remote Access Clients** as shown in Figure 12-6.

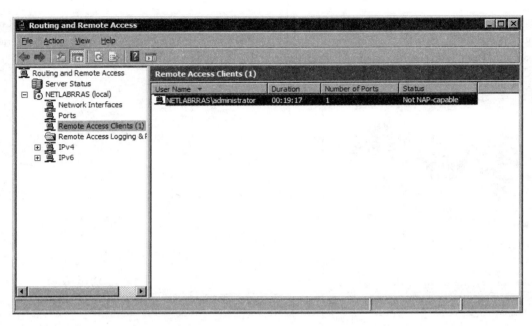

FIGURE 12-6 Remote access clients

 30 MINUTES

Lab Exercise 12.03: Configuring VLANs on a Switch

Virtual local area networks (VLANs) offer the capability of providing security on your network because systems in one VLAN cannot communicate with systems in other VLANs unless the administrator allows routing between the VLANs.

VLANs also offer the capabilities of creating broadcast domains within the switch. When a system in a VLAN broadcasts a message, that broadcast message does not go beyond the VLAN.

Learning Objectives

In this lab, you will create two VLANs on a Cisco multilayer switch. You will then verify that two systems connected to the switch and placed in different VLANs cannot communicate with one another until you enable InterVLAN routing. By the end of this lab you should be able to

- Define the function of a VLAN
- Configure VLANs
- Configure InterVLAN routing

Lab Materials and Setup

The materials you'll need for this lab are

- Pencil and paper

- A Cisco 3560 switch (or similar) or a Cisco simulator

- A console (Yost) cable

- Two client systems

✔ Tech Tip

The Cisco 3560 switch is a multilayer switch providing the capability to create VLANs as well as implement interVLAN routing. There are many manufacturers and models of Layer 3 switches and multilayer switches. If you have access to different model switches or only have access to a Layer 2 switch, you may still follow the steps to create two VLANs; however, you will not be able to configure interVLAN routing without a separate external router.

You will also be working with the Cisco Command-Line Interface (CLI) in the Cisco IOS software. Only the commands needed to complete the Lab Exercise will be introduced. If you would like to explore the IOS further, please visit Cisco at www.cisco.com/en/US/docs/ios/preface/usingios. html.

Many of the commands you will use in this Lab Exercise will be run from the **privileged EXEC mode (Switch#)**. This mode is normally password protected and if the password is lost or forgotten, it can be difficult to reset the password. To perform a password recovery on a Cisco switch, navigate to the following Web site: www.cisco.com/en/US/products/sw/iosswrel/ps1831/products_tech_note09186a00801746e6.shtml. Scroll down to the **Index**. Here you will find hyperlinks to the **Password Recovery Procedure** for many Cisco routers and switches. Follow the hyperlink for your Cisco switch to get the specific password recovery procedure.

Getting Down to Business

Cathy, one of the network technicians at ITCF, is talking with Maggie and learns that you are working on your CompTIA Network+ certification. Cathy is working with a customer who is implementing VLANs and would like to know if you would like to learn how to configure VLANs. As usual, you jump at the chance to work with a mentor, and you invite Cathy to use a switch and two computers in the Network Lab.

Step 1   To set up the small network, power on the switch and then plug the first computer into port number 2. Connect the second computer to port number 8 on the switch.

Step 2   On both systems, disable the Windows Firewall. Configure the first computer (System1) with an IP address of 10.0.0.1/8 and the second computer (System2) with an IP address of 10.0.0.2/8.

Step 3 After configuring the IP addresses, open a command prompt and verify that you can ping from one computer to the other (see Figure 12-7). Can you successfully ping from computer 1 to computer 2?

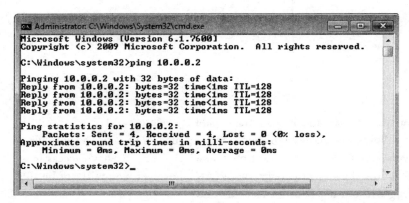

FIGURE 12-7 Results of successfully configured network: System 1 can successfully ping System 2.

Step 4 Connect the console cable to the console port on your switch and then to the serial port on System 1. On System 1, launch PuTTY (you should have already downloaded PuTTY in Step 3 of Lab Exercise 11.02). In the **Basic options for your PuTTY session**, verify that the **Serial** button is selected. Under the **Category:** pane, click the **Serial** menu item. Under the **Options controlling local serial lines** verify the following settings as shown in Figure 12-8:

Serial line to connect to	COM1
Speed (baud)	9600
Data bits	8
Stop bits	1
Parity	None
Flow control	None

Click the **Open** button. You may have to press ENTER in the PuTTY command-line window before you see a prompt, allowing you to type commands.

Step 5 To display a list of VLANs that currently exist, type **show vlan**. You should see that there are a few default VLANs for different network architectures—notice that VLAN 1 is named the default VLAN (see Figure 12-9). The far right column shows you which ports are part of the VLAN. Record the ports that are part of the default VLAN:

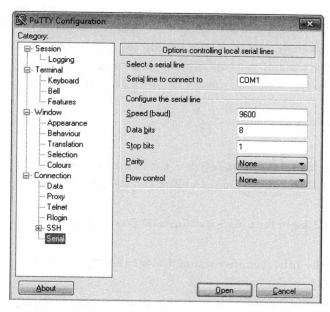

FIGURE 12-8 PuTTY configuration window with serial settings to manage the Cisco 3560 switch

```
COM1 - PuTTY
Switch>show vlan

VLAN Name                             Status    Ports
---- -------------------------------- --------- -------------------------------
1    default                          active    Fa0/1, Fa0/2, Fa0/3, Fa0/4
                                                Fa0/5, Fa0/6, Fa0/7, Fa0/8
                                                Fa0/9, Fa0/10, Fa0/11, Fa0/12
                                                Fa0/13, Fa0/14, Fa0/15, Fa0/16
                                                Fa0/17, Fa0/18, Fa0/19, Fa0/20
                                                Fa0/21, Fa0/22, Fa0/23, Fa0/24
                                                Gi0/1, Gi0/2
1002 fddi-default                     act/unsup
1003 token-ring-default               act/unsup
1004 fddinet-default                  act/unsup
1005 trnet-default                    act/unsup

VLAN Type  SAID    MTU   Parent RingNo BridgeNo Stp  BrdgMode Trans1 Trans2
---- ----- ------- ----- ------ ------ -------- ---- -------- ------ ------
1    enet  100001  1500  -      -      -        -    -        0      0
1002 fddi  101002  1500  -      -      -        -    -        0      0
1003 tr    101003  1500  -      -      -        -    -        0      0
1004 fdnet 101004  1500  -      -      -        ieee -        0      0
1005 trnet 101005  1500  -      -      -        ibm  -        0      0
```

FIGURE 12-9 Looking at the default VLANs on a Cisco switch

> ✔ **Hint**
>
> If you are using a switch that has been in the lab environment, it may already be in some state of configuration as opposed to the default out-of-box state. If you had any trouble pinging between the computers, or there seem to be some VLANs already configured, use the following steps to reset the switch:

a. Press and hold the **Mode button** for approximately 15 seconds (when the four LEDs turn solid green), then release the **Mode button**. The SYST LED should then blink and the terminal should indicate **Reload Requested**.

b. Press ENTER and when prompted **Would you like to terminate autoinstall? [Yes/No]**, type **Yes** and press ENTER.

c. When prompted **Would you like to enter the initial configuration dialog? [Yes/No]**, type **No** and press ENTER.

d. You should now be at the **Switch>** prompt. The settings should be the default configuration of all ports in VLAN 1.

Step 6 To create a VLAN named Acct and one called Marketing, type the following commands, pressing ENTER after each command. You'll start at the Switch> prompt:

```
enable
```

You should now be at the Switch# prompt. Keep going:

```
conf t
```

Now the prompt looks like this: Switch(config)#. Keep going:

```
vlan 2
```

Now the prompt looks like this: Switch(config-vlan)#. Keep going:

```
name Acct
```

You will return to the Switch(config-vlan)# prompt. If you did this correctly, you won't get any feedback. Keep going:

```
exit
```

Now the prompt again looks like this: Switch(config)#. Keep going:

```
vlan 3
```

The prompt will change to Switch(config-vlan)#. Keep going:

```
name Marketing
```

You will return to the Switch(config-vlan)# prompt. If you did this correctly, you won't get any feedback. Keep going:

```
end
```

Step 7 At this point, you should be at the prompt Switch#. You might see a log entry appear, saying that the switch configuration has changed. If so, press ENTER to get back to the prompt.

To view the newly created VLANs, type the following commands. Figure 12-10 shows the results.

```
show vlan
```

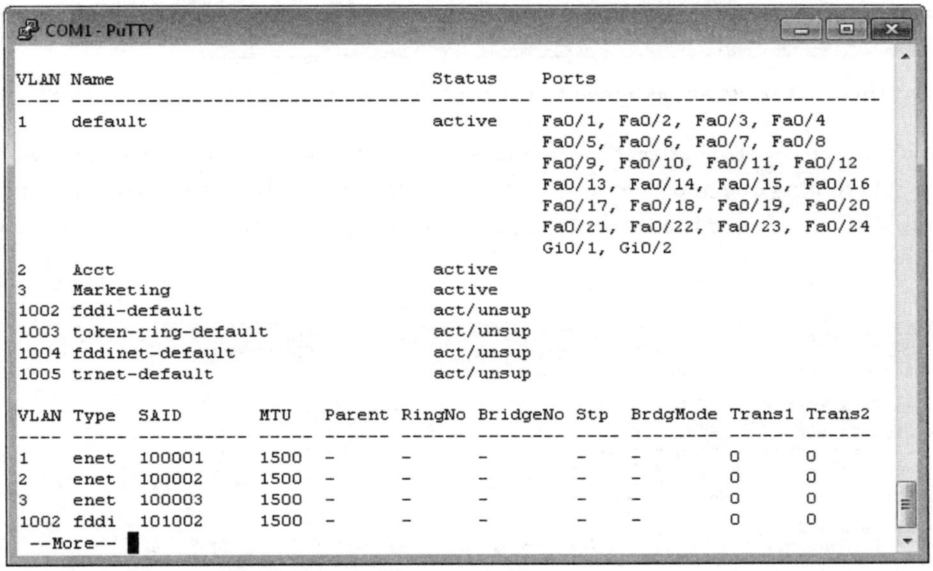

FIGURE 12-10 Looking at the newly created VLANs

Step 8 To place port 2 in the Acct VLAN, type the following commands, and press the ENTER key after each one. Note that the prompt dialog will change as you move through the commands.

```
conf t
interface fa0/2 switchport access vlan 2
exit
```

Step 9 To place port 8 in the Marketing VLAN, type the following commands:

```
interface fa0/8switchport access vlan 3
exit
exit
```

Step 10 To verify that the ports are placed in the appropriate VLANs, use the following command to display VLANs. Figure 12-11 shows the results.

```
show vlan
```

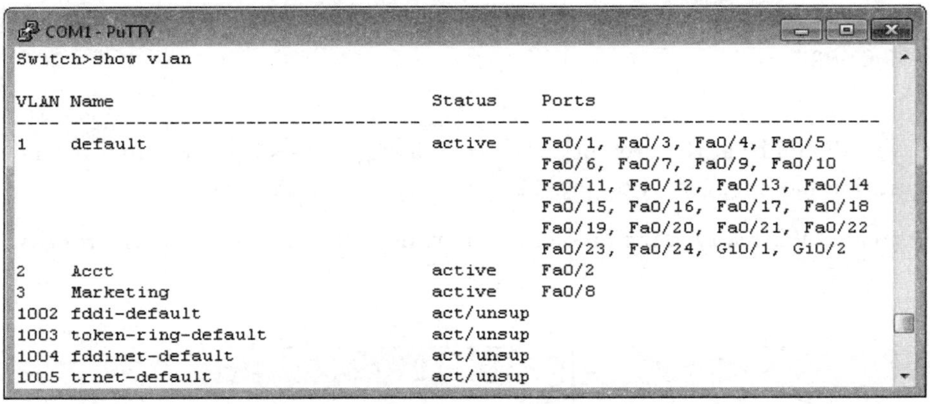

```
COM1 - PuTTY                                                    [_][□][X]
Switch>show vlan

VLAN Name                             Status    Ports
---- -------------------------------- --------- -------------------------------
1    default                          active    Fa0/1, Fa0/3, Fa0/4, Fa0/5
                                                Fa0/6, Fa0/7, Fa0/9, Fa0/10
                                                Fa0/11, Fa0/12, Fa0/13, Fa0/14
                                                Fa0/15, Fa0/16, Fa0/17, Fa0/18
                                                Fa0/19, Fa0/20, Fa0/21, Fa0/22
                                                Fa0/23, Fa0/24, Gi0/1, Gi0/2
2    Acct                             active    Fa0/2
3    Marketing                        active    Fa0/8
1002 fddi-default                     act/unsup
1003 token-ring-default               act/unsup
1004 fddinet-default                  act/unsup
1005 trnet-default                    act/unsup
```

Figure 12-11 Verifying that ports are assigned to the correct VLANs

Step 11   Now that you have the ports that each system is connected to in different VLANs, the two systems should not be able to ping one another (see Figure 12-12). The reason is that VLANs are security boundaries, and unless a Layer 3 device is used, only systems within a single VLAN will be able to communicate with one another.

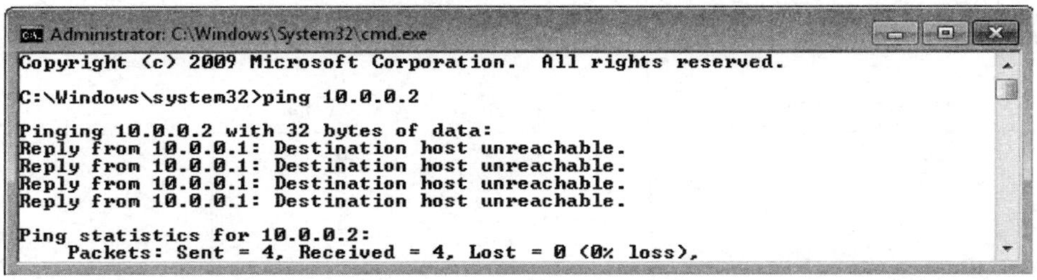

```
Administrator: C:\Windows\System32\cmd.exe                     [_][□][X]
Copyright (c) 2009 Microsoft Corporation.  All rights reserved.

C:\Windows\system32>ping 10.0.0.2

Pinging 10.0.0.2 with 32 bytes of data:
Reply from 10.0.0.1: Destination host unreachable.
Reply from 10.0.0.1: Destination host unreachable.
Reply from 10.0.0.1: Destination host unreachable.
Reply from 10.0.0.1: Destination host unreachable.

Ping statistics for 10.0.0.2:
    Packets: Sent = 4, Received = 4, Lost = 0 (0% loss),
```

Figure 12-12 Once the two systems are in different VLANs, they can no longer communicate.

Can you ping from System 1 to System 2? _____

Can you ping from System 2 to System 1? _____

Step 12   Now you will implement interVLAN routing to allow the two separate VLANs to communicate with each other. To enable interVLAN routing, you will assign a router address to each VLAN, and enable routing using the following commands, pressing ENTER after each command. Note that the prompt will change as you move through the commands.

```
enable
conf t
interface vlan 2
ip address 10.2.0.1 255.255.0.0
```

```
exit
interface vlan 3
ip address 10.3.0.1 255.255.0.0
exit
ip routing
exit
```

Step 13 To verify that the IP addresses have been assigned to the appropriate VLANs, use the following command to display VLANs and IP addresses. Figure 12-13 shows the results.

```
show ip interface
```

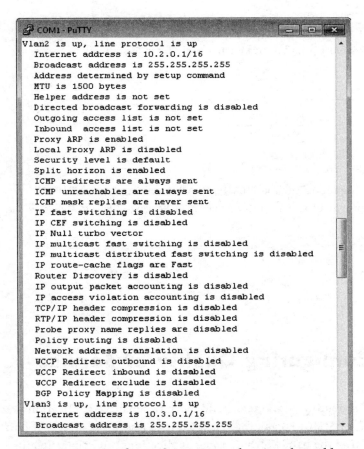

FIGURE 12-13 Verifying the VLANs and assigned IP addresses

Step 14 Now you must place the computer systems in the correct networks. Configure the first computer (System 1) with an IP address of 10.2.0.11/16 and a default gateway of 10.2.0.1. Configure the second computer (System 2) with an IP address of 10.3.0.11/16 and a default gateway of 10.3.0.1.

Step 15   Now that you have the VLANs routed, the two systems should be able to ping one another (see Figure 12-14). The Acct VLAN is network 10.2.0.0/16 and the Marketing VLAN is network 10.3.0.0/16.

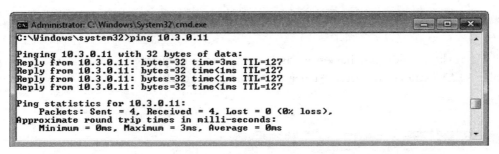

```
C:\Windows\system32>ping 10.3.0.11

Pinging 10.3.0.11 with 32 bytes of data:
Reply from 10.3.0.11: bytes=32 time=3ms TTL=127
Reply from 10.3.0.11: bytes=32 time<1ms TTL=127
Reply from 10.3.0.11: bytes=32 time<1ms TTL=127
Reply from 10.3.0.11: bytes=32 time<1ms TTL=127

Ping statistics for 10.3.0.11:
    Packets: Sent = 4, Received = 4, Lost = 0 (0% loss),
Approximate round trip times in milli-seconds:
    Minimum = 0ms, Maximum = 3ms, Average = 0ms
```

FIGURE 12-14 Successful ping from System 1 (10.2.0.11/16) with a reply from System 2 (10.3.0.11/16)

Can you ping from System 1 to System 2? _____

Can you ping from System 2 to System 1? _____

✖ Cross-Reference

To learn more about advanced switching topics such as VLANs, VLAN Trunking Protocol (VTP), and interVLAN routing, refer to Chapter 12 of the *Mike Meyers' CompTIA Network+ Guide to Managing and Troubleshooting Networks* textbook.

 45 MINUTES

Lab Exercise 12.04: Configuring Quality of Service (QoS)

Quality of Service (QoS) is the practice of providing guaranteed bandwidth to sensitive applications such as audio or video streaming, Voice over IP, or MMORPG gaming. The goal is to lessen the effects of buffering, dropout, jitter, and latency by limiting the bandwidth on some applications, and guaranteeing the bandwidth of the sensitive applications. Many SOHO routers offer QoS utilities allowing the user to prioritize more bandwidth to one or more of the high-demand applications.

One way to demonstrate the concept of QoS is to use a commercial speed-testing Web site such as Speakeasy (www.speakeasy.net) or Speedtest.net (www.speedtest.net). Run the test first with QoS wide open to determine your average bandwidth, note your results, and then throttle down the bandwidth of your router by 50 to 90 percent of your top speed to demonstrate the power of QoS.

Lastly, there are a number of third-party, open-source, Linux-based operating systems available for today's SOHO routers. Firmware with names such as Sveasoft, Tomato, and DD-WRT will allow you to flash the BIOS of the standard router, adding features like advanced QoS, radio output power, overclocking, and even the ability to use SSH to get in and use the native Linux commands to modify the characteristics of the router. You will learn how to install DD-WRT on a WRT54GL router.

Learning Objectives

When you have completed this lab, you will be able to

- Download DD-WRT, and flash a router with the firmware

- Perform a speed test on your Internet connection

- Configure QoS to throttle the bandwidth for demonstration purposes

Lab Materials and Setup

This Lab Exercise should be performed with a non-production router. Optimum conditions would allow the DD-WRT router to be placed between a lab computer system and an Internet connection. The materials you'll need for this lab are

- Pencil and paper

- A PC with Internet connectivity

- One router (Linksys WRT54GL or similar wireless routers will work fine)

- Appropriate UTP cabling

Getting Down to Business

The Networking Lab is really going to get a workout today. You have been concentrating on advanced networking devices and would like to explore QoS a little more deeply. You have been talking with one of your coworkers, Tim, who really promotes the benefits of upgrading one of the wireless routers with an open-source, Linux-based firmware to enhance the capabilities of the router.

You decide to use one of the older routers, download DD-WRT, and flash the BIOS before conducting some QoS experiments.

✖ Caution

The following QoS Lab Exercise can be performed using a standard Linksys or similar wireless router. For this Lab Exercise, I used the WRT54GL wireless router with the DD-WRT alternative OpenSource firmware installed. Please understand that flashing the routers with third-party firmware can sometimes damage the router (known as "bricking") and voids all warranties from Linksys. This procedure should not be performed on critical routers.

Even the programmers state "USE AT YOUR OWN RISK." Please consult with your instructor before flashing any routers!

Step 1   To upgrade a router with the DD-WRT firmware, begin with a stock router (such as the Linksys WRT54GL) with the default out-of-the-box settings. Log on to the router using the default IP address of **192.168.1.1,** the user name **admin** and password **admin**. The default **Setup** page is shown in Figure 12-15.

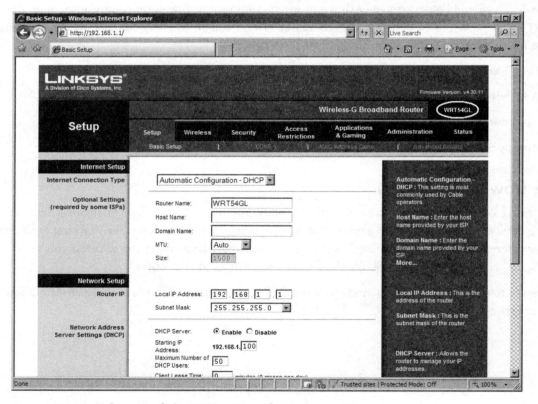

Figure 12-15 Title page of the WRT54GL configuration utility

Step 2   It is very important that you verify the router's model number. In Figure 12-15, make note of the router's model number **WRT54GL** in white letters on a black background. You should be able to verify your router's model number in a similar fashion. As stated multiple times, it is very important to verify the router's model number when downloading the DD-WRT firmware. **Using the wrong firmware on your router will destroy the router (brick the router).**

Step 3 Using your computer connected to the Internet, open your browser and navigate to the DD-WRT Web site at www.dd-wrt.com as shown in Figure 12-16. Click the **Router Database** button and enter your router's model number (in this Lab Exercise example, **WRT54GL**). The results should produce one response.

Figure 12-16 Home page of dd-wrt.com open-source, Linux-based router firmware

Step 4 Verify that the listed information is for your specific router model and click to open the firmware database for this model. Select the most stable build for your router (v24 Build 10020 for the WRT54GL was the most stable build at the time of this writing) and click on the file named **dd-wrt.v24_mini_generic.bin**. See Figure 12-17.

Figure 12-17 Selecting the DD-WRT mini generic build for the WRT54GL router

Step 5   Now from the title page of the Linksys WRT54GL router, select the **Administration** tab and then select **Firmware Upgrade**. Click **Browse** and navigate to the file **dd-wrt.v24_mini_generic.bin**. Click **Upgrade**.

✔ **Hint**

Be careful during this step to not interrupt the installation for any reason. An interrupted install can cause a *bricked* router, meaning one that's no longer usable. Getting the error message in red stating "Upgrade are Failed" means—despite the bad grammar—that the install package stopped the installation before the router was damaged.

Step 6   You should now see a message stating **Upgrade is successful**. Click on the **Continue** button. The browser should now reconnect to the WRT54GL (or similar) router. Note that the IP address and the router name are still the default values. Log on to the router using the **DD-WRT control panel** with the user name **root,** and the password **admin** as shown in Figure 12-18.

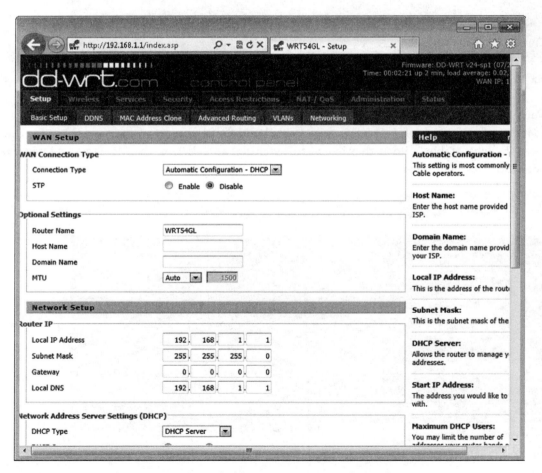

FIGURE 12-18 Linksys WRT54GL with dd-wrt.com …Control Panel

Step 7 Configure the **WAN Connection Type**, **Optional Settings**, **Router IP**, and **Network Address Server Settings (DHCP)** for your network. Click the **Apply Settings** button. Verify that your computer can still access the Internet, and then proceed to the next step.

Step 8 Launch the Web site www.speedtest.net and click **Begin Test**. Note that you can select the location where your test connects. Use the default location and let the test run. Record the results in the following space:

_____

_____

These are the download and upload speeds that your Internet connections are capable of. Note the speeds of the example shown in Figure 12-19.

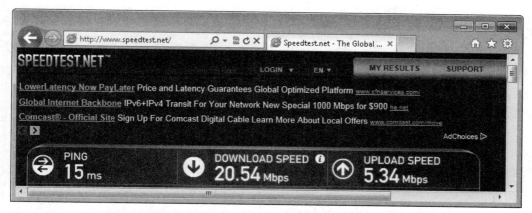

FIGURE 12-19 Output of the Speedtest.net speed test showing both download and upload speeds

Step 9 Now reload the **dd-wrt.com …Control Panel**. Click on the **NAT/QoS** tab and then click on the **QoS** tab. See Figure 12-20. Use the following settings to simulate setting QoS. In actuality, you will be slowing the entire bandwidth. This is strictly for demonstration purposes.

Start QoS: Enable

Port: WAN

Packet Scheduler: HTB

Uplink (kbps): 1000

Downlink (kbps): 1000

Optimize for Gaming: Not Selected

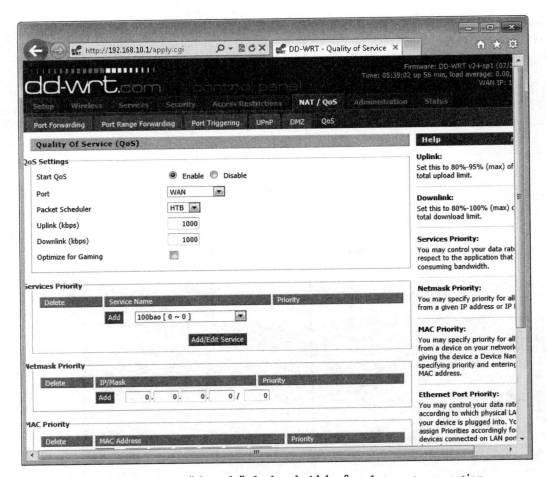

FIGURE 12-20 Setting QoS to "throttle" the bandwidth of an Internet connection

Step 10   Now launch the Web site www.speedtest.net again and then click **Begin Test**. Record the results in the following space:

_____

_____

This displays the download and upload speeds of your Internet connection with QoS throttling the bandwidth of the connection to 1 Mbps. Note the speeds of the example shown in Figure 12-21.

Step 11   To return the router to normal operation, reload the **dd-wrt.com …Control Panel**. Click on the **NAT/QoS** tab and then click on the **QoS** tab and in the **QoS Settings | Start QoS** screen, select **Disable**.

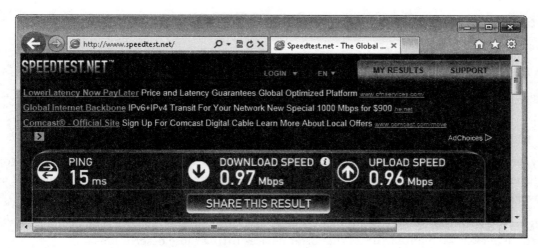

FIGURE 12-21 Output of the Speedtest.net speed test after applying QoS

 20 MINUTES

Lab Exercise 12.05: Exploring Network Protection

You have installed and configured a VPN, VLAN, and QoS. Now to finish your exploration of advanced networking devices, you will explore what Mike terms *network protection*. There are four areas that you will examine:

- Intrusion detection system/intrusion protection system (IDS/IPS)

- Port mirroring

- Proxy serving

- Port authentication

Just as there are manufacturers that provide multilayer switches that are capable of providing VPNs, VLANs, and QoS, there are manufacturers, developers, and methods that provide network protection. You're going to explore some of these manufacturers, developers, and methods.

Learning Objectives

In this lab, you'll explore a few of the manufacturers, developers, and methods that offer various network protection solutions. By the end of this lab, you will be able to

- Define IDS/IPS and profile one or two of the manufacturers

- Define port mirroring

- Contrast the two types of proxy serving

- Detail port authentication

Lab Materials and Setup

The materials you need for this lab are

- A PC with Internet access
- Pencil and paper

Getting Down to Business

As with any network consulting firm, the staff at ITCF work hard to stay informed on the latest networking technologies, especially where network security and protection are concerned! After talking with one of your co-workers about IDS/IPS, you are intrigued and decide to do some further investigation.

Step 1   Beginning with IDS/IPS devices, provide a brief description of each device. Then conduct a Web search to profile one or two manufacturers that offer devices fitting those descriptions.

_____

_____

Step 2   See what you can find out about port mirroring. Record your findings in the following space.

_____

_____

Step 3   You have already read about proxy servers. Now compare the features of a physical proxy server (such as the Blue Coat ProxySG 510) and a public proxy server.

_____

_____

Step 4   Finish with a short discussion about port authentication.

_____

_____

Lab Analysis

1. Michael has just started using Voice over IP (VoIP) to reduce his phone costs. He is not entirely happy though, because the phone experiences frequent drop-outs, making conversations very difficult. What might you recommend to Michael to help with this problem?

   _____

   _____

2. Jennifer knows that using a VPN allows you to safely connect to computers over the Internet using an encrypted channel. She would like to know the difference between PPTP encryption and L2TP encryption. Briefly describe the difference for her.

   _____

   _____

3. Lee is about to purchase five new switches that he will be using in a VLAN configuration. What is the benefit of a multilayer switch?

   _____

   _____

4. Brandon would like to implement the strongest protection available to prevent unwanted access to the corporate network. What is the difference between an IDS and an IPS? Which device would be considered the strongest protection?

   _____

   _____

5. ITCF already implements a robust firewall on their office Internet connection. Why might they want to install a proxy server as well?

   _____

   _____

Key Term Quiz

Use the vocabulary terms from the list below to complete the sentences that follow. Not all of the terms will be used.

client/server

content switch

host-based IDS

interVLAN routing

intrusion detection system (IDS)

load balance

multilayer switch

network-based IDS

port authentication

port mirroring

proxy server

traffic shaping

trunk port

tunnel

virtual local area network (VLAN)

virtual private network (VPN)

1. A VPN is used to create an encrypted _____ between the VPN client and the VPN server.

2. In order to allow VLAN traffic to span multiple switches, you must designate a(n) _____ on each switch.

3. In order to distribute large numbers of requests for a service, you can _____ the workload across multiple servers.

4. A(n) _____ will monitor network traffic for suspicious activity.

5. In order to monitor network traffic on your switch, you will need to configure _____ on the switch.

Chapter 13
IPv6

Lab Exercises

Whether you are a seasoned tech, have been in IT for only a few years, or have just begun your journey toward becoming a networking professional, these are exciting times! IANA has distributed the last IPv4 addresses to the Regional Internet Registries (RIRs). Yep, on February 3, 2011, the last of the approximately 4 billion IPv4 addresses were distributed to the five RIRs. In the not-too-distant future, there will no longer be any IPv4 addresses available for new devices that need direct Internet connectivity.

Enter IPv6! On June 8, 2011, the Internet Society sponsored the World IPv6 Day when large Internet entities (Google, Facebook, Yahoo!, Akamai, and Limelight Networks, to name a few) were asked to implement IPv6 on their sites to test the connectivity of IPv6. It was a resounding success! As you develop your networking skills, you will be called on more and more to configure devices using IPv6 for the network address.

The CompTIA Network+ exam objectives require a network professional to be familiar with IPv6 addressing concepts and some of the supporting technologies such as IPv6-in-IPv4 tunneling protocols. The labs in this chapter are designed to give you an opportunity to practice what you have learned about IPv6 from the *Mike Meyers' CompTIA Network+ Guide to Managing and Troubleshooting Networks* textbook.

First, you will revisit some of the governing bodies that define IPv6. Then you'll review some of the new IPv6 terminology, practice address notation shortcuts, and verify your TCP/IP configuration on a Windows 7 system. Finally, you will experiment with one of the IPv6 tunnel brokers, Hurricane Electric.

 20 MINUTES

Lab Exercise 13.01: Governing Bodies, Part 3

After exploring the governing bodies that handle the specifications and management of the TCP/IP protocol suite, you should know the organizations that are directly responsible for IPv6. To begin your exploration of IPv6, you will examine some of the organizations that specifically relate to IPv6.

Learning Objectives

In this lab, you'll explore various organizations that are responsible for the development, management, and distribution of IPv6. By the end of this lab, you will be able to

- Describe the purposes and features of the organizations responsible for IPv6

- Research and provide some detail on RFCs associated with IPv6

Lab Materials and Setup

The materials you need for this lab are

- A PC with Internet access

- Pencil and paper

Getting Down to Business

As you just learned in the introduction to this chapter (or maybe you already knew this information), the world is running out of IPv4 addresses. Some of the organizations that you have already researched are directly involved with the implementation and distribution of the IPv6 addressing scheme. Take a few moments to reexamine these organizations with a focus on IPv6.

Step 1   Start this exploration of IPv6 with a visit to this Web site, www.iana.org. As you learned in Chapter 8, this is the Internet Assigned Numbers Authority (IANA). Explore the five Regional Internet Registries (RIRs) and write a short summary of what they are and what their main responsibilities are.

Registry	Area Covered	Notes

Step 2   You have also explored the Internet Society (ISOC). Visit the World IPv6 Day Web site at www .worldipv6day.org/ and record some of the facts you learn about the June 8, 2011 event.

Step 3   Open RFC 2460, which defines the specifications of IPv6, at www.ietf.org/rfc/rfc2460.txt and record some of the information from the introduction. How many bits long is an IPv6 address compared to an IPv4 address?

_____

_____

Step 4   While you explore RFCs related to IPv6, you should look at RFC 2373: "IPv6 Addressing Architecture" (www.ietf.org/rfc/rfc2373.txt). This RFC defines the various addresses available in IPv6, such as unicast addresses, anycast addresses, and multicast addresses. Take a moment and read the definition of an _anycast address_. Summarize the definition in the space provided:

_____

_____

 15 MINUTES

Lab Exercise 13.02 Reviewing IPv6 Terminology

Half the battle of becoming proficient in the technology is developing an understanding of the terminology. What does Maggie mean when she says that IPv6 routers will receive their IPv6 addresses and distribute IPv6 addresses to clients based on _aggregation_? You'll have to learn the terminology in order to develop the skills to configure the technology.

In this lab you will review the IPv6 terminology.

Learning Objectives

At the completion of this lab, you will be able to

- Identify the key terms associated with Internet Protocol version 6 (IPv6)

Lab Materials and Setup

The materials you'll need for this lab are

- The *Mike Meyers' CompTIA Network+ Guide to Managing and Troubleshooting Networks* textbook

- Pencil and paper

Getting Down to Business

Alex, a co-worker of yours at ITCF, has been working with a client to implement IPv6 throughout his office. He is having some trouble because the protocol is quite different than IPv4. Alex asks you to help him identify some of the terminology and concepts introduced with the IPv6 protocol. To ensure that you are familiar with the IPv6 terminology before you take the CompTIA Network+ exam, you agree to help Alex, knowing this exercise will help you remember the terms!

✖ Cross-Reference

Before attacking this Lab Exercise, you may want to review the concepts of IPv6 covered in Chapter 13 of the *Mike Meyers' CompTIA Network+ Guide to Managing and Troubleshooting Networks* textbook.

Step 1 Using the knowledge of IPv6 that you have learned from reading the *Mike Meyers' CompTIA Network+ Guide to Managing and Troubleshooting Networks* textbook, complete the following matching exercise:

A. ::1   _____ A unique address used by a system for one-on-one communication

B. Link-local address   _____ The IPv6 version of a public IP address

C. Extended Unique   _____ An address type that is assigned to multiple nodes. Any one of the
   Identifier   nodes could receive data destined to that address — but it is the
                                       node closest to the sending node that will receive the data.

D. Unicast address   _____ A NAT-traversal IPv6 tunneling protocol

E. Global address   _____ The IPv6 equivalent of an APIPA address

F. Stateful DHCPv6   _____ An address type that is assigned to multiple nodes. All of the nodes
                                       receive data destined to that address.

G. Anycast address   _____ An IPv6 DHCP server that only assigns additional TCP/IP settings

H. Stateless DHCPv6   _____ The IPv6 loopback address

I. Multicast address   _____ An IPv6 DHCP server that automatically assigns an IP address,
                                       subnet mask, default gateway, and additional TCP/IP settings

J. Teredo   _____ The last 64 bits of an IPv6 address

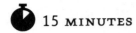 15 MINUTES

Lab Exercise 13.03: Practicing IPv6 Notation Shortcuts

As you have learned, the IPv6 address is an 128-bit address displayed as eight groups of four hexadecimal numbers, such as 2001:0470:B8F9:0001:020C:29FF:FE53:45CA. You probably will not have to manually configure IPv6 addresses as you did IPv4 addresses (except as you will in Lab Exercise 13.04), but it would be good to learn how to recognize these addresses in both their long and short forms.

In this Lab Exercise you will practice using the notation shortcut method to convert various IPv6 addresses between their long forms and their short forms.

Learning Objectives

In this lab, you'll practice converting IPv6 addresses between long form notation and short form notation using the shortcuts introduced in the *Mike Meyers' CompTIA Network+ Guide to Managing and Troubleshooting Networks* textbook. At the end of this lab you will be able to

- Convert IPv6 addresses from long form notation to short form notation

- Convert IPv6 addresses from short form notation to long form notation

Lab Materials and Setup

The materials you'll need for this lab are

- The *Mike Meyers' CompTIA Network+ Guide to Managing and Troubleshooting Networks* textbook

- Pencil and paper

Getting Down to Business

One of the new clients ITCF has taken on is implementing IPv6 exclusively. CJ asks Maggie to explore the various IPv6 addresses and their notation. As usual, Maggie asks you if you would like to work with her to gain the experience. You heartily agree and quickly begin to tackle the problems together.

✖ Cross-Reference

Please use the shortcuts introduced in the "IPv6 Address Notation" section in Chapter 13 of the *Mike Meyers' CompTIA Network+ Guide to Managing and Troubleshooting Networks* textbook.

Step 1   Using the shortcuts, convert the following IPv6 addresses from their long form notation to their short form notation:

1.   Long Form – 2001:0000:0000:3210:0800:200C:00CF:1234

Short Form – _____

2.   Long Form – FE80:0000:0000:0000:020C:000F:0000:FE53

Short Form – _____

3.   Long Form – FF02:0000:0000:0000:0000:0000:0000:0001

Short Form – _____

4.   Long Form – 2001:0000:0000:0001:0200:000E:FFC8:0010

Short Form – _____

5.   Long Form – FE80:0000:0000:0000:205C:2194:3F57:FD71

Short Form – _____

Step 2   Now using the same shortcuts, convert the following IPv6 addresses from their short form notation to their long form notation:

1.   Short Form – ::1

Long Form – _____

2.   Short Form – FE80::A:0:53

Long Form – _____

3.   Short Form – FF02::2

Long Form – _____

4.   Short Form – 2001::6:E00:9:FFC8:11

Long Form – _____

5.   Short Form – FE80::205C:2194:3F57:FD71

Long Form – _____

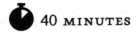 40 MINUTES

Lab Exercise 13.04: IPv6 Configuration and Exploration

All of the major Internet entities have adopted IPv6 as the IPv4 address pool approaches depletion. It is still not common, however, for an organization to run an IPv6-only enabled network.

In this Lab Exercise you will use the Windows 7 client machine and the Windows Server 2008 machine in the Network Lab to implement an IPv6 network. You will manually configure, verify, and test the connectivity of IPv6 addresses assigned to the systems. You will also identify the address type of the IPv6 addresses.

Learning Objectives

In this lab, you'll again work with the TCP/IP settings on your Windows 7 and Windows Server 2008 machines. You will configure and explore your IPv6 address information. At the end of this lab you will be able to

- Verify your IPv6 settings

- Configure IPv6 Unique Local Addresses (ULAs)

- Test and verify IPv6 connectivity

Lab Materials and Setup

The materials you'll need for this lab are

- Pencil and paper

- A system with Internet connectivity to facilitate research

- Windows XP, Windows Vista, or Windows 7 client machine

- Windows Server 2008 machine (it may be configured as in the previous chapter's Lab Exercises, but it is not critical for this Lab Exercise)

- The Linksys WRT54GL (or similar) router that was configured in prior Lab Exercises and appropriate cabling to connect the small network

Getting Down to Business

CJ and Maggie come by the Network Lab and ask how your IPv6 skills are coming along. They have a concept they would like you to explore, an IPv6-native network. They are not able to free up any of the IPv6-capable routers that would enable you to configure your small network with global unicast addresses. Instead, they have generated a random Unique Local IPv6 Unicast Address range. They ask you to take the time to configure the netlabclient and netlabserver systems manually to use IPv6 as the native addressing for TCP/IP.

✖ Cross-Reference

You can learn more about the different address types by checking out the "IPv6 Basics" section in Chapter 13 of the *Mike Meyers' CompTIA Network+ Guide to Managing and Troubleshooting Networks* textbook.

Step 1 Begin by generating a random **Unique Local Address (ULA).** You can accomplish this by navigating to the following Web site, www.simpledns.com/private-ipv6.aspx, and randomly generating the **Private IPv6 address range.**

✔ Tech Tip

The parameters for the ULA are set forth in **RFC 4193: Unique Local IPv6 Unicast Addresses.** Alternatively, you can assign the following IPv6 address parameters that were already generated by **Simple DNS** as detailed here:

Prefix/L:	fd
Global ID:	bfdd19becc
Subnet ID:	de78
Combined/CID:	fdbf:dd19:becc:de78::/64
IPv6 Addresses:	fdbf:dd19:becc:de78:xxxx:xxxx:xxxx:xxxx

The Lab Exercise uses the following addresses for specific devices:

Client System: fdbf:dd19:becc:de78::11/64

Server System: fdbf:dd19:becc:de78::254/64

Router: fdbf:dd19:becc:de78::1/64

Step 2 If you haven't already done so, disable all Windows firewalls and enable IPv6 on both the client and server machines.

Step 3 Configure each system with the appropriate **IPv6 address**, **Subnet prefix length**, **Default gateway**, and **Preferred DNS server** as shown in Figure 13-1.

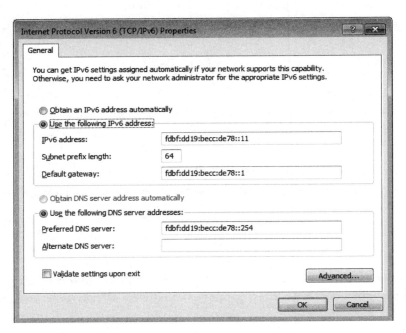

FIGURE 13-1 Client machine IPv6 properties

Step 4 After you have configured both the client system and the server system, open a command prompt with administrative privileges and run **ipconfig /all**. See Figure 13-2. Record the results here:

_____

_____

```
Administrator: C:\Windows\System32\cmd.exe
Ethernet adapter Local Area Connection:

   Connection-specific DNS Suffix  . :
   Description . . . . . . . . . . . : Realtek PCIe GBE Family Controller
   Physical Address. . . . . . . . . : 00-26-B9-16-F6-64
   DHCP Enabled. . . . . . . . . . . : No
   Autoconfiguration Enabled . . . . : Yes
   IPv6 Address. . . . . . . . . . . : fdbf:dd19:becc:de78::11(Preferred)
   Link-local IPv6 Address . . . . . : fe80::d80:a3a5:8d59:b63d%10(Preferred)
   Default Gateway . . . . . . . . . : fdbf:dd19:becc:de78::1
   DHCPv6 IAID . . . . . . . . . . . : 285222585
   DHCPv6 Client DUID. . . . . . . . : 00-01-00-01-12-D4-DF-CC-00-26-B9-16-F6-64

   DNS Servers . . . . . . . . . . . : fdbf:dd19:becc:de78::254
   NetBIOS over Tcpip. . . . . . . . : Disabled
```

FIGURE 13-2 Output of **ipconfig /all** on client machine

→ **Note**

As you have learned by reading Chapter 13 of the *Mike Meyers' CompTIA Network+ Guide to Managing and Troubleshooting Networks* textbook, a link-local address is a private address in IPv6 used for local communication, like APIPA is in IPv4. To get access to the Internet, your system will need a global address in IPv6.

Step 5 Switch over to the console for the Server 2008 machine. Click **Start | Administrative Tools | DNS**. Right-click **troubleticket.local** and select **New Host (A or AAAA)**. Add a record for **netlabserver** with the **IPv6 address fdbf:dd19:becc:de78::254**. This will create a new **AAAA** record as shown in Figure 13-3.

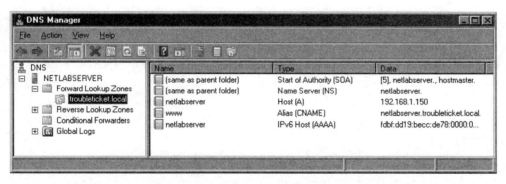

FIGURE 13-3 Adding an IPv6 AAAA record in DNS Manager

Step 6 Now launch a command prompt. Ping each of the addresses listed. An example of one of the responses is shown in Figure 13-4. Record your results in the provided space:

```
C:\Windows\system32>ping www.troubleticket.local

Pinging netlabserver.troubleticket.local [fdbf:dd19:becc:de78::254] with 32 bytes of data:
Reply from fdbf:dd19:becc:de78::254: time=2ms
Reply from fdbf:dd19:becc:de78::254: time=2ms
Reply from fdbf:dd19:becc:de78::254: time=2ms
Reply from fdbf:dd19:becc:de78::254: time=2ms

Ping statistics for fdbf:dd19:becc:de78::254:
    Packets: Sent = 4, Received = 4, Lost = 0 (0% loss),
Approximate round trip times in milli-seconds:
    Minimum = 2ms, Maximum = 2ms, Average = 2ms
```

FIGURE 13-4 Results of pinging www.troubleticket.local

ping ::1 Results: _____

ping fdbf:dd19:becc:de78::11 Results: _____

ping fdbf:dd19:becc:de78::254 Results: _____

ping www.troubleticket.local Results: _____

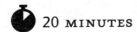 20 minutes

Lab Exercise 13.05: Configuring Windows 7 to Use an IPv6 Tunnel Broker

Hurricane Electric Internet Services provides an IPv6 tunnel broker service. Tunnel brokers provide an IPv6 tunneling protocol, which enables you to access IPv6 resources on the Internet. The reason the tunneling protocol is needed is that although you have IPv6 installed on your system, and the Internet resources you are accessing have IPv6 running, the routers on the Internet that are between your system and the IPv6 resources you are accessing do not. Hurricane Electric provides a 6in4 tunneling protocol that enables IPv6 connectivity through IPv4 devices.

> ✖ **Cross-Reference**
>
> To learn more about tunnels, 6in4, and tunnel brokers, check out the "Moving to IPv6" section in Chapter 13 of the *Mike Meyers' CompTIA Network+ Guide to Managing and Troubleshooting Networks* textbook.

Learning Objectives

In this lab, you will set up a free account with the tunnel broker, Hurricane Electric. You'll then use **netsh**, the network shell programming environment, to configure and enable the 6in4 tunneling standard. When you have completed this lab, you will be able to

- Enable and test IPv6 connectivity
- Navigate the **netsh** programming environment

Lab Materials and Setup

The materials you'll need for this lab are

- A Windows 7 system with Internet connectivity
- A valid e-mail address
- Pencil and paper

Getting Down to Business

ITCF's client has finally decided to implement IPv6 office-wide, only to find out that communication over the Internet with native IPv6 is not fully implemented. Maggie and the client discuss some of the solutions and decide to use one of the commercial tunnel brokers. After doing some research on the various organizations (gogoNET, freenet6, SixXS, and Hurricane Electric), they select Hurricane Electric. Maggie invites you to tag along as she creates an account and configures the tunneling protocol.

Step 1   In the following space, briefly describe why a 6in4 tunneling protocol, provided by tunnel brokers, is needed.

_____

_____

Step 2   Fire up Windows, launch your browser, and enter the URL **http://ipv6.google.com** in the address bar. What are the results?

_____

_____

Step 3   Now navigate to Hurricane Electric at www.tunnelbroker.net. The IPv6 tunnel broker home page is a wealth of information in and of itself. Take a moment and read the introduction. Hurricane Electric offers a free tunnel broker service, but you will have to register, provide personal information and an e-mail address, and create an account. Click the **Sign up now!** button.

→ **Note**

If you are performing this Lab Exercise as part of a class in a school or training center, please follow the instructor's directions. You may be restricted in creating a tunnel through the school or company's Internet connection. As with any service that you sign up with on the Internet, please read the **Terms and Services** before you provide your personal information. Even if you decide not to install the tunnel broker, follow along with the Lab Exercise steps. You will learn about IPv6, tunnel brokers, and even use the netsh programming environment to set up the interface.

Step 4   When you receive the e-mail containing your password, enter your user name and password in the **Tunnelbroker Login** box. Click **Create Regular Tunnel** and follow the onscreen instructions. You will have to provide your external IPv4 address that you receive from your ISP (if this is the first tunnel you are creating, Hurricane Electric will post the address they have for you). Click the **Create Tunnel** button. This will create the tunnel and bring you to the summary page. Note the IPv6 tunnel configuration information (**Description**, **IPv6 Tunnel Endpoints**, **Available DNS Resolvers**, and **Routed IPv6 Prefixes**). Record the information for your IPv6 tunnel endpoints:

Server IPv4 Address _____

Server IPv6 Address _____

Client IPv4 Address _____

Client IPv6 Address _____

→ **Note**

You may enter your actual IP addresses in the spaces in the preceding list, or use fictitious addresses for the Lab Exercise. To use the tunnel, however, the correct addresses will need to be used in the next step.

Step 5   Now you will use **netsh** to configure client-side IPv6 tunnel settings. If you are on the Hurricane Electric Web site, click the **Example Configurations** tab in the **Tunnel Details** window. The addresses shown in the following steps are fictitious; substitute your actual addresses if you are physically configuring the tunnel. Use the following sub-steps to launch a command prompt with Administrative privileges and run the commands to complete the client-side configuration:

a.   Click **Start** and type **cmd** in the **Search programs and file** dialog box. Right-click **cmd.exe** when it appears in the **Programs** list and select to **Run as administrator** from the drop-down menu. Now follow the next steps to configure your client-side settings.

✔ **Tech Tip**

In the following steps you will be using the **network shell (netsh)** utility. The **netsh** commands can be entered as one long string of syntax and run from the C:\> prompt. For example:

```
C:\>netsh interface teredo set state disabled.
```

You can also drill down to sub-contexts by entering the commands one at a time. For example:

```
C:\>netsh
netsh>interface
netsh interface>teredo
netsh interface teredo>set state disabled
```

Either method will work as long as you pay attention to which context you are working within. The following Lab Exercise steps use one long string of syntax for each configuration command.

b.   You will begin by disabling the **Teredo** tunneling protocol by typing the following command:

```
netsh interface teredo set state disabled
```

c.   You will now add the IPv4 information for the 6in4 tunnel between the client-side and server-side endpoints. If you are using a cable modem, FIOS, or a wireless router, you will want to use the actual address of your client machine, not the external IP address provided by your ISP.

```
netsh interface ipv6 add v6v4tunnel IP6Tunnel 192.168.1.101 205.207.124.24
```

d.   Now you will configure your IPv6 address for the IPv6 tunnel that you just created:

```
netsh interface ipv6 add address IP6Tunnel 2001:74:2a0c:d0e::2/64
```

e.   Lastly, you will configure the default gateway (router) address for the 6in4 tunnel:

```
netsh interface ipv6 add route ::/0 IP6Tunnel 2001:74:2a0c:d0e::1/64
```

If everything worked as expected, you should have a working IPv6 tunnel and be able to communicate with IPv6-only sites. Run this last **netsh** command to verify connectivity. Your results should resemble those shown in Figure 13-5.

```
netsh interface ipv6 show interfaces
```

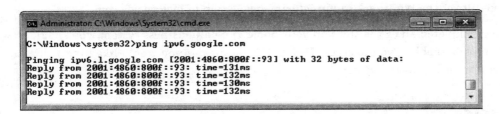

FIGURE 13-5   Connected and disconnected IPv6 interfaces

Step 6   From the command prompt, can you ping ipv6.google.com? Are the results similar to Figure 13-6?

_____

_____

_____

```
C:\Windows\system32>ping ipv6.google.com

Pinging ipv6.l.google.com [2001:4860:800f::93] with 32 bytes of data:
Reply from 2001:4860:800f::93: time=131ms
Reply from 2001:4860:800f::93: time=132ms
Reply from 2001:4860:800f::93: time=130ms
Reply from 2001:4860:800f::93: time=132ms
```

FIGURE 13-6   Reply from ipv6.google.com

Step 7   Type **exit** to close the command prompt.

Step 8   Now you will use one of the tools that you worked with in earlier chapters. Follow the sub-steps to access Google through their IPv6-only Web page and track the packets with Wireshark.

a.   Open the Wireshark Packet Sniffer application and configure the program as before. Turn promiscuous mode off and ready the program to capture packets, but do not start the capture yet.

b.   Open your browser and type **ipv6.google.com** in the URL address bar. Do not press ENTER until you start the capture in Wireshark.

c. Start the Wireshark capture. Navigate back to your Web browser and press ENTER to launch the ipv6.google.com Web site. Confirm that you have loaded the Google Web page. What are the results?

d. Switch to the Wireshark application and **Stop** the capture. Examine the capture file. Is it similar to that shown in Figure 13-7? Note the IPv6 addresses.

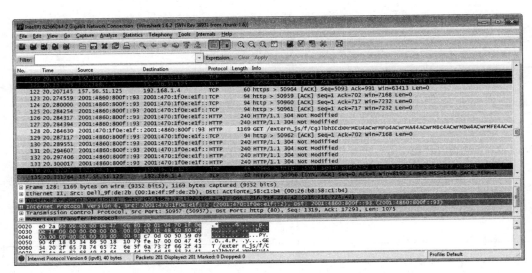

FIGURE 13-7   Results of the Wireshark capture during navigation to ipv6.google.com

Step 9   If you have completed all of the steps on your home or small business system, you should now have a IPv6 tunnel broker enabling you to access IPv6-only Web sites. If you would like to test this interface, point your browser at ipv6.test-ipv6.com.

Lab Analysis

1. Jennifer is studying for the CompTIA Network+ exam. While reading about IPv6, she asks, "What is a link-local address and how can I recognize this address type?"

2. Zach wants to know how a system running IPv6 gets a global unicast address.

3. Scott keeps hearing some fellow techs talking about an IPv6 anycast address. Can you explain to Scott what this is and how it is used?

_____

_____

4. What are the different types of multicast addresses supported by IPv6?

_____

_____

5. Joseph asks you to explain to him some of the rules for the IPv6 address notation. In the space that follows, give a breakdown of the format of an IPv6 address.

_____

_____

Key Term Quiz

Use the vocabulary terms from the list below to complete the sentences that follow. Not all of the terms will be used.

6in4	stateful
6to4	stateless
anycast	Teredo
Extended Unique Identifier	tunnel
global unicast address	tunnel broker
link-local address	unicast address
multicast address	

1. To get on the Internet with IPv6, you will need to have a(n) _____.

2. To access the IPv6 Internet resources, you will need to use a(n) _____ protocol.

3. Hurricane Electric is an example of an IPv6-in-IPv4 tunnel protocol provider. Such a provider is referred to as a(n) _____.

4. When each IPv6 system starts up, it will assign itself a(n) _____.

5. The last 64 bits of an IPv6 address are known as the _____.

Chapter 14

Remote Connectivity

Lab Exercises

In many of the Lab Exercises you have performed thus far, you have integrated both local area networks (LANs) and wide area networks (WANs) as you worked through the Lab Exercise steps. Now, you will delve specifically into the technologies associated with remote connections. Most networks today have at least one router connected to a WAN environment. A large organization might connect to the outside world through a dedicated line, for example. An individual might connect to a high-speed Internet link.

In these labs, you'll examine the different technologies used for remote connectivity. These labs will include a review of WAN technologies and speeds, a closer look at the technologies that provide the "last mile" of connectivity, and two methods to configure a remote desktop to enable someone to administer a system remotely. You'll finish up by lending a helping hand using Windows Remote Assistant.

Now's the time to jump in and get started!

 20 MINUTES

Lab Exercise 14.01: Identifying WAN Technologies

Network technicians have the responsibility of configuring, managing, and troubleshooting the various methods of connecting LANs to WANs. These connections provide Internet access to the clients on the LAN, and access to the LAN by authorized remote clients from outside the LAN.

As a network technician, you need to understand the terminology used to describe the popular WAN-related technologies, such as PSTN, T1, SONET, Frame Relay, and ATM, as well as define the various speeds associated with these WAN technologies.

Learning Objectives

At the completion of this lab, you will be able to

- Define the speeds of popular WAN technologies
- Identify key WAN-related terms

Lab Materials and Setup

The materials you'll need for this lab are

- A PC with Internet access
- The *Mike Meyers' CompTIA Network+ Guide to Managing and Troubleshooting Networks* textbook
- Pencil and paper

Getting Down to Business

CJ and Maggie been very been supportive of your pursuit of the CompTIA Network+ certification. The Networking Lab continues to be an excellent resource for installing, configuring, and troubleshooting various networking scenarios. They know that it is sometimes difficult to simulate all of the WAN technologies that you should be familiar with, so they recommend that you hit the books, so to speak, and review the different WAN technologies you'll need to understand to pass the CompTIA Network+ exam. They put together the following mix-and-match exercises to help you review WAN technologies and their associated speeds.

Step 1   There are basically three transmission media in use today for dedicated point-to-point services: T-carrier over copper, Optical Carrier over fiber, and Ethernet over copper or fiber. The transmission methods may vary, but the speed of the media remains fairly constant. For each of the media types in the table, place the correct letter beside the corresponding definition for the media type and speed.

A. DS0 Channel   _____ A fiber carrier that achieves a speed of 51.85 Mbps

B. DS1   _____ A copper carrier that uses 32 DS0 channels providing a speed of 2.048 Mbps

C. T1 Line   _____ A fiber carrier that achieves a speed of 622.08 Mbps

D. E1 Line   _____ A fiber carrier that achieves a speed of 9.955 Gbps

E. T3 Line   _____ The basic digital signaling rate of 64 Kbps

F. E3 Line   _____ A fiber carrier that achieves a speed of 39.82 Gbps

G. OC-1   _____ A type of media capable of providing 1000 Mbps – 10 Gbps performance

H. OC-3   _____ A fiber carrier that achieves a speed of 2.488 Gbps

I. OC-12   _____ A copper carrier that uses 24 DS0 channels providing a speed of 1.544 Mbps

J. OC-24   _____ A fiber carrier that achieves a speed of 13.22 Gbps

K. OC-48   _____ A term that is more accurate when describing 24 DS0 channels providing a speed of 1.544 Mbps

L. OC-192   _____ A copper carrier that uses 672 DS0 channels providing a speed of 44.736 (45) Mbps

M. OC-256   _____ A fiber carrier that achieves a speed of 1.244 Gbps

N. OC-768   _____ A fiber carrier that achieves a speed of 155.52 Mbps

O. Ethernet   _____ A copper carrier that uses 512 DS0 channels providing a speed of 34.368 (34) Mbps

Step 2   Place the correct letter beside the corresponding definition for the following WAN technologies.

A. CSU/DSU   _____ A packet-switching standard designed for T-carrier lines such as a T1

B. ATM   _____ The European specification for the long-distance, high-speed, fiber-optic transmission defined by the International Telecommunications Union (ITU)

C. DWDM   _____ Connects a copper carrier such as a T1 line to your router

D. Frame relay _____ The point in a building where the ISP/telephony company's responsibility ends and the organization's responsibility begins

E. Demarc   _____ Label-switching technology that inserts a label between Layer 2 header and the Layer 3 information.

F. MPLS   _____ Allows one single-mode fiber cable to carry approximately 150 simultaneous signals

G. SDH   _____ The primary standard for long-distance, high-speed, fiber-optic transmission

H. SONET   _____ Integrates voice, video, and data over a single link that uses a fixed-size 53-byte cell

 20 MINUTES

Lab Exercise 14.02: Explore the "Last Mile"

Individuals and SOHOs use numerous methods to connect to the digital outside world. For these individuals and smaller organizations, this is the connection to the central office (CO) and is known as the "last mile." In the early days, this connection was primarily analog telephone lines. Today, you will see high-speed cable, fiber, or cellular technologies providing connectivity to residential dwellings.

You have used some form of connection to the Internet in many of the prior Lab Exercises, so you have some knowledge of one or two of these "last mile" technologies already. To answer some of the questions that you will encounter on the CompTIA Network+ exam comfortably, you should review these connection methods.

Learning Objectives

At the completion of this lab, you will be able to

- Define the "last mile" technologies

- Detail key specifications and features of each connection technology

Lab Materials and Setup

The materials you'll need for this lab are

- A PC with Internet access

- The *Mike Meyers' CompTIA Network+ Guide to Managing and Troubleshooting Networks* textbook

- Pencil and paper

Getting Down to Business

You already have some experience with one or two of the SOHO connection methods. If you have used dial-up, DSL, cable, or fiber, you have used a "last mile" technology. Maggie will be presenting a report to CJ on the various connection technologies that ITCF will recommend to their clients. Since your clients are from all types of locales (rural farms to urban apartments), Maggie wants to cover all available technologies. She asks you to help with the preliminary information gathering.

Using the Internet and the textbook, research and review the various SOHO connection technologies and provide a definition and short summary of each.

Step 1 Start with the old standard, dial-up. Cover some of the details and requirements for both PSTN/POTS and ISDN.

_____

_____

_____

_____

Step 2 Next you will explore DSL. Make sure to include information about ADSL, SDSL, and VDSL.

_____

_____

_____

_____

Step 3   Cable Internet connectivity has been popular for a number of years and continues to vie for the highest speeds for residential and commercial service. Discuss some of the characteristics of cable Internet service.

_____

_____

_____

_____

Step 4   In rural areas, satellite Internet connectivity may be the most attractive option. What are some of the features of satellite Internet?

_____

_____

_____

_____

Step 5   With the explosive use of portable smart devices (smartphones), the cellular WAN has become the _de facto_ standard for Internet connectivity on the go. Discuss both Mobile Data Services and IEEE 802.16.

_____

_____

_____

_____

Step 6   The most serious competitor for cable Internet services is delivered by fiber-optic cabling right to the house. Record some of the features of fiber Internet connectivity.

_____

_____

_____

_____

Step 7   Finally, explore the experimental Broadband over Power Line (BPL) and discuss the methodology and obstacles to this technology.

_____

_____

_____

_____

 30 MINUTES

Lab Exercise 14.03: Using Remote Desktop Connection (RDC)

Most businesses today support users working at remote locations or from home, and with the increase in the use of virtual servers (see Chapter 17), it is not uncommon to manage those servers from an on-premise or remote client machine. To set up this capability, you can configure the remote system to enable you to use client software to connect remotely to that system when the need arises.

There are a number of remote management software solutions that you can use. One of the popular solutions is to enable Remote Desktop on Windows systems, so that you can then use the Remote Desktop client to initiate a remote session with the system. Once a Remote Desktop Connection is established, you can then fully administer the system as if you were sitting at the computer.

✖ Cross-Reference

Before tackling this lab, read over the "Remote Terminal" section in Chapter 14 of the _Mike Meyers' CompTIA Network+ Guide to Managing and Troubleshooting Networks_ textbook.

Learning Objectives

In this lab, you will enable Remote Desktop on a Windows server so that you can then administer it remotely. Keep in mind that you can enable Remote Desktop on any Windows system, including Windows XP, Windows Vista, and Windows 7. At the end of this lab, you will be able to

- Enable Remote Desktop

- Remotely connect to a system using the Remote Desktop client

Lab Materials and Setup

The materials you'll need for this lab are

- A Windows Server 2008 system (possibly the machine you have been using to perform the Lab Exercises for prior chapters)

- A Windows XP, Windows Vista, or Windows 7 client

- The Linksys WRT54GL (or similar) router and appropriate cabling to connect the small network

- Pencil and paper

Getting Down to Business

ITCF has a number of customers located in remote cities. ITCF techs will occasionally travel to the customer site when the customer has a need for server changes. In a discussion with CJ, he mentions that the growing trend is to manage client servers from the ITCF office. He recommends that you explore the features of the Remote Desktop program that is built into Windows and configure a remote session in the ITCF networking lab.

✔ **Tech Tip**

At this point in your studies, you have performed numerous Lab Exercises using Microsoft Windows XP, Windows Vista, Windows 7, and Windows Server 2008. Ubuntu Linux has been featured in some of the Lab Exercises as well. You have also worked with various switches and routers, including the Linksys WRT54GL. You have cabled the systems, configured TCP/IP, and explored various networking applications and utilities.

Working with your instructor, take a few moments to review the configuration of your networking lab setup. Components and configurations may have changed over time with multiple groups using the equipment, or some of the systems may still be configured for specific Lab Exercises. Review Administrator names and passwords and log in to the systems. Check the cabling. Explore the basic TCP/IP configuration and verify that the client systems, servers, and switches (4-port switch of the WRT54GL) are all on the same network. Run some basic utilities and validate connectivity. Performing this routine now will assist in making the future Lab Exercises run more smoothly.

Step 1   Ensure that the Windows Server 2008 system is powered on and then log on as Administrator.

Step 2   Right-click **Computer** and select **Properties** from the drop-down menu. From the **System** window, select **Remote settings** from the **Tasks** list. This will open the **System Properties** window with the **Remote** tab selected, as shown in Figure 14-1.

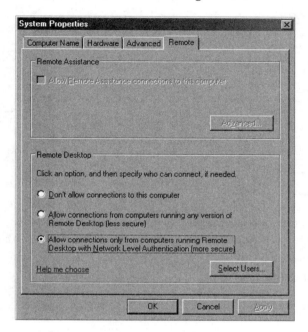

FIGURE 14-1 The Remote tab of the System Properties window of a Windows Server 2008 machine

Step 3   Enable the **Remote Desktop** option by choosing **Allow connections only from computers running Remote Desktop with Network Level Authentication (more secure)**. By default, which versions of Remote Desktop and which user accounts can use Remote Desktop to connect to the server?

_____

_____

Step 4   If you want to allow other users to use Remote Desktop to connect to the system, choose the **Select Users** button and add the users to the list. When you give users the capability to use Remote Desktop to connect to the system in this manner, you add them to a built-in group that has the permission to use Remote Desktop to connect to the server. What is the name of this built-in group?

_____

_____

Choose **OK** to close the **System Properties** window.

Step 5   Now log on to your Windows 7 client machine to see if you can use Remote Desktop to connect to the server. Choose **Start | All Programs | Accessories | Remote Desktop Connection**. This will launch the **Remote Desktop Connection** logon window. Type the IP address of the server you want to connect to and then choose **Connect**. See Figure 14-2.

Figure 14-2 Remote Desktop Connection window

Step 6   When queried to **Enter your credentials**, enter the Administrator user name and password for the Windows Server 2008 machine. Now you can navigate all of the applications and utilities of the Server 2008 machine as if you logged on locally. Look at the System Properties to verify that you are connected to the Server 2008 machine. What are the results?

_____

_____

Step 7   Notice that the **Remote Desktop Connection** window by default fills the entire monitor screen. In typical use, you would click **Start | Log Off** to log off the Server 2008 machine and close the **Remote Desktop Connection**. You could also choose **Start | Shut Down** to perform a remote shutdown of the Server 2008 machine. This would be useful if you received a notice that the location where your server resides lost power and you would like to shut down the system gracefully before the UPS battery backup runs out. Go ahead and **Shut Down** the remote system. What is the warning message that you receive?

_____

_____

Step 8   When you configured the server to accept remote connections, you should have noticed a warning stating that "Remote Desktop Firewall exception will be enabled." If the firewall between the Remote Desktop client and the Remote Desktop server is enabled, how would this exception allow the Remote Desktop client to connect to the server?

_____

_____

30 MINUTES

Lab Exercise 14.04: Configuring Virtual Network Computing (VNC) Remote Connections

Sometimes the operating systems you work with will not be Microsoft products. Linux servers, Linux clients, and Macintosh clients continue to gain market share, and a good network tech will develop skills on these products as well. Even if you use one of these alternate operating systems, you may still want to manage remotely or enable remote management of the system. Virtual Network Computing (VNC) is remote desktop software that works nicely in Linux, Mac, and Windows operating systems.

Many of the various versions of Linux operating systems (often called Linux "distros," for "distributions") come with VNC utilities built in. In this Lab Exercise, you will explore the configuration and use of the VNC server in the Ubuntu 11.04 Linux distribution.

Learning Objectives

In this Lab Exercise, you will enable VNC on an Ubuntu Linux system so that you can then administer it remotely. You will then connect to the Ubuntu system using VNC on a Windows 7 system. At the end of this lab, you will be able to

- Enable VNC remote desktop on a Ubuntu Linux system

- Remotely manage a Linux system from a Windows system using the VNC client

Lab Materials and Setup

The materials you'll need for this lab are

- A system connected to the Internet

- An Ubuntu Linux system

- A Windows 7 system

- A network switch and appropriate cabling to connect the small network

- Pencil and paper

Getting Down to Business

The Windows Remote Desktop Connection is a wonderful tool for remotely managing Windows machines, but what happens if you are running a number of Linux servers hosting all of your Web sites? CJ now recommends that you explore the configuration and use of alternate remote desktop connection software. You fire up the Ubuntu and Windows 7 systems in the Networking Lab and get down to business!

Step 1   To begin this Lab Exercise, you will download a VNC client/server program. Try the popular and free Tight VNC. On the system connected to the Internet, download the self-installing package for Windows at this Web site: www.tightvnc.com/download.php. After downloading, copy the installer package onto the Windows 7 client you will use in the Lab Exercise.

Step 2   Now log on to the Ubuntu Linux system, and perform the steps to configure the VNC server included with distribution 11.04 as follows:

a.   Open the Remote Desktop utility by clicking the **Power Button** icon and selecting **System Settings** from the drop-down menu.

b.   Click on the **Remote Desktop** icon in the **Internet and Network** section. This will launch the **Remote Desktop Preferences**, where you will enable the Ubuntu machine to accept Remote Desktop connections. Check the following components (see Figure 14-3):

- Allow other users to view your desktop

- Allow other users to control your desktop

- You must confirm each access to this machine

- Require the user to enter this password: **netlab**

- Only display an icon when there is someone connected

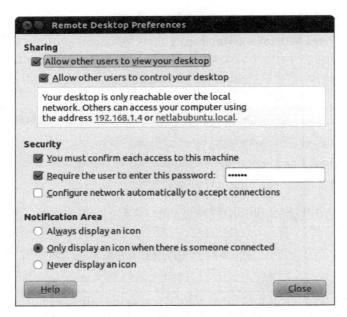

FIGURE 14-3 Remote Desktop Preferences in Ubuntu Linux

c. To provide compatibility with TightVNC, which you will be using on the Windows 7 machine to connect and control this Ubuntu machine remotely, you will have to configure one of the remote desktop settings manually. Perform the following steps on the Ubuntu system:

   - Press ALT-F2 to open the **Run a command** dialog box.

   - Type **gconf-editor** in the dialog box and press ENTER. This launches the **Configuration Editor**.

   - In the Configuration Editor, navigate to **desktop | gnome | remote_access** and check **disable_xdamage** as shown in Figure 14-4. (Disabling the XDamage extension provides compatibility with video cards that otherwise won't work with some of the 3D effects in Ubuntu.)

- Close the Configuration Editor.

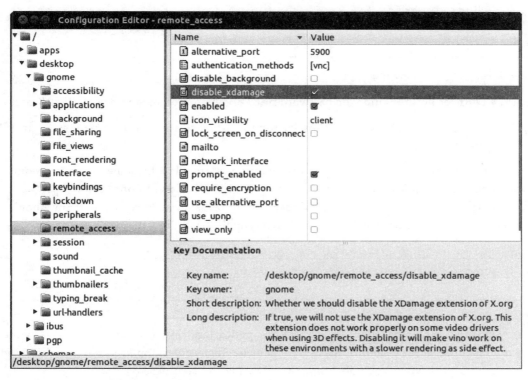

FIGURE 14-4 Configuration Editor – remote_access

Step 3 Log on to the Windows 7 machine and perform the following steps to configure TightVNC Viewer. After installing TightVNC Viewer and logging on to the Ubuntu machine, you will be able to manage and configure the Linux system remotely from the Windows system.

    a.   Launch the **tightvnc-2.0.4-setup.exe** file to begin the installation of TightVNC.

    b.   Follow the steps to install the TightVNC Viewer, selecting all of the defaults. When prompted, reboot the system to complete the installation.

    c.   Open the TightVNC Viewer application, and enter the IP address of the Ubuntu Linux system as shown in Figure 14-5.

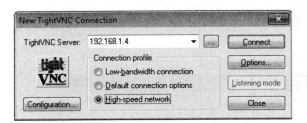

FIGURE 14-5 New TightVNC connection

    d.   Click the **Connect** button. Enter the password **netlab** when prompted and click the **OK** button.

    e.   On the Ubuntu system, choose the **Allow** button to authorize another user to view or control the computer remotely.

    f.   Now use the remote desktop to navigate the Ubuntu system. Click on some of the icons and launch one of the applications. You can open the **TightVNC Viewer Connection Options** to configure items such as the **Mouse Pointer**. Figure 14-6 shows a screenshot of the **About Ubuntu** application in Windows 7 Explorer. What application did you open?

_____

_____

Step 4 When you finish exploring Ubuntu and the VNC application, close the TightVNC Viewer window on the Windows 7 machine. On the Ubuntu machine, open the Remote Desktop Preferences utility and disable **Allow other users to view your desktop**. Shut down both machines.

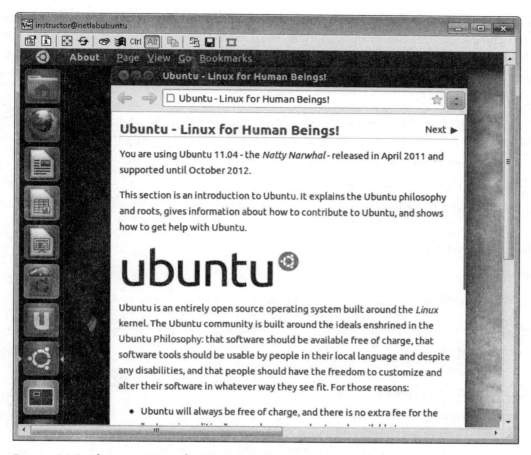

FIGURE 14-6 Ubuntu – Linux for Human Beings!

 30 MINUTES

Lab Exercise 14.05: "Helping Out" with Windows Remote Assistance

Remote Desktop and VNC are great solutions when you want to take control of a remote machine, but what if you would like to help someone configure his desktop settings? What can you do to help trouble-shoot problems when a remote user calls for help? One of the methods you can use is to have the user invite you to "share" control of his desktop, guiding him in the steps required to resolve his issue.

Microsoft offers a unique solution known as Windows Remote Assistance. Windows Remote Assistance enables a user to invite a technician to connect to a system remotely and then share pointer movement and keystrokes of that system with the tech. This method gives you (the tech) complete access to the remote machine, but at the same time, the user can view and contribute to the session.

Windows Remote Assistance differs therefore from Remote Desktop because Windows Remote Assistance continues the user's currently running session. The user doesn't have to log off at all. When you log in with Remote Desktop, in contrast, you start a completely new session.

Learning Objectives

In this lab, you will negotiate a Windows Remote Assistance session on two Windows 7 systems. Windows Remote Assistance is backward-compatible, and will work on older Microsoft operating systems, such as Windows XP and Vista. At the end of this lab, you will be able to

- Initiate a Windows Remote Assistance session
- Remotely assist a Windows 7 client

Lab Materials and Setup

The materials you'll need for this lab are

- Two Windows client machines (Windows 7 systems were used in the Lab Exercise)
- A network switch and appropriate cabling to connect the small network
- Pencil and paper

Getting Down to Business

You may have noticed in the last Lab Exercise that not only did VNC offer remote desktop capability, but that both the local and remote users had access to the desktop. This is a great feature of VNC, but a number of additional steps were involved. Implementing VNC would probably be cumbersome to ITCF's clients since most of them use Windows operating systems, and Windows Remote Assistance is built in.

CJ has you wrap up your exploration of remote connectivity applications with the configuration, initiation, and use of the Microsoft Windows Remote Assistance feature in Windows 7.

Step 1   Power up the two Windows 7 machines and make sure that they are configured to communicate with each other in the small Networking Lab. Log on to both machines with an administrative account. For the purposes of this Lab Exercise, consider one machine as the **Office Tech** machine and the other as the **Remote Client** machine.

Step 2   Start the preparation for this Lab Exercise on the Office Tech machine. Windows Remote Assistance begins the session by having the remote client send an e-mail request to the office tech. You probably have not set up an e-mail system or accounts in the Networking Lab, so you will create an invitation and place it in a shared folder on the **Office Tech** machine.

  a.   On the **Office Tech** machine, open the **C:** drive and create a folder named **Invitations**.

  b.   Right-click the **Invitations** folder and choose **Share with | Homegroup (Read/Write)** from the drop-down menu.

c.   Verify that the **Invitations** folder is shared by highlighting the folder and observing the information at the bottom of the window as shown in Figure 14-7.

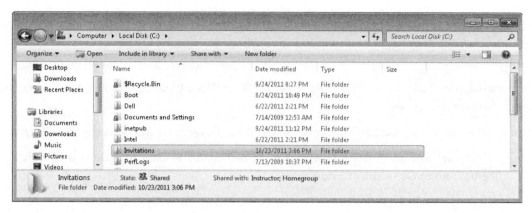

FIGURE 14-7 Verifying that the Invitations folder is shared and that the owner and Homegroup have access

Step 3   Now, on the Remote Client machine, perform the steps to configure the user to accept Remote Assistance and create an invitation:

a.   Right-click **Computer** and select **Properties** from the drop-down menu. Click the **System Protection** option, then select the **Remote** tab. This will open the **System Properties** window with the **Remote** tab selected, as shown in Figure 14-8.

FIGURE 14-8 The Remote tab of the System Properties of the Remote Client Windows 7 machine

b.   Under **Remote Assistance,** check the box next to **Allow Remote Assistance connections to this computer.** Click the **Advanced** button. What are the default settings?

_____

_____

c.   Close the Remote Assistance settings by clicking **OK** or **Cancel** and then select **Apply** and **OK** to accept **Remote Assistance.**

d.   To begin the process of requesting Remote Assistance, perform the tasks in the following steps:

- Click **Start** and enter the following line of text in the **Search programs and files** dialog box: **Remote Assistance**

- Click on **Windows Remote Assistance** in the list of programs that appear.

- In the **Windows Remote Assistance** window, select **Invite someone you trust to help you**, as shown in Figure 14-9.

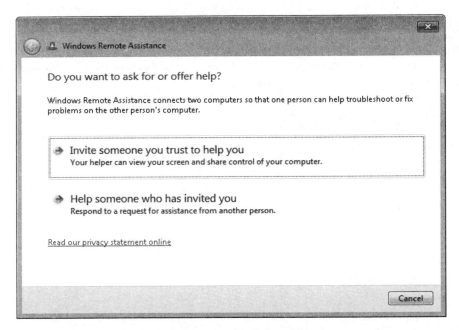

FIGURE 14-9 Inviting a tech you trust to help with system configuration or troubleshooting

- You probably have not configured an e-mail system for the Networking Lab, so you should select **Save this invitation as a file** and save it in the **Invitations** share on the Office Tech machine.

- This will create a password, open a **Windows Remote Assistance** window, and prompt you to **Give your helper the invitation file and password**. See Figure 14-10.

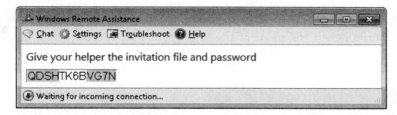

FIGURE 14-10 Windows Remote Assistance password entry screen, waiting for incoming connection

- To facilitate the next steps, you could copy the password to a text file and place it in the **Invitation** share on the Office Tech machine.

Step 4 To complete the invitation and connect using **Remote Assistance**, you will now perform steps on both the **Office Tech** system and the **Remote Client** system. The step explanations will tell you which machine to use during that step.

a. On the **Office Tech** machine, open the **C:\Invitations** folder and double-click the **Invitation.msrc** incident file. This will open the **Windows Remote Assistance** window and prompt you to enter the password. If you have also saved the password in a text file, you can simply open the text document and copy and paste the password into the dialog box, as shown in Figure 14-11. Select **OK** and then switch over to the **Remote Client** machine.

FIGURE 14-11 The password to connect to the remote computer

b. On the **Remote Client** machine, click the **Yes** button to allow the office tech to view the remote client desktop. At this point, what is the office tech able to do?

_____

_____

c. Now switch to the Office Tech machine and select **Request Control** in the upper left-hand corner of the menu bar. This will request the ability to control the keyboard and mouse of the Remote Client machine.

d. Back on the Remote Client machine, click **Allow %username% to respond to User Account Control prompts** where %username% is the name of the Office Tech user account. Click **Yes** to allow. See Figure 14-12.

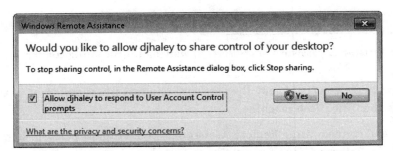

FIGURE 14-12 Windows Remote Assistance allowing Office Tech to control Remote Client while Remote Client is also able to view and control the keyboard and mouse

e. Now the Office Tech and the Remote Client should have co-control of the Remote Client machine's keyboard and mouse functions. Verify that the Office Tech can do something on the Remote Client.

f. Once you've verified capability, click the **Close** button to close the **Windows Remote Assistance** window and end the remote assistance session.

Lab Analysis

1. Seth is running a small graphic arts business out of his home. He often transfers high-resolution images to a drop box on the Internet for his customers to access these images. What are the different types of DSL, and which would you suggest Seth use for his business?

_____

_____

2. Alexis has been your lab partner for the Lab Exercises in this chapter. She remembers reading about Voice over IP in the textbook, but did not see any Lab Exercises related to this technology. Alexis asks you to describe briefly the VoIP protocols RTP and SIP.

_____

_____

3. Many routers offer modules or interface cards that directly support CSU/DSU connections. Jesse asks you to explain what a CSU/DSU is and what it is used for.

   _____

   _____

4. Mike has been reading up on long-distance, high-speed WAN technologies and has noticed various terms like SONET, OC-1, OC-3, STS-256, and STS-768. What can you tell Mike about these terms?

   _____

   _____

5. Many of the ITCF employees work from their homes a few days a week. Sam, one of your Webmasters, needs access to the Apache servers when working from home just as if he were in the office. What solution might you recommend?

   _____

   _____

Key Term Quiz

Use the vocabulary terms from the list below to complete the sentences that follow. Not all of the terms will be used.

asymmetric DSL (ADSL)

Asynchronous Transfer Mode (ATM)

Basic Rate Interface (BRI)

Broadband over Power Line (BPL)

cable Internet

Channel Service Unit/Digital Service Unit (CSU/DSU)

digital subscriber line (DSL)

fiber Internet

Frame Relay

last mile

Optical Carrier (OCx)

public switched telephone network (PSTN)

Real-time Transport Protocol (RTP)

Remote Desktop Protocol (RDP)

satellite Internet

symmetric DSL (SDSL)

Synchronous Optical Network (SONET)

T1

T3

Virtual Network Computing (VNC)

Voice over IP (VoIP)

Windows Remote Assistance

1. The _____ protocol is the VoIP protocol that defines the type of packet used to transfer voice over the Internet.

2. Remote Desktop uses the _____ protocol to send screen information to the remote user.

3. A(n) _____ connection uses separate download and upload speeds over the phone lines.

4. A(n) _____ connection has a transfer rate of 1.544 Mbps.

5. The _____ tool enables a technician to troubleshoot a remote computer with the user able to observe and interact at the same time.

Chapter 15
Wireless Networking

Lab Exercises

Wireless networking is the solution to, and the cause of, many network technicians' headaches. Wireless networking is being adopted at a phenomenal rate in all corners of the globe, from small home and office networks to large corporate enterprises, school campuses to local libraries. You'll also find wireless networking in hotels, airports, and even cafes, fast food restaurants, and donut shops. As a networking solution, wireless is an exciting evolution that provides flexibility, scalability, and ever-increasing throughput speeds. On the downside, wireless networks can be finicky to configure, prone to interference, and insecure.

I say "can be" because there are a number of things you, the network tech, can do to overcome the weaknesses of wireless networking to make it a robust, secure, and available solution. The CompTIA Network+ exam expects you to be competent in all aspects of wireless networking. In this chapter, you're going to install, configure, and manage Wi-Fi wireless technology and security. You will explore the basic facts and figures of each wireless technology, the accepted industry standards that apply to them, and how to implement and troubleshoot these technologies. Welcome to wireless networking!

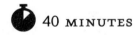 40 MINUTES

Lab Exercise 15.01: Wireless Networking Standards

The world of wireless networking is currently dominated by 802.11g- and 802.11n-based Wi-Fi Ethernet. Understanding the various specifications, operating ranges, speeds, compatibility issues, security methods, and so on enables you to make informed decisions when planning a wireless network rollout.

Learning Objectives

In this lab, you will review the specifications of the various flavors of the IEEE 802.11 wireless networking technologies. When you have completed this lab, you will be able to

- Define the important specifications of wireless networking technologies

Lab Materials and Setup

The materials required for this lab are

- The *Mike Meyers' CompTIA Network+ Guide to Managing and Troubleshooting Networks* textbook

- A computer with Internet access

- Pencil and paper

Getting Down to Business

Remember Maggie's excitement when she was talking about the wireless connectivity that ITCF's client is implementing in all of the rest stops along the interstates and autobahns? Well, now it is time to install these sites and make sure that they will function well into the future. Maggie asks you to research the current offerings in the world of Wi-Fi and make your recommendations on the technologies to use in each of the installments.

Step 1 Your first step is to research the specifications and features of the devices that meet the various Wi-Fi standards. Using the *Mike Meyers' CompTIA Network+ Guide to Managing and Troubleshooting Networks* textbook and the Internet, research and record the specifications for the IEEE 802.11 standards in the following table.

✖ Cross-Reference

To assist in your review of the specifications, functions, and security associated with wireless networking, consult the "Wi-Fi Standards" section of Chapter 15 in the *Mike Meyers' CompTIA Network+ Guide to Managing and Troubleshooting Networks* textbook.

Standard	Frequency	Spectrum	Maximum Speed	Maximum Range	Compatibility
802.11					
802.11a					
802.11b					
802.11g					
802.11n					

Step 2 Due to the actual architecture of wireless networking, it would be impractical to use Carrier Sense Multiple Access with Collision Detection (CSMA/CD). Wireless networks use Carrier Sense Multiple Access with Collision Avoidance (CSMA/CA) to enable nodes to communicate with each other without

interfering with each other's broadcasts and corrupting data. Explain why the CSMA/CD access method wouldn't work with wireless technology, and describe how the CSMA/CA access method functions.

_____

_____

Step 3   Provide an appropriate description for the following components of security associated with Wi-Fi technology:

✖ Cross-Reference

Many of the wireless security measures may be found in the "Wireless Networking Security" section of Chapter 15 in the *Mike Meyers' CompTIA Network+ Guide to Managing and Troubleshooting Networks* textbook. Additional, detailed specifications may be found by conducting Internet searches on the named security components.

✔ Exam Tip

The CompTIA Network+ certification exam objectives include **MAC address filtering** as one of the appropriate wireless security measures. Though MAC address filtering (along with disabling SSID broadcast) will deter the casual uninvited user from leeching a connection to the Internet, these components should not be considered strong security measures to protect a wireless network from being hacked. In the real world, make sure that you have enabled WPA or WPA2 encryption to protect your wireless network from unwanted access.

If you get a question referring to wireless security on the CompTIA Network+ certification exam and the only probable answer is **MAC address filtering**, then there is a good chance that it is the correct answer.

Security Component	Description
MAC address filtering	
RADIUS	
EAP	
WEP	
WPA	
TKIP	

Security Component	Description
WPA2	
AES	
WPA2-PSK	
IEEE 802.1X	
IEEE 802.11i	

Step 4 Wireless access points (WAPs), sometimes referred to as access points (APs), use various antenna technologies such as omnidirectional and directional antennas. Research and define the characteristics of the following antenna technologies:

Antenna Technology	Characteristics
Dipole antenna	
Parabolic antenna	
Yagi antenna	
Patch antenna	

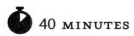 40 MINUTES

Lab Exercise 15.02: Planning the Wireless Network

Now, armed with the specifications, characteristics, and features of Wi-Fi wireless technology, you can look at the requirements for the rest stops. You will want to plan for future growth—including both increased traffic as population and travel continue to expand, and performance as technology improves.

Wireless networking is becoming increasingly important to individuals in their homes as well as businesses that cater to the public. It provides instant connectivity and is the solution to many wired network physical barriers. Plus, it's cool!

Learning Objectives

In this lab, you will analyze the basic information of how wireless networks function to make recommendations for the implementation of wireless networks in the highway rest stops. When you have completed this lab, you'll be able to

- Recommend wireless technology based on application

- Design appropriate wireless models based on usage

- Devise a plan to implement wireless connectivity in highway rest stops

Lab Materials and Setup

The only materials required for this lab are a pencil and some paper.

Getting Down to Business

The various rest stops along the most traveled highways have facilities that are fairly standard in size and the number of travelers they support per hour. There is usually one building with a number of restaurants and fast-food eateries around the edges of the space with a large common area in the center with tables and chairs. Most of the common areas are wide open with a minimum of obstacles, but they can span hundreds of feet from wall to wall. The general goals for each rest stop are as follows:

- The network should be able to support from 20 to 60 devices at one time.
- The network must be secure against unauthorized wireless access, but allow authorized visitors to join with minimal configuration.
- The network should use industry-standard technology that is widely available.

Step 1   Explain the basic hardware and software required to implement wireless networking.

_____

_____

Step 2   Explain the differences between ad hoc and infrastructure modes.

_____

_____

Step 3   Describe at least two methods to implement security on wireless networks. For a public wireless solution, name two security methods that are not practical.

_____

_____

Step 4   Given the typical size of the rest stops, a standard single wireless access point probably won't provide enough range to cover the entire space. How can you increase the wireless coverage area?

_____

_____

Step 5 Based on the goals listed for the rest stops, describe the wireless networking solution you plan to implement.

_____

_____

Step 6 Explain how you will connect the wireless network nodes to the existing 1000BaseT network and ultimately the Internet.

_____

_____

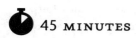 45 MINUTES

Lab Exercise 15.03: Configuring Wireless Networking

With only slight variations, installing and configuring wireless network equipment is much like doing so for a wired network. Since you already know how to install network adapters and network switches, I'll forego a detailed discussion of those procedures here and concentrate on steps for configuring your wireless network nodes to talk to each other in ad hoc and infrastructure modes.

Learning Objectives

In this lab, you will configure PCs for wireless networking. When you have completed this lab, you will be able to

- Configure PCs for Wi-Fi wireless networking in ad hoc and infrastructure mode
- Configure a wireless access point for wireless networking in infrastructure mode

Lab Materials and Setup

The materials you will need for this lab are

- Two Windows PCs equipped with Wi-Fi network adapters (Windows XP, Windows Vista, or Windows 7)
- Wireless access point (802.11g or 802.11n recommended)

Getting Down to Business

After you've delivered a report of your suggested wireless network implementation to Maggie, she recommends that you build a prototype of the wireless network in the Networking Lab. If possible, you should try to model the actual usage that will take place in the rest stops. For instance, many of the travelers will have laptop computers, netbooks, tablets, or smartphones. Generally, any of the devices come with integrated wireless network interfaces, so working with various makes and models of wireless network adapters and access points will help prepare you for real-world application.

Step 1   If you have not already done so, install a wireless network adapter into an available slot on your PC, following the manufacturer's instructions. If you're using a PCIe or ExpressCard NIC, this should be a simple matter of inserting the hardware and then, once PnP detects the device, following the prompts to install the hardware drivers. If you're using a USB device, install the hardware drivers before connecting the device to the PC. Once you've successfully installed the device and device drivers, you should see an icon for the wireless network (signal strength bars with a yellow asterisk) in your PC's notification area (the system tray). Right-click the icon and select **Network and Sharing Center**, then select **Set up a new connection or network**. The Windows 7 **Set Up a Connection or Network** Wizard is shown in Figure 15-1. The appearance of your wireless configuration utility may vary somewhat, but they all function in practically the same manner. Select **Set up a wireless ad hoc (computer-to-computer) network**, then click **Next**.

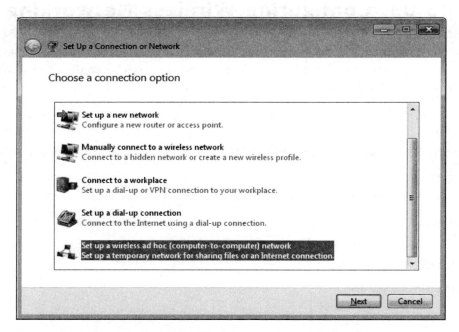

Figure 15-1 The Windows 7 Set Up a Connection or Network Wizard

Step 2 On each PC that you want to operate in ad hoc mode, change the following settings:

- Set the network adapter to operate in ad hoc mode.

- Configure a unique (nondefault) SSID name, such as NETPLUSLAB.

- Configure a common broadcasting channel.

What are the results?

_____

_____

Step 3 Configuring a wireless network to operate in infrastructure mode requires several extra steps when compared to ad hoc mode: clear, configure, and then connect.

First, plug the WAP into an electrical outlet. If it's been installed in a network before, you should reset it to factory defaults. That will clear out any sort of configurations, and you'll be able to use the default user name and password to configure it. Almost every WAP has a reset button that you hold for a certain length of time to reset it. If you don't have documentation for the WAP, go for 10 seconds or longer.

Second, plug a stand-alone computer or portable into the WAP using an Ethernet or USB cable (depending on which connection the WAP has). Most consumer-grade WAPs, like the Linksys WRT54G, come bundled with an enabled DHCP server, so as long as the computer you use is set up for DHCP, it'll get an IP address that will enable you to access the WAP's Web interface and configure the WAP.

Configuration is done using—you guessed it—a configuration utility supplied by the wireless access point's maker. In some cases, the utility is browser-based, and you simply open your Web browser, point to a special local IP address (such as 192.168.1.1), and enter a password when prompted to access the utility. Other access points require that you install a dedicated configuration utility program. Figure 15-2 shows the configuration utility for a Linksys wireless access point.

As with the wireless network adapter configuration utility, the wireless access point configuration utility may vary in appearance depending on the make and model, but the functions should be practically identical. Launch your access point configuration utility and do the following:

- Configure a unique (nondefault) SSID name, such as TRAVELSTOP.

- Change from the default broadcasting channel to a different channel.

- If the access point is configured as a DHCP server, disable this setting.

- Change the WAP's IP address so that it fits in the same network ID as your wired network. Be careful not to use an IP address that can be assigned to another device via DHCP.

Save the new configuration settings on the access point.

Finally, connect the WAP to your wired network segment. Installation is a simple matter of connecting it to a network outlet, switch, or patch panel via a patch cable.

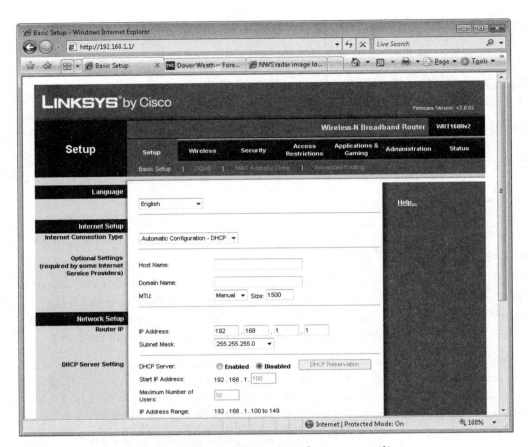

FIGURE 15-2 The Linksys WRT160N Web-based configuration utility

What are the results? Are wireless network nodes able to communicate with the access point? Are wireless network nodes able to communicate with each other?

_____

_____

Step 4   Now configure your wireless network nodes with settings that match the new configuration of your wireless access point (SSID, broadcast channel). What are the results? Are wireless network nodes able to communicate with the access point? Are wireless network nodes able to communicate with each other?

_____

_____

Step 5   In a real-world setting, you would never leave the WAP wide open. To bring the security up to an acceptable level, locate and configure the following settings on your wireless access point:

- Change the default user name (if possible) and password for the configuration utility.

- Enable WPA2-Personal encryption on the WAP and configure each wireless network node with the appropriate passphrase.

- What are the results?

_____

_____

✔ **Exam Tip**

The CompTIA Network+ exam might ask a question about securing wireless networks that calls for more than encryption and changing the default user name and password. If MAC filtering is one of the other options, select it, even though you shouldn't rely on MAC filtering for security today.

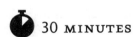 30 MINUTES

Lab Exercise 15.04: Troubleshooting Wireless Networks

The famous science fiction writer Arthur C. Clarke coined one of my favorite sayings when he stated in his third law, "Any sufficiently advanced technology is indistinguishable from magic." Wireless networking isn't quite that advanced, but the results are nonetheless quite impressive—when they work correctly. When they don't work correctly, wireless networks afford network techs some unique opportunities to display their troubleshooting acumen.

Learning Objectives

In this lab, you will troubleshoot some common wireless networking issues. When you have completed this lab, you will be able to

- Diagnose and troubleshoot common wireless networking problems

Lab Materials and Setup

The materials you'll need for this lab are

- Two Windows PCs equipped with Wi-Fi network adapters (Windows XP, Vista, or Windows 7)

- A wireless access point (802.11g or 802.11n recommended)

Getting Down to Business

You have successfully installed and configured the wireless network model to be implemented in the highway rest stops. Maggie now asks you to demonstrate steps for troubleshooting simple problems before you tear down the wireless networking lab.

Step 1   List at least three steps you should take to determine if a loss of wireless connectivity is due to your wireless network adapter's hardware or software configuration.

Step 2   After determining that your wireless network adapter is functioning correctly, how can you find out whether your network node has proper connectivity and signal strength to the wireless network?

Step 3   Name at least three factors that could cause poor signal strength between wireless network nodes.

Step 4   Assuming that a loss of wireless connectivity is not caused by improper hardware or software configuration, excessive distance between wireless network nodes, or environmental factors, what should you check next?

Lab Analysis

1. Max has just purchased an 802.11n AP for his home network. He installs the device and configures the network, but seems to have some intermittent drops of connectivity. Explain the types of wireless consumer electronics that may cause interference with an 802.11n wireless network.

_____

_____

2. Brian has been doing some research on the various RF broadcasting methods that are in use for Wi-Fi devices. He asks you to explain the different broadcast methods used by direct sequence spread spectrum (DSSS), frequency-hopping spread spectrum (FHSS), and orthogonal frequency-division multiplexing (OFDM) devices.

_____

_____

3. Mary has just purchased a dual-band 802.11n wireless router. While reviewing the specifications, she notices that it claims to be backward-compatible not only with 802.11b/g, but also with 802.11a. How is this possible? Would you recommend that Mary purchase any 802.11a NICs for her network since they are compatible?

_____

_____

4. Willy has been looking over your proposal for the wireless network implementation for the highway rest stops and would like to know why you do not recommend using MAC address filtering as an added security measure. What is your explanation?

_____

_____

5. Justin is a network administrator for a local university. He is configuring a wireless network to cover the student and faculty common areas. The wireless network will tie into the campus network, so all of the students and faculty will use their existing user names and passwords. How should Justin configure the wireless authentication?

_____

_____

Key Term Quiz

Use the vocabulary terms from the list below to complete the sentences that follow. Not all of the terms will be used.

ad hoc mode

association

basic service set (BSS)

direct sequence spread spectrum (DSSS)

Extended Basic Service Set (EBSS)

Extended Service Set Identifier (ESSID)

frequency-hopping spread spectrum (FHSS)

infrastructure mode

orthogonal frequency-division multiplexing (OFDM)

Service Set Identifier (SSID)

Wi-Fi

Wi-Fi Protected Access 2 (WPA2)

Wired Equivalent Privacy (WEP)

wireless access point

1. When multiple access points (APs) are used on the same network segment and share the same network name, this is referred to as a(n) _____.

2. A study group at your school consisting of 7 to 10 students meets regularly to exchange notes and research. The group members all have Wi-Fi–equipped laptop computers. The meetings take place at different locations on and off the school campus. The group members should configure their laptops to use _____ when they meet.

3. One of the specifications that changed between 802.11-based wireless networking flavors is that 802.11a/b-based technology uses the _____ broadcasting method, while 802.11g/n uses the _____ broadcasting method.

4. The _____ method of data encryption provides a considerable security improvement as compared to the _____ method of data encryption.

5. Wireless access points enable network techs to connect wireless network nodes to a wired network segment in _____.

Chapter 16
Protecting Your Network

Lab Exercises

Network protection covers many different security aspects. You have probably already explored the various anti-virus, anti-spyware, and anti-adware programs that fight against the infections of malware (especially if you are a CompTIA A+ certified technician). Likewise, the topic of RAID (Redundant Array of Inexpensive Disks) should be familiar from your prior studies. You have worked with encryption in Chapter 11, "Secure TCP/IP Applications," and VPNs in Chapter 12, "Advanced Networking Devices." Now it's time to review some of these components and some new concepts too, because they apply to the protection of both computer networks and critical data.

Given the many options available, these labs concentrate on a number of fundamental concepts and components that demonstrate technology and techniques for protecting your network. In the first lab, you will analyze some of the common types of threats that could possibly affect your network and corrupt or destroy the important data. Next, you will implement password policies in Windows to protect the network from uninvited access. The third lab covers the management of user accounts, groups, and access to resources with the principle of least privilege. The next two labs cover the same issue—firewalls—but show how even this fairly narrow topic can manifest itself in both hardware devices (usually combined with other protective mechanisms) and software implementations.

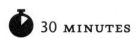 30 MINUTES

Lab Exercise 16.01: Analyzing Threats

As briefly described in the opening paragraphs of this chapter, there are countless threats, malicious or otherwise, that can affect the security of a network and therefore the data contained within. These threats range from the simple but possibly time-consuming loss of data from a hard drive or server crash to the devastating results of information stolen through a mismanaged administrative account or a Trojan horse.

Effective protection of the network (and the data) requires due diligence on the part of the network administrator when it comes to analyzing these threats and warding them off or planning contingency measures. Employers (and the CompTIA Network+ exam) expect the network tech to have a working knowledge of the various threats that are waiting to pounce on the unsuspecting network.

Learning Objectives

In this lab, you will review the common threats you may encounter when working as a network technician. When you have completed this lab, you will be able to

- Describe the methods to protect systems from hardware failure

- Define account management

- List and detail the various forms of malware

- Explain the concept of social engineering

- Define man-in-the-middle attacks

- Provide the definition of a Denial of Service (DoS) attack

- Implement physical security

- Guard against attacks on wireless connections

Lab Materials and Setup

The materials you'll need for this lab are

- A computer with Internet access

- The *Mike Meyers' CompTIA Network+ Guide to Managing and Troubleshooting Networks* textbook

- Pencil and paper

Getting Down to Business

Now that you are progressing well through your studies and are almost ready to sit the CompTIA Network+ exam, CJ has a request. It has been a while since the department has provided an update to the business managers on the security measures in place to protect the network and corporate data. He asks you to conduct a study of the most common threats affecting networks today (from small home networks to large corporate enterprises) and present a report as part of the team's presentation to management.

Use both the textbook and the Internet for your research. Work through the following steps and further refine your knowledge of threats to the network.

Step 1 Provide a brief description of each of the following hardware fault-tolerance measures:

Fault-Tolerance Measure	Description
RAID 1	
RAID 5	
Redundant power supply	
Redundant NIC	
Load balancing	

Step 2   Outline some common steps to fully protect access to the administration of networking components such as routers, switches, file servers, domain controllers, and the administrative tools found within.

_____

_____

Step 3   Provide an appropriate definition for each of the listed types of malware:

Malware	Definition
Virus	
Worm	
Macro virus	
Trojan horse	
Rootkit	

Step 4   Define the method and purpose of social engineering.

_____

_____

Step 5   What is phishing?

_____

_____

Step 6   Provide a scenario depicting a man-in-the-middle attack.

_____

_____

Step 7   Document a Denial of Service (DoS) attack.

_____

_____

Step 8 Discuss some of the methods used to provide the physical security of networks.

_____

_____

Step 9 Explain the factors that might lead to network intrusion through wireless connections.

_____

_____

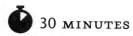 30 MINUTES

Lab Exercise 16.02: Managing Password Policies

One of the most important safeguards against unwanted access to corporate client PCs and servers (and therefore, the network) is a strong password. Many systems, including Microsoft Windows Vista, Windows 7, Windows Server 2003, and Windows Server 2008, include security policies that allow you to configure various settings that control how a user's password can be formulated.

Your part of the job that includes managing users and security will have you address account passwords, ensuring that only the people who should have access to the particular system they are trying to access actually do have access.

Learning Objectives

In this lab, you will configure computer security and develop a template for assigning a strong password. When you have completed this lab, you will be able to

- Create a password policy

- Edit account security settings

- Log on to a system with a valid account and change the password to meet strong password requirements

Lab Materials and Setup

The materials you'll need for this lab are

- Access to a computer with at least one of the following operating systems installed:

  Windows XP Professional
  Windows Vista (Business or Ultimate)
  Windows 7 (Professional, Enterprise, or Ultimate)
  Windows Server 2003 or Windows Server 2008

Getting Down to Business

Maggie has been asked to set up a group policy structure for the marketing department of a new client. She invites you to tag along as she defines and tests the user account password policy that she will implement.

→ **Note**

In a corporate environment such as ITCF and many of their clients, the password policy would be configured for the various departments and all of the users on a global basis. If the corporation is using Microsoft architecture, the corporate network will be defined by Active Directory domains, various organization units, and Group Policy Objects. Typically, the actual configuration of system settings will take place on a Windows Server 2003 or Windows Server 2008 Domain Controller using the Active Directory Group Policy Object editor.

For the purposes of the Lab Exercise, the exploration and configuration of the password policy can be completely facilitated on a PC running Windows XP Professional; Windows Vista Business or Ultimate; Windows 7 Professional, Enterprise, or Ultimate; Windows Server 2003; or Windows Server 2008. The author used Windows 7 Enterprise for this Lab Exercise.

Step 1 Log on to the lab system with an administrator account. On a Windows 7 Enterprise machine, select **Start | Control Panel | System and Security | Administrative Tools | Local Security Policy | Account Policies | Password Policy**. Depending on the version of Windows you are using, the navigation may vary. (See Figure 16-1.)

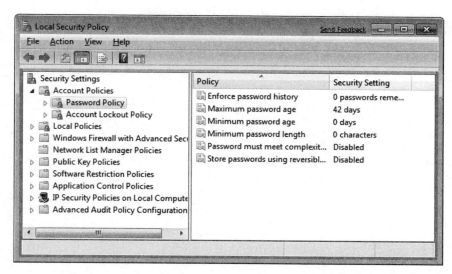

FIGURE 16-1 Password policy configuration screen

Step 2   In the **Local Security Settings** screen, set the following values for the various password policy security settings:

Enforce password history	10
Maximum password age	30
Minimum password age	0
Minimum password length	8
Password must meet complexity requirements	Enabled
Store passwords using reversible encryption	Disabled

Step 3   If you are working with Windows 7, right-click **Computer** and select **Manage** from the drop-down menu; this selects the Computer Management Console. Open the **Local Users and Groups** system tool, and then open **Users**. Create a new user named **TheresaR** and attempt to use the following password. (See Figure 16-2.)

secret

What are the results? Are they similar to the message shown in Figure 16-3?

FIGURE 16-2 Microsoft Windows 7 New User applet

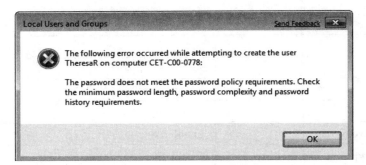

FIGURE 16-3 Local Users and Groups error message

Now, using the same user name, TheresaR, make sure that the **User must change password at next logon** check box is selected, and attempt to use the following password.

$3cR3+101

→ **Note**

Make sure that the password is typed exactly as it appears in the example. The use of both upper- and lowercase characters, special characters, and numerical characters is imperative to meet password complexity requirements.

Step 4   Log off the machine and log back on as TheresaR. When prompted to change the password, enter the same password and click OK. What are the results?

_____

_____

_____

Step 5   If the same password is unsuccessful, try to use the following password.

$3cR3+2o2

What are the results?

_____

_____

_____

 30 MINUTES

Lab Exercise 16.03: Controlling the User's Access to Resources

Now that you have addressed the account passwords, ensuring that only the people who should have access to the particular system are the ones who do, you need to address the level of access they have to the various resources on the system. This is where you apply the "principle of least privilege." The concept is to assign the lowest access permissions possible that allow the users to still do their jobs.

Obviously, only administrators should have access to the administrative resources and infrastructure components such as the management of servers, switches, and routers. However, even various users from different departments should be restricted as to what they can access outside of their area of responsibility. For instance, an employee from the marketing department will probably be restricted from access to the financial department's records, but will have limited access to sales department information.

Since there are usually multiple employees in each department who will need access to certain data and will need to be restricted from access to other data, most network operating systems provide some way to organize the users into security groups. These groups are then assigned the proper access permissions for the various data on the network systems.

Learning Objectives

In this lab, you will create a number of security groups and assign various share rights to resources by group membership. When you have completed this lab, you will be able to

- Create security groups

- Make users members of the various groups

- Assign proper permissions to resources based on group membership

Lab Materials and Setup

The materials you'll need for this lab are

- Two Windows computers networked together, each with one of the following operating systems installed:

  Windows XP Professional
  Windows Vista (Business or Ultimate)
  Windows 7 (Professional, Enterprise, or Ultimate)
  Windows Server 2003 or Windows Server 2008

Getting Down to Business

Maggie is still working with the new structure for the marketing department of the new client. She has implemented the password policy and is now going to create the marketing group, assign members, and configure the various rights to the resources on the systems.

Step 1 Log on to the first lab system with an administrator account, right-click **Computer**, and select **Manage** from the drop-down menu. Open the **Local Users and Groups** system tool, and then open **Groups**. Create new groups named **Finance**, **Marketing**, and **Sales**. (See Figure 16-4.)

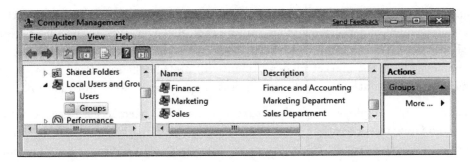

FIGURE 16-4 Creating groups in Local Users and Groups

Step 2 Now double-click the **Marketing** group and select **Add | Members**. Use the **Advanced | Find Now** tool or manually add the TheresaR user account to the marketing group. In Figure 16-5, the **Select Users** screen, observe that the user account TheresaR on computer CET-C00-0778 has been selected. When you click the **OK** button, TheresaR will be added as a member of the Marketing group.

Step 3 You need to create three document folders, one for each department, share them out, and assign permissions for proper access. Begin by creating the marketing folder MarketDocs and assigning the Marketing group the share permission of **Change**. (See Figure 16-6.)

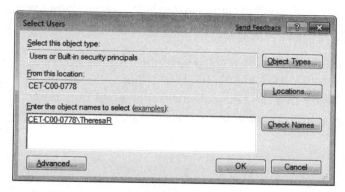

FIGURE 16-5 Adding a member to the Marketing group

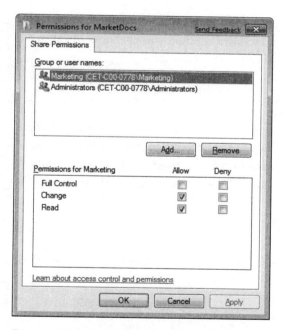

FIGURE 16-6 Assigning the Marketing group the Change permission in the Share Permissions tab for MarketDocs

Next, create the SalesDocs folder and assign the Sales group the share permission of **Change** and the Marketing group the share permission of **Read**. Last, create the FinanceDocs folder and assign the Finance group the share permission of **Change**.

✔ **Tech Tip**

If you are a CompTIA A+ Certified Technician, you have worked with Microsoft Windows Share permissions and NTFS Security permissions. The CompTIA Network+ exam will not test your knowledge of these components; however, you should be familiar with their contribution to protecting your network and the resources on your network.

To facilitate this Lab Exercise, you will not configure any NTFS security (leaving the Everyone group with Full Control). For each of the three folders you create, in addition to the specific groups mentioned in Step 3, you should verify that the Everyone group is removed from the share permissions and that the Administrators group is added to the share permissions with Full Control.

Step 4   To simulate a real corporate environment, you are now going to add a file or two to each of the folders you just created. While still logged on with an administrative account, create a new text document in each of these folders: MarketDocs, SalesDocs, and FinanceDocs.

Step 5   Now log on to the second computer and using whichever method you prefer, connect to the first computer using the user account TheresaR and explore the shared folders.

✔ **Hint**

One of the methods to log on to a remote computer and explore the shared folders is to use the Run dialog box and type the UNC of the computer you want to connect to. For instance, if the name of the first computer is Computer1, then you would type **\\Computer1** in the Run dialog box. You will be prompted for a user name and password. This is where you would log on as TheresaR.

If you have configured the folders correctly, you should see a window similar to the one in Figure 16-7.

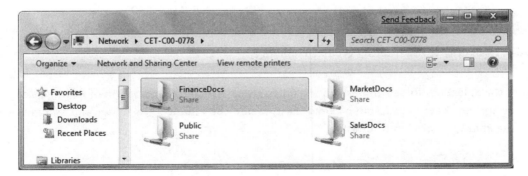

FIGURE 16-7 Shared folders available on the first computer

Step 6 Attempt to access the MarketDocs folder. Are you are able to access the folder? If yes, attempt to read the sample file contained within. Were you able to read it? Now right-click anywhere in the window space of the MarketDocs folder and create a new text document. What are the results?

_____

_____

Step 7 Next, attempt to access the SalesDocs folder. Are you are able to access the folder? If yes, attempt to read the sample file contained within. Were you able to read it? Now right-click anywhere in the window space of the SalesDocs folder and create a new text document. What are the results?

_____

_____

Step 8 Lastly, attempt to access the FinanceDocs folder. Are you are able to access the folder? If yes, attempt to read the sample file contained within. Were you able to read it? Now right-click anywhere in the window space of the FinanceDocs folder and create a new text document. What are the results?

_____

_____

 45 MINUTES

Lab Exercise 16.04: Hardware Firewalls: Linksys Firewall Configuration

With the proliferation of the Internet and the wonderful communication capabilities it affords comes the proliferation of dishonest people and programs attempting to exploit that communications capability for illicit gain. There is no question that educating individuals and organizations on how to practice safe Internet usage is the first step toward protecting the network from these unscrupulous thieves. However, sophisticated infiltration programs require sophisticated intrusion protection to keep the network safe. Enter _firewalls_!

Firewalls are devices that protect networks and computers by filtering TCP/IP traffic. There are many companies offering firewall products, most of which fall into two categories. The first type is a network-based firewall. This is a firewall that is incorporated into another device such as a router, and along with some other features, works to keep harmful traffic off the network. Since the router is a physical device, this type of firewall is often called a *hardware firewall*. The second type is a host-based firewall. This firewall protects individual computers from harmful traffic. This host-based firewall is also known as a *software firewall* because there is no special hardware; it is just another program on your computer.

You will work with a software firewall in the next Lab Exercise. For now you are going to research hardware firewalls and configure a Linksys wireless router to protect your network.

Learning Objectives

In this lab, you'll explore hardware firewalls. When you have completed this lab, you'll be able to

- Identify hardware firewalls provided by various manufacturers
- Define the components that typically make up a hardware firewall
- Configure and optimize a Linksys wireless router to protect the network

Lab Materials and Setup

The materials you need for this lab are

- A PC with Internet connectivity
- The *Mike Meyers' CompTIA Network+ Guide to Managing and Troubleshooting Networks* textbook
- Pencil and paper
- A Linksys wireless router such as the WRT160N router

Getting Down to Business

Hardware firewalls, by design, are physical devices with a collection of features designed to protect your network from the unwanted entry of programs or people from the outside world. These devices can be dedicated security sentry devices, robust edge routers, or simple SOHO wireless routers with various components to ward off uninvited access.

The distinction between "hardware" and "software" firewalls really comes down to where the firewall software resides. If it is on a dedicated device such as a Cisco Adaptive Security Appliance (ASA) or a router, it is considered a hardware firewall. If it is host-based (on an individual computer), it is considered a software firewall.

Step 1   Research the current offerings in the hardware firewall market. Identify the make, model, and key features of at least three devices.

1. _____

2. _____

3. _____

Step 2 One of the benefits of using a hardware firewall device is that the traditional firewall protection (usually the Stateful Packet Inspection [SPI] component is considered to be the actual firewall) is not the only protection included. Define some of the other features that are offered by hardware firewalls.

_____

_____

_____

_____

Step 3 Now it is time to configure a simple SOHO wireless router to protect your network from outside intrusion. Start by logging on to the administrative application of the wireless router. Figure 16-8 shows the **Security** page of a Linksys WRT160N wireless router. By default, most of the firewall protection will be enabled on Linksys routers, so this will most likely be a review of the settings.

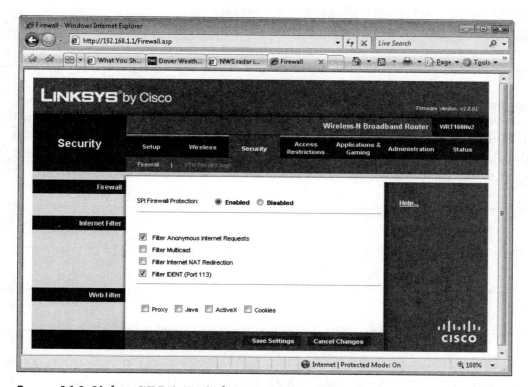

FIGURE 16-8 Linksys WRT160N wireless router Security page

Is your firewall enabled? What specific filters are enabled?

_____

_____

✔ **Hint**

To understand better some of the functions of the Linksys routers that you are exploring in Steps 3, 4, and 5, Linksys provides excellent help files for all of the configurable options on their routers. Take a moment to scroll through the different options for the security settings, advanced router settings, and application and gaming settings.

Step 4   Now navigate over to the **Advanced Routing** menu screen. This is where you can configure Network Address Translation (NAT). Again the default setting for this is enabled, and it is recommended to use the default settings if the router is the gateway to your Internet.

Is NAT enabled?

_____

Step 5   When you're working in the corporate environment, it would not be unusual to host either e-mail servers or Web servers for the corporation. As discussed in the textbook, the outside world will need less restricted access to these servers in order for the public to have access to them. The method to provide this lightly protected access to the servers is known as a demilitarized zone (DMZ). Provide a brief summary of how a DMZ is configured.

_____

_____

_____

Linksys routers actually provide a method to create a DMZ (see Figure 16-9). Navigate to the **Applications & Gaming** menu item and click the submenu **DMZ**. How does the Linksys router facilitate a DMZ? What are the recommendations for alternative methods?

_____

_____

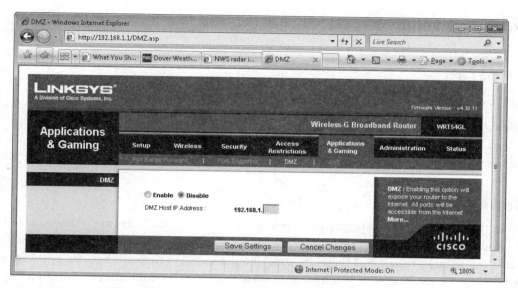

FIGURE 16-9 Linksys WRT54GL wireless router DMZ configuration screen

 45 MINUTES

Lab Exercise 16.05: Software Firewalls: Windows Firewall Configuration

The popularity of (and need for) software firewalls motivated the folks at Microsoft to build a software firewall into Windows XP called Internet Connection Firewall (ICF). With the introduction of Service Pack 2 for Windows XP through Windows 7, Microsoft now includes the (renamed) Windows Firewall as a standard security application.

Learning Objectives

In this lab, you will review the functions of a software firewall and run the Windows Firewall in a Windows environment. When you have completed this lab, you'll be able to

- Describe the function of the Windows Firewall
- Configure Windows Firewall on a Windows XP, Windows Vista, or Windows 7 machine

Lab Materials and Setup

The materials you need for this lab are

- Pencil and paper

- Access to a computer with at least one of the following operating systems installed:

  Windows XP (Service Pack 2 or better)
  Windows Vista
  Windows 7

Getting Down to Business

As you learned in the last exercise, the distinction between "hardware" and "software" firewalls really comes down to where the firewall software resides. The Microsoft Windows Firewall is a host-based (on an individual computer) firewall and therefore considered a software firewall. You can't go wrong with enabling Windows Firewall; even if you have a wireless router with a firewall, you'll just end up enhancing the security.

Step 1   There are a number of ways to access the Windows Firewall configuration applet, so use the method that you prefer. I find it easy to just click **Start | Control Panel | System and Security** and select **Windows Firewall**. What is your current Windows Firewall status? (See Figure 16-10.)

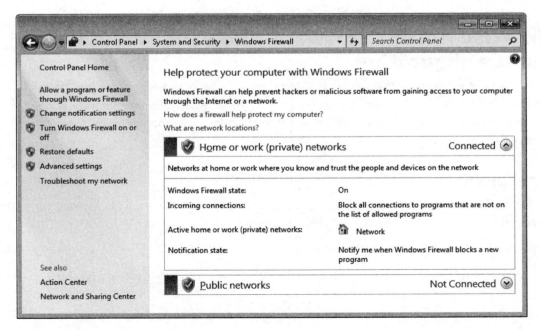

Figure 16-10 Windows Firewall

Step 2 As you have learned, Windows Firewall is a host-based, software firewall. Using the Internet, determine if the Windows Firewall is of the Stateful Packet Inspection (SPI) type. Provide a short definition of SPI.

_____

_____

_____

_____

Step 3 Could you run a Web server on the system running Windows Firewall? What would you need to do?

_____

_____

Step 4 Your cousin Brandon wants to operate a game server on the computer running Windows Firewall. This game server needs ports 7777 and 7787. Can you open these ports in Windows Firewall to allow a system to act as a game server? What steps would you need to take?

_____

_____

Lab Analysis

1. Sandra and Cathy are having a slight disagreement. They have just visited the physical site where a large Internet retailer houses their servers. There are hundreds of servers configured to service the thousands of customers that access the site. Sandra believes that the main function of the server farm is load balancing, while Cathy thinks it is to provide fault tolerance. Who do you think is correct?

_____

_____

2. Kyle is working in his cubicle one day when the phone rings. He answers it and is surprised to hear that it is one of the network administrators from the IT department. The gentleman identifies

himself as Mike, and says that he needs to verify Kyle's user name and password. Kyle hesitates, leans over his cubicle wall, and tells you what's happening. What would you recommend Kyle do?

_____

_____

3. Austin has been attempting to get on the company Web site for over a half an hour and has not been able to connect. He calls the helpdesk and they tell him that the company network is under a DDoS attack. Austin would like to know what this is. How would you explain a DDoS attack to Austin?

_____

_____

4. Daniel is using Windows Vista at home and has implemented the Windows Firewall to protect his computer. It works great, and he wonders why network administrators at his company spend so much money on dedicated firewall devices. His company hosts a couple of Web servers and about 100 employees. What would you tell Dan to clarify when to use one or the other?

_____

_____

5. Robbie, one of the employees at your company, keeps forgetting his password. He would like to know why he has to use all of these goofy characters and change it every 30 days. He confides in you that he is going to jot down his password this time and hide it under the keyboard. How would you help Robbie understand the reason for the difficult password and the 30-day restriction, and encourage him not to write down his password?

_____

_____

Key Term Quiz

Use the vocabulary terms from the list below to complete the sentences that follow. Not all of the terms will be used.

authentication

demilitarized zone (DMZ)

Denial of Service (DoS) attack

encryption

external threat

firewall

hacker

honeypot

internal threat

man-in-the-middle attack

Network Address Translation (NAT)

network threat

packet filtering

port blocking

port filtering

Secure Sockets Layer (SSL)

social engineering

Windows Firewall

zombie attack

1. A user with improperly configured file access permissions who accidentally deletes an important file is a classic example of a(n) _____.

2. Someone posing as an IT support person and calling a user to get her user name and password is an example of _____.

3. You are at a local coffee shop and begin to log on to the wireless network when you notice that the SSID is CAFENOT. This could be an indication of a(n) _____ since the normal SSID is CAFENET.

4. Any device that filters TCP/IP traffic based on IP address or port number is by definition a(n) _____.

5. _____ enables a gateway system to convert IP addresses, thereby hiding the IP addresses of your local network from the Internet.

Chapter 17

Virtualization

Lab Exercises

At this point in your studies, you have already worked with virtual environments. You have configured virtual local area networks (VLANs) to organize groups of physical ports on a switch logically, placing the machines connected to those ports into separate networks. You have also worked with virtual private networks (VPNs) to tunnel safely through the Internet as if you were directly connected to a remote machine. In essence, even the non-virtual Lab Exercises that you have worked through are simulations of what you might deal with in the real world—a *virtual* example of the real situation, if you will!

Now you're going to go from using virtual environments to creating virtual machines! A major trend in desktops and servers is to use one physical computer, install a host operating system, and then deploy multiple virtual machines on top of the hosting OS to meet the needs of the users. The ultimate example of virtualization would be the modern data center where thousands of servers are now hosted on just a few hundred physical machines.

There are various implementations of virtual hardware (desktops, servers, switches, and PBXes) offered by multiple vendors (VMware, Citrix, Microsoft, Oracle, and Parallels, to name a few). These virtualization technologies set up the environment so that you may install and run various operating systems on the same hardware platform simultaneously! Not only does this promote efficient use of hardware and energy resources, but virtualization also enables you to create images of the virtual machine easily, providing excellent fault tolerance and disaster recovery options.

No need to don your 3D glasses here; just work through the Lab Exercises in this chapter to develop your "virtual" understanding!

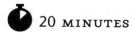 20 MINUTES

Lab Exercise 17.01: Identifying Virtualization Technologies

Virtualization takes on many aspects of the physical devices used every day in the computing environment. Organizations may choose to install multiple virtual servers on one physical machine to handle Web services, e-mail services, file sharing, and print services, to name a few.

In the Lab Exercises for this chapter, you will have the opportunity to install three of the most popular virtual machine technologies available today, but this is only one component of virtualization. Before you work with the actual virtualization programs and before you take the CompTIA Network+ certification exam, you will want to explore all of the technologies associated with virtualization. This Lab Exercise covers virtual desktops, virtual servers, virtual switches, virtual PBXes, and Network as a Service (NaaS) implementations.

Time to explore!

Learning Objectives

At the completion of this lab, you will be able to

- Define virtual desktop technologies

- Define virtual server technologies

- Detail the characteristics of virtual switches

- Describe the function of a virtual PBX

- Detail key components and features of Network as a Service (NaaS)

Lab Materials and Setup

The materials you'll need for this lab are

- A PC with Internet access

- The *Mike Meyers' CompTIA Network+ Guide to Managing and Troubleshooting Networks* textbook

- Pencil and paper

Getting Down to Business

You will install and configure a number of virtualization technologies and operating systems in the next few Lab Exercises. Before you do, it is important that you understand the underlying solutions that virtualization technology provides. Maggie collects a list of virtual technologies and asks you to use your textbook and the Internet to develop a brief description and summary of the characteristics of each of the technologies.

Step 1   Start by researching virtual desktop technology. What are the key features and typical applications for virtual desktop technology?

_____

_____

_____

_____

Step 2   Virtual servers are similar to virtual desktops, but provide some advanced features and support for applications not found in the virtual desktop offerings. Describe some of these advanced features.

_____

_____

_____

_____

Step 3   There are two methods to handle the connection and communication between multiple virtual machines on the same host as well as with the outside world. One method bridges the virtual machines to a physical NIC, and the other employs a _virtual switch_ to interface between the virtual machines and the physical NIC. Discuss the aspects of a virtual switch.

_____

_____

_____

_____

Step 4   When you have a large organization, one of the methods to satisfy a large number of phone extensions is to install a PBX (Private Branch eXchange) to enable the internal phone extensions to use a smaller number of external public extensions. A trend that looks as if it will continue to grow is the migration to virtual PBXes. What are some of the features of virtual PBXes?

_____

_____

_____

_____

Step 5   When researching the virtualization technologies mentioned, you may have seen some reference to onsite versus offsite implementations. Dig a little deeper and discuss onsite vs. offsite virtual solutions.

_____

_____

_____

_____

Step 6   When you start talking about offsite virtual solutions, inevitably discussions turn to cloud computing and Network as a Service (NaaS). What is NaaS?

_____

_____

_____

_____

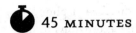

45 MINUTES

Lab Exercise 17.02: Installing and Configuring VMware Player

VMware is arguably the leader in large-scale, enterprise-wide virtualization. With scalable products from vSphere and ESXi, which are fully featured solutions for datacenters and cloud providers, to VMware Player, which is free to individuals exploring virtual solutions for their personal PC, VMware offers solutions at every level.

To introduce you to VMware, you will download VMware Player and install it on a Windows 7 machine, and then you will run Ubuntu Linux in the virtual machine. Many training organizations have adopted virtualization to enable swift reconfiguration of systems for specific demonstrations or to implement complex lab exercises. When working through this Lab Exercise, you may have access to VMware vCenter Lab Manager or ESXi. If so, your instructor may have you apply the basic steps that follow using one of these solutions.

✔ Tech Tip

In the next three Lab Exercises in this chapter, you will use virtualization software to create virtual machines. Virtual machines are exactly like physical computers in that they need operating systems to work. Prior to beginning the Lab Exercises, you will want to prepare the operating system installation media. Two of the Lab Exercises will use Ubuntu Linux as their operating system, and the others will use Windows XP.

At the time of this writing, **Ubuntu 10.04 LTS** seems like a good choice for the Linux systems as it will be supported for five years from April 2010 to April 2015. That's what the LTS stands for, *long-term support*. Plus it's a free Linux distribution. You can download the operating system (OS) at www.ubuntu.com.

Create an installation disc or copy the installation disc image (.iso) to a flash drive for use in the Lab Exercises.

Learning Objectives

In this Lab Exercise, you will use VMware Player virtualization software to install a virtual Ubuntu machine on a Windows 7 PC. You will then explore a few of the Ubuntu programs and commands. At the end of this Lab Exercise, you will be able to

a.   Install and configure VMware Player on a Windows 7 host system

b.   Install and run Ubuntu 10.04 LTS as a guest OS in VMware Player

Lab Materials and Setup

The materials you'll need for this lab are

- A system connected to the Internet or access to VMware Player

- Ubuntu installation media

- A Windows 7 system

- Pencil and paper

Getting Down to Business

CJ and Maggie would like you to take advantage of the networking lab yet again. This time they want you to explore virtualization! You will be working with three virtualization products over the next three Lab Exercises: VMware Player, Microsoft Virtual PC, and Oracle VM VirtualBox. The networking lab offers an excellent environment to work through the idiosyncrasies of each of the products to see how they work before deploying them on production systems.

You'll start with VMware Player, a hosted Virtual Machine Manager.

Step 1 Launch your browser and navigate to www.vmware.com. This is the home of VMware. Run your pointer over the **Support & Downloads** tab at the top of the page. Under **Product Downloads**, click the hyperlink for **All Downloads**, and then select **VMware Player** under the **Desktop & End-User Computing menu**. Click on the **Download** button as shown in Figure 17-1. To download **VMware Player**, you will have to register with a valid e-mail address. Complete the registration and download **VMware Player 4.0 for 32-bit and 64-bit Windows**.

Step 2 Copy the file **VMware-player-4.0.0-471780.exe** to the Windows 7 system that will host the virtual Ubuntu system (if other than the system you just used to download the installation program) and follow the instructions in sub-steps 2a through 2e:

a. Double-click the file **VMware-player-4.0.0-471780.exe** to launch the installation program. At the **Welcome to the installation wizard for VMware Player** screen, click **Next** (see Figure 17-2).

b. The next screen is the **Destination Folder** screen, where you may choose the default location or select **Change** to install in a different folder. Choose the default location or change the folder where the VMware Player program will be installed.

c. Click **Next** once again, choose the check box to **Check for product updates on startup**, and click **Next**. Now deselect the check box to **Help improve VMware Player** and click **Next**. Select where you would like to create shortcuts for VMware Player and click **Next**.

d. Now you will see the window **Ready to Perform the Requested Operations**. Click **Continue** to begin the process. VMware Player setup will perform the installation. This may take several minutes.

e. You will now be instructed that the setup wizard needs to restart your system. Click **Restart Now** to reboot the Windows 7 machine.

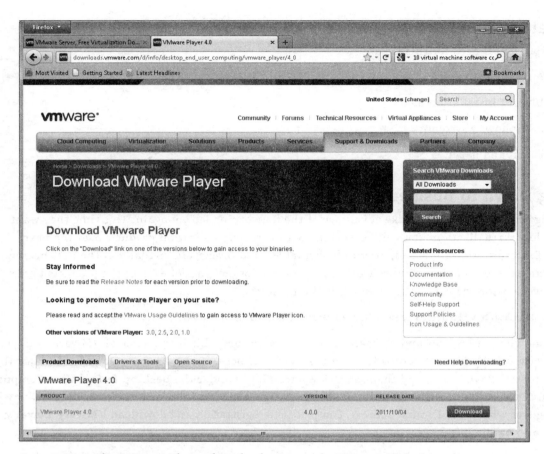

FIGURE 17-1 The VMware Player download page on the VMware Web site

FIGURE 17-2 VMware Player 4 welcome screen

Step 3 On restart, launch the **VMware Player**, create a new virtual machine, and use **Easy Install** to install Ubuntu on the new virtual machine automatically. Perform the tasks in the following instructions to create a new virtual machine:

a. Double-click the **VMware Player** icon and accept the **VMWARE END USER LICENSE AGREEMENT**.

b. At the **Welcome to VMware Player** screen, click the **Create a New Virtual Machine** icon to create a new virtual machine. This will launch the **New Virtual Machine Wizard**. (See Figure 17-3.)

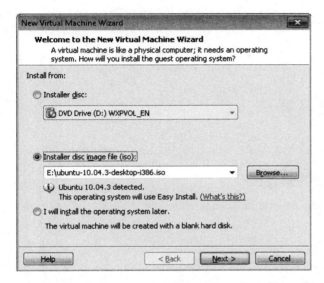

FIGURE 17-3 The VMware Player New Virtual Machine Wizard

c. At this screen, you will choose from where to install the operating system or if you will install the operating system later. You are going to use the **Easy Install** method, installing the operating system as you build the virtual machine. Using your Ubuntu installation media, either insert the CD into the system and choose to install from: **Installer disc** or browse to the disc image and choose to install from: **Installer disc image file (.iso)**. Click **Next**.

d. Next, set up a user name and password for the Ubuntu guest operating system. Enter the name **Student** in the dialog box. Then enter the user name **student** in lowercase and enter a password of your choosing. Click **Next**.

e. You will now name the virtual machine and choose the location for the virtual machine folder. You may use the defaults or change the name and location. Click **Next**.

f. Specify the disk capacity. The recommended size for Ubuntu is 20 GB; however, these systems will probably not go into production, so you may choose a smaller disk capacity for the Lab Exercise. Leave the default setting for **Split virtual disk into multiple files** and click **Next**, splitting the virtual disk (vmdk) into multiple, smaller files. This helps facilitate copying the virtual machine to other media such as a flash drive.

g.   Now you are ready to create the virtual machine. Review the virtual machine settings as shown in Figure 17-4, check the box **Power on this virtual machine after creation**, and then click **Finish** to begin building the virtual machine.

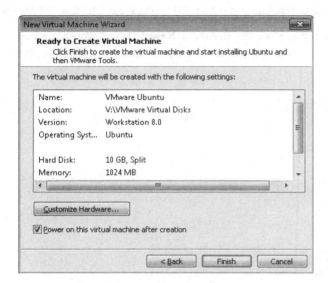

FIGURE 17-4 VMware Player new virtual machine summary page

h.   Depending on your physical hardware, you will receive several hints:

- VMware Player requires a 64-bit processor to run a 64-bit guest operating system. Click **OK**.

- Removable media, such as flash drives, cannot be mounted to both the host operating system and guest operating system simultaneously. You may mount the removable media at a later time. Click **OK** to accept the default.

i.   If your machine is connected to the Internet, you may choose to install **VMware Tools for Ubuntu**. VMware Tools is a suite of utilities that enhances the performance of the virtual machine's guest operating system and improves management of the virtual machine.

If you choose to install the tools at a later time, you will receive an error message at the bottom of the VMware Player window when the system boots. You may ignore this for the Lab Exercise.

Step 4   When the VMware Ubuntu virtual machine reboots, you will be prompted for your user name and password. After entering your information, you will now have a fully functioning installation of

Ubuntu as a guest operating system on top of the host operating system, Windows 7. To explore some of the features of VMware Player, complete the following steps:

a.   Insert a flash drive into the physical host machine.

b.   At the top of the VMware Ubuntu virtual machine window, click on the **Virtual Machine** tab item to open a drop-down menu.

c.   Click on **Removable Devices** and from the expanded menu, choose the flash drive (it may identify the manufacturer such as **SanDisk Cruzer**) and select **Connect (Disconnect from host)**. You will receive the message "A USB device is about to be unplugged from the host and connected to this virtual machine." Click **OK**.

d.   Now in the Ubuntu system, click **Places** and navigate down to the **Computer** icon. Click **Computer** to open the window. Do you see the icon for the flash drive? (See Figure 17-5.)

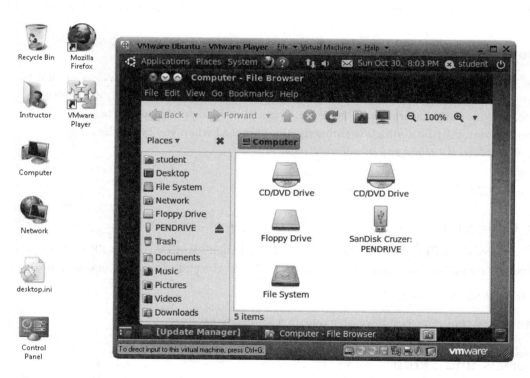

FIGURE 17-5 Ubuntu running in a VMware Player virtual machine on Windows 7. Note the flash drive icon.

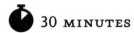

30 MINUTES

Lab Exercise 17.03: Installing and Configuring Windows XP Mode and Windows Virtual PC

As is fairly typical with Microsoft, if there is a technology related to computer applications or operating systems, they have probably designed a product to compete in the market. This is the case with virtualization. Microsoft offers two current products, Windows Virtual PC and Windows Server 2008 R2 Hyper-V. They also provide support for Virtual PC 2007 for backward compatibility (on Microsoft operating systems other than Windows 7).

Microsoft has continued to offer their Virtual PC virtualization software with the inclusion of "Windows XP mode" in Windows 7 to facilitate running legacy programs on a virtual machine running Windows XP, rather than in "compatibility mode." You may also launch new virtual machines and install various Windows operating systems (Windows XP Professional; Windows Vista Business, Enterprise, and Ultimate; and all versions of Windows 7 except Starter) to experience the power of Windows Virtual PC.

✔ **Tech Tip**

Microsoft is very particular with the distribution of Windows XP Mode and Windows Virtual PC. These products will only install on the following systems: Windows 7 Professional, Windows 7 Ultimate, or Windows 7 Enterprise. In addition, you will have to download and install a Windows Activation Update, which is automatically launched when you begin the steps to download Windows XP Mode and Windows Virtual PC.

Learning Objectives

In this Lab Exercise, you will install Windows Virtual PC and then install Windows XP Mode (a preconfigured Windows XP Professional virtual hard disk, or VHD). At the end of this lab, you will be able to

- Install Windows Virtual PC

- Install and configure Windows XP mode on a Windows 7 system

Lab Materials and Setup

The materials you'll need for this lab are

- Windows 7 Professional, Enterprise, or Ultimate

- Internet connectivity

- Pencil and paper

Getting Down to Business

Microsoft has offered a number of Virtual PC products over the years. Microsoft Virtual PC 2004 and Microsoft Virtual PC 2007 supported a number of Microsoft operating systems as guests, including Windows Server 2003 and Windows Server 2008. As previously mentioned, the current offering, Windows Virtual PC, is somewhat limited in the number of Windows operating systems it supports as guests. However, to facilitate legacy applications in Windows 7, Microsoft introduced the Windows XP Mode virtual machine. Windows XP Mode is a virtual machine package for Windows Virtual PC containing a pre-installed, licensed copy of Windows XP Professional with Service Pack 3 as its guest operating system. The Windows XP Mode virtual machine is seamlessly integrated into Windows 7, and offers "one-click launch of Windows XP Mode applications."

Maggie requests that you install Windows XP Mode and Windows Virtual PC and evaluate their functionality.

Step 1 Boot your Windows 7 Professional, Ultimate, or Enterprise system, launch a browser, and navigate to www.microsoft.com/windows/virtual-pc/default.aspx. Click on **Get Windows XP Mode and Windows Virtual PC now,** then select your system and language as shown in Figure 17-6. After you have entered your operating system and language information, a list of four steps will be displayed.

Use the following instructions to complete the four steps:

a. In **Step 1** it is recommended that you either e-mail or print the instructions before restarting your computer.

b. In **Step 2,** click **Windows XP Mode [Download]** to begin the download. Microsoft will install an Activation Update and run a Windows validation process. Once the validation process completes successfully, click **Continue** and save the file **WindowsXPMode_en-us.exe**.

c. In **Step 3** of the online instructions, click **Windows Virtual PC [Download]** and save the file **Windows6.1KB958559-x86-RefreshPkg.msu.**

d. You will only need to perform **Step 4** if you are running Windows 7 without Service Pack 1 (SP1) installed. If you are not running SP1, click on **Windows XP Mode Update.** Verify that all of the required files are in the Download folder and close the browser window.

✔ **Hint**

Earlier versions of Windows 7 and Windows Virtual PC required Hardware Assisted Virtualization Technology. **Step 4** enables Windows XP Mode for PCs without Hardware Assisted Virtualization Technology. If you are running Windows 7 with Service Pack 1 (SP1), you will not be required to run **Step 4.**

Step 2 Now click **Start | Computer | Downloads** and launch the **Windows6.1-KB958559-x86-RefreshPkg.msu** installation file located in the Downloads folder, as shown in Figure 17-7.

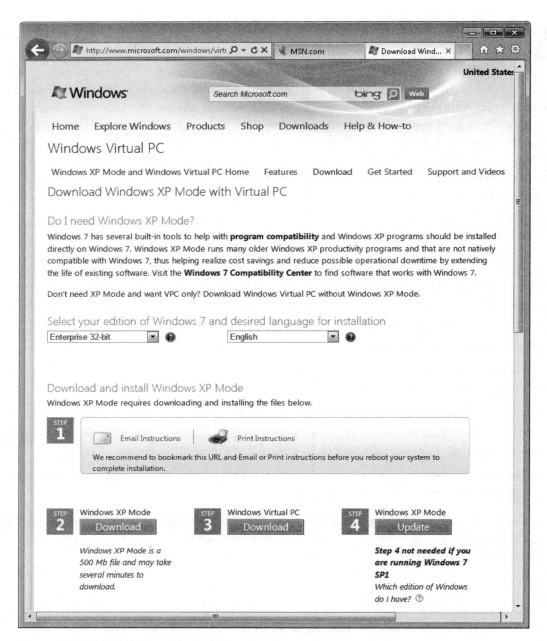

Figure 17-6 The Windows Virtual PC page

Depending on the version of Windows 7, you will either install the x86 (32-bit) or the x64 (64-bit) Windows Virtual PC Update installation file. Some versions of Windows 7 also ship with Windows Virtual PC preinstalled. If your system displays the following message "The update is not applicable to your computer," as shown in Figure 17-8, then check the **Start | All Programs** menu to see if Windows Virtual PC is already installed. What are your results?

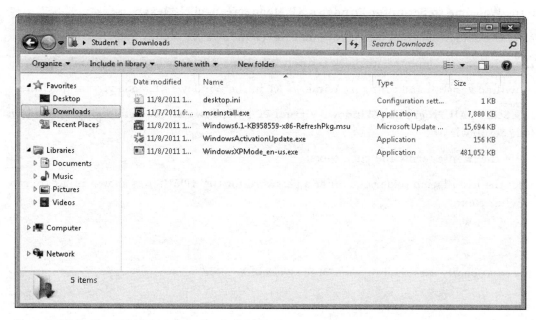

FIGURE 17-7 The Windows Downloads folder showing the Windows Virtual PC Update file and the Windows XP Mode file

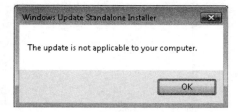

FIGURE 17-8 Windows Update Standalone Installer message

If Windows Update KB958559 (Windows Virtual PC) was not previously installed, follow the directions to install it.

a. Select **Yes** to install the **Update for Windows (KB958559).**

b. Read and accept the license terms to begin the installation.

c. When the installation has completed, you will be instructed to restart your computer for the updates to take effect. Click **Restart Now.**

Step 3 After your computer reboots, you will install the Windows XP Mode virtual machine. Open **Start | Computer | Downloads** and double-click the **WindowsXPMode_en-us.exe** file located in the Downloads folder, as shown earlier in Figure 17-7. Perform the installation directions as follows:

a. Select **Run** when you receive the **Open File - Security Warning.**

b. In the **Welcome to Setup for Windows XP Mode** screen, click **Next.**

c. Select the default location of **c:\Program Files\Windows XP Mode** and click **Next.**

d. When the setup completes, uncheck **Launch Windows XP Mode** and click **Finish.**

Step 4 You will now install and configure Windows XP in the Windows XP Mode virtual machine.

a. Click **Start | All Programs | Windows Virtual PC | Windows XP Mode** to begin the Windows XP Mode Setup wizard.

b. Accept the license terms and click **Next.**

c. Select the installation folder and enter a password for the XPMUser as shown in Figure 17-9, and click **Next.**

✔ **Hint**

Microsoft occasionally uses the initials *XPM* for *Windows XP Mode.*

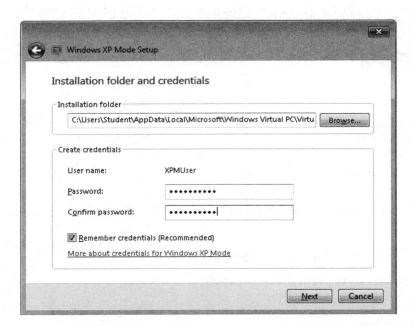

FIGURE 17-9 Installation folder and credentials window in the Windows XP Mode Setup

d. You may now select to help protect your computer by selecting Automatic Updates. Choose either **Help protect my computer by turning on Automatic Updates now. (recommended)** or **Not right now** and then click **Next.**

e. Now click **Start Setup** to start the Windows XP Mode setup. This will take a few minutes and while setting up, the wizard will display some features of Window XP Mode and the steps that are being performed.

f. When the setup completes, you may check the box to launch the Windows XP Mode virtual machine, and then click **Finish.** The Windows XP Mode virtual machine will launch, as shown in Figure 17-10.

FIGURE 17-10 Windows XP Mode – Windows Virtual PC

Step 5 Microsoft has added an interesting feature to the Windows XP Mode virtual machine. If you install a legacy application in the Windows XP Mode virtual machine, it can be made available on the Windows 7 Start menu, as shown in Figure 17-11.

If you have a legacy application installation CD available, follow these steps to explore this feature:

a. Launch the Windows XP Mode virtual machine.

b. Insert the CD or DVD into the optical drive and install the application.

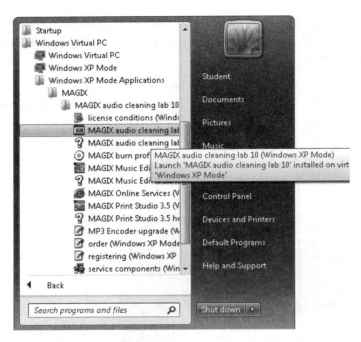

Figure 17-11 Legacy application on Windows XP Mode virtual machine in Windows 7 Start menu

   c.   Shut down the Windows XP Mode virtual machine.

   d.   Click **Start | All Programs | Windows Virtual PC | Windows XP Mode Applications** and select the folder or application that has been installed. The application will launch in its own Windows XP Mode virtual machine.

   e.   When you close the application, the Windows XP Mode virtual machine also closes, seamlessly!

 30 MINUTES

Lab Exercise 17.04: Installing and Configuring Oracle VM VirtualBox

Oracle is a company that built its reputation on a number of outstanding products, not the least of which is their large-scale enterprise database solutions. In the last few years, Oracle has introduced or acquired a new line of "Free and Open Source Software." You may already be familiar with OpenOffice, the word processor, spreadsheet, and presentation software suite. Now you will explore one of their other open source products, VirtualBox.

VirtualBox offers many of the features of VMware, like support for multiple platforms hosting multiple operating systems. One component that sets it apart from the others is that it is completely free and open source, meaning that software developers can seriously modify its operation.

✔ **Tech Tip**

As mentioned earlier, this Lab Exercise will use Ubuntu Linux for the guest operating system. Try an LTS version, downloaded from www.ubuntu.com. Create an installation disc or copy the installation disc image (.iso) to a flash drive for use in this Lab Exercise.

Learning Objectives

In this Lab Exercise, you will use Oracle VirtualBox virtualization software to install a virtual Ubuntu machine on a Windows 7 PC. You will then navigate a few of the Ubuntu programs and commands. At the end of this lab, you will be able to

- Install and configure Oracle VirtualBox on a Windows 7 host system

- Install and run Ubuntu 10.04 LTS as a guest operating system in VirtualBox

Lab Materials and Setup

The materials you'll need for this lab are

- A system connected to the Internet

- A Windows 7 system

- Pencil and paper

Getting Down to Business

Though not as popular as the "big name" virtualization packages, VirtualBox is a viable alternative to VMware, Citrix, and Microsoft offerings. VirtualBox installs relatively quickly, is straightforward to configure, and runs on multiple host platforms. It enables you to host a number of operating systems as guest virtual machines. As you bring your study of virtualization to a close, Maggie recommends you put VirtualBox through its paces by installing it on a Windows 7 host system, launching VirtualBox, and then installing Ubuntu as a guest operating system on the virtual machine.

Step 1 Launch your browser and navigate to www.virtualbox.org. This is the home of VirtualBox. Click on the **Downloads** hyperlink in the left-hand menu list as shown in Figure 17-12. Under **VirtualBox platform packages**, click on the hyperlink **x86/amd64** next to the package for **VirtualBox 4.1.4 for Windows hosts** (or the current version if newer). Save the file.

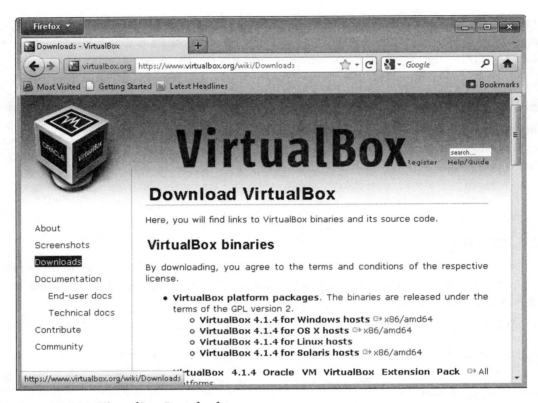

FIGURE 17-12 VirtualBox Download page

Step 2 Copy the file **VirtualBox-4.1.4-74291-Win.exe** to the Windows 7 system that will be hosting the virtual Ubuntu system (if other than the system you just used to download the installation program) and follow the instructions in sub-steps 2a through 2d:

a. Double-click the file **VirtualBox-4.1.4-74291-Win.exe** to launch the installation program. At the **Welcome to the Oracle VM VirtualBox 4.1.4 Setup Wizard** screen, click **Next**.

b. At the **Custom Setup** screen, choose the default values for the way that you want features installed and the location of the program files. Click **Next** and decide where to create shortcuts. Click **Next** once again, and you will then see a **Warning: Network Interfaces** dialog cautioning you that you will be temporarily disconnected from the network. Choose **Yes** (see Figure 17-13).

c. When the next screen appears, click **Install** to begin the installation of VirtualBox.

d. The installation may take a few minutes. You will be asked if you would like to install various device software for the Universal Serial Bus, network services, and network adapters. Choose to install all device software, and when the installation completes, click **Finish** to close the Setup Wizard.

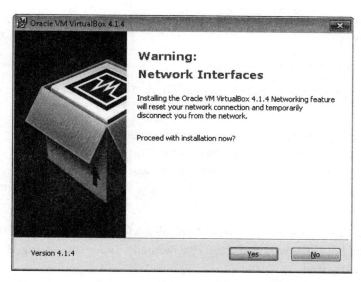

FIGURE 17-13 VirtualBox Warning: Network Interfaces

Step 3   Now you will launch the **Oracle VM VirtualBox Manager** and create a new virtual machine. Perform the tasks in sub-steps 3a through 3f to create a new VirtualBox virtual machine:

a.   Double-click the **Oracle VM VirtualBox** icon to launch the **Oracle VM VirtualBox Manager**.

b.   Click the **New** icon to create a new virtual machine. The screen will read **Welcome to the New Virtual Machine Wizard**. Read the introduction and navigation instructions, then click **Next**.

c.   This will bring you to the **VM Name and OS Type** screen. Name the virtual machine (**Virtual Ubuntu**, for example) and select the **Operating System** and **Version** as shown in Figure 17-14.

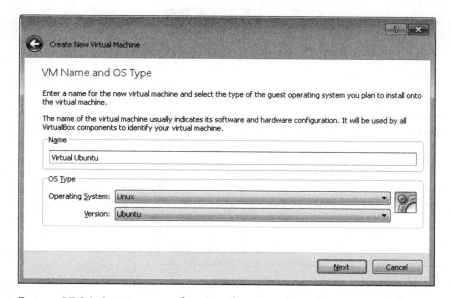

FIGURE 17-14 Setup screen showing the virtual machine name and OS type

d.   Click **Next** and select the amount of memory to allocate to the virtual machine. The recommended base memory size is **512** MB.

e.   In the next few steps, you configure the virtual hard disk:

• Click **Next**. On this screen you will create the virtual hard disk. The recommended size of the startup disk is **8.00** GB.

• Click **Next** to choose the file type for the new virtual hard disk. Depending on whether you would like to use this virtual hard disk with other virtualization software such as VMware (VMDK) or Microsoft (VHD), you may choose one of those formats. If you do not plan to use cross-platform virtual hard disks, just choose the native VirtualBox Disk Image (VDI) format.

• Click **Next**. Now choose how the space on the virtual hard disk will be allocated. Read the descriptions of both dynamically allocated and fixed-size methods. Leave the setting as the default, **Dynamically allocated**.

• Click **Next** and type the name of the new virtual disk file into the dialog box. At this time you may select a different folder for the location of the new file. You may also select the size of the disk that is reported to the guest operating system as the maximum size of this virtual disk.

• Click **Next** to display the Summary page for the new virtual disk. Select the **Create** button to create the new virtual disk.

f.   Now the Summary page for the new virtual machine is displayed as shown in Figure 17-15. Select the **Create** button to create the new virtual machine.

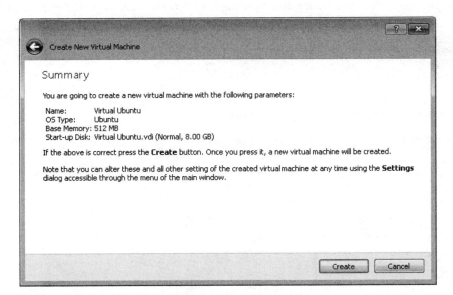

FIGURE 17-15 New Virtual Machine Summary page

Step 4   Now you will boot the new virtual machine and install the Ubuntu operating system. Perform the tasks in the following instructions to install Ubuntu on the new virtual machine:

a.   In the Oracle VM VirtualBox Manager, highlight the **Virtual Ubuntu** machine icon and click the **Start** icon to launch the installation of Ubuntu on the new virtual machine. An information box will open informing you that the **Auto capture keyboard** option is turned on. This option captures the keyboard strokes and mouse movements every time the virtual machine window is active. You can press the *host key* at any time to release the keyboard and mouse from the virtual machine and return them to normal operation. By default, the host key is the right CTRL key on the keyboard. Check the **Do not show this message again** option and click the **OK** button.

b.   Now the **First Run Wizard** welcome screen will launch. Briefly read the instructions and then click the **Next** button to perform the steps to install an operating system.

c.   You will now be prompted to **Select Installation Media**. In the **Media Source** selection box, you may select either the optical media drive containing the Ubuntu operating system installation disk, or you may choose a USB flash drive with the .iso installation file. Choose the proper media and click **Next**.

d.   You will now receive a Summary of the Type and Source of the boot media. Review the information and click the **Start** button.

e.   If you have selected the correct media and have the Ubuntu installation media installed on the device, the Ubuntu installation will launch. You may now follow the Ubuntu installation steps just as if you were installing Ubuntu on a physical machine. The basic installation steps are outlined in the instructions that follow:

- At the Welcome page, choose **Install Ubuntu 10.04.3 LTS** to begin the installation.

- Now set the Region and Time Zone and click **Forward**.

- Next, select the **Keyboard layout** (default USA) and click **Forward**.

- When preparing the disk space, choose **Erase and use the entire disk**. Notice that the disk reads approximately 8.00 GB. Click **Forward**.

- Now you will set up a user name and password. Enter the name **Student** in the dialog box. Notice that the user name **student** in lowercase and the computer name **student-desktop** are created automatically. Now enter a password of your choosing. The Ubuntu installation program will rate your password as weak, fair, good, or strong. How did your password rate?

- Click **Forward** and review the **Ready to install** summary page. If you are happy with the settings, click **Install**.

f.   Just as if you had installed Ubuntu on a physical machine, the installation software will prompt you that the installation is complete and you must restart the computer to use the new OS. Click the **Restart Now** button.

g.   Ubuntu will prompt you to **Please remove the disk and close the tray (if any) then press ENTER.** Press ENTER.

Step 5   When the Ubuntu virtual machine reboots, you will be prompted for your user name and password. After entering the information, you will have a fully functioning installation of Ubuntu as a guest operating system on top of the host operating system, Windows 7. Explore some of the programs in Ubuntu. See Figure 17-16.

FIGURE 17-16 Ubuntu running in a VirtualBox virtual machine on Windows 7

Step 6   There is one last feature of VirtualBox that you will want to explore: snapshots. Complete the following steps to configure a snapshot of the Ubuntu virtual machine you have just created.

a.   Launch the Virtual Ubuntu system and log on with your user name and password.

b.   I know that you are not supposed to play games while in a class, but for strictly educational purposes, open **Applications | Games | Mahjongg** and play a few moves of the game.

c. In the VirtualBox menu, select **Machine** and then select **Take Snapshot** from the drop-down menu. Type **Mahjongg** in the **Snapshot Name** dialog box as shown in Figure 17-17 and click **OK** to create the snapshot.

FIGURE 17-17 VirtualBox Snapshot tool

d. Perform a graceful shutdown of the Ubuntu virtual machine.

e. Open the Oracle VM VirtualBox Manager. The default window will display the virtual machine **Virtual Ubuntu (Mahjongg) | Powered Off** and the **Details** pane as shown in Figure 17-18.

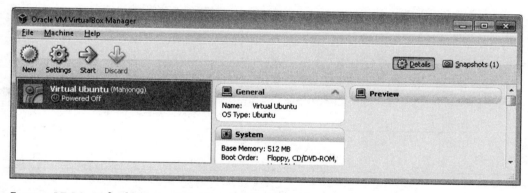

FIGURE 17-18 Default view of the Oracle VM VirtualBox Manager

f. Click **Snapshots** in the top-right of the menu bar. A list of the snapshots for the Virtual Ubuntu machine should be displayed in the right pane including the Mahjongg snapshot that you just created.

g. Right-click the **Mahjongg** snapshot and select **Restore Snapshot** from the drop-down menu. In the **VirtualBox – Question** window that opens, uncheck **Create a snapshot of the current machine state** and click **Restore**. This will load the Mahjongg snapshot into the **Current State** and the virtual machine **Virtual Ubuntu (Mahjongg) | Saved** and the **Snapshots** pane will be displayed, as shown in Figure 17-19.

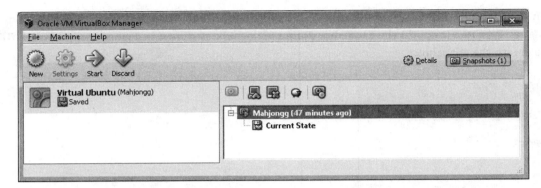

FIGURE 17-19 The Oracle VM VirtualBox Manager with the saved Snapshot loaded

h. Start the saved Virtual Ubuntu machine. You should be returned to the exact point where you saved the Mahjongg game (though the time will have elapsed). Congratulations, you have just created and restored a virtual machine snapshot!

Lab Analysis

1. Matthew has been working through the Lab Exercises, but is still unclear on the exact differences between a "virtual desktop" and a "virtual server." Detail some of the characteristics of each to help Matthew with his studies.

_____

_____

2. Trevor is implementing VoIP for his company and plans on using a virtual PBX. What is a virtual PBX?

_____

_____

3. While downloading VMware Player, Jonathan notices some of the other free products that VMware offers. He asks if you know the differences between the various offerings. Using the Web site www.vmware.com, write a short description of each of the free products that VMware offers.

_____

_____

4. Tim is planning on upgrading one of his virtual installations of Ubuntu with a major, untested application suite. What steps would you recommend Tim follow to minimize any problems if the application suite does not meet expectations?

_____

_____

5. When Cynthia made the decision to adopt the cloud computing model, her IT department mentioned the term NaaS. Can you explain the concept of NaaS to Cynthia? How does virtualization enhance this model?

_____

_____

Key Term Quiz

Use the vocabulary terms from the list below to complete the sentences that follow. Not all of the terms will be used.

bare-metal virtual machine	virtual machine manager (VMM)
hosted virtual machine	virtual PBX
hypervisor	virtual server
Network as a Service (Naas)	virtual switch
snapshot	VMware Player
VirtualBox	Windows Virtual PC
virtual desktop	

1. The two terms typically used to describe virtualization software are _____ or _____.

2. VMware is one of the leaders in the virtualization software market. They currently offer two free products. One of these is a _____ running on another operating system such as Windows 7 Professional and is named _____.

3. When working with virtual machines, one of the convenient features is to be able to take a _____ to capture the current configuration of the machine.

4. Typically, when building a virtual server, the virtualization software is going to be of the _____ variety. This is also known as a "native" virtual machine.

5. _____ is a full-featured, open-source virtualization software solution.

Chapter 18
Network Management

Lab Exercises

There are two key aspects to network management. First, you must ensure that users have access to the resources they need to perform their jobs. File servers, printers, e-mail, and Internet access must all be accessible with seamless performance. Second, if something happens to disrupt the users' access—some disaster strikes—you must have a comprehensive, documented, disaster recovery plan and the resources to implement it!

Performance is measured by first establishing baselines of standard or "normal" network utilization and then monitoring overall network utilization for changes. High availability is maintained by incorporating multiple fault-tolerance methods using RAID, redundant devices (power supplies, NICs, server farms or clustering, switches, and routers), virtualization, and the protection of data through firewalls and uninterruptible power supplies (UPSes). Many organizations strive for an uptime of 99.9 percent.

Being able to react in a timely manner to a disaster requires detailed configuration and change management documentation. Where is that critical edge router, and when was it last updated? Timely recovery also relies on diligent backup procedures, either on individual servers or, for critical organizations, through the use of hot, warm, or cold backup sites.

With the importance of network management practices, many hiring managers will use open-ended questions such as "How would you implement a GFS backup routine?" to validate your understanding of these components. Like potential employers, the CompTIA Network+ exam will expect you to have in-depth knowledge of configuration documentation, performance optimization, fault tolerance, and backup techniques, so you'll need to explore these concepts.

1 HOUR

Lab Exercise 18.01: Configuration Management Documentation

Configuration and change management documentation is a requirement for all but the smallest SOHO network environments. Network administrators and techs will be responsible for defining and documenting the layout and operation of the network. The physical, logical, and functional aspects of the network and devices will be recorded in both diagrams and written documents. The proper use of technology and the roles and responsibilities of the support staff and end users are defined in personnel documentation.

Once the documentation is in place, managing the changes to that documentation—like updating when a portion of the network is upgraded from 100-Mbps equipment and wiring to Gigabit performance— must be attended to diligently. When changes to the network happen—or worse, some component or system fails—the configuration management documentation is the roadmap and guide to bring the network back to full operation.

Learning Objectives

In this lab, you will develop basic configuration management documentation. When you have completed this lab, you will be able to do the following:

- Use Microsoft PowerPoint or Visio to document the network layout

- Analyze configuration management documentation for validity

- Implement change management documentation

- Define an Acceptable Use Policy (AUP)

Lab Materials and Setup

The materials you'll need for this lab are

- A computer with Internet access

- A Windows system with Microsoft Office PowerPoint, OpenOffice Impress, or Microsoft Visio installed

- Optionally (adhering to the organization's security policy), access to the network configuration of your classroom or department for documentation purposes

→ **Note**

In the following lab steps, the details of a fictitious network are provided. Using this fictitious network, you will create a network diagram and a network map as part of a configuration management documentation process. If your instructor or manager will allow you to have access to the parameters of your classroom or department network, substitute your actual network for the fictitious network.

Getting Down to Business

One of the tasks that can really get ahead of you if you're not careful is that of documenting the network configuration and the changes that occur over time. Good administrators and techs will make a point of staying on top of this critical element, documenting when new Gigabit switches are installed, recording the expansion of new departments in the organization with the new devices, PCs, subnets, and so on.

There are four general categories that need to be addressed when you are managing the configuration documentation.

The first category, *network connectivity*, is composed of three related components:

- *Wiring schemes*, or as the CompTIA Network+ exam objectives describe them, *wire schemes*, are usually created by the telecommunication cabling professionals. Wiring schemes document what type of cable is in place (UTP, CAT 5e, CAT 6) and what TIA/EIA standards are used to terminate the cables in RJ-45 connectors and keystones (TIA/EIA 568-B or TIA/EIA 568-A). When major changes are implemented, the wiring schemes will be updated to represent the current structure.

- *Network diagrams* document actual devices on the network (switches, routers, servers, PCs, and so on) and how they connect to each other.

- *Network maps* provide more detail on the individual components of the network such as the IP addressing scheme, DHCP servers, DNS servers, Web servers, e-mail servers, DMZs, and the like.

✔ **Tech Tip**

Network diagrams and *network maps* are terms that are often interchanged, reversed, and even combined when techs and companies actually develop the configuration management documentation. As you study for the CompTIA Network+ exam, just remember that the processes of mapping out nodes, including IP addresses, and noting key routers, switches, and servers are all components of *configuration management documentation*.

Baselines present a snapshot of the network parameters when the network is under normal usage. If something seems to be amiss with network performance, you can quickly assess whether a parameter is out of range, indicating a potential device or application that is not operating correctly.

Policies, procedures, and configuration documentation should cover the broad categories of what is and is not allowed on the network, the various procedures for tasks that users perform (such as retrieving e-mail), and how the users will be trained on those procedures. Also, the configuration of the devices on the network should be well documented. For instance, if the DHCP server crashes, along with a good documented backup routine, there should be good physical documentation specifying the DHCP scopes and scope options for routers (default gateway), DNS servers, and client systems.

Regulations are the laws governing the proper usage of materials in the workplace to keep both the facilities and the workers safe. An example you have already studied is the use of plenum cable in walls and drop ceilings to meet fire code. This should be a part of the configuration management documentation.

You have already worked with wiring schematics and regulations in the Lab Exercises in Chapter 3 and Chapter 6. You are going to develop a baseline using the Performance Monitor tool in the next Lab Exercise.

So for now, I want you to dig into network diagrams, network maps, policies, procedures, and configuration!

➜ **Note**

Over the years, Cisco has become the leading manufacturer of networking routers and switches. With their leadership, many of the icons that have been developed to document Cisco products have been adopted by the industry when documenting network configurations. You may download these icons for use in PowerPoint or Visio at the following URL: www.cisco.com/web/about/ac50/ac47/2.html.

As throughout this Lab Manual, I caution you that Web sites change often. If you find that the link in the preceding paragraph does not bring you to the Cisco network icons, use a search engine and you should be able to find the current location.

Step 1 Using either PowerPoint or Visio and the Cisco networking symbols and icons, develop both a network diagram and network map to document the following fictitious remote office network. All internal cabling is CAT 6 UTP running at Gbps performance level, and the ISP has provided a 100-Mbps fiber connection to the Internet.

- **FileServer1** FileServer1 is the primary server in this remote office network. It provides storage space for the nine employees and also handles the roles of DHCP server and DNS server. The configuration details are included in the following table.

- **BackupServer1** BackupServer1 is the network backup server. The configuration details are included in the following table.

- **Printer** An HP LaserJet 4100N network printer with an integrated JetDirect card is configured as a shared printer. The configuration details are included in the following table.

- **Edge Router** A Cisco 2811 router has been configured as the gateway to the Internet (through a service provider). The configuration details are included in the following table.

- **Switches** A Cisco 3560 managed switch will be used as the primary switch in the main distribution frame (MDF) where the edge router, file server, and backup server are all located. Three workgroup switches will be cascaded off the primary switch to handle multiple clients in each of the three office workspaces.

- **Client computers** To accommodate the nine employees, six desktop PCs and three laptops are installed. All of the machines are initially configured to receive their configuration information through DHCP. The laptops are also used outside of the office by the employees they are assigned to.

Device	Functions	Internal Interface IP Address	External Interface IP Address	Default Gateway
FileServer1	Primary File Server DHCP Scope 172.16.250.51/16– 172.16.250.150/16 Scope Option 003 Router–172.16.1.1 Scope Option 006 DNS Server–172.16.1.254/16	172.16.1.254/16	N/A	172.16.1.1
BackupServer1	Network Backup Server	172.16.1.253/16	N/A	172.16.1.1
Cisco 2811 Router	Edge Router	172.16.1.1/16	101.150.36.239/21	101.150.32.1/21
HP LaserJet 4100N	Network Printer	172.16.1.192/16	N/A	N/A

✖ Cross-Reference

To see examples of network diagrams and network maps, consult Figures 2 through 7 in Chapter 18 of the *Mike Meyers' CompTIA Network+ Guide to Managing and Troubleshooting Networks* textbook.

To refresh your memory on subnetting, such as understanding the differences among /16, /19, /21, and /24 subnets, refer to Chapter 7 in the textbook.

Step 2 One of your colleagues, Tim, has acquired three additional desktop PCs from one of the other branch offices and has installed them for the employees who use the laptops so that they have permanent machines in the office. Tim updates the configuration management documentation. The updated network map is shown in Figure 18-1.

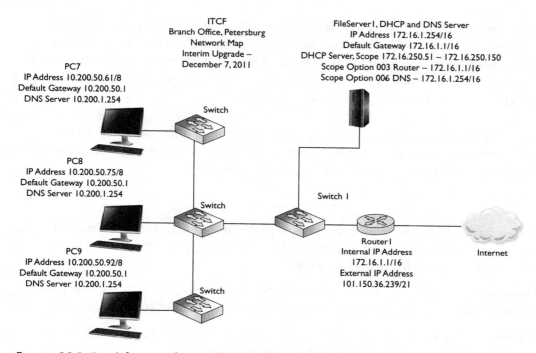

FIGURE 18-1 Partial network map showing three new machines

Now the three employees are complaining that they cannot access any of their files on FileServer1. They also have no Internet connectivity. Analyze the updated network map, diagnose the problem, and provide a solution to restore the users' connectivity.

_____

_____

_____

_____

Step 3   A network configuration management documentation plan is only as good as the most recent update. The term for these updates is *change management documentation.*

→ Note

Change management documentation includes updates to both network diagrams and network maps. Network diagrams include documentation on the devices such as switches, routers, servers, and PCs, along with their connections, connection speeds, make, model, and firmware revision when available. Network maps include documentation on IP addressing, DHCP servers, DNS servers, Web servers, e-mail servers, DMZs, and the like.

When updating the documentation, depending on the modifications, you may only have to update the network diagram or the network map. In the following scenario, you should update both the network diagram and the network map you created in Step 1.

The branch office has expanded the network, adding a public Web server placed in a Demilitarized Zone (DMZ), a Cisco firewall (Adaptive Security Appliance ASA 5510), and a wireless access point. The detailed specifications are provided in the following list:

- **WebServer1**   A public Web server for up-to-date traffic information. This will be placed in a DMZ with light security. The configuration details are included in the following table.

- **Firewall**   A Cisco ASA 5510 Adaptive Security Device will be placed at the internal access point to the DMZ, providing a high level of security to the LAN.

- **Edge router**   The Cisco 2811 router will need to be reconfigured to continue operating as the gateway to the Internet (through a service provider). The configuration details are included in the following table.

- **Wireless access point**   A Linksys WRT54G will be used to provide wireless access for the three laptop computers when the employees are in the office.

- **Client computers**   The three laptops should be modified in the network diagram and the network map to show that they are now wireless clients. You may want to update the documentation with the three desktop PCs that Tim added in the prior step. All client machines should be configured to obtain IP settings automatically.

Building on the network diagram and network map you created in Step 1, update the configuration management documentation. Don't forget to record the date and revisions of the network diagram and network map for the change management documentation records.

Device	Functions	Internal Interface IP Address	External Interface IP Address	Default Gateway
WebServer1	Traffic Update Web site–Public Web server in a lightly protected DMZ	10.200.73.252/19	N/A	10.200.72.2
Cisco ASA 5510	Firewall	172.16.1.1/16	10.200.73.1/19	10.200.72.2
Cisco 2811 router	Edge router	10.200.72.2/19	101.150.36.239/21	101.150.32.1
Linksys WRT54G	Access Point LAN & WLAN DHCP Scope 192.168.40.100–192.168.40.150	WAN Port 172.16.1.3/16	LAN & WLAN 192.168.40.1/24	WAN 172.16.1.1

✔ Hint

When building on the network diagram and network map, you will place the public Web servers in the lightly protected area known as the Demilitarized Zone (DMZ). One method of creating the DMZ is to place the edge router as the first device between the Internet (WAN) and the internal network (LAN). This will have very light security enabled to facilitate access from the outside world. At the other end of the DMZ, you would place the firewall (Cisco ASA 5510) to secure all of the internal machines from external access, thus creating a lightly protected area between the LAN and WAN where the Web server can be placed.

Step 4 With the proliferation of information technology used in every industry, the need for policies to define what is and is not allowed is greater than ever. At all levels, from administrative assistants to corporate financial officers, the acceptable usage of e-communications must be a component of the corporate policy and diligently enforced. Using either the Internet or a copy of your school's or business's Acceptable Use Policy, outline the key features of an AUP.

_____

_____

_____

_____

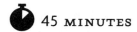 45 MINUTES

Lab Exercise 18.02: Monitoring Performance and Connectivity

Along with staying on top of the network documentation, technology, and network applications such as e-mail and Internet, it is the responsibility of the network team (often the entry-level network tech) to ensure the continued performance of network components and connectivity. Is the Internet connectivity slowing to a crawl when all of the users are accessing Web sites to complete their tasks? Can upper management use the video conferencing system without experiencing lags in both video and audio data?

Obviously, the initial design of the network must take into account the needs of the users as well as the business application being serviced. If you are designing a system for an organization that provides a search engine, the network design should take into account concurrent connections, load balancing, and overall bandwidth. Even small network installations can benefit from careful design and monitoring of the network's performance.

After the initial design is complete, the network tech should establish a baseline of the performance under "normal load," that is, the normal daily use of the network when the business is performing normal operating procedures. The network should then be measured under times of extreme usage to determine bottlenecks, the devices that will hold back the performance when driven to their operating capacities. Is one server being overused? Is the T1 line too small for the organization when it is in full swing?

Various tools are included with most of the popular operating systems as well as benchmark test engines from third-party developers. As usual, Microsoft provides many utilities as part of their various operating systems. You are now going to explore two of these tools in Windows 7, Performance Monitor and Event Viewer.

Learning Objectives

In this lab, you will

- Create a baseline of a system under normal load

- Stress a system and record the change in performance

- Explore the various logs created in Event Viewer

Lab Materials and Setup

The materials you'll need for this lab are

- Pencil and paper

- A computer running Windows XP, Windows Vista, or Windows 7

Getting Down to Business

To develop a baseline for the performance of an entire organization, you will monitor and record all of the critical devices during a time of "normal load," or normal operation. Then, during times of increased activity, you can capture additional data on these devices, store the information in log reports, and compare the data captured during normal load to that of the high-stress load. This will help you identify bottlenecks, providing direction on where the next equipment updates are needed.

Maggie knows the importance of guaranteeing performance to the network users (this is actually one of her responsibilities). She recommends that you use the Network Lab to experiment with the Performance Monitor tool that is included with every version of the Windows operating system.

→ **Note**

Over the years, Microsoft has called the performance monitoring tool by many names; System Monitor, Performance Monitor, Reliability and Performance Monitor, and just Performance have all seen the light of day. Depending on the version of Windows you are using, there will be slight differences in implementation, but all versions will allow you to create a log of various objects and counters. A Windows 7 machine running Performance Monitor was used for this Lab Exercise.

Step 1 Begin by opening the Performance Monitor utility in Windows 7. This can be done in a variety of ways. You can select **Start** and type **perfmon** in the **Search programs and files** dialog box, then press ENTER. You may right-click the **Computer** icon and select **Manage** from the drop-down menu, then expand the menu under **Performance** in the left-hand pane and select **Performance Monitor**. You can even add **Administrative Tools** to the **Start** menu and choose **Performance Monitor** from the submenu.

Step 2 Performance Monitor can show and record statistics about almost anything happening inside the computer. You can customize the collection by clicking the green + symbol in the main pane or clicking CTRL+N to add a counter. Select the **Performance Monitor** under the Monitoring Tools, then use either method to add the following objects and counters:

Object	Instance	Counter
Processor	Total	% Processor Time
Memory	N/A	Pages/sec
Physical Disk	Total	Avg. Disk Queue Length
		Avg. Disk sec/Transfer
Network Interface	<All Instances>	Bytes Total/sec
		Current Bandwidth
IPv4	N/A	Datagrams/sec

✖ Cross-Reference

To analyze additional objects and counters that would be helpful in creating a networking performance baseline, refer to the "Monitoring Performance and Connectivity" section of Chapter 18 of the *Mike Meyers' CompTIA Network+ Guide to Managing and Troubleshooting Networks* textbook.

Once you have added the counters, you should see a graphic representation of the current usage of each of the objects and counters displayed in Performance Monitor, similar to Figure 18-2. What are some of the values for your system?

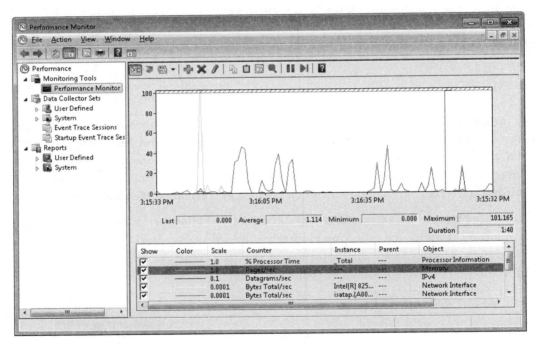

Figure 18-2 Performance Monitor in Microsoft Windows 7

Step 3   Using the Performance Monitor to view current transient data is great if you have a specific slowdown that you are trying to diagnose, but if you want to create baselines and peak usage reports, you will have to create a data collector set. This will be used to collect data over an extended period of time, which you can then use to create reports of network usage.

To use the current objects and counters for your data collector set, right-click Performance Monitor in the left-hand pane and select **New | Data Collector Set**. Name the data collector set **ITCF Baseline**. When prompted, select **Start this data collector set now**.

Step 4 Allow the data collector set to run for a few minutes, and then in the Data Collector Sets folder, expand **User Defined** and right-click **ITCF Baseline**. Select **Stop** from the drop-down menu. This will create a system monitor log under **Reports | User Defined | ITCF Baseline** (see Figure 18-3). Open the system monitor log. You may have to add some of the objects and counters that you captured, such as the Network Interface: Bytes Total/sec, as they may not appear in the default report. Record some of the average performance data in the following space:

_____

_____

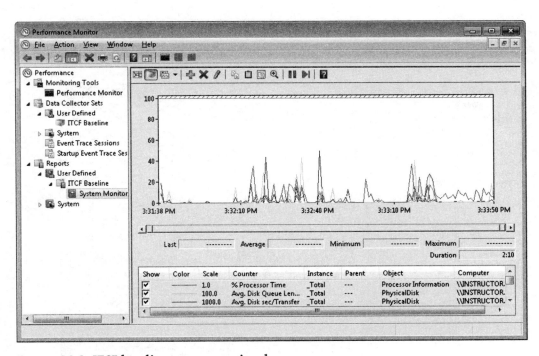

FIGURE 18-3 ITCF baseline system monitor log

Step 5 Create a second data collector set and name it **ITCF High Load**. Before you launch the data capture, run the following activities on your system:

- Open www.pandora.com and stream some music you like.

- View a www.youtube.com video.

- Download Service Pack 1 for Windows 7 from www.microsoft.com/downloads/en/default.aspx.

✔ **Tech Tip**

The applications listed in Step 5 really test your Internet connection and may not produce "high load" conditions on the local devices such as the hard disk or network interface. To increase the overall load, you could set up a network share on another machine and download large files across the LAN while watching a DVD and streaming some information from the Internet.

Now start the ITCF High Load data collector set and let it run while the applications are performing their duties. When the Service Pack download completes (or after a few minutes), stop the data collection and open the System Monitor log to view the performance during high-load conditions. See Figure 18-4. Again, you may have to add some of the objects and counters that are not displayed in the default report. Record some of the performance data. How does it compare to the baseline?

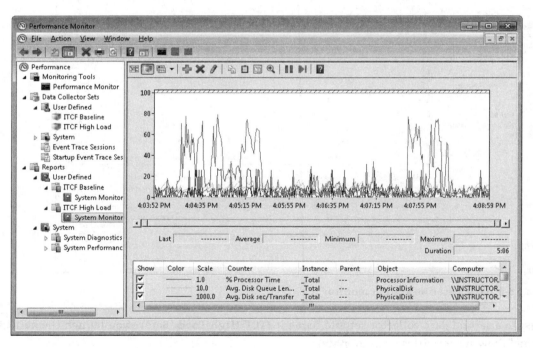

Figure 18-4 ITCF High Load system monitor log

Step 6 Event Viewer has been around almost as long as Windows, and provides standard logs of Application, Security, and System events. Further specialized events such as DHCP, DNS, Active Directory, and so on are included with the Microsoft Windows Server operating systems.

Open Event Viewer, and explore some of the Application, Security, and System logs. I received the DHCP system error, shown in Figure 18-5, when I tried to get a DHCP address for both my wireless adapter and the wired adapter while they were both active on the same Linksys router.

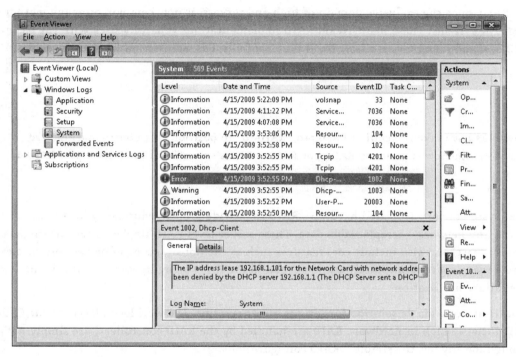

FIGURE 18-5 DHCP error in Event Viewer's system log

Record a few items from your system's information, warnings, errors, and audit failures in the following space:

_____

_____

 45 MINUTES

Lab Exercise 18.03: Fault Tolerance

You have already explored various hardware fault-tolerance methods in "Lab Exercise 16.01: Analyzing Threats." One of the sure-fire methods to avoid disaster in the first place, which is certainly a threat, is to manage the devices and systems that you know have the capacity to fail. The standard method to protect against these failures is to double or even triple the number of devices or systems. If a power supply is critical, add a second to back up the first. If a server is critical, go ahead, add a second one! Don't forget to add two or more hard drives and configure them in a Redundant Array of Independent (or Inexpensive) Disks (RAID) array to guarantee that data is always readily available.

Hardware RAID, once the exclusive domain of high-end servers, is now common on many motherboards and prebuilt systems. These mainstream RAID implementations generally stick with the basics, providing RAID 0, 1, and sometimes 1+0 (10). You'll find few frills, but mainstream RAID is better than nothing!

→ **Note**

Marketing folks have taken to calling RAID 1+0 "RAID 10" to position this nonstandard nested RAID format as somehow superior to RAID 5 or RAID 6. There's no official RAID level past RAID 6.

Most server systems sport dedicated hardware RAID to provide proper redundancy for the most expensive part of any network—irreplaceable data. These server-level RAID implementations support RAID 0, 1, and 5 at least, and also include cool features such as the hot-swapping of drives, automatic failover (where a ready spare immediately starts to rebuild the RAID array in case of failure), and e-mail or voice failure notification.

Software RAID is not a viable solution for serious server systems. The workload placed on the CPU(s) to handle RAID duties (which in hardware RAID are handled by the RAID controllers) are simply not responsive enough for any but the simplest RAID configurations.

The software RAID provided with Microsoft Windows Server 2003 or Server 2008 is an excellent tool to understand how RAID works. The goal of this lab is to inspect different types of RAID configurations, focusing on software RAID in Windows. You will see what you need to do to install and maintain a RAID array, and what to do in case of a drive failure in a RAID array.

→ **Note**

Microsoft Windows Server 2003 and Server 2008 support software-based RAID 0, RAID 1, and RAID 5 configurations using Microsoft's proprietary Dynamic Disk technology. Windows XP Professional; Windows Vista Business, Enterprise, and Ultimate; and Windows 7 Professional, Enterprise, and Ultimate only support software RAID 0 and RAID 1 configurations.

Learning Objectives

In this lab, you will examine some software RAID solutions and determine how to do the following:

- Configure RAID for RAID 0, 1, or 5
- Perform basic drive maintenance
- Rebuild arrays in case of failure

Lab Materials and Setup

The materials you'll need for this lab are

- Pencil and paper

- A computer with Internet access

- A Windows Server 2003 or Windows Server 2008 system. If possible, the instructor should assist the students with the installation of the operating system on one hard drive. Then they should install three additional hard drives to support the RAID configuration.

- Optionally, a Windows Server 2003 or Windows Server 2008 system with SCSI or SAS RAID controllers and multiple hard drives

✔ Hint

To facilitate this Lab Exercise, it may be more feasible to use an older PC with three or four disks installed. Many IT training environments have plenty of old equipment that can be put to good use for this RAID implementation. With this goal in mind, you will use Windows Server 2003, which will install and operate on older systems with less performance degradation. This will allow you to use machines with slower processors, smaller amounts of memory, and small PATA or SATA hard drives to run this Lab Exercise.

If you would prefer to use a Windows Server 2008 system (or another server system), you should still be able to perform these lab steps to implement software RAID. Disk Management is virtually identical in either Windows Server 2003 or Windows Server 2008.

Getting Down to Business

The actual management of network servers and fault tolerance is somewhat beyond the scope of the CompTIA Network+ exam; however, you will be thoroughly tested on the concepts. Working as a network administrator, you will often be involved with the upkeep of these components while attending to network management.

→ Note

This lab assumes a basic familiarity with the Windows Disk Management applet.

With this in mind, CJ asks you to use the Windows Server 2003 machine he donated to the Network Lab to experiment with the configuration of RAID 0, 1, and 5. He recommends using the software implementation that is included with Server 2003 for convenience but is open to assisting you if you decide to configure the server's onboard RAID controller. You should develop a small reference table with the details and requirements for each of the RAID levels.

Note

Because RAID 0 provides no fault tolerance at all, you should not use it with a server. I've included it here to provide flexibility in the classroom if you don't have a copy of Windows Server handy in the lab and also to give you extra practice with Disk Management and RAID.

Step 1   Create a table summarizing RAID 0, RAID 1, RAID 5, RAID 6, and RAID 1+0 (10) for your records. Use the following as a template.

RAID Level	Short Description	Benefits	Drawbacks	Minimum Drives
0				
1				
5				
6				
1+0 (10)				

✔ Hint

You will not be expected to know the various levels of RAID for the CompTIA Network+ examination, nor will the textbook go into great detail regarding the implementations of RAID. As you work to become an IT professional, you should build a strong knowledge base that you can tap into when applying concepts as real-world solutions.

A few moments of Internet research will provide all of the information for the preceding table and, along with the foundation you have established studying for the CompTIA A+ certification, will serve you well into your career.

Step 2   Depending on your system, you may be using PATA, SATA, SCSI, or SAS hard drives. Using the hardware documentation included with most server systems, install three additional hard drives in the Windows Server system.

Go into Disk Management and confirm that the three hard drives are completely blank. Remove any volumes or partitions if any exist. Initialize each drive and then convert the drives to Dynamic Disks. Do this in one of the following ways:

- Use the Initialize and Convert Wizard that pops up automatically when you start Disk Management.

- Manually open Disk Management, right-click one of the three drives, and select **Initialize**. Then right-click one of the three disks and select **Convert to Dynamic Disk**. Repeat the process to initialize and convert the other two drives. The result should look like Figure 18-6.

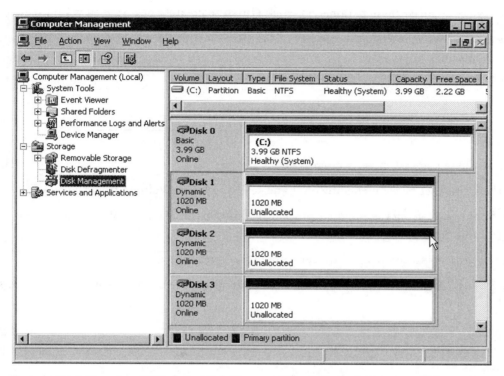

Figure 18-6 Four hard drives in Disk Management (Windows Server 2003)

What are the results? Include the capacities of the drives.

_____

_____

_____

Step 3 Now follow these steps to create a stripe set using Disk 1 and Disk 2:

a. Open Computer Management, expand the **Storage** node, and click the **Disk Management** icon.

b. Right-click an unconfigured disk volume and select **New Volume** from the pop-up menu to start the New Volume Wizard.

c. Click **Next**, and then at the **Volume Type** screen, select **Striped** (different versions of server have different names here, but it should be obvious), and click **Next**.

  d.   Select the volumes you want to stripe, and configure the volume size (to save time, configure
       the size of the striped set to something small, such as 250 MB), and then follow the prompts
       to assign a drive letter to the volume and specify a format (FAT, FAT32, or NTFS).

  e.   After you've configured these parameters, click **Finish** to create a new striped volume set.

What are the results? What is the total capacity of the stripe set? Could you have made a stripe set
using Disk 1, Disk 2, and Disk 3?

_____

_____

Step 4   Now follow these steps to create a mirror set:

  a.   Delete the striped set by right-clicking on it and selecting **Delete Volume** from the pop-up menu.

  b.   Repeat steps 1 and 2 from the previous procedure, only this time choose **Mirror Set** in the
       Select Volume Type dialog.

  c.   Follow the prompts to create a mirror set across Disk 1 and Disk 2.

What are the results? What is the total capacity of the mirror set? Could you have made a mirror set
using Disk 1, Disk 2, and Disk 3?

_____

_____

Step 5   Now delete the mirrored volumes and follow the same steps to create a RAID 5 set using all three
disks. What is the total capacity of the RAID 5 set? Could you have made a RAID 5 set using only Disk 1
and Disk 2?

_____

_____

Step 6   Shut down the system, remove one of the three drives from the RAID 5 set, and then reboot
the system. What are the results? Can you still access the RAID set? What is the process to replace a bad
drive in a real-world environment?

_____

_____

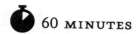

60 MINUTES

Lab Exercise 18.04: Disaster Recovery

Lab Exercise 18.03 dealt with fault tolerance and the art of ensuring the high availability of critical data. Fault tolerance, however, should not be the end-all of data security. In keeping with the philosophy that the most important part of a network is the data, a comprehensive backup strategy is the point of last defense and should be one of the kingpins in the administrator's network management routines. When RAID arrays fail, when users accidentally delete that critical database, or when viruses corrupt your file server, the ability to restore the systems to their most recent state will allow the organization to recover from the disaster gracefully.

Numerous technologies are available to implement quality system backups: tape drives and media, Blu-ray Disc optical drives and media, removable hard drives, and Network Attached Storage (NAS). All of these technologies are used alone or in combination—along with tried-and-true backup strategies—to protect the data when disaster strikes. Mission-critical organizations such as world financial institutions, government agencies, or national security operations will even employ entire alternate locations that will have some level of network infrastructure ready to go in case of a complete failure of the primary location.

Data backup technology, techniques, and strategies are tools that you can apply immediately from the smallest of organizations to large enterprise networks. Along with preparing for the CompTIA Network+ exam, honing your skills as a network administrator or tech, you can also adopt these techniques to keep your precious photos and music safe from disaster!

Learning Objectives

In this lab, you'll learn to perform the following:

- Run a backup using Windows Backup

- Develop a practical tape (or removable drive) backup strategy for a small business, applying best-practice techniques

- Define the requirements for a hot, warm, and cold backup site

Lab Materials and Setup

The materials you'll need for this lab are

- Pencil and paper

- A computer with Internet Access

- A Windows PC (XP, Vista, or 7)

- Some form of removable or remote storage. A CD, DVD, BD, removable hard drive, or network storage will work fine for this exercise. A tape drive and tapes are handy but not necessary.

Getting Down to Business

You have almost completed your studies for the Network+ exam! Along the way, you have developed a deep understanding of networking concepts and applied these skills to daily responsibilities in your position as a desktop support specialist. Now a Network Tech, Level 1 position has opened up at ITCF, and you would like to apply for the position.

Maggie is confident of your capabilities and agrees to be one of your professional references. She recommends that you focus on one last area of network management before your interview: disaster recovery! She explains that no organization can ever prepare "too much" to avoid the devastating results of a poorly planned backup and recovery strategy. As such, she coaches you to expect a few detailed questions concerning backup techniques: Grandfather-Father-Son (GFS), and of course, hot, warm, and cold sites. You hit the Network Lab to prepare yourself in case you are asked to explain one of these disaster recovery components.

Step 1   To begin this exercise, you should create a few text files or choose some existing data that you can afford to lose in the event that your disaster recovery plan goes awry. Store the files in the user's Documents folder. What are the names of the files you have created?

_____

_____

Step 2   To practice the application of backup concepts using the Windows 7 Backup and Restore utility, log on to your system with administrative privileges and launch the Backup and Restore applet. If this is the first time you have launched the utility, it will indicate that "Windows Backup has not been set up." Click the **Set up Backup** button to start the configuration of the backup.

Step 3   You will have to select a location for the backup files to be saved, such as a recordable or ReWritable CD/DVD, a removable hard drive, or a network share. For the purposes of this Lab Exercise, you may choose a share on the Windows Server 2003 or Windows Server 2008 machine that CJ has donated to the Network Lab, as shown in Figure 18-7. What media will you use for the backup?

_____

Once the proper credentials are entered, click the **Next** button and select the **Let me choose** radio button when prompted "What do you want to back up?" Choose the sample files you just created (or maybe user data files or some files that you can delete to make the restore process more authentic), and deselect the **Include a system image** check box (including the image would take some time). See Figure 18-8.

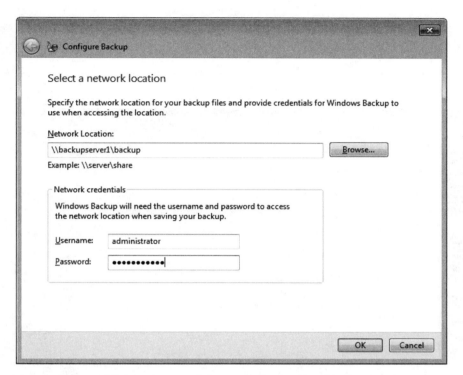

FIGURE 18-7 Selecting a network location for backup files in Windows 7

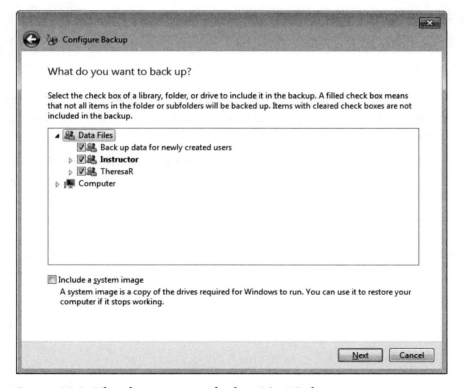

FIGURE 18-8 What do you want to back up? in Windows 7

Step 4   Click **Next**. The backup will run and display a status window similar to the one shown in Figure 18-9. What backup schedule have you selected?

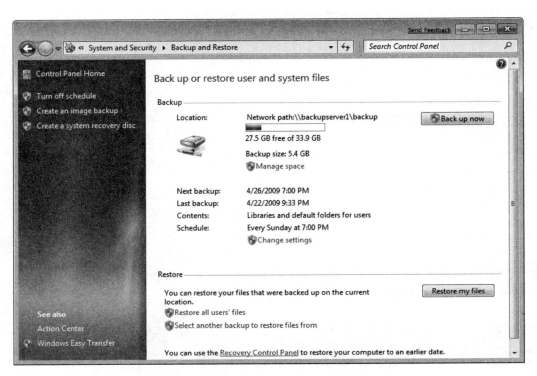

FIGURE 18-9 Back up or restore user and system files in Windows 7

Step 5   After you have successfully created a backup of your important data, delete one or two of the unimportant files that you have saved in the backup. Use the Restore utility to recover these files and bring the system back to current status.

Step 6   Using the concept of best practice, develop a backup strategy for some of ITCF's larger clients using traditional digital linear tape (DLT) tape drives and media. First define the Grandfather-Father-Son (GFS) tape rotation methodology.

Now devise a weekly backup using both the full/incremental and the full/differential methods. Explain the benefits and shortcomings for each method.

_____

_____

The following templates should help you organize your backup routines:

Full/Incremental

Monday	Tuesday	Wednesday	Thursday	Friday

Full/Differential

Monday	Tuesday	Wednesday	Thursday	Friday

Step 7 The database server crashes on Thursday. Using the full/incremental backup strategy, what tapes will you need to restore the system?

_____

_____

Step 8 The database server crashes on Wednesday. Using the full/differential backup strategy, what tapes will you need to restore the system?

_____

_____

Step 9 CJ used to work for a large trading company that was involved in multimillion-dollar online transactions. He mentions that they had a complete hot backup site for the transaction servers; if the system was down more than a few hours or so, they could lose millions of dollars. Conduct an Internet search and provide the definitions for hot, warm, and cold backup sites.

_____

_____

_____

Lab Analysis

1. Brandon has just finished an exhilarating game of Counter-Strike when his supervisor steps into his cubicle and gives him a verbal warning concerning gaming during business hours. She explains to Brandon that there is a company policy that defines what is allowed and not allowed in the workplace. After his supervisor leaves, Brandon asks you what she is talking about. What do you tell Brandon?

    _____

    _____

2. Ben is scheduled for an interview with the DESTOK Corporation. They are a corporate backup services organization, with a disaster-proof physical storage facility. He was told to brush up on his knowledge of backup strategies, especially Grandfather-Father-Son (GFS). What can you tell Ben about GFS?

    _____

    _____

3. You have explored Event Viewer, observing entries in the Application, Security, and System logs. What are the various status indicators that are used in Event Viewer?

    _____

    _____

4. Stan is responsible for all of the backups of five critical financial servers on your network. He has devised a backup routine in which he performs a normal backup on Friday evening after all of the business is done for the week. There are a large number of transactions that take place every weekday, causing large changes to the data. What type of nightly backup would you recommend Stan use?

    _____

    _____

5. Brittney has just upgraded all of the 100-Mbps switches and routers to Gigabit switches and routers for your organization. She asks for your assistance in recording all of the pertinent information for the switches and routers. What method will you employ?

    _____

    _____

Key Term Quiz

Use the vocabulary terms from the list below to complete the sentences that follow. Not all of the terms will be used.

Acceptable Use Policy (AUP)

baseline

bottleneck

change management documentation

cold recovery site

configuration management documentation

counters

differential backup

disk striping

disk striping with double parity

disk striping with parity

drive duplexing

drive mirroring

Event Viewer

hot recovery site

incremental backup

Network Attached Storage (NAS)

network diagram

network map

normal backup

objects

Performance Monitor

Redundant Array of Independent/Inexpensive
 Disks (RAID)

uninterruptible power supply (UPS)

warm recovery site

wiring scheme

1. Network administrators will often use a set of standardized symbols in Microsoft Visio or PowerPoint to draft both a(n) _____ to document devices on the network and a(n) _____ to provide details about the individual components of the network—such as the IP addressing scheme—for their organization.

2. The definition of a(n) _____ is a hardware component that is operating at maximum performance but is still the slowest component in the system affecting the overall performance of the system.

3. A(n) _____ provides a few minutes of power to your server in the event of power loss.

4. RAID 6, also referred to as _____, is the technique of using four or more disks to protect the data, even if two of the disks fail.

5. In Microsoft's _____, various _____ can be configured to track the operation of hardware components known as _____.

Chapter 19

Building a SOHO Network

Lab Exercises

The end of the text is near, and it's time to view the big picture of building a SOHO network. The information presented in this chapter isn't terribly technical—earlier chapters have covered those details. This chapter looks at the process of installing a network as a single project, one that you need to take from the beginning to the end.

There's no single right answer when it comes to building a SOHO network. If at the end of the job the users are happy with the network and it's doing the job it was designed to do, then you've succeeded. To that end, the goals of the labs in this chapter are unlike anything you've seen in previous chapters. As a whole, all of these labs come together to build a complete SOHO network "from the ground up." Individually, each of these labs reinforces the chapter and refers back to earlier chapters as well. The goal here is to make you look at the overall project and appreciate how each step affects the next. Don't look for the right answers for the labs; find the right answers for yourself and prepare to defend your choices!

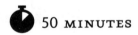 50 MINUTES

Lab Exercise 19.01: Planning the Network

Well, all your boasting to your friends about how much you've learned about networking has suddenly brought you to a very important place. A good friend of yours has asked you to install a network in her new townhouse. Time to put those skills to work and design your first SOHO network!

This first exercise requires you to design a typical SOHO network. To perform this lab, you'll need skills from Chapter 19 of the textbook, as well as Chapters 6 and 18 of this lab manual.

Learning Objectives

At the completion of this lab, you will be able to

- Create a list of requirements for a new network installation
- Recognize environmental limitations of a new network installation
- Create a network map for a new SOHO network

Lab Materials and Setup

The materials you'll need for this lab are

- A PC with Internet access

- The *Mike Meyers' CompTIA Network+ Guide to Managing and Troubleshooting Networks* textbook

- Pencil and paper

Getting Down to Business

Your friend is very proud of her new home and can't wait for you to get to work designing her network. You come over to her new place and sit down at a table (still surrounded by packing boxes) and ask her what she needs from her new network. Here's her answer:

Her office is on the first floor. She has a Windows 7 Ultimate desktop system that she uses to store large numbers of graphics files and little else. It has three 2-TB drives installed as C:, D:, and E:. She also has a laptop on which she does most of her work. This laptop is connected to two printers via an external USB hub, a typical home laser printer and a very high-end, large-format inkjet printer that she uses to make prints of her work.

The second floor is the main part of the townhouse. It is an open layout, with a kitchen and massive living area that she wants to turn into a dining area and living area. She wants a home theater PC driving a 52-inch screen on the second floor of the home. She has the 52-inch TV, but hasn't purchased the PC yet and is looking to you for guidance.

The third floor is her bedroom and another small office area. The office area overlooks the main floor. She feels the view helps inspire her art. There is a powerful Windows Vista Ultimate machine with a 24-inch monitor and a Wacom digitizer tablet. She also wants to be able to use her laptop anywhere on the third floor as she likes to check her e-mail while sitting on her bed.

Last, she shows you that the previous owner left two Axis 214 PTZ cameras installed in the front and the back of the townhouse, overlooking the front and back entrances. She assures you the cameras are in good working order and asks you if you can "make these work so I can see what's happening outside from any computer in the house."

All walls of the house are standard home construction, drywall and studs. The townhouse has a crawlspace attic that covers the entire house and is easily accessible. There is no existing wiring in the house with the exception of four runs of speaker wire to support the side and back channels of a 7.1 sound system.

Figures 19-1, 19-2, and 19-3 show the floor plan of each floor of the townhouse. Note the locations of cameras, speaker outlet, and desired location of the home theater.

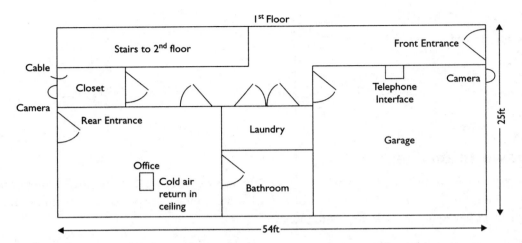

FIGURE 19-1 Floor plan of first floor

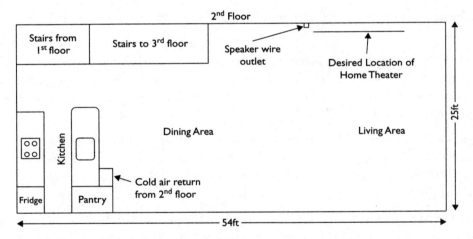

FIGURE 19-2 Floor plan of second floor

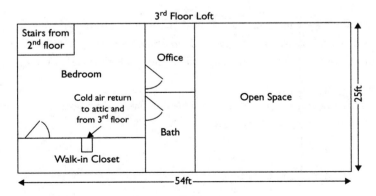

FIGURE 19-3 Floor plan of third floor

Step 1   Your friend has a great start here, but she doesn't really appreciate what she's asking the network to do. Get someone to role-play the friend, and discuss the network needs. Create a list of requirements based on that conversation. Here are a few hints to get you started:

1. Is she getting cable TV or does she just want to watch Internet TV?

2. Which computers need access to the printers?

3. Has she considered making the downstairs desktop a standard file server?

4. Does she have any backup options?

5. How does she feel about wireless?

6. What speed does the wired network need to run?

Step 2   Using the "list of requirements" as a guide, create a network map of the network. This is a great time to decide on the internal network ID and start assigning IP addresses! Be sure to include the home theater, two desktop computers, the printers, the two cameras, a router, and a switch (although the switch won't need an IP address). Ignore wireless for the moment, as a later exercise will cover wireless.

✱ Cross Reference

You'll find a list of requirements for setting up a network in Chapter 19 of the *Mike Meyers' Comp-TIA Network+ Guide to Managing and Troubleshooting Networks* textbook.

Step 3   Consider any environmental limitations of this network. What parts of the house might you need to watch out for in terms of heat, cold, or moisture?

_____

_____

Step 4   Update the network map to include a DHCP server and the IP address scheme.

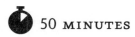 50 MINUTES

Lab Exercise 19.02: Installing the Physical Network

You're off to a good start. You know what the network needs to do, and you've generated a network map to cover everything but the wireless. It's now time to grab your work clothes and a drywall saw and install the physical network.

This Lab Exercise requires you to design and install the physical network in a typical SOHO network fashion. Whether you do the actual installation or hire a professional is for you to determine. To perform this Lab Exercise, you'll need skills from Chapter 19 of the textbook, as well as Chapters 6 and 18 of this lab manual.

Learning Objectives

At the completion of this lab, you will be able to

- Generate a network diagram for the network

- Determine the best location for the demarc and MDF for a SOHO network

- Recognize challenges in pulling cable in a SOHO network

Lab Materials and Setup

The materials you'll need for this lab are

- A PC with Internet access

- The *Mike Meyers' CompTIA Network+ Guide to Managing and Troubleshooting Networks* textbook

- Pencil and paper

Getting Down to Business

In this world of wireless everything, it's tempting to ignore a wired network and just do everything wirelessly. While this sounds great in concept, the reality is that a wired network is always far faster and far more dependable than a wireless one. With this attitude in mind, you need to successfully design and install the physical network.

Remember, all walls of the house are standard home construction, with drywall and studs. The townhouse has a crawlspace attic that covers the entire house and is easily accessible. There is no existing network wiring in the house, with the exception of four runs of speaker wire to support the side and back channels of a 7.1 sound system.

Step 1   Make photocopies of the floor plans in this book (Figures 19-1, 19-2, and 19-3) for the next steps.

Step 2   Your friend is trying to decide between using a cable modem or fiber Internet service provider. Each offers excellent television service as well as Internet. They are roughly the same speed and cost. The only real difference is that the fiber will terminate in the garage and the cable terminates in the first-floor closet. Decide which to use, and write down the criteria that made you come to that decision. Use personal experience as well as the floor plan to make your decision.

_____

_____

Step 3   Using your decision from Step 2, decide on an MDF for the SOHO network. Assume that your first option isn't agreeable to your friend, and come up with a second area. Sketch the MDF on the floor plan, and then on a separate sheet of paper show the layout of the MDF. Include the type of rack you would use, as well as the type of patch panel, power, environmental controls, switch, and router.

Step 4 Draw out the cable runs for the townhouse. You may use any of the images, including Figure 19-4. Keep in mind that the floor joists in the house run from one side of the house to the other, making horizontal runs in the floors expensive if they run from the front to the back of the house. Horizontal runs going from one side of the house to the other are easy. Also, it's very easy to run cables up and down the walls. Are there alternatives to the runs to make them easier to do? Use Figure 19-4 to help you make sure all the runs stay within the length requirements of the network you choose.

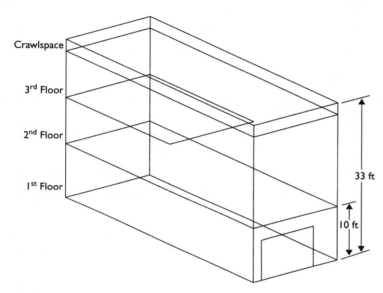

FIGURE 19-4 Isometric of the house

Step 5 Locate a cable installer in your area and ask them to give you an estimate for the house. (Don't be afraid to ask! You'd be amazed how much most companies enjoy helping people learn about their business!) Get a price quote and weigh that against installing the network yourself. How would you test the cables? What if you run into problems? Write a short paragraph on the benefits and the liabilities of "do it yourself" versus a professional installation.

 50 MINUTES

Lab Exercise 19.03: Going Wireless

Despite the earlier remarks about wireless, it's hard to imagine any network without an 802.11 wireless network. Wireless may not be as fast or as dependable as cable, but its ease of installation and convenience at such a low price make it hard to resist. Your friend clearly stated she wants the laptop to work anywhere in the house, so let's get this townhouse set up for wireless.

This exercise requires you to design and install the wireless network in a typical SOHO network. Whether you do the actual installation or hire a professional is for you to determine in the lab. To perform this lab, you'll need skills from Chapter 19 of the textbook, as well as Chapters 15 and 18 of this lab manual.

Learning Objectives

At the completion of this lab, you will be able to

- Properly install a wireless access point to ensure good coverage

- Configure multiple wireless access points to work in an Extended Service Set (ESS)

- Properly configure wireless access points for encryption

- Verify that the wireless network works seamlessly with the wired network

✔ **Hint**

You have two different options for setting up a wireless network, ad hoc and infrastructure. Ad hoc gets you a small, decentralized network with no access to the world outside the network. Will that work here?

Lab Materials and Setup

The materials you'll need for this lab are

- A PC with Internet access

- The *Mike Meyers' CompTIA Network+ Guide to Managing and Troubleshooting Networks* textbook

- Pencil and paper

Getting Down to Business

For the scope of this lab, assume that a wireless access point's signal will easily pass through a single floor but not two floors. Also, the wireless signal will pass through two walls but not three.

Remember, all walls of the house are standard home construction, drywall and studs. The townhouse has a crawlspace attic that covers the entire house and is easily accessible. There is no existing network wiring in the house with the exception of four runs of speaker wire to support the side and back channels of a 7.1 sound system.

Step 1 Make photocopies of the floor plans in this book (Figures 19-1, 19-2, and 19-3) for the next steps.

Step 2 Using the criteria given for this Lab Exercise, choose the number of wireless access points (WAPs) you will use to ensure full coverage. Take the copies of the network diagram and include these WAPs. Demonstrate your decision to fellow students or your instructor and prepare to defend it.

Step 3   Extend the cable runs on the network diagram to include the wireless access points. Be sure to include cable runs to all WAPs.

Step 4   Now update the network map you created earlier to include the WAPs. Don't forget the IP addresses!

Step 5   Choose the brand and model of WAP the network will use: 802.11g or 802.11n? If 802.11n, dual or single band? Decide how you are going to power the WAPs. Will you run AC adapters or will you use Power over Ethernet (PoE)? If you use PoE, will you use Power Injectors or will you purchase a PoE-capable switch? Document your decision and update your network map to include these decisions.

_____

_____

Step 6   Many SOHO options are available today for devices that are routers/switches/WAPs all in one. Is there any room for that type of device in your network, or should you use all separate pieces? Make your decision and write down your reasons or present them to your instructor or fellow students. Prepare to defend it!

_____

_____

Step 7   Create a list of necessary steps to configure your WAPs for encryption. (Be sure to choose an encryption first!) Then go to http://ui.linksys.com and choose two different Linksys WAPs to configure (all Linksys WAPs start with the letters WAP) and configure them to meet the criteria you chose. Demonstrate your configuration to your instructor or a fellow student. These are emulators, not real WAPs. Do not click Save Changes at any time as it will only reset the page to defaults.

 50 MINUTES

Lab Exercise 19.04: Configuring Routers

One of the greatest problems with SOHO networks is the purpose-built SOHO routers that are so common today. Most of these routers, assuming you can plug them in correctly, will work out of the box. Unfortunately, the default configurations are also the most dangerous to use as they lack any form of security.

This exercise requires you to configure a typical SOHO router. To perform this lab, you'll need skills from Chapter 19 of the textbook, as well as Chapters 7 and 8 of this lab manual.

Learning Objectives

At the completion of this lab, you will be able to

- Properly configure IP information for a SOHO router

- Properly configure DHCP for a SOHO network

- Activate the firewall features for a basic SOHO router

- Configure a basic ACL for a SOHO router

Lab Materials and Setup

The materials you'll need for this lab are

- A Windows Vista or 7 PC with Internet access

- The *Mike Meyers' CompTIA Network+ Guide to Managing and Troubleshooting Networks* textbook

- Pencil and paper

Getting Down to Business

SOHO routers are wonderful tools that make connecting a small network to the Internet an easy job. Nevertheless, you must know how to make a number of basic configurations to make the router work well. This Lab Exercise challenges you to use the knowledge you gained from multiple chapters in the textbook to make a safer, well-configured router.

Step 1   Go to http://ui.linksys.com and locate the WRVS4400N router. Remember, this is only an emulator. Do not click Save Changes at any time as it will only reset the page to defaults.

Step 2   Using the IP addressing scheme you chose for your network, configure the router with the IP address and subnet mask you chose for its internal address.

Step 3   Configure the router's DHCP server to work for your network. (Disable/Enable the DHCP server to get the DHCP settings to update.)

Step 4   Poke around the settings for this router for Firewall. What is this firewall that is turned on or off? How is this different from making your own ACL option?

_____

_____

Step 5   Your friend has a son who likes to play certain games using the popular Steam client (www .steampowered.com). Provide a written or oral presentation on how to create an ACL on the router that will prevent him from using his Steam client after 10 P.M. on school nights. (Note: The WRVS4400N emulator does not function on ACLs. Try the WRT54GL emulator, which works a bit better.)

_____

_____

Step 6 Going back to the WRV4400N, what else would you do on this router to lock it down? Make a list and prepare to defend it.

_____

_____

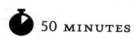 50 MINUTES

Lab Exercise 19.05: Configuring Clients

It's time to finalize the network by configuring the clients' IP information so they can access each other, as well as the Internet. In this case there are four computers: a home theater system, two desktops, and a laptop, but there are also the two AXIS 214 PTZ cameras to configure as well.

This exercise requires you to configure IP information for wired and wireless clients in a typical SOHO network. To perform this lab, you'll need skills from Chapter 19 of the textbook, as well as Chapters 7 and 10 of this lab manual.

Learning Objectives

At the completion of this lab, you will be able to

- Properly configure a wired Windows system for network and Internet access
- Properly configure a wireless Windows system for network and Internet access
- Configure IP information on a non-PC device (in this case, IP cameras)
- Consider different DNS client configuration options

Lab Materials and Setup

The materials you'll need for this lab are

- A Windows Vista or 7 PC using a wired connection with Internet access
- A Windows Vista or 7 PC using a wireless connection

- The *Mike Meyers' CompTIA Network+ Guide to Managing and Troubleshooting Networks* textbook

- Pencil and paper

Getting Down to Business

With any luck at all, this should be the easiest of all the Lab Exercises in this chapter. This is a simple review of the skills you should already know from previous chapters, culminating in your using those skills to determine how to configure a device you've probably never encountered before: an IP-based Point-Tile-Zoom (PTZ) camera.

Step 1   Configure the wired client for Internet access. If the client is set up for DHCP, can you reconfigure for static IP address, even if it's just temporary? Where would you get the IP address, subnet mask, and default gateway information? If the client is currently on the Internet, can you make a subtle misconfiguration to make it not work? Give the misconfigured system to a fellow student to see if he or she can fix the problem.

_____

_____

Step 2   Connect a wireless client to an SSID. If the client was already on the wireless network, delete the profile in the wireless client and start from the beginning.

Step 3   If you have access to a WAP, create an SSID and have the client connect. Then, without changing the SSID, change the encryption. What do you need to do to get the client to connect successfully?

Step 4   Assume for a moment that you're having DNS problems. Go online and find some public DNS servers to use in your DNS settings. What are two of the popular Google public DNS server IP addresses?

_____

_____

Step 5   Go online and determine how to configure the AXIS 214 PTZ cameras to use valid IP information for your network ID. Do you need special software, or can you use a Web browser? What is the default IP address for these cameras? Can these cameras act as DHCP clients? After the cameras are running, how do you see what they see: a special application or your Web browser? What would you do so that your friend can see these cameras on any computer in her home?

_____

_____

Lab Analysis

1. Bill wants to create a SOHO network in an old warehouse space that's been completely gutted. How would his network needs differ from those of your friend's townhouse SOHO network?

2. Bill's warehouse needs the Internet! Assuming the warehouse is located right next door to you, what would you recommend he use? What if you learned that he planned to start a video production business in the space, creating high-definition instructional videos designed for posting to YouTube? How would your recommendation change?

3. Bill wants two creative teams working in two separate wireless network spaces in his warehouse during the video shooting times. (After the shoot, everybody will be on the same wired network.) Can he create two wireless networks in essentially a single physical space? What steps would you recommend (if it's possible) for the wireless setup? Rather than setting up two ad hoc networks, could he somehow connect the two wireless networks in infrastructure mode to the wired network and get Internet access through his default gateway? Explain.

4. Bill's video production company is part of a larger network of companies that want to coordinate the videos produced to optimize training options and reduce any overlap. Bill anticipates a lot of VoIP and video conferencing via Skype between the various companies, but he's worried that the video uploads are going to cause the video and voice chatting to suffer. What's your recommendation?

5. Bill notices that his network tech has systematically added manual DNS settings for the gateway and a few key machines, rather than letting DHCP do the serving. Explain to Bill the relative merits of using manual DNS settings, such as Google's public DNS.

Key Term Quiz

Use the vocabulary terms from the list below to complete the sentences that follow. Not all of the terms will be used.

802.11g	network diagram
802.11n	network map
ad hoc mode	peripheral
Extended Service Set (ESS)	Power over Ethernet (PoE)
infrastructure mode	quality of service (QoS)
lights-out management (LOM)	security
list of requirements	Wi-Fi Protected Access (WPA)
main distribution frame	Wi-Fi Protected Access 2 (WPA2)
network design	Wired Equivalent Privacy (WEP)

1. The _____ in a building stores the demarc, telephone cross-connects, and LAN cross-connects.

2. If given the choice of all three wireless encryption options, always go with _____ over _____, and never use _____.

3. A(n) _____ is a highly detailed illustration of a network, down to individual computers. It will show IP addresses, ports, protocols, and more.

4. You can use _____ to connect several wireless nodes without the need for a WAP.

5. Configuring _____ on a router or managed switch enables you to prioritize specific types of network traffic.

Chapter 20
Network Troubleshooting

Lab Exercises

Similar to the discussion back in Chapter 4 concerning the "art of making cables," the skills and processes you will need to learn and refine to troubleshoot networks are also referred to as an "art." The art of troubleshooting can be difficult to master. In order to hone your skills, you need to familiarize yourself with the terms and processes and to practice with the many network troubleshooting tools available (both hardware and software).

In the following Lab Exercises, you'll examine the different hardware and software tools that are used to help troubleshoot network problems. You will also take time to identify some useful troubleshooting questions that you would ask a user in a troubleshooting situation to help you identify the problem. The CompTIA Network+ exam expects you to be familiar with the different troubleshooting tools used by network professionals—so put some time into these Lab Exercises, and don't forget to reference Chapter 20 in the *Mike Meyers' CompTIA Network+ Guide to Managing and Troubleshooting Networks* textbook.

 20 MINUTES

Lab Exercise 20.01: Identifying Hardware Troubleshooting Tools

When troubleshooting network problems, you will utilize hardware tools to help identify physical issues with the network. The hardware tools will help you identify and correct problems with the physical components of the network, such as network cabling, connectors, and physical connectivity. You will start your study of troubleshooting techniques with a review of the popular tools available to diagnose and correct problems with the physical components of the network.

Learning Objectives

When you have completed this lab, you will be able to

- Identify the various tools used to work with the physical components of a network

- Contrast and compare the different tools you would use to troubleshoot the physical network versus the tools you would use to assemble and repair the physical components of the network

Lab Materials and Setup

The materials you'll need for this lab are

- Pencil and paper

- The *Mike Meyers' CompTIA Network+ Guide to Managing and Troubleshooting Networks* textbook

- A PC with access to the Internet for research

Getting Down to Business

Lee, one of the other network techs at ITCF, is helping one of his friends outside of work with a small office upgrade. They are upgrading the old cabling to CAT 6 and running a piece of fiber-optic cable between two buildings. Lee invites you to tag along for the experience. He recommends that you put together a list of some of the tools you should have on hand and asks you to review the function of each of the tools.

Step 1 In the following mix-and-match exercise, identify the description that corresponds with each hardware tool by recording the correct letter.

Tool	Description
A. Time domain reflectometer (TDR)	_____ Used to capture and analyze network traffic
B. Butt set	_____ Can tell you how much voltage is on the line
C. Protocol analyzer	_____ Removes the insulation from a cable exposing the conductor
D. Certifier	_____ Can identify where a break in copper cable is
E. Temperature monitor	_____ Places UTP wires into a 66- or 110-block
F. Multimeter	_____ Can identify if the cable is handling its rated capacity
G. Punchdown tool	_____ Used to firmly connect RJ-45 connectors to CAT cables
H. Cable tester	_____ Can identify where a break in fiber cable is
I. Toner probe	_____ Can indicate if there is continuity between the two ends of a wire
J. Optical time domain reflectometer	_____ Can tap into a 66- or 110-block to see if a particular line is working
K. Wire stripper	_____ Can help you locate a particular cable
L. Crimping tool	_____ Can be used to monitor and ensure the temperature level

Step 2 Now, utilizing the Internet, conduct a search for each of the tools listed and provide the name of one or two popular manufacturers. Make note of whether the tool is primarily an assembly/repair tool or is typically used to verify/troubleshoot connectivity issues.

Tool	Manufacturer	Typical Use
A. Time domain reflectometer (TDR)		
B. Butt set		
C. Protocol analyzer		
D. Certifier		
E. Temperature monitor		
F. Multimeter		
G. Punchdown tool		
H. Cable tester		
I. Toner probe		
J. Optical time domain reflectometer		
K. Wire stripper		
L. Crimping tool		

 30 MINUTES

Lab Exercise 20.02: Working with a Cable Verifier

When you worked with the physical network back in Chapter 6, you worked with various hardware tools to troubleshoot network connectivity. Well, the troubleshooting process is important enough, both in practice and to pass the CompTIA Network+ exam, that you should run through a few more steps related to troubleshooting network connectivity!

In the previous Lab Exercises, you worked with cable testers, time domain reflectometers, and toner probes. Now you will use a device that provides a number of these functions from the same unit, displaying information such as a graphical wire map, the length of the cable, distance to fault (if the cable is damaged), even speed, such as 10/100/1000 Mbps. A number of manufacturers offer models that test all of these parameters, usually called *cable verifiers*. Greenlee, JDSU, Paladin, and Fluke all offer models in the range of US$400 to $600, some with additional functionality covering voice and video cabling in addition to data cabling.

Even if you do not have a cable verifier available to you, follow through the Lab Exercise steps to refresh yourself with the steps to follow when troubleshooting structured cabling connectivity.

Learning Objectives

In this lab, you will go through some basic network connectivity troubleshooting scenarios, so by the time you complete this lab, you'll be able to

- Troubleshoot simple physical network connectivity issues

Lab Materials and Setup

The materials you'll need for this lab are

- Multiple lengths of patch cable

- Multiple lengths of crossover cables

- Various damaged cables or poorly assembled cables

- A PC with a NIC

- A 10/100/1000 Ethernet switch

- A cable verifier (a Fluke Microscanner2 was used for the Lab Exercise)

- Pencil and paper

Getting Down to Business

When you're working in a SOHO environment, depending on the size of the organization, the network design and installation may be handled by the IT department or professional cable installers. Once the structured cabling is in place, the keystones and the faceplates are fixed to the wall outlets, and the patch bays are punched down, the network infrastructure can remain stable for years. But what happens if you start to experience intermittent connectivity on one or two of the runs? Do you immediately call the cable installers, or do you handle it in-house?

Many SOHO organizations will begin with an in-house assessment of the situation. The seasoned tech, following the time-honored practice of the troubleshooting process, will begin with the simplest components first (NICs, patch cables, switches), working toward a solution step by step. When a cable run is suspected, various tools may be employed to test the cable. An inexpensive cable tester will tell you if the cable is broken, but that's about it. A cable verifier will give you additional information such as the distance to the break or the speed of the connection (10 Mbps, 100 Mbps, or 1000 Mbps). Cable certifiers, though pricey, will provide advanced features such as measurements for near-end crosstalk (NEXT) and far-end crosstalk (FEXT).

Maggie has a number of Fluke Microscanner2 cable verifiers. She offers you access to one of them so you may conduct some experiments with various lengths of patch cable, crossover cables, damaged cables, and a few switches to see the cable troubleshooting process in action.

✔ Exam Tip

In this Lab Exercise, you will be working with a device referred to as a *cable verifier*. Cable verifiers are really just devices that combine a few of the useful test tools that you have already worked with. The cable verifier will check for continuity (cable tester), length of cable or distance to break (time domain reflectometer [TDR]), and help identify individual cables or ports with the addition of a probe (toner). When questioned on the CompTIA Network+ certification exam, you should be careful to respond with the correct tool. Use a cable tester to check for continuity or connectivity, use a TDR to check the distance to cable breaks, and use a toner and probe to identify individual cables or ports.

Step 1   To make this scenario a thorough troubleshooting exercise, you will start by simulating a basic network run. If this were in a typical office, the computer would plug into an RJ-45 wall jack and the signal would travel over the cable run through a patch panel to a switch in the MDF or IDF. As you have done a number of times now, take a patch cable and make a connection between a PC and an Ethernet switch. Examine the status lights on both the PC's NIC and the switch. Describe what you observe and what you might deduce from this observation.

_____

_____

Step 2   Gather a few lengths of known-good CAT 5e or CAT 6 patch cable and your cable verifier. For the Lab Exercise, a Fluke Microscanner2 cable verifier was used, so some of the tests may not be available on your model. Connect the cable verifier's main unit and the detachable wire map adapter to the cable. Observe the graphical wire map results and the length of cable, and verify connectivity between all pairs. Record the results of three of the patch cables in the following space:

Patch Cable # 1: _____

Patch Cable # 2: _____

Patch Cable # 3: _____

Step 3   Now, using the crossover cable, connect the cable verifier's main unit and the detachable wire map adapter to the crossover cable. Observe the graphical wire map results and the length of cable, and verify connectivity between all pairs. Record the results in the following space:

Crossover Cable: _____

Step 4   If you have any damaged or improperly assembled cables, they can give this Lab Exercise a real-world feel. Using the suspect cables, connect the cable verifier's main unit and the detachable wire map adapter to the cable. Observe the graphical wire map results and the length of cable, and verify connectivity between all pairs. Record the results of three of the patch cables in the following space:

Patch Cable # 1: _____

Patch Cable # 2: _____

Patch Cable # 3: _____

Step 5   Using one of the known-good patch cables, plug one end into the main unit of the cable verifier and the other end into a switch. If you have 10-Mbps, 100-Mbps, and 1000-Mbps switches, try all three. Observe the results on the cable verifier's display. What are the results?

_____

_____

Step 6 Many advanced switches offer Power over Ethernet (PoE) to provide power to downstream switches, wireless access points, and digital phone equipment. If you have access to a switch with PoE, plug a patch cable into the switch and plug the other end into the cable verifier. Did the cable verifier identify that PoE is available?

_____

_____

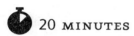 20 MINUTES

Lab Exercise 20.03: Using Software Troubleshooting Tools

When troubleshooting network problems, you first check the hardware aspects of the network, for example, making sure that everything is connected. After verifying that everything is connected, you then look to the visual indicators, such as the link light on the network card or the "online" light on the printer. What do you do after verifying that everything is physically in place and appears to be working?

The next step is to jump into the operating system and use some of the useful commands that you have learned that allow you to troubleshoot network problems!

Learning Objectives

In this lab, you'll review the different Windows commands that are used to troubleshoot network problems. At the end of this lab, you will be able to

- Verify your IP address

- Verify connectivity to another system

- Verify that DNS name resolution is working

- View systems that are connected to you

Lab Materials and Setup

The materials you'll need for this lab are

- Pencil and paper

- A Windows XP, Windows Vista, or Windows 7 system with Internet connectivity

Getting Down to Business

Ken calls you over to his desk and appears to be very frustrated. He can't seem to get on the Internet and needs you to show him some of the tools he can use to verify network connectivity.

✖ Cross-Reference

It would be a good idea to review the different troubleshooting utilities presented in Chapter 15 of the *Mike Meyers' CompTIA Network+ Guide to Managing and Troubleshooting Networks* textbook before performing this lab.

You start by verifying the physical network components. You have verified that the network cable is connected to Ken's system and that the link light is on. You are now ready to verify the configuration of his system using some of the software tools available in Windows.

Step 1   In the following space, list some of the utilities you might use to troubleshoot the problem.

_____

_____

_____

_____

What are some of the tools that would be available to you if you were working on a Linux machine such as Ubuntu?

_____

_____

Step 2   You will first verify that the system has an IP address by typing the **ipconfig** command at a Windows command prompt. Record the IP configuration information in the following spaces:

IP address: _____

Subnet mask: _____

Default gateway: _____

➜ Note

The `ipconfig` command can be used by itself to view the connection-specific DNS suffix, link-local IPv6 address, IPv4 IP address, subnet mask, and default gateway of a system, or you can use `ipconfig /all` to display all TCP/IP settings, including your DNS Server address and your system's physical MAC address.

Step 3   After verifying that the system has an IP address, you will need to verify that the system is configured for a DNS server. Type the **ipconfig /all** command and record the following information.

DNS server: _____

Step 4   Once you have recorded the IP address of the default gateway and DNS server, you will verify that they are running by using the ping command. Ping the IP address of the default gateway by typing **ping <ip_address_of_default gateway>** and pressing ENTER.

Now ping the IP address of the DNS server by typing **ping <ip_address_of_DNS_server>** and pressing ENTER. Do you get replies from both systems? (Circle your answers on the following lines.)

Default gateway?   Yes   No

DNS server?   Yes   No

Step 5   Along the same lines as the ping utility, another TCP/IP utility that allows you to troubleshoot connectivity is known as traceroute (tracert). Tracert will allow you to record the number of "hops" or routers a packet has to pass through to get from a source computer to a destination computer (usually on a far-removed remote network).

Open a command prompt and type **tracert www.comptia.org**. This will trace the route from your computer to the server hosting www.comptia.org. Often, tracert will time out well before reaching the destination host. This could indicate an actual connectivity problem, but tracert may just be blocked by firewalls or other security measures.

Open a browser and navigate to www.comptia.org. If you are able to open the Web site, there are no connectivity problems between your computer and the CompTIA Web site.

Record a few of the hops in the following space.

_____

_____

_____

Step 6 Next you will use the `nslookup` command to troubleshoot DNS. To find out the IP address of the Web site for google.com, type **nslookup www.google.com**. Record the IP address of the Web site in the following space (record multiple addresses if there is more than one). See Figure 20-1.

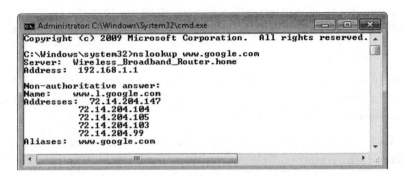

FIGURE 20-1 Output of the **nslookup** command with www.google.com

Step 7 Now you will try to find out the mail servers for google.com using the `nslookup` utility. Type the following commands to find out the e-mail server for Google.

```
nslookup
set type=mx
google.com
```

Your results should resemble those shown in Figure 20-2. MX records in DNS are used to refer to the mail exchange servers for a company.

```
C:\Windows\system32>nslookup
Default Server:  Wireless_Broadband_Router.home
Address:  192.168.1.1

> set type=mx
> google.com
Server:  Wireless_Broadband_Router.home
Address:  192.168.1.1

Non-authoritative answer:
google.com      MX preference = 40, mail exchanger = alt3.aspmx.l.google.com
google.com      MX preference = 50, mail exchanger = alt4.aspmx.l.google.com
google.com      MX preference = 10, mail exchanger = aspmx.l.google.com
google.com      MX preference = 30, mail exchanger = alt2.aspmx.l.google.com
google.com      MX preference = 20, mail exchanger = alt1.aspmx.l.google.com

aspmx.l.google.com       internet address = 74.125.115.26
alt2.aspmx.l.google.com internet address = 74.125.79.27
alt1.aspmx.l.google.com internet address = 209.85.229.26
alt3.aspmx.l.google.com internet address = 74.125.39.26
>
```

FIGURE 20-2 A list of mail exchange (MX) records for google.com

Record the mail server settings in the following space:

_____

_____

_____

➔ **Note**

The `nslookup` command is used to troubleshoot DNS-related issues. It can be used the way it is presented in the previous step, or you can use it to resolve a single host address to IP address by typing `nslookup www.totalsem.com`.

Step 8   You have shown Ken how to verify the TCP/IP settings with the `ipconfig` command and how to verify connectivity with the `ping` command. You have also verified that he can communicate with the DNS server using the `nslookup` command. Next you will show Ken how to use commands to see the active connections to the system. Open a Web browser and navigate to www.totalsem.com.

Step 9   Now open a command prompt and type **netstat –n** and press ENTER. The `netstat` command is used to display current connections, including both connections you initiate and connections initiated by someone else!

In the `netstat` output, record the line of information that is related to your connection to the Total Seminars Web site. Identify what each column in the output is used for. See Figure 20-3.

_____

_____

FIGURE 20-3 Output of the **netstat –n** command after launching the www.totalsem.com Web site

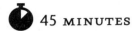 45 MINUTES

Lab Exercise 20.04: Network Mapping and Port Scanning

With the heightened need for cyber security, maintaining and troubleshooting the various components that can compromise the network's security will continue to be the focus of the skilled network technician. Nmap (Network Mapper) is a wonderful tool that not only allows you to create a virtual map of the devices on your network but also generates a report listing the host names, MAC addresses, IP addresses, and all of the open ports for each device.

The Nmap suite of tools also includes Zenmap. Zenmap is a GUI front end and results viewer for Nmap. It allows you to scan your network, examine the network map, and view some of the detailed information related to the devices on your network, all from a convenient Windows interface. Zenmap provides an excellent tool to troubleshoot host names, IP addressing, and firewall configuration.

Learning Objectives

In this lab, you'll install and run Zenmap. When you've completed this lab, you will be able to

- Install and run the Nmap and Zenmap port scanning applications

- Examine the resultant network map

- Review the port data generated by the scan

Lab Materials and Setup

The materials you'll need for this lab are

- A PC with Internet connectivity to download the Nmap and Zenmap installation files or access to the installation files

- Pencil and paper

- Multiple Windows XP, Windows 7, or Ubuntu Linux client machines

- One or two Windows Server 2008 systems

- The Linksys WRT54GL (or similar) router that was configured in Lab Exercise 9.03 and appropriate cabling to connect the small network

Getting Down to Business

Nmap/Zenmap provides an excellent method to create a network map of all of the systems and devices available on your network. It also provides a detailed report on each of the devices, including operating systems and host names (when available), MAC addresses, IP addresses, and open port information.

This information can then be analyzed and used to troubleshoot security holes such as IP addressing schemes, open ports, and firewall issues.

To generate a more realistic scenario, Maggie recommends you use the machines and devices in the networking lab to construct a simple network consisting of one or two client systems, one or two servers, and a wireless router. You can then run Zenmap and use the data to troubleshoot network security.

Take a few moments, build the small network, and then launch Zenmap and commence your exploration!

Step 1 To begin your exploration of your network and the Nmap/Zenmap network mapping tool, you will first download the installation files from Nmap's Web site.

a. Go to http://nmap.org and click on the **Download** hyperlink.

b. On the download page, scroll down to the **Microsoft Windows Binaries** section and navigate to the **Latest stable release self-installer** and then click the **nmap-5.51-setup.exe** hyperlink.

c. Download the Nmap executable installation file (the current version at the time of this writing is 5.51) to your Windows desktop or downloaded files folder.

d. Copy the executable installation file to a flash drive for installation on your networking lab Windows client machine.

✔ **Tech Tip**

To provide a richer experience when using Nmap, Maggie has recommended that you perform the Lab Exercise on a small closed local area network. Configure two Microsoft Server 2008 systems (one as the DNS server), two or more clients, and a wireless router (used as a wired switch/router). Enable the firewalls on all devices. You may choose an IP addressing scheme of your own or use 192.168.10.0/24 as shown in the figures for this Lab Exercise.

Step 2 On one of the Microsoft client machines, copy the Nmap installation file and use the following instructions to install Nmap/Zenmap:

a. Launch the Nmap setup program **nmap-5.51-setup.exe.**

b. Select **I Agree** on the License Agreement screen.

c. Verify that all of the components are checked as shown in Figure 20-4, and click **Next.**

d. Select the destination location (the default location is fine) and click **Install.**

e. **Nmap Setup** will now install all of the files needed to configure and run the Nmap/Zenmap utility. When the installation of the files is complete, click **Next.**

f. Create the shortcuts and click **Next.**

g. When you're finished, Nmap will be installed on your computer. Click **Finish.**

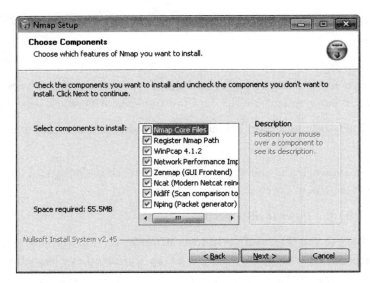

Figure 20-4 Choosing components such as Nmap Core Files and Zenmap (GUI front end)

Step 3   Now launch the **Nmap – Zenmap** application. In the **Target** dialog box, type the Network ID of the IP address and an "*" for the Host ID, such as **192.168.10.***. This will scan all hosts on the 192.168.10.0/24 network. Click **Scan** to begin the process, as shown in Figure 20-5.

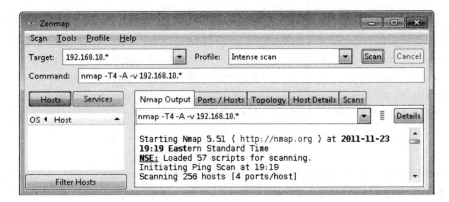

Figure 20-5 Beginning the network scan with the Zenmap GUI for Nmap

Step 4   After the scan of your network completes, you should have a list of devices (depending on how many systems you have running) and a large amount of data (scanned addresses, scanned ports, operating system types, and so on). When the scan completes, click the **Topology** tab and then click the **Fisheye** tab. Your display should look similar to the network map shown in Figure 20-6.

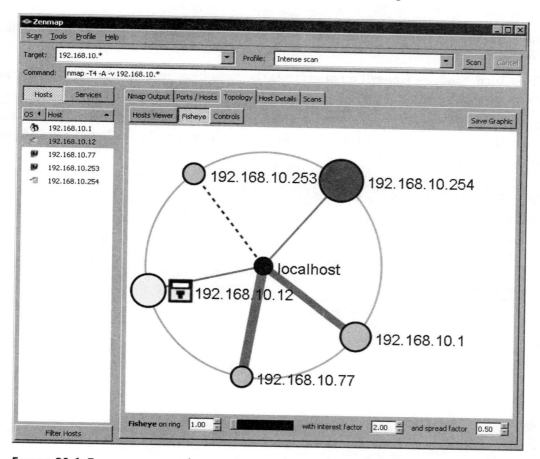

FIGURE 20-6 Zenmap-generated network map of the ITCF networking lab setup

Using the detailed information discovered during the Nmap/Zenmap scan of your network, record the device names and IP addresses of the various systems in the following space.

_____

_____

_____

_____

Step 5 Next, select one of the remote Windows systems (either a Windows 7 client or a Windows Server 2008 machine that you are not running Nmap/Zenmap from). This will be the **Target** machine for the port scans. Configure the firewall to block all incoming connections as follows:

  a. Open the Windows Firewall configuration utility by selecting **Start | Control Panel | Windows Firewall**.

  b. Select **Turn Windows Firewall on or off** from the menu items listed on the left-hand side of the window.

  c. Confirm that the Windows Firewall is turned on for both private and public network locations. Check the box **Block all incoming connections, including those in the list of allowed programs**, as shown in Figure 20-7.

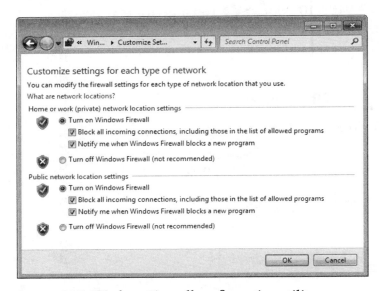

Figure 20-7 Windows Firewall configuration utility

Step 6 Now, to scan the specific Windows machine you configured in Step 5 (the target machine), open Nmap/Zenmap on another machine on the same network and complete the following steps:

  a. Enter the IP address for the machine that you just configured into the **Target** dialog box.

  b. Click on the **Scan** button and let the scan complete.

c.   Select the **Host Details** tab and record the following information:

Operating System Icon: _____

Open Ports: _____

Filtered Ports: _____

Closed Ports: _____

Security Icon: _____

✔ **Hint**

The Zenmap GUI front end includes a number of icons to indicate which operating system is installed on the system that has been scanned. Zenmap also includes icons that indicate the status of the security of the system based on the number of open ports. A full list of the icons along with additional information can be found in the *Zenmap GUI Users' Guide*. This guide can be found at http://nmap.org/book/zenmap-results.html#zenmap-tab-topology.

The following list is a simple description of the security icons:

Safe Icon:	0–2 open ports
Chest Icon:	3–4 open ports
Open Box Icon:	5–6 open ports
Swiss Cheese Icon:	7–8 open ports
Bomb Icon:	9 or more open ports

Step 7   Now, on the Windows target machine, uncheck the box for **Block all incoming connections, including those in the list of allowed programs** to open some of the ports. Scan the target machine again and record the results as follows:

Operating System Icon: _____

Open Ports: _____

Filtered Ports: _____

Closed Ports: _____

Security Icon: _____

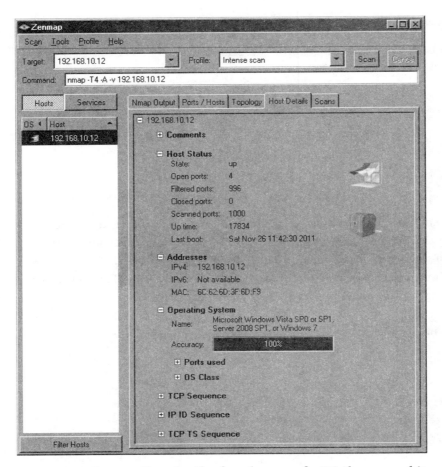

FIGURE 20-8 Zenmap Host details after the scan of a Windows 7 machine with the Windows Firewall enabled

How do your results compare to those shown in Figure 20-8?

Step 8   To complete your exploration of port scanning, on the Windows target machine, completely disable the Windows Firewall. Scan the target machine again and record the results as follows:

Operating System Icon: _____

Open Ports: _____

Filtered Ports: _____

Closed Ports: _____

Security Icon: _____

How do your results compare to those shown in Figure 20-9?

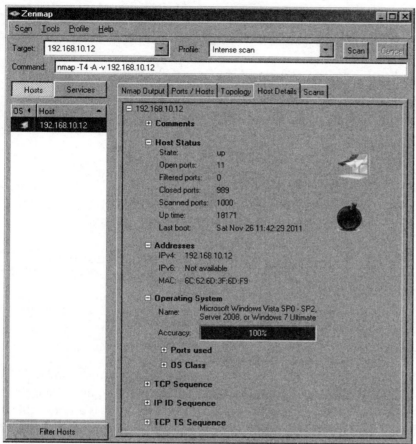

FIGURE 20-9 Zenmap Host details after the scan of a Windows 7 machine with the Windows Firewall disabled

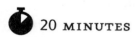 20 MINUTES

Lab Exercise 20.05: Identifying the Troubleshooting Process

When troubleshooting any problem, it is important to have a plan of attack to develop a solution to that problem. The CompTIA Network+ certification exam objectives set forth a methodology to troubleshoot networking issues. The Network+ exam expects you to know these steps to troubleshooting network-related issues. As a network tech, you should not only commit these steps to memory but should work to master the art of troubleshooting, gradually applying simple to complex techniques to arrive at a solution.

The key to troubleshooting is to be mentally prepared when a problem arises. As with any skill, the best way to develop a troubleshooting technique is practice, practice, practice.

Learning Objectives

In this lab, you'll review the troubleshooting process. When you have completed this lab, you will be able to

- Identify the steps of the troubleshooting process
- Describe what each process does
- Develop a number of basic probing questions

Lab Materials and Setup

The materials you'll need for this lab are

- The *Mike Meyers' CompTIA Network+ Guide to Managing and Troubleshooting Networks* textbook
- A PC with Internet access for research
- Pencil and paper

Getting Down to Business

You have now been working with Maggie for a number of months. After watching her troubleshoot network issues, you would like to know how she seems to be able to fix problems fairly quickly. Maggie explains that it is one thing to know how to use the hardware and software tools, but it is another thing to know when to use them. She explains that troubleshooting network issues is like learning to play a musical instrument—it is much easier if there is a process to follow and you must practice.

> ### ✖ Cross-Reference
>
> Before performing this Lab Exercise, re-read the section titled "The Troubleshooting Process" in Chapter 20 of the *Mike Meyers' CompTIA Network+ Guide to Managing and Troubleshooting Networks* textbook.

Step 1   The following is a list of the steps to properly troubleshoot a problem. Place a number beside each step to indicate the order in which the steps should be performed.

_____ Test the theory to determine cause

_____ Document findings, actions, and outcomes

_____ Identify the problem

_____ Implement the solution or escalate as necessary

_____ Establish a theory of probable cause

_____ Verify full system functionality and implement preventative measures

_____ Establish a plan of action and identify potential effects

Step 2   You have been asked by CJ to give a brief explanation of each step in the troubleshooting process. In the space provided, record a brief description of each step in the troubleshooting process.

_____

_____

_____

_____

_____

_____

_____

Step 3   During the "Identify the Problem" phase of the troubleshooting process, you will need to be prepared with some questions that you can ask users to help identify the problem. In the space provided, list three or four potential questions you could ask a user after she complains that she does not have Internet access.

✔ **Hint**

The troubleshooting process and basic questioning techniques are not unique to the IT industry or to networking. If you conduct an Internet search, you can augment the basic questions you may find in the textbook. Search on terms like "basic troubleshooting questions."

_____

_____

_____

_____

Lab Analysis

1. Doug has often used a multimeter to check the voltages of a PC's power supply, especially when a component is not working. How can Doug use a multimeter to help him troubleshoot network problems?

   _____

   _____

2. Tymere has been studying a number of the command-line utilities used to troubleshoot networks. She asks if you could briefly describe the difference between the netstat command and the nbtstat command. Can you provide an example of common switches used with each command?

   _____

   _____

3. Cynthia is exploring Linux using an Ubuntu desktop machine. She would like to know what functions the Linux commands mtr and dig provide.

   _____

   _____

4. Joshua is running a monthly security check on the office network. One of the tools he is using is a port scanner. What is the purpose of a port scanner?

   _____

   _____

5. After studying the steps that CompTIA recommends when troubleshooting networks, Trevor wonders if he will actually apply this technique when he is troubleshooting a real problem. Why is it important to know the troubleshooting process?

   _____

   _____

Key Term Quiz

Use the vocabulary terms from the list below to complete the sentences that follow. Not all of the terms will be used.

cable stripper	nbtstat
cable tester	netstat
certifier	Nmap
dig	nslookup
DNS	ping
hostname	port scanner
ifconfig	protocol analyzer
ipconfig	punchdown tool
multimeter	Zenmap

1. _____ is the Linux command to view your TCP/IP settings.

2. FQDNs are resolved to IP addresses using _____.

3. A(n) _____ is responsible for testing a cable to ensure that it can handle its rated capacity.

4. _____ and _____ are software tools used to query DNS servers.

5. If you want to analyze a remote system for open ports that may allow for security breaches, you can use a(n) _____.

GLOSSARY

6IN4 One of the most popular of all the IPv6 tunneling standards, and one of only two IPv6 tunneling protocols that can go through a NAT.

6TO4 The dominant IPv6 tunneling protocol because it is the only IPv6 tunnel that doesn't require a tunnel broker. It is generally used to connect two routers directly because it normally requires a public IPv4 address.

10BASEFL Fiber-optic implementation of Ethernet that runs at 10 megabits per second (Mbps) using baseband signaling. Maximum segment length is 2 km.

10BASET An Ethernet LAN designed to run on UTP cabling. Runs at 10 Mbps and uses baseband signaling. Maximum length for the cabling between the NIC and the hub (or the switch, the repeater, and so forth) is 100 m.

10GBASEER/10GBASEEW A 10 GbE standard using 1550-nm single-mode fiber. Maximum cable length up to 40 km.

10GBASELR/10GBASELW A 10 GbE standard using 1310-nm single-mode fiber. Maximum cable length up to 10 km.

10GBASESR/10GBASESW A 10 GbE standard using 850-nm multimode fiber. Maximum cable length up to 300 m.

10GBASET A 10 GbE standard designed to run on CAT 6a UTP cabling. Maximum cable length of 100 m.

10 GIGABIT ETHERNET (10 GBE) Currently (2012) the fastest Ethernet designation available, with a number of fiber-optic and copper standards.

100BASEFX An Ethernet LAN designed to run on fiber-optic cabling. Runs at 100 Mbps and uses baseband signaling. Maximum cable length is 400 m for half-duplex and 2 km for full-duplex.

100BASET An Ethernet LAN designed to run on UTP cabling. Runs at 100 Mbps, uses baseband signaling, and uses two pairs of wires on CAT 5 or better cabling.

100BASET4 An Ethernet LAN designed to run on UTP cabling. Runs at 100 Mbps and uses four-pair CAT 3 or better cabling. Made obsolete by 100BaseT.

100BASETX The technically accurate but little-used name for 100BaseT.

110-PUNCHDOWN BLOCK The most common connection used on the back of an RJ-45 jack and patch panels.

110-PUNCHDOWN TOOL *See* Punchdown Tool.

802 COMMITTEE The IEEE committee responsible for all Ethernet standards.

802.1X A port-authentication network access control mechanism for networks.

802.3 (ETHERNET) *See* Ethernet.

802.3AB The IEEE standard for 1000BaseT.

802.3z The umbrella IEEE standard for all versions of Gigabit Ethernet other than 1000BaseT.

802.11 *See* IEEE 802.11.

802.11a A wireless standard that operates in the frequency range of 5 GHz and offers throughput of up to 54 Mbps.

802.11b The first popular wireless standard, which operates in the frequency range of 2.4 GHz and offers throughput of up to 11 Mbps.

802.11g Currently (2012) the wireless standard with the widest use, 802.11g operates on the 2.4-GHz band with a maximum throughput of 54 Mbps.

802.11i A wireless standard that added security features.

802.11n An updated 802.11 standard that increases transfer speeds and adds support for multiple in/multiple out (MIMO) by using multiple antennas. 802.11n can operate on either the 2.4- or 5-GHz frequency band and has a maximum throughput of 400 Mbps.

802.16 A wireless standard (also known as WiMax) with a range of up to 30 miles.

1000BaseCX A Gigabit Ethernet standard using unique copper cabling, with a 25-m maximum cable distance.

1000BaseLX A Gigabit Ethernet standard using single-mode fiber cabling, with a 220- to 500-m maximum cable distance.

1000BaseSX A Gigabit Ethernet standard using multimode fiber cabling, with a 5-km maximum cable distance.

1000BaseT A Gigabit Ethernet standard using CAT 5e/6 UTP cabling, with a 100-m maximum cable distance.

1000BaseX An umbrella Gigabit Ethernet standard. Also known as 802.3z. Comprises all Gigabit standards with the exception of 1000BaseT, which is under the 802.3ab standard.

A Records A list of the IP addresses and names of all the systems on a DNS server domain.

AAA (Authentication, Authorization, and Accounting) *See* Authentication, Authorization, and Accounting (AAA).

Acceptable Use Policy A document that defines what a person may and may not do on an organization's computers and networks.

Access Control List (ACL) A clearly defined list of permissions that specifies what actions an authenticated user may perform on a shared resource.

Active Directory A form of directory service used in networks with Windows servers. Creates an organization of related computers that share one or more Windows domains.

Activity Light An LED on a NIC, hub, or switch that blinks rapidly to show data transfers over the network.

Ad-Hoc Mode A wireless networking mode where each node is in direct contact with every other node in a decentralized free-for-all. Ad-hoc mode is similar to the mesh topology.

Address Resolution Protocol (ARP) A protocol in the TCP/IP suite used with the command-line utility of the same name to determine the MAC address that corresponds to a particular IP address.

ADSL (Asymmetric Digital Subscriber Line) *See* Asymmetric Digital Subscriber Line (ADSL).

Advanced Encryption Standard (AES) A block cipher created in the late 1990s that uses a 128-bit block size and a 128-, 192-, or 256-bit key size. Practically uncrackable.

Adware A program that monitors the types of Web sites you frequent and uses that information to generate targeted advertisements, usually pop-up windows.

Aggregation A router hierarchy in which every router underneath a higher router always uses a subnet of that router's existing routes.

Algorithm A set of rules for solving a problem in a given number of steps.

Anycast A method of addressing groups of computers as though they were a single computer. Anycasting starts by giving a number of computers (or clusters of computers) the same IP address. Advanced routers then send incoming packets to the closest of the computers.

Apache HTTP Server An open-source HTTP server program that runs on a wide variety of operating systems.

Application Layer *See* Open Systems Interconnection (OSI) Seven-Layer Model.

Application Log Tracks application events, such as when an application opens or closes. Different types of application logs record different events.

Archive Bit An attribute of a file that shows whether the file has been backed up since the last change. Each time a file is opened, changed, or saved, the archive bit is turned on. Some types of backups turn off this archive bit to indicate that a good backup of the file exists on tape.

Area ID Address assigned to routers in an OSPF network to prevent flooding beyond the routers in that particular network. *See also* Open Shortest Path First (OSPF).

arping A command used to discover hosts on a network, similar to ping, but that relies on ARP rather than ICMP. The arping command won't cross any routers, so it will only work within a broadcast domain. *See also* Address Resolution Protocol (ARP) and ping.

Asset Management Managing each aspect of a network, from documentation to performance to hardware.

Asymmetric Digital Subscriber Line (ADSL) A fully digital, dedicated connection to the telephone system that provides download speeds of up to 9 Mbps and upload speeds of up to 1 Mbps.

Asymmetric-Key Algorithm An encryption method in which the key used to encrypt a message and the key used to decrypt it are different, or asymmetrical.

Asynchronous Transfer Mode (ATM) A network technology that runs at speeds between 25 and 622 Mbps using fiber-optic cabling or CAT 5 or better UTP.

Attenuation The degradation of signal over distance for a networking cable.

Authentication A process that proves good data traffic truly came from where it says it originated by verifying the sending and receiving users and computers.

Authentication, Authorization, and Accounting (AAA) A security philosophy wherein a computer trying to connect to a network must first present some form of credential in order to be authenticated and then must have limitable permissions within the network. The authenticating server should also record session information about the client.

Authentication Server (AS) In Kerberos, a system that hands out Ticket-Granting Tickets to clients after comparing the client hash to its own. *See also* Ticket-Granting Ticket (TGT).

Authoritative DNS Servers DNS servers that hold the IP addresses and names of systems for a particular domain or domains in special storage areas called *forward lookup zones*.

Authorization A step in the AAA philosophy during which a client's permissions are decided upon. *See also* Authentication, Authorization, and Accounting (AAA).

Automatic Private IP Addressing (APIPA) A networking feature in operating systems that enables DHCP clients to self-configure an IP address and subnet mask automatically when a DHCP server isn't available.

Autonomous System (AS) One or more networks that are governed by a single protocol within that AS, which provides routing for the Internet backbone.

Back Up To save important data in a secondary location as a safety precaution against the loss of the primary data.

Backup Designated Router (BDR) A second router set to take over if the designated router fails. *See also* Designated Router (DR).

Backup Generator An onsite generator that provides electricity if the power utility fails.

Bandwidth A piece of the spectrum occupied by some form of signal, whether it is television, voice, fax data, and so forth. Signals require a certain size and location of bandwidth to be transmitted. The higher the bandwidth, the faster the signal transmission, thus allowing for a more complex signal such as audio or video. Because bandwidth is

a limited space, when one user is occupying it, others must wait their turn. Bandwidth is also the capacity of a network to transmit a given amount of data during a given period.

Baseband Digital signaling that has only one signal (a single signal) on the cable at a time. The signals must be in one of three states: one, zero, or idle.

Baseline Static image of a system's (or network's) performance when all elements are known to be working properly.

Basic NAT A simple form of NAT that translates a computer's private or internal IP address to a global IP address on a one-to-one basis.

Basic Rate Interface (BRI) The basic ISDN configuration, which consists of two B channels (which can carry voice or data at a rate of 64 Kbps) and one D channel (which carries setup and configuration information, as well as data, at 16 Kbps).

Basic Service Set (BSS) In wireless networking, a single access point servicing a given area.

Basic Service Set Identifier (BSSID) Naming scheme in wireless networks.

Baud One analog cycle on a telephone line.

Baud Rate The number of bauds per second. In the early days of telephone data transmission, the baud rate was often analogous to bits per second. Due to advanced modulation of baud cycles as well as data compression, this is no longer true.

Bearer Channel (B Channel) A type of ISDN channel that carries data and voice information using standard DS0 channels at 64 Kbps.

Biometric Devices Devices that scan fingerprints, retinas, or even the sound of the user's voice to provide a foolproof replacement for both passwords and smart devices.

Bit Error Rate Test (BERT) An end-to-end test that verifies a T-carrier connection.

Block Cipher An encryption algorithm in which data is encrypted in "chunks" of a certain length at a time. Popular in wired networks.

BNC Connector A connector used for 10Base2 coaxial cable. All BNC connectors have to be locked into place by turning the locking ring 90 degrees.

Bonding Two or more NICs in a system working together to act as a single NIC to increase performance.

BOOTSTRAP PROTOCOL (BOOTP) A component of TCP/IP that allows computers to discover and receive an IP address from a DHCP server prior to booting the OS. Other items that may be discovered during the BOOTP process are the IP address of the default gateway for the subnet and the IP addresses of any name servers.

BORDER GATEWAY PROTOCOL (BGP-4) An exterior gateway routing protocol that enables groups of routers to share routing information so that efficient, loop-free routes can be established.

BOTNET A group of computers under the control of one operator, used for malicious purposes.

BPS (BITS PER SECOND) A measurement of how fast data is moved across a transmission medium. A Gigabit Ethernet connection moves 1,000,000,000 bps.

BRIDGE A device that connects two networks and passes traffic between them based only on the node address, so that traffic between nodes on one network does not appear on the other network. For example, an Ethernet bridge only looks at the MAC address. Bridges filter and forward frames based on MAC addresses and operate at Layer 2 (Data Link layer) of the OSI seven-layer model.

BRIDGE LOOP A negative situation in which bridging devices (usually switches) are installed in a loop configuration, causing frames to loop continuously. Switches using Spanning Tree Protocol (STP) prevent bridge loops by automatically turning off looping ports.

BRIDGED CONNECTION An early type of DSL connection that made the DSL line function the same as if you snapped an Ethernet cable into your NIC.

BROADBAND Analog signaling that sends multiple signals over the cable at the same time. The best example of broadband signaling is cable television. The zero, one, and idle states exist on multiple channels on the same cable. *See also* Baseband.

BROADCAST A frame or packet addressed to all machines, almost always limited to a broadcast domain.

BROADCAST ADDRESS The address a NIC attaches to a frame when it wants every other NIC on the network to read it. In TCP/IP, the general broadcast address is 255.255.255.255. In Ethernet, the broadcast MAC address is FF-FF-FF-FF-FF-FF.

BROADCAST DOMAIN A network of computers that will hear each other's broadcasts. The older term *collision domain* is the same, but rarely used today.

BROADCAST STORM The result of one or more devices sending a nonstop flurry of broadcast frames on the network.

BROWSER A software program specifically designed to retrieve, interpret, and display Web pages.

BUILDING ENTRANCE Location where all the cables from the outside world (telephone lines, cables from other buildings, and so on) come into a building.

BUS TOPOLOGY A network topology that uses a single bus cable that connects all of the computers in line. Bus topology networks must be terminated to prevent signal reflection.

BUTT SET Device that can tap into a 66- or 110-punchdown block to see if a particular line is working.

BYTE Eight contiguous bits, the fundamental data unit of personal computers. Storing the equivalent of one character, the byte is also the basic unit of measurement for computer storage. Bytes are counted in powers of two.

CAB FILES Short for "cabinet files." These files are compressed and most commonly used during Microsoft operating system installation to store many smaller files, such as device drivers.

CABLE CERTIFIER A very powerful cable testing device used by professional installers to test the electrical characteristics of a cable and then generate a certification report, proving that cable runs pass TIA/EIA standards.

CABLE DROP Location where the cable comes out of the wall at the workstation location.

CABLE MODEM A bridge device that interconnects the cable company's DOCSIS service to the user's Ethernet network. In most locations, the cable modem is the demarc.

CABLE STRIPPER Device that enables the creation of UTP cables.

CABLE TESTER A generic name for a device that tests cables. Some common tests are continuity, electrical shorts, crossed wires, or other electrical characteristics.

CABLE TRAY A device for organizing cable runs in a drop ceiling.

CACHE A special area of RAM that stores frequently accessed data. In a network there are a number of applications that take advantage of cache in some way.

CACHE-ONLY DNS SERVERS (CACHING-ONLY DNS SERVERS) DNS servers that do not have any forward lookup zones. They resolve names of systems on the Internet for the network, but are not responsible for telling other DNS servers the names of any clients.

Cached Lookup The list kept by a DNS server of IP addresses it has already resolved, so it won't have to re-resolve an FQDN it has already checked.

Caching Engine A server dedicated to storing cache information on your network. These servers can reduce overall network traffic dramatically.

Canonical Name (CNAME) Less common type of DNS record that acts as a computer's alias.

Capturing a Printer A process by which a printer uses a local LPT port that connects to a networked printer. This is usually only done to support older programs that are not smart enough to know how to print directly to a UNC-named printer; it's quite rare today.

Card Generic term for anything that you can snap into an expansion slot.

Carrier Sense Multiple Access with Collision Avoidance (CSMA/CA) See CSMA/CA (Carrier Sense Multiple Access with Collision Avoidance).

Carrier Sense Multiple Access with Collision Detection (CSMA/CD) See CSMA/CD (Carrier Sense Multiple Access with Collision Detection).

CAT 3 Category 3 wire, a TIA/EIA standard for UTP wiring that can operate at up to 16 Mbps.

CAT 4 Category 4 wire, a TIA/EIA standard for UTP wiring that can operate at up to 20 Mbps. This wire is not widely used, except in older Token Ring networks.

CAT 5 Category 5 wire, a TIA/EIA standard for UTP wiring that can operate at up to 100 Mbps.

CAT 5e Category 5e wire, a TIA/EIA standard for UTP wiring with improved support for 100 Mbps using two pairs and support for 1000 Mbps using four pairs.

CAT 6 Category 6 wire, a TIA/EIA standard for UTP wiring with improved support for 1000 Mbps.

Category (CAT) Rating A grade assigned to cable to help network installers get the right cable for the right network technology. CAT ratings are officially rated in megahertz (MHz), indicating the highest-frequency bandwidth the cable can handle.

CCITT (Comité Consutatif Internationale Télépho-nique et Télégraphique) European standards body that established the V standards for modems.

Central Office Building that houses local exchanges and a location where individual voice circuits come together.

Certificate A public encryption key signed with the digital signature from a trusted third party called a *certificate authority (CA)*. This key serves to validate the identity of its holder when that person or company sends data to other parties.

Certifier A device that tests a cable to ensure that it can handle its rated amount of capacity.

Challenge Handshake Authentication Protocol (CHAP) A remote access authentication protocol. It has the serving system challenge the remote client, which must provide an encrypted password.

Change Management Documentation A set of documents that defines procedures for changes to the network.

Channel A portion of the wireless spectrum on which a particular wireless network operates. Setting wireless networks to different channels enables separation of the networks.

Channel Bonding Wireless technology that enables WAPs to use two channels for transmission.

Channel Service Unit/Digital Service Unit (CSU/DSU) See CSU/DSU (Channel Service Unit/Data Service Unit).

Chat A multiparty, real-time text conversation. The Internet's most popular version is known as Internet Relay Chat (IRC), which many groups use to converse in real time with each other.

Checksum A simple error-detection method that adds a numerical value to each data packet, based on the number of data bits in the packet. The receiving node applies the same formula to the data and verifies that the numerical value is the same; if not, the data has been corrupted and must be re-sent.

Cipher A series of complex and hard-to-reverse mathematics run on a string of ones and zeroes in order to make a new set of seemingly meaningless ones and zeroes.

Ciphertext The output when cleartext is run through a cipher algorithm using a key.

Circuit Switching The process for connecting two phones together on one circuit.

Cisco IOS Cisco's proprietary operating system.

Cladding The part of a fiber-optic cable that makes the light reflect down the fiber.

Class License Contiguous chunk of IP addresses passed out by the Internet Assigned Numbers Authority (IANA).

CLASSLESS INTER-DOMAIN ROUTING (CIDR) Method of categorizing IP addresses in order to distribute them. *See also* Subnetting.

CLASSLESS SUBNET A subnet that does not fall into the common categories such as Class A, Class B, and Class C.

CLEARTEXT *See* Plaintext.

CLIENT A computer program that uses the services of another computer program; software that extracts information from a server. Your autodial phone is a client, and the phone company is its server. Also, a machine that accesses shared resources on a server.

CLIENT-TO-SITE A type of VPN connection where a single computer logs into a remote network and becomes, for all intents and purposes, a member of that network.

CLIENT/SERVER A relationship in which client software obtains services from a server on behalf of a user.

CLIENT/SERVER APPLICATION An application that performs some or all of its processing on an application server rather than on the client. The client usually only receives the result of the processing.

CLIENT/SERVER NETWORK A network that has dedicated server machines and client machines.

CLOUD COMPUTING Using the Internet to store files and run applications. For example, Google Documents is a cloud computing application that enables you to run productivity applications over the Internet from your Web browser.

COAXIAL CABLE A type of cable that contains a central conductor wire surrounded by an insulating material, which in turn is surrounded by a braided metal shield. It is called coaxial because the center wire and the braided metal shield share a common axis or centerline.

COLLISION The result of two nodes transmitting at the same time on a multiple access network such as Ethernet. Both frames may be lost or partial frames may result.

COLLISION DOMAIN *See* Broadcast Domain.

COLLISION LIGHT A light on some older NICs that flickers when a network collision is detected.

COMMAND A request, typed from a terminal or embedded in a file, to perform an operation or to execute a particular program.

COMMON INTERNET FILE SYSTEM (CIFS) The protocol that NetBIOS used to share folders and printers. Still very common, even on UNIX/Linux systems.

COMPATIBILITY ISSUE When different pieces of hardware or software don't work together correctly.

COMPLETE ALGORITHM A cipher and the methods used to implement that cipher.

CONCENTRATOR A device that brings together at a common center connections to a particular kind of network (such as Ethernet) and implements that network internally.

CONFIGURATION MANAGEMENT A set of documents, policies, and procedures designed to help you maintain and update your network in a logical, orderly fashion.

CONFIGURATION MANAGEMENT DOCUMENTATION Documents that define the configuration of a network. These would include wiring diagrams, network diagrams, baselines, and policy/procedure/configuration documentation.

CONFIGURATIONS The settings stored in devices that define how they are to operate.

CONNECTION A term used to refer to communication between two computers.

CONNECTION-ORIENTED COMMUNICATION A protocol that establishes a connection between two hosts before transmitting data and verifies receipt before closing the connection between the hosts. TCP is an example of a connection-oriented protocol.

CONNECTIONLESS COMMUNICATION A protocol that does not establish and verify a connection between the hosts before sending data; it just sends the data and hopes for the best. This is faster than connection-oriented protocols. UDP is an example of a connectionless protocol.

CONTENT SWITCH Advanced networking device that works at least at Layer 7 (Application layer) and hides servers behind a single IP.

CONTINUITY The physical connection of wires in a network.

CONTINUITY TESTER Inexpensive network tester that can only test for continuity on a line.

CONVERGENCE Point at which the routing tables for all routers in a network are updated.

COPY BACKUP A type of backup similar to Normal or Full, in that all selected files on a system are backed up. This type of backup does *not* change the archive bit of the files being backed up.

CORE The central glass of the fiber-optic cable that carries the light signal.

COST Routers can use a connection's monetary cost when determining a route's metric.

COUNTER A predefined event that is recorded to a log file.

CRC (CYCLIC REDUNDANCY CHECK) A mathematical method that is used to check for errors in long streams of transmitted data with high accuracy. Before data is sent, the main computer uses the data to calculate a CRC value from the data's contents. If the receiver calculates a different CRC value from the received data, the data was corrupted during transmission and is re-sent. Ethernet frames have a CRC code.

CRIMPER Also called a *crimping tool*, the tool used to secure a crimp (or an RJ-45 connector) onto the end of a cable.

CROSS-PLATFORM SUPPORT Standards created to enable terminals (and now operating systems) from different companies to interact with one another.

CROSSOVER CABLE A special UTP cable used to interconnect hubs/switches or to connect network cards without a hub/switch. Crossover cables reverse the sending and receiving wire pairs from one end to the other.

CROSSOVER PORT Special port in a hub that crosses the sending and receiving wires, thus removing the need for a crossover cable to connect the hubs.

CROSSTALK Electrical signal interference between two cables that are in close proximity to each other.

CSMA/CA (CARRIER SENSE MULTIPLE ACCESS WITH COLLISION AVOIDANCE) Access method used mainly on wireless networks. Before hosts send out data, they send out a signal that checks to make sure the network is free of other signals. If data is detected on the channel, the hosts wait a random time period before trying again. If the channel is free, the data is sent out.

CSMA/CD (CARRIER SENSE MULTIPLE ACCESS WITH COLLISION DETECTION) Access method that Ethernet systems use in LAN technologies, enabling frames of data to flow through the network and ultimately reach address locations. Known as a contention protocol, hosts on CSMA/CD networks send out data without checking to see if the wire is free first. If a collision occurs, then both hosts wait a random time period before retransmitting the data.

CSU/DSU (CHANNEL SERVICE UNIT/DATA SERVICE UNIT) A piece of equipment that connects a T-carrier leased line from the telephone company to a customer's equipment (such as a router). It performs line encoding and conditioning functions, and it often has a loopback function for testing.

DAILY BACKUP Also called a *daily copy backup*, makes a copy of all files that have been changed on that day without changing the archive bits of those files.

DAISY-CHAIN A method of connecting together several devices along a bus and managing the signals for each device.

DATA BACKUP The process of creating extra copies of data to be used in case the primary data source fails.

DATA ENCRYPTION STANDARD (DES) A symmetric-key algorithm developed by the U.S. government in the 1970s and formerly in use in a variety of TCP/IP applications. DES used a 64-bit block and a 56-bit key. Over time, the 56-bit key made DES susceptible to brute-force attacks.

DATA LINK LAYER *See* Open Systems Interconnection (OSI) Seven-Layer Model.

DATA OVER CABLE SERVICE INTERFACE SPECIFICATION (DOCSIS) The unique protocol used by cable modem networks.

DATAGRAM A connectionless transfer unit created with User Datagram Protocol designed for quick transfers over a packet-switched network.

DECIBEL (DB) A measurement of the quality of a signal.

DEDICATED CIRCUIT A circuit that runs from a breaker box to specific outlets.

DEDICATED LINE A telephone line that is an always open, or connected, circuit. Dedicated telephone lines usually do not have telephone numbers.

DEDICATED SERVER A machine that does not use any client functions, only server functions.

DEFAULT A software function or operation that occurs automatically unless the user specifies something else.

DEFAULT GATEWAY In a TCP/IP network, the IP address of the router that interconnects the LAN to a wider network, usually the Internet. This router's IP address is part of the necessary TCP/IP configuration for communicating with multiple networks using IP.

DELTA CHANNEL (D CHANNEL) A type of ISDN line that transfers data at 16 Kbps.

DEMARC A device that marks the dividing line of responsibility for the functioning of a network between internal users and upstream service providers.

DEMARC EXTENSION Any cabling that runs from the network interface to whatever box is used by the customer as a demarc.

Demilitarized Zone (DMZ) A lightly protected or unprotected subnet network positioned between an outer firewall and an organization's highly protected internal network. DMZs are used mainly to host public address servers (such as Web servers).

Denial of Service (DoS) Attack An attack that floods a networked server with so many requests that it becomes overwhelmed and ceases functioning.

Designated Router (DR) The main router in an OSPF network that relays information to all other routers in the area.

Destination Port A fixed, predetermined number that defines the function or session type in a TCP/IP network.

Device Driver A subprogram to control communications between the computer and some peripheral hardware.

Device ID The last six digits of a MAC address, identifying the manufacturer's unique serial number for that NIC.

DHCP Lease Created by the DHCP server to allow a system requesting DHCP IP information to use that information for a certain amount of time.

DHCP Scope The pool of IP addresses that a DHCP server may allocate to clients requesting IP addresses or other IP information like DNS server addresses.

Dial-up Lines Telephone lines with telephone numbers; they must dial to make a connection, as opposed to a dedicated line.

Differential Backup Similar to an incremental backup in that it backs up the files that have been changed since the last backup. This type of backup does not change the state of the archive bit.

DIG (Domain Information Groper) *See* Domain Information Groper.

Digital Signature A string of characters, created from a private encryption key, that verifies a sender's identity to those who receive encrypted data or messages.

Digital Subscriber Line (DSL) A high-speed Internet connection technology that uses a regular telephone line for connectivity. DSL comes in several varieties, including Asymmetric (ADSL) and Symmetric (SDSL), and many speeds. Typical home-user DSL connections are ADSL with a download speed of up to 9 Mbps and an upload speed of up to 1 Kbps.

Dipole Antenna The standard straight-wire antenna that provides most omni-directional function.

Direct Current (DC) A type of electric circuit where the flow of electrons is in a complete circle.

Direct-Sequence Spread-Spectrum (DSSS) A spread-spectrum broadcasting method defined in the 802.11 standard that sends data out on different frequencies at the same time.

Directional Antenna An antenna that focuses its signal into a beam of sorts.

Discretionary Access Control (DAC) Authorization method based on the idea that there is an owner of a resource who may at his or her discretion assign access to that resource. DAC is considered much more flexible than MAC.

Disk Mirroring Process by which data is written simultaneously to two or more disk drives. Read and write speed is decreased, but redundancy, in case of catastrophe, is increased. Also known as RAID level 1. *See also* Duplexing.

Disk Striping Process by which data is spread among multiple (at least two) drives. It increases speed for both reads and writes of data, but provides no fault tolerance. Also known as RAID level 0.

Disk Striping with Parity Process by which data is spread among multiple (at least three) drives, with parity information as well to provide fault tolerance. The most commonly implemented type is RAID 5, where the data and parity information is spread across three or more drives.

Dispersion Diffusion over distance of light propagating down fiber cable.

Distance Vector Set of routing protocols that calculates the total cost to get to a particular network ID and compares that cost to the total cost of all the other routes to get to that same network ID.

Distributed Coordination Function (DCF) One of two methods of collision avoidance defined by the 802.11 standard and the only one currently implemented. DCF specifies strict rules for sending data onto the network media.

Distributed Denial of Service (DDoS) Attack A DoS attack that uses multiple (as in hundreds or up to hundreds of thousands) of computers under the control of a single operator to conduct a devastating attack.

DLL (Dynamic Link Library) A file of executable functions or data that can be used by a Windows application. Typically, a DLL provides one or more particular functions, and a program accesses the functions by creating links to the DLL.

DNS DOMAIN A specific branch of the DNS name space. First-level DNS domains include .com, .gov, and .edu.

DNS RESOLVER CACHE A cache used by Windows DNS clients to keep track of DNS information.

DNS ROOT SERVERS The highest in the hierarchy of DNS servers running the Internet.

DNS SERVER A system that runs a special DNS server program.

DNS TREE A hierarchy of DNS domains and individual computer names organized into a tree-like structure, the top of which is the root.

DOCUMENT A medium and the data recorded on it for human use; for example, a report sheet or book. By extension, any record that has permanence and that can be read by a human or a machine.

DOCUMENTATION A collection of organized documents or the information recorded in documents. Also, instructional material specifying the inputs, operations, and outputs of a computer program or system.

DOMAIN A term used to describe a grouping of users, computers, and/or networks. In Microsoft networking, a domain is a group of computers and users that shares a common account database and a common security policy. For the Internet, a domain is a group of computers that shares a common element in their DNS hierarchical name.

DOMAIN CONTROLLER A Microsoft Windows Server system specifically configured to store user and server account information for its domain. Often abbreviated as "DC." Windows domain controllers store all account and security information in the *Active Directory* directory service.

DOMAIN INFORMATION GROPER (dig) Command-line tool in non-Windows systems used to diagnose DNS problems.

DOMAIN NAME SYSTEM (DNS) A TCP/IP name resolution system that resolves host names to IP addresses.

DOMAIN USERS AND GROUPS Users and groups that are defined across an entire network domain.

DOTTED DECIMAL NOTATION Shorthand method for discussing and configuring binary IP addresses.

DOWNLOAD The transfer of information from a remote computer system to the user's system. Opposite of *upload*.

DRIVE DUPLEXING *See* Duplexing.

DRIVE MIRRORING The process of writing identical data to two hard drives on the same controller at the same time to provide data redundancy.

DS0 The digital signal rate created by converting analog sound into 8-bit chunks 8000 times a second, with a data stream of 64 Kbps. This is the simplest data stream (and the slowest rate) of the digital part of the phone system.

DS1 The signaling method used by T1 lines, which uses a relatively simple frame consisting of 25 pieces: a framing bit and 24 channels. Each DS1 channel holds a single 8-bit DS0 data sample. The framing bit and data channels combine to make 193 bits per DS1 frame. These frames are transmitted 8000 times/sec, making a total throughput of 1.544 Mbps.

DSL ACCESS MULTIPLEXER (DSLAM) A device located in a telephone company's central office that connects multiple customers to the Internet.

DSL MODEM A device that enables customers to connect to the Internet using a DSL connection. A DSL modem isn't really a modem—it's more like an ISDN terminal adapter—but the term stuck, and even the manufacturers of the devices now call them DSL modems.

DSP (DIGITAL SIGNAL PROCESSOR) A specialized microprocessor-like device that processes digital signals at the expense of other capabilities, much as the floating-point unit (FPU) is optimized for math functions. DSPs are used in such specialized hardware as high-speed modems, multimedia sound cards, MIDI equipment, and real-time video capture and compression.

DUPLEXING Also called *disk duplexing* or *drive duplexing*, similar to mirroring in that data is written to and read from two physical drives for fault tolerance. In addition, separate controllers are used for each drive, for both additional fault tolerance and additional speed. Considered RAID level 1. *See also* Disk Mirroring.

DYNAMIC ADDRESSING A way for a computer to receive IP information automatically from a server program. *See also* Dynamic Host Configuration Protocol (DHCP).

DYNAMIC DNS (DDNS) A protocol that enables DNS servers to get automatic updates of IP addresses of computers in their forward lookup zones, mainly by talking to the local DHCP server.

DYNAMIC HOST CONFIGURATION PROTOCOL (DHCP) A protocol that enables a DHCP server to set TCP/IP settings automatically for a DHCP client.

Dynamic Link Library (DLL) *See* DLL (Dynamic Link Library).

Dynamic NAT Type of NAT in which many computers can share a pool of routable IP addresses that number fewer than the computers.

Dynamic Port Numbers Port numbers 49152–65535, recommended by the IANA to be used as ephemeral port numbers.

Dynamic Routing Process by which routers in an internetwork automatically exchange information with other routers. Requires a dynamic routing protocol, such as OSPF or RIP.

Dynamic Routing Protocol A protocol that supports the building of automatic routing tables, such as OSPF or RIP.

E1 The European counterpart of a T1 connection that carries 32 channels at 64 Kbps for a total of 2.048 Mbps—making it slightly faster than a T1.

E3 The European counterpart of a T3 line that carries 16 E1 lines (512 channels), for a total bandwidth of 34.368 Mbps—making it a little bit slower than an American T3.

Edge Router Router that connects one automated system (AS) to another.

Effective Permissions The permissions of all groups combined in any network operating system.

Electro-Magnetic Interference (EMI) Interference from one device to another, resulting in poor performance in the device's capabilities. This is similar to having static on your TV while running a hair dryer, or placing two monitors too close together and getting a "shaky" screen.

E-mail (Electronic Mail) Messages, usually text, sent from one person to another via computer. E-mail can also be sent automatically to a large number of addresses, known as a *mailing list*.

E-mail Client Program that runs on a computer and enables you to send, receive, and organize e-mail.

E-mail Server Also known as *mail server*, a server that accepts incoming mail, sorts the mail for recipients into mailboxes, and sends mail to other servers using SMTP.

Emulator Software or hardware that converts the commands to and from the host machine to an entirely different platform. For example, a program that enables you to run Nintendo games on your PC.

Encapsulation The process of putting the packets from one protocol inside the packets of another protocol. An example of this is TCP/IP encapsulation in Ethernet, which places TCP/IP packets inside Ethernet frames.

Encryption A method of securing messages by scrambling and encoding each packet as it is sent across an unsecured medium, such as the Internet. Each encryption level provides multiple standards and options.

Endpoint In the TCP/IP world, the session information stored in RAM. *See also* Socket.

Endpoints Correct term to use when discussing the data each computer stores about the connection between two computers' TCP/IP applications. *See also* Socket Pairs.

Enhanced Interior Gateway Routing Protocol (EIGRP) Cisco's proprietary hybrid protocol that has elements of both distance vector and link state routing.

Environmental Monitor Device used in telecommunications rooms that keeps track of humidity, temperature, and more.

Ephemeral Port In TCP/IP communication, an arbitrary number generated by a sending computer that the receiving computer uses as a destination address when sending a return packet.

Ephemeral Port Numbers *See* Ephemeral Port.

Equipment Rack A metal structure used in equipment rooms to secure network hardware devices and patch panels. Most racks are 19" wide. Devices designed to fit in such a rack use a height measurement called *units*, or simply *U*.

ESD (Electro-Static Discharge) The movement of electrons from one body to another. ESD is a real menace to PCs because it can cause permanent damage to semiconductors.

Ethernet Name coined by Xerox for the first standard of network cabling and protocols. Ethernet is based on a bus topology. The IEEE 802.3 subcommittee defines the current Ethernet specifications.

Evil Twin An attack that lures people into logging into a rogue access point that looks similar to a legitimate access point.

Executable Viruses Viruses that are literally extensions of executables and that are unable to exist by themselves. Once an infected executable file is run, the virus loads into memory, adding copies of itself to other EXEs that are subsequently run.

Extended Service Set (ESS) A single wireless access point servicing a given area that has been extended by adding more access points.

EXTENDED SERVICE SET ID (ESSID) An SSID applied to an Extended Service Set as a network naming convention.

EXTENDED UNIQUE IDENTIFIER, 64-BIT (EUI-64) The last 64 bits of the IPv6 address, which are determined based on a device's MAC address.

EXTENSIBLE AUTHENTICATION PROTOCOL (EAP) Authentication wrapper that EAP-compliant applications can use to accept one of many types of authentication. While EAP is a general-purpose authentication wrapper, its only substantial use is in wireless networks.

EXTERNAL CONNECTIONS A network's connection to the wider Internet. Also a major concern when setting up a SOHO network.

EXTERNAL DATA BUS (EDB) The primary data highway of all computers. Everything in your computer is tied either directly or indirectly to the EDB.

EXTERNAL NETWORK ADDRESS A number added to the MAC address of every computer on an IPX/SPX network that defines every computer on the network; this is often referred to as a *network number*.

EXTERNAL THREATS Threats to your network through external means; examples include virus attacks and the exploitation of users, security holes in the OS, or the network hardware itself.

FAQ (FREQUENTLY ASKED QUESTIONS) Common abbreviation coined by BBS users and spread to Usenet and the Internet. This is a list of questions and answers that pertains to a particular topic, maintained so that users new to the group don't all bombard the group with similar questions. Examples are "What is the name of the actor who plays *X* on this show, and was he in anything else?" or "Can anyone list all of the books by this author in the order that they were published so that I can read them in that order?" The common answer to this type of question is "Read the FAQ!"

FAR-END CROSSTALK (FEXT) Crosstalk on the opposite end of a cable from the signal's source.

FAST ETHERNET Nickname for the 100-Mbps Ethernet standards. Originally applied to 100BaseT.

FAULT TOLERANCE The capability of any system to continue functioning after some part of the system has failed. RAID is an example of a hardware device that provides fault tolerance for hard drives.

FEDERAL COMMUNICATIONS COMMISSION (FCC) In the United States, regulates public airwaves and rates PCs and other equipment according to the amount of radiation emitted.

FIBER-OPTIC CABLE A high-speed physical medium for transmitting data that uses light rather than electricity to transmit data and is made of high-purity glass fibers sealed within a flexible opaque tube. Much faster than conventional copper wire.

FILE SERVER A computer designated to store software, courseware, administrative tools, and other data on a local or wide area network. It "serves" this information to other computers via the network when users enter their personal access codes.

FILE TRANSFER PROTOCOL (FTP) A set of rules that allows two computers to talk to one another as a file transfer is carried out. This is the protocol used when you transfer a file from one computer to another across the Internet.

FIRE RATINGS Ratings developed by Underwriters Laboratories (UL) and the National Electrical Code (NEC) to define the risk of network cables burning and creating noxious fumes and smoke.

FIREWALL A device that restricts traffic between a local network and the Internet.

FIREWIRE An IEEE 1394 standard to send wide-band signals over a thin connector system that plugs into TVs, VCRs, TV cameras, PCs, and so forth. This serial bus developed by Apple and Texas Instruments enables connection of 60 devices at speeds ranging from 100 to 800 Mbps.

FLAT NAME SPACE A naming convention that gives each device only one name that must be unique. NetBIOS uses a flat name space. TCP/IP's DNS uses a hierarchical name space.

FORWARD LOOKUP ZONE The storage area in a DNS server to store the IP addresses and names of systems for a particular domain or domains.

FQDN (FULLY QUALIFIED DOMAIN NAME) The complete DNS name of a system, from its host name to the top-level domain name.

FRACTIONAL T1 ACCESS A service provided by many telephone companies wherein customers can purchase a number of individual channels in a T1 line in order to save money.

FRAME A defined series of binary data that is the basic container for a discrete amount of data moving across a network. Frames are created at Layer 2 of the OSI model.

FRAME CHECK SEQUENCE (FCS) A sequence of bits placed in a frame that is used to check the primary data for errors.

FRAME RELAY An extremely efficient data transmission technique used to send digital information such as voice, data,

LAN, and WAN traffic quickly and cost-efficiently to many destinations from one port.

FreeRADIUS Free RADIUS server software for UNIX/Linux systems.

Freeware Software that is distributed for free with no license fee.

Frequency Division Multiplexing (FDM) A process of keeping individual phone calls separate by adding a different frequency multiplier to each phone call, making it possible to separate phone calls by their unique frequency range.

Frequency-Hopping Spread-Spectrum (FHSS) A spread-spectrum broadcasting method defined in the 802.11 standard that sends data on one frequency at a time, constantly shifting (or *hopping*) frequencies.

FUBAR Fouled Up Beyond All Recognition.

Full Duplex Any device that can send and receive data simultaneously.

Fully Meshed Topology A mesh network where every node is directly connected to every other node.

Gain The strengthening and focusing of radio frequency output from a wireless access point (WAP).

Gateway Router A router that acts as a default gateway in a TCP/IP network.

General Logs Logs that record updates to applications.

Giga The prefix that generally refers to the quantity 1,073,741,824. One gigabyte is 1,073,741,824 bytes. With frequencies, in contrast, giga- often refers to one billion. One gigahertz is 1,000,000,000 hertz.

Gigabit Ethernet *See* 1000BaseT.

Gigabyte 1024 megabytes.

Global Unicast Address A second IPv6 address that every system needs in order to get on the Internet.

Grandfather, Father, Son (GFS) A tape rotation strategy used in data backups.

Group Policy A feature of Windows Active Directory that allows an administrator to apply policy settings to network users *en masse*.

Group Policy Object (GPO) Enables network administrators to define multiple rights and permissions to entire sets of users all at one time.

Groups Collections of network users who share similar tasks and need similar permissions; defined to make administration tasks easier.

H.323 A VoIP standard that handles the initiation, setup, and delivery of VoIP sessions.

Hackers People who break into computer systems with malicious intent.

Half Duplex Any device that can only send or receive data at any given moment.

Hardware Tools Tools such as cable testers, TDRs, OTDRs, certifiers, voltage event recorders, protocol analyzers, cable strippers, multimeters, tone probes/generators, butt sets, and punchdown tools used to configure and troubleshoot a network.

Hash A mathematical function used in cryptography that is run on a string of binary digits of any length that results in a value of some fixed length.

Hex (Hexadecimal) Hex symbols based on a numbering system of 16 (computer shorthand for binary numbers), using 10 digits and 6 letters to condense 0s and 1s to binary numbers. Hex is represented by digits 0 through 9 and alpha *A* through *F*, so that 09h has a value of 9, and 0Ah has a value of 10.

Hierarchical Name Space A naming scheme where the full name of each object includes its position within the hierarchy. An example of a hierarchical name is www.totalseminars.com, which includes not only the host name, but also the domain name. DNS uses a hierarchical name space scheme for fully qualified domain names (FQDNs).

High Availability A collection of technologies and procedures that work together to keep an application available at all times.

High-Speed WAN Internet Cards A type of router expansion card that enables connection to two different ISPs.

History Logs Logs that track the history of how a user or users access network resources, or how network resources are accessed throughout the network.

Home Page Either the Web page that your browser is set to use when it starts up or the main Web page for a business, organization, or person. Also, the main page in any collection of Web pages.

Honeynet The network created by a honeypot in order to lure in hackers.

Honeypot An area of a network that an administrator sets up for the express purpose of attracting a computer hacker.

If a hacker takes the bait, the network's important resources are unharmed and network personnel can analyze the attack to predict and protect against future attacks, making the network more secure.

Hop The passage of a packet through a router.

Horizontal Cabling Cabling that connects the equipment room to the work areas.

Host A single device (usually a computer) on a TCP/ IP network that has an IP address; any device that can be the source or destination of a data packet. Also, a computer running multiple virtualized operating systems.

Host ID The portion of an IP address that defines a specific machine in a subnet.

Host Name An individual computer name in the DNS naming convention.

Hostname Command-line tool that returns the host name of the computer it is run on.

Hosts File The predecessor to DNS, a static text file that resides on a computer and is used to resolve DNS host names to IP addresses. The HOSTS file is checked before the machine sends a name resolution request to a DNS name server. The HOSTS file has no extension.

HTML (Hypertext Markup Language) An ASCII-based script-like language for creating hypertext documents like those on the World Wide Web.

HTTP (Hypertext Transfer Protocol) Extremely fast protocol used for network file transfers on the World Wide Web.

HTTP over SSL (HTTPS) A secure form of HTTP, used commonly for Internet business transactions or any time where a secure connection is required. *See also* Hypertext Transfer Protocol (HTTP) *and* Secure Sockets Layer (SSL).

Hub An electronic device that sits at the center of a star topology network, providing a common point for the connection of network devices. In a 10BaseT Ethernet network, the hub contains the electronic equivalent of a properly terminated bus cable. Hubs are rare today and have been replaced by switches.

Hybrid Topology A mix or blend of two different topologies. A star-bus topology is a hybrid of the star and bus topologies.

Hypertext A document that has been marked up to enable a user to select words or pictures within the document, click them, and connect to further information. The basis of the World Wide Web.

Hypervisor An extra layer of sophisticated programming to manage the vastly more complex interactions required for virtualization.

ICF (Internet Connection Firewall) The software firewall built into Windows XP that protects your system from unauthorized access from the Internet. Microsoft changed the name to the Windows Firewall in Windows Service Pack 2.

ICS (Internet Connection Sharing) Also known simply as *Internet sharing*, the technique of enabling more than one computer to access the Internet simultaneously using a single Internet connection. When you use Internet sharing, you connect an entire LAN to the Internet using a single public IP address.

IEEE (Institute of Electrical and Electronics Engineers) The leading standards-setting group in the United States.

IEEE 802.2 IEEE subcommittee that defined the standards for Logical Link Control (LLC).

IEEE 802.3 IEEE subcommittee that defined the standards for CSMA/CD (a.k.a. *Ethernet*).

IEEE 802.11 IEEE subcommittee that defined the standards for wireless.

IEEE 802.14 IEEE subcommittee that defined the standards for cable modems.

IEEE 1284 The IEEE standard for the now obsolete parallel communication.

IEEE 1394 IEEE standard for FireWire communication.

IETF (Internet Engineering Task Force) The primary standards organization for the Internet.

ifconfig A command-line utility for Linux servers and workstations that displays the current TCP/IP configuration of the machine, similar to ipconfig for Windows systems.

IMAP (Internet Message Access Protocol) An alternative to POP3. IMAP retrieves e-mail from an e-mail server like POP3; IMAP uses TCP port 143.

Impedance The amount of resistance to an electrical signal on a wire. It is used as a relative measure of the amount of data a cable can handle.

INCREMENTAL BACKUP Backs up all files that have their archive bits turned on, meaning they have been changed since the last backup. This type of backup turns the archive bits off after the files have been backed up.

INDEPENDENT BASIC SERVICE SET (IBSS) A basic unit of organization in wireless networks formed by two or more wireless nodes communicating in ad-hoc mode.

INDEPENDENT COMPUTING ARCHITECTURE (ICA) A Citrix-created standard that defines how a server and a client exchange terminal information.

INFRASTRUCTURE MODE Mode in which wireless networks use one or more wireless access points to connect the wireless network nodes centrally. This configuration is similar to the *star topology* of a wired network.

INHERITANCE A method of assigning user permissions, in which folder permissions flow downward into subfolders.

INSULATING JACKET The external plastic covering of a fiber-optic cable.

INTEGRATED SERVICES DIGITAL NETWORK (ISDN) *See* ISDN (Integrated Services Digital Network).

INTERFRAME GAP (IFG) A short, predefined silence used in CSMA/CA.

INTERFRAME SPACE (IFS) Short, predefined period of silence in CSMA/CA appended to the waiting time when a device detects activity on the line.

INTERMEDIATE DISTRIBUTION FRAME (IDF) The room where all the horizontal runs from all the work areas on a given floor in a building come together.

INTERMEDIATE SYSTEM TO INTERMEDIATE SYSTEM (IS-IS) Protocol similar to, but not as popular as, OSPF, but with support for IPv6 since inception.

INTERNAL CONNECTIONS The connections between computers in a network.

INTERNAL NETWORK A private LAN, with a unique network ID, that resides behind a router.

INTERNAL THREATS All the things that a network's own users do to create problems on the network. Examples include accidental deletion of files, accidental damage to hardware devices or cabling, and abuse of rights and permissions.

INTERNET ASSIGNED NUMBERS AUTHORITY (IANA) The organization responsible for assigning public IP addresses. IANA no longer directly assigns IP addresses, having delegated this to the five Regional Internet Registries. *See* Regional Internet Registries.

INTERNET AUTHENTICATION SERVICE (IAS) Popular RADIUS server for Microsoft environments.

INTERNET CONNECTION FIREWALL (ICF) *See* ICF (Internet Connection Firewall).

INTERNET CONNECTION SHARING (ICS) *See* ICS (Internet Connection Sharing).

INTERNET CONTROL MESSAGE PROTOCOL (ICMP) Protocol in which messages consist of a single packet and are connectionless. ICMP packets determine connectivity between two hosts.

INTERNET GROUP MANAGEMENT PROTOCOL (IGMP) Protocol that routers use to communicate with hosts to determine a "group" membership in order to determine which computers want to receive a multicast.

INTERNET INFORMATION SERVICES (IIS) Microsoft's Web server program for managing Web servers.

INTERNET MESSAGE ACCESS PROTOCOL VERSION 4 (IMAP4) An alternative to POP3 for receiving e-mail from an e-mail server. Supports searching through messages stored on a server and supports using folders to organize e-mail.

INTERNET PROTOCOL (IP) The Internet standard protocol that handles the logical naming for the TCP/IP protocol using IP addresses.

INTERNET PROTOCOL VERSION 4 (IPV4) Protocol in which addresses consist of four sets of numbers, each number being a value between 0 and 255, using a period to separate the numbers. Often called *dotted decimal* format. No IPv4 address may be all 0s or all 255s. Examples include 192.168.0.1 and 64.176.19.164.

INTERNET PROTOCOL VERSION 6 (IPV6) Protocol in which addresses consist of eight sets of four hexadecimal numbers, each number being a value between 0000 and FFFF, using a colon to separate the numbers. No IP address may be all 0s or all FFFFs. Here's an example:

FEDC:BA98:7654:3210:0800:200C:00CF:1234.

INTERNIC The organization that maintained the DNS services, registrations, and so forth run by Network Solutions, General Atomics, and AT&T in the early days of the Internet. ICANN assumed these roles in 1998, so the only time you'll see this organization mentioned currently is on certification exams.

INTERVLAN ROUTING A feature on some switches to create virtual routers.

INTRA-SITE AUTOMATIC TUNNEL ADDRESSING PROTOCOL (ISATAP) An IPv6 tunneling protocol that adds the IPv4 address to an IPv6 prefix.

INTRANET A private TCP/IP network inside a company or organization.

INTRUSION DETECTION SYSTEM (IDS)/INTRUSION PREVENTION SYSTEM (IPS) An application (often running on a dedicated IDS box) that inspects incoming packets, looking for active intrusions. The difference between an IDS and an IPS is that an IPS can react to an attack.

IP ADDRESS The numeric address of a computer connected to a TCP/IP network, such as the Internet. IPv4 addresses are 32 bits long, written as four octets of 8-bit binary. IPv6 addresses are 128 bits long, written as eight sets of four hexadecimal characters. IP addresses must be matched with a valid subnet mask, which identifies the part of the IP address that is the network ID and the part that is the host ID.

IP FILTERING A method of blocking packets based on IP addresses.

IP SECURITY (IPSEC) A IP packet encryption protocol. IPsec is the only IP encryption protocol to work at Layer 3 of the OSI seven-layer model. IPsec is most commonly seen on Virtual Private Networks. *See* Virtual Private Network (VPN).

ipconfig A command-line utility for Windows that displays the current TCP/IP configuration of the machine; similar to UNIX/Linux's ifconfig.

IRC (INTERNET RELAY CHAT) An online group discussion. Also called *chat*.

ISDN (INTEGRATED SERVICES DIGITAL NETWORK) The CCITT (Comité Consutatif Internationale Téléphonique et Télégraphique) standard that defines a digital method for telephone communications. Originally designed to replace the current analog telephone systems. ISDN lines have telephone numbers and support up to 128-Kbps transfer rates. ISDN also allows data and voice to share a common phone line. Never very popular, ISDN is now relegated to specialized niches.

ISP (INTERNET SERVICE PROVIDER) An institution that provides access to the Internet in some form, usually for a fee.

IT (INFORMATION TECHNOLOGY) The business of computers, electronic communications, and electronic commerce.

JAVA A network-oriented programming language invented by Sun Microsystems and specifically designed for writing programs that can be safely downloaded to your computer through the Internet and immediately run without fear of viruses or other harm to your computer or files. Using small Java programs (called *applets*), Web pages can include functions such as animations, calculators, and other fancy tricks.

JUST A BUNCH OF DISKS (JBOD) An array of hard drives that are simply connected with no RAID implementations.

K- Most commonly used as the suffix for the binary quantity 1024. For instance, 640 K means 640 × 1024 or 655,360. Just to add some extra confusion to the IT industry, K is often misspoken as "kilo," the metric value for 1,000. For example, 10 KB, spoken as "10 kilobytes," means 10,240 bytes rather than 10,000 bytes. Finally, when discussing frequencies, K means 1000. So, 1 KHz = 1000 kilohertz.

KBPS (KILOBITS PER SECOND) Data transfer rate.

KERBEROS An authentication standard designed to allow different operating systems and applications to authenticate each other.

KEY DISTRIBUTION CENTER (KDC) System for granting authentication in Kerberos.

KEY PAIR Name for the two keys generated in asymmetric-key algorithm systems.

KILOHERTZ (KHZ) A unit of measure that equals a frequency of 1000 cycles per second.

LAN (LOCAL AREA NETWORK) A group of PCs connected together via cabling, radio, or infrared that use this connectivity to share resources such as printers and mass storage.

LAST MILE The connection between a central office and individual users in a telephone system.

LATENCY A measure of a signal's delay.

LAYER A grouping of related tasks involving the transfer of information. Also, a particular level of the OSI seven-layer model, for example, Physical layer, Data Link layer, and so forth.

LAYER 2 SWITCH Any device that filters and forwards frames based on the MAC addresses of the sending and receiving machines. What is normally called a "switch" is actually a "Layer 2 switch."

LAYER 2 TUNNELING PROTOCOL (L2TP) A VPN protocol developed by Cisco that can be run on almost any connection imaginable. LT2P has no authentication or encryption, but uses IPsec for all its security needs.

LAYER 3 SWITCH Also known as a *router*, filters and forwards data packets based on the IP addresses of the sending and receiving machines.

LC A duplex type of Small Form Factor (SFF) fiber connector, designed to accept two fiber cables.

LED (Light Emitting Diodes) Solid-state devices that vibrate at luminous frequencies when current is applied.

Leeching Using another person's wireless connection to the Internet without that person's permission.

Light Leakage The type of interference caused by bending a piece of fiber-optic cable past its maximum bend radius. Light bleeds through the cladding, causing signal distortion and loss.

Lights-out Management Special "computer within a computer" features built into better servers, designed to give you access to a server even when the server itself is shut off.

Lightweight Directory Access Protocol (LDAP) The tool that programs use to query and change a database used by the network. LDAP uses TCP port 389 by default.

Lightweight Extensible Authentication Protocol (LEAP) A proprietary EAP authentication used almost exclusively by Cisco wireless products. LEAP is an interesting combination of MS-CHAP authentication between a wireless client and a RADIUS server.

Link Light An LED on NICs, hubs, and switches that lights up to show good connection between the devices.

Link-Local Address The address that a computer running IPv6 gives itself after first booting. The first 64 bits of a link-local address are always FE80::/64.

Link Segments Segments that link other segments together but are unpopulated or have no computers directly attached to them.

Link State Type of dynamic routing protocol that announces only changes to routing tables, as opposed to entire routing tables. Compare to distance vector routing protocols. *See also* Distance Vector.

Linux The popular open source UNIX-clone operating system.

List of Requirements A list of all the things you'll need to do to set up your SOHO network, as well as the desired capabilities of the network.

Listening Port A socket that is prepared to respond to any IP packets destined for that socket's port number.

LMHOSTS File A static text file that resides on a computer and is used to resolve NetBIOS names to IP addresses. The LMHOSTS file is checked before the machine sends a name resolution request to a WINS name server. The LMHOSTS file has no extension.

Load Balancing The process of taking several servers and making them look like a single server.

Local Refers to the computer(s), server(s), and/or LAN that a user is physically using or that is in the same room or building.

Local Connector (LC) One popular type of Small Form Factor (SFF) connector, considered by many to be the predominant fiber connector.

Local User Accounts The accounts unique to a single Windows system. Stored in the local system's registry.

Localhost The HOSTS file alias for the loopback address of 127.0.0.1, referring to the current machine.

Logical Address A programmable network address, unlike a physical address that is burned into ROM.

Logical Link Control (LLC) The aspect of the NIC that talks to the operating system, places data coming from the software into frames, and creates the FCS on each frame. The LLC also deals with incoming frames—processing those that are addressed to this NIC and erasing frames addressed to other machines on the network.

Logical Network Diagram A document that shows the broadcast domains and individual IP addresses for all devices on the network. Only critical switches and routers are shown.

Logical Topology A network topology defined by signal paths as opposed to the physical layout of the cables. *See also* Physical Topology.

Loopback Address Sometimes called the localhost, a reserved IP address used for internal testing: 127.0.0.1.

Loopback Plug Network connector that connects back into itself, used to connect loopback tests.

Loopback Test A special test often included in diagnostic software that sends data out of the NIC and checks to see if it comes back.

MAC (Media Access Control) Address Unique 48-bit address assigned to each network card. IEEE assigns blocks of possible addresses to various NIC manufacturers to help ensure that each address is unique. The Data Link layer of the OSI seven-layer model uses MAC addresses for locating machines.

MAC Address Filtering A method of limiting access to a wireless network based on the physical addresses of wireless NICs.

MAC Filtering *See* MAC Address Filtering.

Macro A specially written application macro (collection of commands) that performs the same functions as a virus. These macros normally autostart when the application is run and then make copies of themselves, often propagating across networks.

Mailbox Special holding area on an e-mail server that separates out e-mail for each user.

Main Distribution Frame (MDF) The room in a building that stores the demarc, telephone cross-connects, and LAN cross-connects.

Malware Any program or code (macro, script, and so on) that's designed to do something on a system or network that you don't want to have happen.

Man in the Middle A hacking attack where a person inserts him- or herself into a conversation between two others, covertly intercepting traffic thought to be only between those other people.

Managed Device Networking devices, such as routers and advanced switches, that must be configured to use.

Managed Switch *See* Managed Device.

Management Information Base (MIB) SNMP's version of a server. *See* Simple Network Management Protocol (SNMP).

Mandatory Access Control (MAC) A security model in which every resource is assigned a label that defines its security level. If the user lacks that security level, they do not get access.

Maximum Transfer Unit (MTU) Specifies the largest size of a data unit in a communications protocol, such as Ethernet.

MB (Megabyte) 1,048,576 bytes.

MD5 (Message-Digest Algorithm version 5) Arguably the most popular hashing function.

Mechanical Transfer Registered Jack (MT-RJ) The first type of Small Form Factor (SFF) fiber connector, still in common use.

Media Access Control (MAC) The part of a NIC that remembers the NIC's own MAC address and attaches that address to outgoing frames.

Media Converter A device that lets you interconnect different types of Ethernet cable.

Mega- A prefix that usually stands for the binary quantity 1,048,576. One megabyte is 1,048,576 bytes. One megahertz, however, is 1,000,000 hertz. Sometimes shortened to *meg*, as in "a 286 has an address space of 16 megs."

Mesh Topology Topology in which each computer has a direct or indirect connection to every other computer in a network. Any node on the network can forward traffic to other nodes. Popular in cellular and many wireless networks.

Metric Relative value that defines the "cost" of using a particular route.

Metropolitan Area Network (MAN) Multiple computers connected via cabling, radio, leased phone lines, or infrared that are within the same city. A typical example of a MAN is a college campus. No firm dividing lines dictate what is considered a WAN, MAN, or LAN.

MHz (Megahertz) A unit of measure that equals a frequency of 1 million cycles per second.

MIME (Multipurpose Internet Mail Extensions) A standard for attaching binary files, such as executables and images, to the Internet's text-based mail (24-Kbps packet size).

Mirroring Also called *drive mirroring*, reading and writing data at the same time to two drives for fault-tolerance purposes. Considered RAID level 1.

Modal Distortion A light distortion problem unique to multimode fiber-optic cable.

Modem (Modulator-Demodulator) A device that converts both digital bit streams into analog signals (modulation) and incoming analog signals back into digital signals (demodulation). Most commonly used to interconnect telephone lines to computers.

Mounting Bracket Bracket that acts as a holder for a faceplate in cable installations.

MS-CHAP Microsoft's dominant variation of the CHAP protocol, uses a slightly more advanced encryption protocol.

MTU (Maximum Transfer Unit) *See* Maximum Transfer Unit (MTU).

MTU Black Hole When a router's firewall features block ICMP requests, making MTU worthless.

MTU Mismatch The situation when your network's packets are so large that they must be fragmented to fit into your ISP's packets.

Multicast Method of sending a packet in which the sending computer sends it to a group of interested computers.

MULTICAST ADDRESSES In IPv6, a set of reserved addresses designed to go only to certain systems.

MULTIFACTOR AUTHENTICATION A form of authentication where a user must use two or more factors to prove his or her identity.

MULTILAYER SWITCH A switch that has functions that operate at multiple layers of the OSI seven-layer model.

MULTIMETER A tool for testing voltage (AC and DC), resistance, and continuity.

MULTIMODE FIBER (MMF) Type of fiber-optic cable that uses LEDs.

MULTIPLE IN/MULTIPLE OUT (MIMO) A feature in 802.11 WAPs that enables them to make multiple simultaneous connections.

MULTIPLEXER A device that merges information from multiple input channels to a single output channel.

MULTIPROTOCOL LABEL SWITCHING (MPLS) A router feature that labels certain data to use a desired connection. It works with any type of packet switching (even Ethernet) to force certain types of data to use a certain path.

MULTISOURCE AGREEMENT (MSA) Interchangeable modular transceivers used in 10 GbE networking devices.

MULTISPEED HUB Any hub that supports more than one network speed for otherwise similar cabling systems. Multispeed hubs come in two flavors: one has mostly dedicated slower ports, with a few dedicated faster ports, whereas the other has only special auto-sensing ports that automatically run at either the faster or the slower speed.

MX RECORDS Records used by SMTP servers to determine where to send mail.

MY TRACEROUTE (MTR) Terminal command in Linux that dynamically displays the route a packet is taking. Similar to traceroute.

NAME RESOLUTION A method that enables one computer on the network to locate another to establish a session. All network protocols perform name resolution in one of two ways: either via *broadcast* or by providing some form of *name server*.

NAME SERVER A computer whose job is to know the name of every other computer on the network.

NAT TRANSLATION TABLE Special database in a NAT router that stores destination IP addresses and ephemeral source ports from outgoing packets and compares them against returning packets.

nbtstat A command-line utility used to check the current NetBIOS name cache on a particular machine. The utility compares NetBIOS names to their corresponding IP addresses.

NEAR-END CROSSTALK (NEXT) Crosstalk at the same end of a cable from which the signal is being generated.

NetBEUI (NetBIOS EXTENDED USER INTERFACE) Microsoft's first networking protocol, designed to work with NetBIOS. NetBEUI is long obsolesced by TCP/IP. NetBEUI did not support routing.

NetBIOS (NETWORK BASIC INPUT/OUTPUT SYSTEM) A protocol that operates at the Session layer of the OSI seven-layer model. This protocol creates and manages connections based on the names of the computers involved.

NetBIOS NAME A computer name that identifies both the specific machine and the functions that machine performs. A NetBIOS name consists of 16 characters: the first 15 are an alphanumeric name, and the 16th is a special suffix that identifies the role the machine plays.

NETSTAT A universal command-line utility used to examine the TCP/IP connections open on a given host.

NETWORK A collection of two or more computers interconnected by telephone lines, coaxial cables, satellite links, radio, and/or some other communication technique. A computer *network* is a group of computers that are connected together and communicate with one another for a common purpose. Computer networks support "people and organization" networks, users who also share a common purpose for communicating.

NETWORK ACCESS CONTROL (NAC) Control over information, people, access, machines, and everything in between.

NETWORK ACCESS SERVER (NAS) Systems that control the modems in a RADIUS network.

NETWORK ADDRESS TRANSLATION (NAT) A means of translating a system's IP address into another IP address before sending it out to a larger network. NAT manifests itself by a NAT program that runs on a system or a router. A network using NAT provides the systems on the network with private IP addresses. The system running the NAT software has two interfaces: one connected to the network and the other connected to the larger network.

The NAT program takes packets from the client systems bound for the larger network and translates their internal private IP addresses to its own public IP address, enabling many systems to share a single IP address.

NETWORK AS A SERVICE (NaaS) The act of renting virtual server space over the Internet. *See* Cloud Computing.

NETWORK DESIGN The process of gathering together and planning the layout for the equipment needed to create a network.

NETWORK DIAGRAM An illustration that shows devices on a network and how they connect.

NETWORK ID A number used in IP networks to identify the network on which a device or machine exists.

NETWORK INTERFACE A device by which a system accesses a network. In most cases, this is a NIC or a modem.

NETWORK INTERFACE CARD (NIC) Traditionally, an expansion card that enables a PC to link physically to a network. Modern computers now use built-in NICs, no longer requiring physical cards, but the term "NIC" is still very common.

NETWORK INTERFACE UNIT (NIU) Another name for a demarc. *See* Demarc.

NETWORK LAYER Layer 3 of the OSI seven-layer model. *See* Open Systems Interconnection (OSI) Seven-Layer Model.

NETWORK MANAGEMENT SOFTWARE (NMS) Tools that enable you to describe, visualize, and configure an entire network.

NETWORK MAP A highly detailed illustration of a network, down to the individual computers. A network map will show IP addresses, ports, protocols, and more.

NETWORK NAME Another name for the SSID.

NETWORK PROTOCOL Special software that exists in every network-capable operating system that acts to create unique identifiers for each system. It also creates a set of communication rules for issues like how to handle data chopped up into multiple packets and how to deal with routers. TCP/IP is the dominant network protocol today.

NETWORK SHARE A shared resource on a network.

NETWORK THREAT Any number of things that share one essential feature: the potential to damage network data, machines, or users.

NETWORK TIME PROTOCOL (NTP) Protocol that gives the current time.

NETWORK TOPOLOGY Refers to the way that cables and other pieces of hardware connect to one another.

NEWSGROUP The name for a discussion group on Usenet.

NEXT HOP The next router a packet should go to at any given point.

NFS (NETWORK FILE SYSTEM) A TCP/IP file system–sharing protocol that enables systems to treat files on a remote machine as though they were local files. NFS uses TCP port 2049, but many users choose alternative port numbers. Though still somewhat popular and heavily supported, NFS has been largely replaced by Samba/CIFS. *See also* Samba *and* Common Internet File System (CIFS).

NMAP A network utility designed to scan a network and create a map. Frequently used as a vulnerability scanner.

NODE A member of a network or a point where one or more functional units interconnect transmission lines.

NOISE Undesirable signals bearing no desired information and frequently capable of introducing errors into the communication process.

NON-DISCOVERY MODE A setting for Bluetooth devices that effectively hides them from other Bluetooth devices.

NONREPUDIATION The process that guarantees the data is as originally sent and that it came from the source you think it should have come from.

NORMAL BACKUP A full backup of every selected file on a system. This type of backup turns off the archive bit after the backup.

NOVELL NETWARE A powerful, unique, and once dominant network operating system that operated on a client/server model.

NS (NANOSECOND) A billionth of a second. Light travels a little over 11 inches in 1 ns.

NS RECORDS Records that list the DNS servers for a Web site.

NSLOOKUP A once handy tool that advanced techs used to query the functions of DNS servers. Most DNS servers now ignore all but the most basic nslookup queries.

NTFS (NT FILE SYSTEM) A file system for hard drives that enables object-level security, long filename support, compression, and encryption. NTFS 4.0 debuted with Windows NT 4.0. Windows 2000 offered NTFS 5.0; Windows XP saw the debut of NTFS 5.1. Later Windows versions continued the updates, so Windows Vista uses NTFS 6.0 and Windows 7 uses NTFS 6.1.

NTFS PERMISSIONS Groupings of what Microsoft calls special permissions that have names like Execute, Read, and Write, and that allow or disallow users certain access to files.

NTLDR A Windows NT/2000/XP/2003 boot file. Launched by the MBR or MFT, NTLDR looks at the BOOT.INI configuration file for any installed operating systems.

Object A group of related counters used in Windows logging utilities.

OEM (Original Equipment Manufacturer) Contrary to the name, does not create original hardware, but rather purchases components from manufacturers and puts them together in systems under its own brand name. Dell, Inc. and Gateway, Inc., for example, are for the most part OEMs. Apple, Inc., which manufactures most of the components for its own Macintosh-branded machines, is not an OEM. Also known as *VARs (value-added resellers)*.

Offsite The term for a virtual computer accessed and stored remotely.

Ohm Rating Electronic measurement of a cable's or an electronic component's impedance.

Onsite The term for a virtual computer stored at your location.

Open Port *See* Listening Port.

Open Shortest Path First (OSPF) An interior gateway routing protocol developed for IP networks based on the *shortest path first* or *link-state algorithm*.

Open Source Applications and operating systems that offer access to their source code; this enables developers to modify applications and operating systems easily to meet their specific needs.

Open Systems Interconnection (OSI) An international standard suite of protocols defined by the International Organization for Standardization (ISO) that implements the OSI seven-layer model for network communications between computers.

Open Systems Interconnection (OSI) Seven-Layer Model An architecture model based on the OSI protocol suite, which defines and standardizes the flow of data between computers. The following lists the seven layers:

Layer 1 The *Physical layer* defines hardware connections and turns binary into physical pulses (electrical or light). Repeaters and hubs operate at the Physical layer.
Layer 2 The *Data Link layer* identifies devices on the Physical layer. MAC addresses are part of the Data Link layer. Bridges operate at the Data Link layer.
Layer 3 The *Network layer* moves packets between computers on different networks. Routers operate at the Network layer. IP and IPX operate at the Network layer.

Layer 4 The *Transport layer* breaks data down into manageable chunks. TCP, UDP, SPX, and NetBEUI operate at the Transport layer.
Layer 5 The *Session layer* manages connections between machines. NetBIOS and Sockets operate at the Session layer.
Layer 6 The *Presentation layer*, which can also manage data encryption, hides the differences among various types of computer systems.
Layer 7 The *Application layer* provides tools for programs to use to access the network (and the lower layers). HTTP, FTP, SMTP, and POP3 are all examples of protocols that operate at the Application layer.

OpenSSH A series of secure programs developed by the OpenBSD organization to fix SSH's limitation of only being able to handle one session per tunnel.

Operating System (OS) The set of programming that enables a program to interact with the computer and provides an interface between the PC and the user. Examples are Microsoft Windows 7, Apple Macintosh OS X, and SUSE Linux.

Optical Carrier (OC) Specification used to denote the optical data carrying capacity (in Mbps) of fiber-optic cables in networks conforming to the SONET standard. The OC standard is an escalating series of speeds, designed to meet the needs of medium-to-large corporations. SONET establishes OCs from 51.8 Mbps (OC-1) to 39.8 Gbps (OC-768).

Optical Time Domain Reflectometer (OTDR) Tester for fiber-optic cable that determines continuity and reports the location of cable breaks.

Organizationally Unique Identifier (OUI) The first 24 bits of a MAC address, assigned to the NIC manufacturer by the IEEE.

Orthogonal Frequency-Division Multiplexing (OFDM) A spread-spectrum broadcasting method that combines the multiple frequencies of DSSS with FHSS's hopping capability.

OS (Operating System) *See* Operating System (OS).

Oscilloscope A device that gives a graphical/visual representation of signal levels over a period of time.

Packet Basic component of communication over a network. A group of bits of fixed maximum size and well-defined format that is switched and transmitted as a complete whole through a network. It contains source and destination address, data, and control information. *See also* Frame.

PACKET FILTERING A mechanism that blocks any incoming or outgoing packet from a particular IP address or range of IP addresses. Also known as *IP filtering*.

PACKET SNIFFER A tool that intercepts and logs network packets.

PAD Extra data added to an Ethernet frame to bring the data up to the minimum required size of 64 bytes.

PARTIALLY MESHED TOPOLOGY A mesh topology in which not all of the nodes are directly connected.

PASSIVE OPTICAL NETWORK (PON) A fiber architecture that uses a single fiber to the neighborhood switch and then individual fiber runs to each final destination.

PASSWORD A series of characters that enables a user to gain access to a file, a folder, a PC, or a program.

PASSWORD AUTHENTICATION PROTOCOL (PAP) The oldest and most basic form of authentication and also the least safe because it sends all passwords in cleartext.

PATCH CABLES Short (2 to 5 foot) UTP cables that connect patch panels to the hubs.

PATCH PANEL A panel containing a row of female connectors (ports) that terminate the horizontal cabling in the equipment room. Patch panels facilitate cabling organization and provide protection to horizontal cabling.

PATH MTU DISCOVERY (PMTU) A method for determining the best MTU setting that works by adding a new feature called the "Don't Fragment (DF) flag" to the IP packet.

PBX (PRIVATE BRANCH EXCHANGE) A private phone system used within an organization.

PDA (PERSONAL DIGITAL ASSISTANT) A hand-held computer that blurs the line between the calculator and computer. Earlier PDAs were calculators that enabled the user to program in such information as addresses and appointments. Newer machines, such as the Palm Pilot, are fully programmable computers. Most PDAs use a pen/stylus for input rather than a keyboard. A few of the larger PDAs have a tiny keyboard in addition to the stylus.

PEER-TO-PEER A network in which each machine can act as either a client or a server.

PEER-TO-PEER MODE *See* Ad-Hoc Mode.

PERFORMANCE MONITOR (PERFMON) The Windows XP logging utility.

PERIPHERALS Noncomputer devices on a network, for example, fax machines, printers, or scanners.

PERMISSIONS Sets of attributes that network administrators assign to users and groups that define what they can do to resources.

PERSISTENT CONNECTION A connection to a shared folder or drive that the computer immediately reconnects to at logon.

PERSONAL AREA NETWORK (PAN) The network created among Bluetooth devices such as smartphones, tablets, printers, keyboards, mice, and so on.

PHISHING A social engineering technique where the attacker poses as a trusted source in order to obtain sensitive information.

PHYSICAL ADDRESS An address burned into a ROM chip on a NIC. A MAC address is an example of a physical address.

PHYSICAL LAYER *See* Open Systems Interconnection (OSI) Seven-Layer Model.

PHYSICAL NETWORK DIAGRAM A document that shows all of the physical connections on a network. Cabling type, protocol, and speed are also listed for each connection.

PHYSICAL TOPOLOGY The manner in which the physical components of a network are arranged.

PING (PACKET INTERNET GROPER) A small network message sent by a computer to check for the presence and response of another system. A ping uses ICMP packets. *See* Internet Control Message Protocol (ICMP).

PLAIN OLD TELEPHONE SERVICE (POTS) *See* Public Switched Telephone Network (PSTN).

PLAINTEXT Data that is in an easily read or viewed industry-wide standard format.

PLATFORM Hardware environment that supports the running of a computer system.

PLENUM Usually a space between a building's false ceiling and the floor above it. Most of the wiring for networks is located in this space. Plenum is also a fire rating for network cabling.

POINT COORDINATION FUNCTION (PCF) A method of collision avoidance defined by the 802.11 standard, which has yet to be implemented.

POINT-TO-MULTIPOINT Topology in which one device communicates with more than one other device on a network.

Point-to-Point Protocol (PPP) A protocol that enables a computer to connect to the Internet through a dial-in connection and to enjoy most of the benefits of a direct connection. PPP is considered to be superior to SLIP because of its error detection and data compression features, which SLIP lacks, and the capability to use dynamic IP addresses.

Point-to-Point Protocol over Ethernet (PPPoE) A protocol that was originally designed to encapsulate PPP frames into Ethernet frames. Used by DSL providers to force customers to log into their DSL connections instead of simply connecting automatically.

Point-to-Point Topology A network of two single devices communicating with each other.

Point-to-Point Tunneling Protocol (PPTP) A protocol that works with PPP to provide a secure data link between computers using encryption.

Pointer Record (PTR) A record that points to canonical names. *See also* Reverse Lookup Zone.

Polyvinyl Chloride (PVC) A material used for the outside insulation and jacketing of most cables. Also a fire rating for a type of cable that has no significant fire protection.

Port That portion of a computer through which a peripheral device may communicate. Often identified with the various plug-in jacks on the back of your computer. On a network hub, it is the connector that receives the wire link from a node. In TCP/IP, ports are 16-bit numbers between 0 and 65535 assigned to a particular TCP/IP session.

Port Address Translation (PAT) The most commonly used form of Network Address Translation, where the NAT uses port numbers to map traffic from specific machines in the network. *See* Network Address Translation.

Port Authentication Function of many advanced networking devices that authenticates a connecting device at the point of connection.

Port Blocking Preventing the passage of any TCP or UDP segments or datagrams through any ports other than the ones prescribed by the system administrator.

Port Filtering *See* Port Blocking.

Port Forwarding Preventing the passage of any IP packets through any ports other than the ones prescribed by the system administrator.

Port Mirroring The capability of many advanced switches to mirror data from any or all physical ports on a switch to a single physical port. Useful for any type of situation where an administrator needs to inspect packets coming to or from certain computers.

Port Number Number used to identify the requested service (such as SMTP or FTP) when connecting to a TCP/IP host. Some example port numbers include 80 (HTTP), 20 (FTP), 69 (TFTP), 25 (SMTP), and 110 (POP3).

Post Office Protocol Version 3 (POP3) One of the two protocols that receive e-mail from SMTP servers. POP3 uses TCP port 110. Most e-mail clients use this protocol, although some use IMAP4.

PostScript A language defined by Adobe Systems, Inc., for describing how to create an image on a page. The description is independent of the resolution of the device that will create the image. It includes a technology for defining the shape of a font and creating a raster image at many different resolutions and sizes.

Power over Ethernet (PoE) A standard that enables WAPs to receive their power from the same Ethernet cables that transfer their data.

Power Users A user account that has the capability to do many, but not all, of the basic administrator functions.

PPPoE (PPP over Ethernet) *See* Point-to-Point Protocol over Ethernet (PPPoE).

Preamble A 64-bit series of alternating 1s and 0s, ending with 11, that begins every Ethernet frame. The preamble gives a receiving NIC time to realize a frame is coming and to know exactly where the frame starts.

Presentation Layer *See* Open Systems Interconnection (OSI) Seven-Layer Model.

Primary Lookup Zone A forward lookup zone stored in a text file. *See* Forward Lookup Zone.

Primary Rate Interface (PRI) A type of ISDN that is actually just a full T1 line carrying 23 B channels.

Private Port Numbers *See* Dynamic Port Numbers.

Program A set of actions or instructions that a machine is capable of interpreting and executing. Used as a verb, it means to design, write, and test such instructions.

Promiscuous Mode A mode of operation for a NIC in which the NIC processes all frames that it sees on the cable.

Prompt A character or message provided by an operating system or program to indicate that it is ready to accept input.

PROPRIETARY Term used to describe technology that is unique to, and owned by, a particular vendor.

PROTECTED EXTENSIBLE AUTHENTICATION PROTOCOL (PEAP) An authentication protocol that uses a password function based on MS-CHAPv2 with the addition of an encrypted TLS tunnel similar to EAP-TLS.

PROTOCOL An agreement that governs the procedures used to exchange information between cooperating entities; usually includes how much information is to be sent, how often it is sent, how to recover from transmission errors, and who is to receive the information.

PROTOCOL ANALYZER A tool that monitors the different protocols running at different layers on the network and that can give Application, Session, Network, and Data Link layer information on every frame going through a network.

PROTOCOL STACK The actual software that implements the protocol suite on a particular operating system.

PROTOCOL SUITE A set of protocols that are commonly used together and operate at different levels of the OSI seven-layer model.

PROXY ARP The process of making remotely connected computers act as though they are on the same LAN as local computers.

PROXY SERVER A device that fetches Internet resources for a client without exposing that client directly to the Internet. Most proxy servers accept requests for HTTP, FTP, POP3, and SMTP resources. The proxy server often caches, or stores, a copy of the requested resource for later use.

PSTN (PUBLIC SWITCHED TELEPHONE NETWORK) *See* Public Switched Telephone Network (PSTN).

PUBLIC-KEY CRYPTOGRAPHY A method for exchanging digital keys securely.

PUBLIC-KEY INFRASTRUCTURE (PKI) The system for creating and distributing digital certificates using sites like VeriSign, Thawte, or GoDaddy.

PUBLIC SWITCHED TELEPHONE NETWORK (PSTN) Also known as *Plain Old Telephone Service (POTS)*. The most common type of phone connection, which takes your sounds, translated into an analog waveform by the microphone, and transmits them to another phone.

PUNCHDOWN TOOL A specialized tool for connecting UTP wires to a 110-block.

QUALITY OF SERVICE (QOS) Policies that control how much bandwidth a protocol, PC, user, VLAN, or IP address may use.

RACEWAY Cable organizing device that adheres to walls, making for a much simpler, though less neat, installation than running cables in the walls.

RADIO FREQUENCY INTERFERENCE (RFI) The phenomenon where a Wi-Fi signal is disrupted by a radio signal from another device.

RADIO GRADE (RG) RATINGS Ratings developed by the U.S. military to provide a quick reference for the different types of coaxial cables.

RADIUS SERVER A system that enables remote users to connect to a network service.

REAL-TIME PROCESSING The processing of transactions as they occur, rather than batching them. Pertaining to an application, processing in which response to input is fast enough to affect subsequent inputs and guide the process, and in which records are updated immediately. The lag from input time to output time must be sufficiently small for acceptable timeliness. Timeliness is a function of the total system: missile guidance requires output within a few milliseconds of input, whereas scheduling of steamships requires a response time in days. Real-time systems are those with a response time of milliseconds; interactive systems respond in seconds; and batch systems may respond in hours or days.

REAL-TIME TRANSPORT PROTOCOL (RTP) Protocol that defines the type of packets used on the Internet to move voice or data from a server to clients. The vast majority of VoIP solutions available today use RTP.

REDUNDANT ARRAY OF INDEPENDENT [OR INEXPENSIVE] DEVICES [OR DISKS] (RAID) A way to create a fault-tolerant storage system. RAID has six levels. Level 0 uses byte-level striping and provides no fault tolerance. Level 1 uses mirroring or duplexing. Level 2 uses bit-level striping. Level 3 stores error-correcting information (such as parity) on a separate disk and data striping on the remaining drives. Level 4 is level 3 with block-level striping. Level 5 uses block-level and parity data striping.

REGEDIT.EXE A program used to edit the Windows registry.

REGIONAL INTERNET REGISTRIES (RIRs) Entities under the oversight of the Internet Assigned Numbers Authority (IANA), which parcels out IP addresses.

REGISTERED PORTS Port numbers from 1024 to 49151. Anyone can use these port numbers for their servers or for ephemeral numbers on clients.

REGULATIONS Rules of law or policy that govern behavior in the workplace, such as what to do when a particular event occurs.

REMOTE Refers to the computer(s), server(s), and/or LAN that cannot be physically used due to its distance from the user.

REMOTE ACCESS The capability to access a computer from outside a building in which it is housed. Remote access requires communications hardware, software, and actual physical links.

REMOTE ACCESS SERVER (RAS) Refers to both the hardware component (servers built to handle the unique stresses of a large number of clients calling in) and the software component (programs that work with the operating system to allow remote access to the network) of a remote access solution.

REMOTE AUTHENTICATION DIAL-IN USER SERVICE (RADIUS) An AAA standard created to support ISPs with hundreds if not thousands of modems in hundreds of computers to connect to a single central database. RADIUS consists of three devices: the RADIUS server that has access to a database of user names and passwords, a number of network access servers (NASs) that control the modems, and a group of systems that dial into the network.

REMOTE COPY PROTOCOL (RCP) Provides the capability to copy files to and from the remote server without the need to resort to FTP or Network File System (NFS, a UNIX form of folder sharing). RCP can also be used in scripts and shares TCP port 514 with RSH.

REMOTE DESKTOP PROTOCOL (RDP) A Microsoft-created remote terminal protocol.

REMOTE INSTALLATION SERVICES (RIS) A tool introduced with Windows 2000 that can be used to initiate either a scripted installation or an installation of an image of an operating system onto a PC.

REMOTE LOGIN (RLOGIN) Program in UNIX that enables you to log into a server remotely. Unlike Telnet, rlogin can be configured to log in automatically.

REMOTE SHELL (RSH) Allows you to send single commands to the remote server. Whereas rlogin is designed to be used interactively, RSH can be easily integrated into a script.

REMOTE TERMINAL A connection on a faraway computer that enables you to control that computer as if you were sitting in front of it and logged in. Remote terminal programs all require a server and a client. The server is the computer to be controlled. The client is the computer from which you do the controlling.

REPEATER A device that takes all of the frames it receives on one Ethernet segment and re-creates them on another Ethernet segment. This allows for longer cables or more computers on a segment. Repeaters operate at Layer 1 (Physical) of the OSI seven-layer model.

REPLICATION A process where multiple computers might share complete copies of a database and constantly update each other.

RESISTANCE The tendency for a physical medium to impede electron flow. It is classically measured in a unit called *ohms*. *See also* Impedance.

RESOURCE Anything that exists on another computer that a person wants to use without going to that computer. Also an online information set or an online interactive option. An online library catalog and the local school lunch menu are examples of information sets. Online menus or graphical user interfaces, Internet e-mail, online conferences, Telnet, FTP, and Gopher are examples of interactive options.

REVERSE LOOKUP ZONE A DNS setting that resolves IP addresses to FQDNs. In other words, it does exactly the reverse of what DNS normally accomplishes using forward lookup zones.

RING TOPOLOGY A network topology in which all the computers on the network attach to a central ring of cable.

RIPv1 The first version of RIP, which had several shortcomings, such as a maximum hop count of 15 and a routing table update interval of 30 seconds, which was a problem because every router on a network would send out its table at the same time.

RIPv2 The current version of RIP. Fixed many problems of RIPv1, but the maximum hop count of 15 still applies.

RISER Fire rating that designates the proper cabling to use for vertical runs between floors of a building.

RIVEST CIPHER 4 (RC4) A popular streaming symmetric-key algorithm.

RIVEST SHAMIR ADLEMAN (RSA) An improved public-key cryptography algorithm that enables secure digital signatures.

RJ (REGISTERED JACK) Connectors used for UTP cable on both telephone and network connections.

RJ-11 Type of connector with four-wire UTP connections; usually found in telephone connections.

RJ-45 Type of connector with eight-wire UTP connections; usually found in network connections and used for 10/100/1000BaseT networking.

ROGUE ACCESS POINT An unauthorized wireless access point (WAP) installed in a computer network.

ROLE-BASED ACCESS CONTROL (RBAC) The most popular authentication model used in file sharing, defines a user's access to a resource based on the roles the user plays in the network environment. This leads to the idea of creation of groups. A group in most networks is nothing more than a name that has clearly defined accesses to different resources. User accounts are placed into various groups.

ROM (READ-ONLY MEMORY) The generic term for non-volatile memory that can be read from but not written to. This means that code and data stored in ROM cannot be corrupted by accidental erasure. Additionally, ROM retains its data when power is removed, which makes it the perfect medium for storing BIOS data or information such as scientific constants.

ROOT DIRECTORY The directory that contains all other directories.

ROOTKIT A Trojan that takes advantage of very low-level operating system functions to hide itself from all but the most aggressive of anti-malware tools.

ROUTE A command that enables a user to display and edit the local system's routing table.

ROUTER A device that connects separate networks and forwards a packet from one network to another based only on the network address for the protocol being used. For example, an IP router looks only at the IP network number. Routers operate at Layer 3 (Network) of the OSI seven-layer model.

ROUTING AND REMOTE ACCESS SERVICE (RRAS) A special remote access server program, originally only available on Windows Server, on which a PPTP endpoint is placed in Microsoft networks.

ROUTING INFORMATION PROTOCOL (RIP) Distance vector routing protocol that dates from the 1980s.

ROUTING LOOP A situation where interconnected routers loop traffic, causing the routers to respond slowly or not respond at all.

ROUTING TABLE A list of paths to various networks required by routers. This table can be built either manually or automatically.

RS-232 The recommended standard (RS) upon which all serial communication takes place on a PC.

RUN A single piece of installed horizontal cabling.

SAMBA An application that enables UNIX systems to communicate using Server Message Blocks (SMBs). This, in turn, enables them to act as Microsoft clients and servers on the network.

SC CONNECTOR One of two special types of fiber-optic cable used in 10BaseFL networks.

SCALABILITY The capability to support network growth.

SCANNER A device that senses alterations of light and dark. It enables the user to import photographs, other physical images, and text into the computer in digital form.

SECONDARY LOOKUP ZONE A backup lookup zone stored on another DNS servers. *See also* Forward Lookup Zone.

SECURE COPY PROTOCOL (SCP) One of the first SSH-enabled programs to appear after the introduction of SSH. SCP was one of the first protocols used to transfer data securely between two hosts and thus might have replaced FTP. SCP works well but lacks features such as a directory listing.

SECURE FTP (SFTP) Designed as a replacement for FTP after many of the inadequacies of SCP (such as the inability to see the files on the other computer) were discovered.

SECURE HASH ALGORITHM (SHA) A popular cryptographic hash.

SECURE SHELL (SSH) A terminal emulation program that looks exactly like Telnet but encrypts the data. SSH has replaced Telnet on the Internet.

SECURE SOCKETS LAYER (SSL) A protocol developed by Netscape for transmitting private documents over the Internet. SSL works by using a public key to encrypt sensitive data. This encrypted data is sent over an SSL connection and then decrypted at the receiving end using a private key.

SECURITY A network's resilience against unwanted access or attack.

SECURITY LOG A log that tracks anything that affects security, such as successful and failed logons and logoffs.

SECURITY POLICY A set of procedures defining actions employees should perform to protect the network's security.

SEGMENT The bus cable to which the computers on an Ethernet network connect.

SENDMAIL A popular e-mail server program.

SEQUENTIAL A method of storing and retrieving information that requires data to be written and read sequentially. Accessing any portion of the data requires reading all the preceding data.

Server A computer that shares its resources, such as printers and files, with other computers on the network. An example of this is a Network File System Server that shares its disk space with a workstation that has no disk drive of its own.

Server-Based Network A network in which one or more systems function as dedicated file, print, or application servers, but do not function as clients.

Service Set Identification (SSID) A 32-bit identification string, sometimes called a *network name*, that's inserted into the header of each data packet processed by a wireless access point.

Session A networking term used to refer to the logical stream of data flowing between two programs and being communicated over a network. Many different sessions may be emanating from any one node on a network.

Session Initiation Protocol (SIP) A signaling protocol for controlling voice and video calls over IP. SIP competes with H.323 for VoIP dominance.

Session Layer *See* Open Systems Interconnection (OSI) Seven-Layer Model.

Session Software Handles the process of differentiating among various types of connections on a PC.

Share Level Security A security system in which each resource has a password assigned to it; access to the resource is based on knowing the password.

Share Permissions Permissions that only control the access of other users on the network with whom you share your resource. They have no impact on you (or anyone else) sitting at the computer whose resource is being shared.

Shareware Software that is protected by copyright, but the copyright holder allows (encourages!) you to make and distribute copies, under the condition that those who adopt the software after preview pay a fee. Derivative works are not allowed, and you may make an archival copy.

Shell Generally refers to the user interface of an operating system. A shell is the command processor that is the actual interface between the kernel and the user.

Shielded Twisted Pair (STP) A cabling for networks composed of pairs of wires twisted around each other at specific intervals. The twists serve to reduce interference (also called *crosstalk*). The more twists, the less interference. The cable has metallic shielding to protect the wires from external interference. *See also* Unshielded Twisted Pair (UTP) for the more commonly used cable type in modern networks.

Short Circuit Allows electricity to pass between two conductive elements that weren't designed to interact together. Also called a *short*.

Shortest Path First Networking algorithm for directing router traffic. *See also* Open Shortest Path First (OSPF).

Signal Strength A measurement of how well your wireless device is connecting to other devices.

Signaling Topology Another name for logical topology. *See* Logical Topology.

Simple Mail Transfer Protocol (SMTP) The main protocol used to send electronic mail on the Internet.

Simple Network Management Protocol (SNMP) A set of standards for communication with devices connected to a TCP/IP network. Examples of these devices include routers, hubs, and switches.

Single-Mode Fiber (SMF) Fiber-optic cables that use lasers.

Site Survey A process that enables you to determine any obstacles to creating the wireless network you want.

Site-to-Site A type of VPN connection using two Cisco VPN concentrators to connect two separate LANs permanently.

Small Form Factor (SFF) A description of later-generation, fiber-optic connectors designed to be much smaller than the first iterations of connectors. *See also* LC *and* Mechanical Transfer Registered Jack (MT-RJ).

Small Form Factor Pluggable (SFP) A Cisco module that enables you to add additional features to its routers.

Smart Device Devices (such as credit cards, USB keys, etc.) that you insert into your PC in lieu of entering a password.

Smart Jack Type of NIU that enables ISPs or telephone companies to test for faults in a network, such as disconnections and loopbacks.

SMB (Server Message Block) Protocol used by Microsoft clients and servers to share file and print resources.

Smurf A type of hacking attack in which an attacker floods a network with ping packets sent to the broadcast address. The trick that makes this attack special is that the return address of the pings is spoofed to that of the intended victim. When all the computers on the network respond to the initial ping, they send their response to the intended victim.

Snap-Ins Small utilities that can be used with the Microsoft Management Console.

Snapshot A tool that enables you to save an extra copy of a virtual machine as it is exactly at the moment the snapshot is taken.

Sneakernet Saving a file on a portable medium and walking it over to another computer.

Sniffer Diagnostic program that can order a NIC to run in promiscuous mode. *See* Promiscuous Mode.

Snip *See* Cable Stripper.

Social Engineering The process of using or manipulating people inside the networking environment to gain access to that network from the outside.

Socket A combination of a port number and an IP address that uniquely identifies a connection.

Socket Pairs *See* Endpoints.

Software Programming instructions or data stored on some type of binary storage device.

Solid Core A cable that uses a single solid wire to transmit signals.

SONET (Synchronous Optical Network) A standard for connecting fiber-optic transmission systems. SONET was proposed in the mid-1980s and is now an ANSI standard. SONET defines interface standards at the Physical layer of the OSI seven-layer model.

Source Address Table (SAT) An electronic table of the MAC addresses of each computer connected to a switch.

Spanning Tree Protocol (STP) A protocol that enables switches to detect and repair bridge loops automatically.

Spyware Any program that sends information about your system or your actions over the Internet.

SQL (Structured Query Language) A language created by IBM that relies on simple English statements to perform database queries. SQL enables databases from different manufacturers to be queried using a standard syntax.

SSL (Secure Sockets Layer) *See* Secure Sockets Layer (SSL).

SSL VPN A type of VPN that uses SSL encryption. Clients connect to the VPN server using a standard Web browser, with the traffic secured using SSL. The two most common types of SSL VPNs are SSL portal VPNs and SSL tunnel VPNs.

ST Connector One of two special types of fiber-optic cable used in 10BaseFL networks.

Star Topology A network topology in which all computers in the network connect to a central wiring point.

Star-Bus Topology A hybrid of the star and bus topologies that uses a physical star, where all nodes connect to a single wiring point such as a hub and a logical bus that maintains the Ethernet standards. One benefit of a star-bus topology is *fault tolerance*.

Star-Ring Topology A hybrid of the Token Ring topology and the physical star.

Stateful Describes a DHCPv6 server that works very similarly to an IPv4 DHCP server, passing out IPv6 addresses, subnet masks, and default gateways as well as optional items like DNS server addresses.

Stateful Filtering/Stateful Inspection A method of filtering in which all packets are examined as a stream. Stateful devices can do more than allow or block; they can track when a stream is disrupted or packets get corrupted and act accordingly.

Stateless Describes a DHCPv6 server that only passes out optional information.

Stateless Filtering A method of filtering where the device that does the filtering just checks the packet for IP addresses and port numbers and blocks or allows accordingly.

Static Addressing The process of assigning IP addresses by manually typing them into client computers.

Static NAT (SNAT) A type of NAT that maps a single routable IP address to a single machine, allowing you to access that machine from outside the network.

Static Routing A process by which routers in an internetwork obtain information about paths to other routers. This information must be supplied manually.

Storage A device or medium that can retain data for subsequent retrieval.

STP (Spanning Tree Protocol) *See* Spanning Tree Protocol (STP).

Straight-through Cable A cable that enables you to connect the uplink ports of two hubs together.

Stranded Core A cable that uses a bundle of tiny wire strands to transmit signals. Stranded core is not quite as good a conductor as solid core, but it will stand up to substantial handling without breaking.

Stream Cipher An encryption method that encrypts a single bit at a time. Popular when data comes in long streams (such as with older wireless networks or cell phones).

Stripe Set Two or more drives in a group that are used for a striped volume.

Structured Cabling Standards defined by the Telecommunications Industry Association/Electronic Industries Alliance (TIA/EIA) that define methods of organizing the cables in a network for ease of repair and replacement.

STS Overhead   Carries the signaling and protocol information in Synchronous Transport Signal (STS).

STS Payload   Carries data in STS.

Subnet   Each independent network in a TCP/IP internetwork.

Subnet Mask   The value used in TCP/IP settings to divide the IP address of a host into its component parts: network ID and host ID.

Subnetting   Taking a single class of IP addresses and chopping it into multiple smaller groups.

Supplicant   A client computer in a RADIUS network.

Switch   A device that filters and forwards traffic based on some criteria. A bridge and a router are both examples of switches.

Switching Loop   When you connect multiple switches together to cause a loop to appear.

Symmetric DSL (SDSL)   Type of DSL connection that provides equal upload and download speed and, in theory, provides speeds up to 15 Mbps, although the vast majority of ISPs provide packages ranging from 192 Kbps to 9 Mbps.

Symmetric-Key Algorithm   Any encryption method that uses the same key for both encryption and decryption.

Synchronous   Describes a connection between two electronic devices where neither must acknowledge (ACK) when receiving data.

Synchronous Digital Hierarchy (SDH)   European fiber carrier standard equivalent to SONET.

Synchronous Optical Network (SONET)   American fiber carrier standard. *See also* SONET (Synchronous Optical Network).

Synchronous Transport Signal (STS)   Signal method used by SONET. It consists of the STS payload and the STS overhead. A number is appended to the end of STS to designate signal speed.

System Log   A log file that records issues dealing with the overall system, such as system services, device drivers, or configuration changes.

System Restore   A Windows utility that enables you to return your PC to a recent working configuration when something goes wrong. System Restore returns your computer's system settings to the way they were the last time you remember your system working correctly—all without affecting your personal files or e-mail.

T1   A leased-line connection capable of carrying data at 1,544,000 bps.

T1 Line   The specific, shielded, two-pair cabling that connects the two ends of a T1 connection.

T3 Line   A leased-line connection capable of carrying data at 44,736,000 bps.

TCP Segment   The connection-oriented payload of an IP packet. A TCP segment works on the Transport layer.

TCP/IP Model   An architecture model based on the TCP/IP protocol suite, which defines and standardizes the flow of data between computers. The following lists the four layers:

> **Layer 1**   The *Link layer (Network Interface layer)* is similar to OSI's Data Link and Physical layers. The Link layer consists of any part of the network that deals with frames.
> **Layer 2**   The *Internet layer* is the same as OSI's Network layer. Any part of the network that deals with pure IP packets—getting a packet to its destination—is on the Internet layer.
> **Layer 3**   The *Transport layer* combines the features of OSI's Transport and Session layers. It is concerned with the assembly and disassembly of data, as well as connection-oriented and connectionless communication.
> **Layer 4**   The *Application layer* combines the features of the top three layers of the OSI model. It consists of the processes that applications use to initiate, control, and disconnect from a remote system.

Telecommunications Room   A central location for computer or telephone equipment and, most importantly, centralized cabling. All cables usually run to the telecommunications room from the rest of the installation.

Telephony   The science of converting sound into electrical signals, moving those signals from one location to another, and then converting those signals back into sounds. This includes modems, telephone lines, the telephone system, and any products used to create a remote access link between a remote access client and server.

Telnet   A program that enables users on the Internet to log onto remote systems from their own host systems.

Temperature Monitor   Device for keeping a telecommunications room at an optimal temperature.

Temporal Key Integrity Protocol (TKIP)   The extra layer of security that WPA adds on top of WEP.

Teredo A NAT-traversal IPv6 tunneling protocol, built into Microsoft Windows.

Terminal Access Controller Access Control System Plus (TACACS+) A proprietary protocol developed by Cisco to support AAA in a network with many routers and switches. It is similar to RADIUS in function, but uses TCP port 49 by default and separates authorization, authentication, and accounting into different parts.

Terminal Adapter (TA) The most common interface used to connect a computer to an ISDN line.

Terminal Emulation Software that enables a PC to communicate with another computer or network as if it were a specific type of hardware terminal.

TIA/EIA (Telecommunications Industry Association/ Electronics Industry Association) The standards body that defines most of the standards for computer network cabling. Many of these standards are defined under the TIA/ EIA 568 standard.

TIA/EIA 568A One of two four-pair UTP crimping standards for 10/100/1000BaseT networks. Often shortened to T568A. The other standard is TIA/EIA 568B.

TIA/EIA 568B One of two four-pair UTP crimping standards for 10/100/1000BaseT networks. Often shortened to T568B. The other standard is TIA/EIA 568A.

TIA/EIA 606 Official methodology for labeling patch panels.

Ticket-Granting Ticket (TGT) Sent by an Authentication Server in a Kerberos setup if a client's hash matches its own, signaling that the client is authenticated but not yet authorized.

Time Division Multiplexing (TDM) The process of having frames that carry a bit of every channel in every frame sent at a regular interval in a T1 connection.

Time Domain Reflectometer (TDR) Advanced cable tester that tests the length of cables and their continuity or discontinuity, and identifies the location of any discontinuity due to a bend, break, unwanted crimp, and so on.

Tone Generator *See* Toners.

Tone Probe *See* Toners.

Toners Generic term for two devices used together—a tone generator and a tone locator (probe)—to trace cables by sending an electrical signal along a wire at a particular frequency. The tone locator then emits a sound when it distinguishes that frequency. Also referred to as *Fox and Hound*.

Top-Level Domain Servers A set of DNS servers—just below the root servers—that handle the top-level domain names, such as .com, .org, .net, and so on.

Topology The pattern of interconnections in a communications system among devices, nodes, and associated input and output stations. Also describes how computers connect to each other without regard to how they actually communicate.

tracert (also traceroute) A command-line utility used to follow the path a packet takes between two hosts.

Traffic Analysis Tools that chart a network's traffic usage.

Traffic Shaping Controlling the flow of packets into or out of the network according to the type of packet or other rules.

Transceiver The device that transmits and receives signals on a cable.

Transmission Control Protocol (TCP) Part of the TCP/ IP protocol suite, operates at Layer 4 (Transport) of the OSI seven-layer model. TCP is a connection-oriented protocol.

Transmission Control Protocol/Internet Protocol (TCP/IP) A set of communication protocols developed by the U.S. Department of Defense that enables dissimilar computers to share information over a network.

Transmit Beamforming A multiple-antenna technology in 802.11n WAPs that helps get rid of dead spots.

Transport Layer *See* Open Systems Interconnection (OSI) Seven-Layer Model.

Transport Layer Security (TLS) A robust update to SSL that works with almost any TCP application.

Trivial File Transfer Protocol (TFTP) A protocol that transfers files between servers and clients. Unlike FTP, TFTP requires no user login. Devices that need an operating system, but have no local hard disk (for example, diskless workstations and routers), often use TFTP to download their operating systems.

Trojan A virus that masquerades as a file with a legitimate purpose, so that a user will run it intentionally. The classic example is a file that runs a game, but also causes some type of damage to the player's system.

Trunk Port A port on a switch configured to carry all data, regardless of VLAN number, between all switches in a LAN.

Trunking The process of transferring VLAN data between two or more switches.

TUNNEL An encrypted link between two programs on two separate computers.

TUNNEL BROKER In IPv6, a service that creates the actual tunnel and (usually) offers a custom-made endpoint client for you to use, although more advanced users can often make a manual connection.

TUNNEL INFORMATION AND CONTROL PROTOCOL (TIC) One of the protocols that set up IPv6 tunnels and handle configuration as well as login.

TUNNEL SETUP PROTOCOL (TSP) One of the protocols that set up IPv6 tunnels and handle configuration as well as login.

TWISTED PAIR Twisted pairs of cables, the most overwhelmingly common type of cabling used in networks. The two types of twisted pair cabling are UTP (unshielded twisted pair) and STP (shielded twisted pair). The twists serve to reduce interference, called *crosstalk*; the more twists, the less crosstalk.

TWO-FACTOR AUTHENTICATION A method of security authentication that requires two separate means of authentication, for example, some sort of physical token that, when inserted, prompts for a password.

U (UNITS) The unique height measurement used with equipment racks; 1 U equals 1.75 inches.

UART (UNIVERSAL ASYNCHRONOUS RECEIVER/TRANSMITTER) A device that turns serial data into parallel data. The cornerstone of serial ports and modems.

UDP (USER DATAGRAM PROTOCOL) Part of the TCP/IP protocol suite, a connectionless protocol that is an alternative to TCP.

UDP DATAGRAM A connectionless networking container used in UDP communication.

UNC (UNIVERSAL NAMING CONVENTION) Describes any shared resource in a network using the convention \\<server name>\<name of shared resource>.

UNICAST A message sent from one computer to one other computer.

UNICAST ADDRESS A unique IPv6 address that is exclusive to a system. Link-local addresses are unicast addresses.

UNIFIED COMMUNICATION (UC) A system that rolls many different network services into one, for example, instant messaging (IM), telephone service, video conferencing, and more.

UNINTERRUPTIBLE POWER SUPPLY (UPS) A device that supplies continuous clean power to a computer system the whole time the computer is on. Protects against power outages and sags. The term *UPS* is often used mistakenly when people mean stand-by power supply or system (SPS).

UNIVERSAL ASYNCHRONOUS RECEIVER TRANSMITTER (UART) A device inside a modem that takes the 8-bit-wide digital data and converts it into 1-bit-wide digital data and hands it to the modem for conversion to analog data. The process is reversed for incoming data.

UNIX A popular computer software operating system used on many Internet host systems.

UNSHIELDED TWISTED PAIR (UTP) A popular cabling for telephone and networks composed of pairs of wires twisted around each other at specific intervals. The twists serve to reduce interference (also called *crosstalk*). The more twists, the less interference. The cable has no metallic shielding to protect the wires from external interference, unlike its cousin, *STP*. 10BaseT uses UTP, as do many other networking technologies. UTP is available in a variety of grades, called categories, as defined in the following:

Category 1 UTP Regular analog phone lines, not used for data communications
Category 2 UTP Supports speeds up to 4 Mbps
Category 3 UTP Supports speeds up to 16 Mbps
Category 4 UTP Supports speeds up to 20 Mbps
Category 5 UTP Supports speeds up to 100 Mbps
Category 5e UTP Supports speeds up to 100 Mbps with two pairs and up to 1000 Mbps with four pairs
Category 6 UTP Improved support for speeds up to 10 Gbps
Category 6a UTP Extends the length of 10-Gbps communication to the full 100 meters commonly associated with UTP cabling.

UPLINK PORT Port on a hub that enables you to connect two hubs together using a straight-through cable.

UPLOAD The transfer of information from a user's system to a remote computer system. Opposite of download. *See also* Download.

URL (UNIFORM RESOURCE LOCATOR) An address that defines the type and the location of a resource on the Internet. URLs are used in almost every TCP/IP application. A typical HTTP URL is http://www.totalsem.com.

USENET The network of UNIX users, generally perceived as informal and made up of loosely coupled nodes, that exchanges mail and messages. Started by Duke University and UNC–Chapel Hill. An information cooperative linking around 16,000 computer sites and millions of people.

Usenet provides a series of "news groups" analogous to online conferences.

USER Anyone who uses a computer. You.

USER ACCOUNT A container that identifies a user to the application, operating system, or network, including name, password, user name, groups to which the user belongs, and other information based on the user and the OS or NOS being used. Usually defines the rights and roles a user plays on a system.

USER DATAGRAM PROTOCOL (UDP) A protocol used by some older applications, most prominently TFTP (Trivial FTP), to transfer files. UDP datagrams are both simpler and smaller than TCP segments, and they do most of the behind-the-scenes work in a TCP/IP network.

USER-LEVEL SECURITY A security system in which each user has an account, and access to resources is based on user identity.

USER PROFILES A collection of settings that corresponds to a specific user account and may follow the user, regardless of the computer at which he or she logs on. These settings enable the user to have customized environment and security settings.

V STANDARDS Standards established by CCITT for modem manufacturers to follow (voluntarily) to ensure compatible speeds, compression, and error correction.

V.92 STANDARD The current modem standard, which has a download speed of 57,600 bps and an upload speed of 48 Kbps. V.92 modems have several interesting features, such as Quick Connect and Modem on Hold.

VERTICAL CROSS-CONNECT Main patch panel in a telecommunications room. *See also* Patch Panel.

VERY HIGH BITRATE DSL (VDSL) The latest form of DSL with download and upload speeds of up to 100 Mbps. VDSL was designed to run on copper phone lines, but many VDSL suppliers use fiber-optic cabling to increase effective distances.

VIEW The different displays found in Performance Monitor.

VIRTUAL LOCAL AREA NETWORK (VLAN) A LAN that, using VLAN-capable switches, places some (or any on the more expensive VLANs) systems on virtual broadcast domains.

VIRTUAL MACHINE (VM) A virtual computer accessed through a class of program called a hypervisor or virtual machine manager. A virtual machine runs *inside* your actual operating system, essentially enabling you to run two or more operating systems at once.

VIRTUAL MACHINE MANAGER (VMM) *See* Hypervisor.

VIRTUAL PBX Software that functionally replaces a physical PBX telephone system.

VIRTUAL PRIVATE NETWORK (VPN) A network configuration that enables a remote user to access a private network via the Internet. VPNs employ an encryption methodology called *tunneling*, which protects the data from interception.

VIRTUAL SWITCH Special software that enables VMs to communicate with each other without going outside of the host system.

VIRTUAL TRUNK PROTOCOL (VTP) A proprietary Cisco protocol to automate the updating of multiple VLAN switches.

VIRUS A program that can make a copy of itself without you necessarily being aware of it. Some viruses can destroy or damage files, and generally the best protection is always to maintain backups of your files.

VIRUS DEFINITION OR DATA FILES Enables the virus protection software to recognize the viruses on your system and clean them. These files should be updated often. Also called *signature files*, depending on the virus protection software in use.

VOICE OVER IP (VoIP) Using an IP network to transfer voice calls.

VOLTAGE The pressure of the electrons passing through a wire.

VOLTAGE EVENT RECORDER Tracks voltage over time by plugging into a power outlet.

VOLTS (V) Units of measurement for voltage.

VPN CONCENTRATOR The new endpoint of the local LAN in L2TP.

VULNERABILITY SCANNER A tool that scans a network for potential attack vectors.

WAN (WIDE AREA NETWORK) A geographically dispersed network created by linking various computers and LANs over long distances, generally using leased phone lines. There is no firm dividing line between a WAN and a LAN.

WARM BOOT A system restart performed after the system has been powered and operating. This clears and resets the memory, but does not stop and start the hard drive.

WATTAGE (WATTS OR W) The amount of amps and volts needed by a particular device to function.

Web Server A server that enables access to HTML documents by remote users.

Well-Known Port Numbers Port numbers from 0 to 1204 that are used primarily by client applications to talk to server applications in TCP/IP networks.

Wi-Fi The most widely adopted wireless networking type in use today. Technically, only wireless devices that conform to the extended versions of the 802.11 standard—802.11a, 802.11b, and 802.11g—are Wi-Fi certified.

Wi-Fi Protected Access (WPA) A wireless security protocol that addresses the weaknesses and acts as a sort of upgrade to WEP. WPA offers security enhancements such as dynamic encryption key generation (keys are issued on a per-user and per-session basis), an encryption key integrity-checking feature, user authentication through the industry-standard Extensible Authentication Protocol (EAP), and other advanced features that WEP lacks.

Wi-Fi Protected Access 2 (WPA2) An update to the WPA protocol that uses the Advanced Encryption Standard algorithm, making it much harder to crack.

WiMax *See* 802.16.

Windows Domain A group of computers controlled by a computer running Windows Server, which is configured as a domain controller.

Windows Firewall The firewall that has been included in Windows operating systems since Windows XP; originally named Internet Connection Firewall (ICF) but renamed in XP Service Pack 2.

Windows Internet Name Service (WINS) A name resolution service that resolves NetBIOS names to IP addresses.

winipcfg A graphical program used on Windows 95, Windows 98, and Windows Me machines to display the current TCP/IP configuration of the machine; similar to more modern Windows's ipconfig and UNIX/ Linux's ifconfig.

WINS Proxy Agent A WINS relay agent that forwards WINS broadcasts to a WINS server on the other side of a router to keep older systems from broadcasting in place of registering with the server.

Wire Scheme *See* Wiring Diagram.

Wired Equivalent Privacy (WEP) A wireless security protocol that uses a 64-bit encryption algorithm to scramble data packets.

Wireless Access Point (WAP) Connects wireless network nodes to wireless or wired networks. Many WAPs are combination devices that act as high-speed hubs, switches, bridges, and routers, all rolled into one.

Wireless Bridge Device used to connect two wireless network segments together, or to join wireless and wired networks together in the same way that wired bridge devices do.

Wireless Network *See* Wi-Fi.

Wiremap Term that techs use to refer to the proper connectivity of wires in a network.

Wireshark A popular packet sniffer.

Wiring Diagram A document, also known as a *wiring schematic*, that usually consists of multiple pages and that shows the following: how the wires in a network connect to switches and other nodes, what types of cables are used, and how patch panels are configured. It usually includes details about each cable run.

Wiring Schematic *See* Wiring Diagram.

Work Area In a basic structured cabling network, often simply an office or cubicle that potentially contains a PC attached to the network.

Workgroup A convenient method of organizing computers under Network/My Network Places in Windows operating systems.

Workstation A general-purpose computer that is small enough and inexpensive enough to reside at a person's work area for his or her exclusive use.

Worm A very special form of virus. Unlike other viruses, a worm does not infect other files on the computer. Instead, it replicates by making copies of itself on other systems on a network by taking advantage of security weaknesses in networking protocols.

WPA2-Enterprise A version of WPA2 that uses a RADIUS server for authentication.

WWW (World Wide Web) The (graphical) Internet that can be accessed using Gopher, FTP, HTTP, Telnet, Usenet, WAIS, and some other tools.

X.25 The first generation of packet-switching technology, enables remote devices to communicate with each other across high-speed digital links without the expense of individual leased lines.

Yost Cable Cable used to interface with a Cisco device.

Zombie A single computer under the control of an operator that is used in a botnet attack. *See also* Botnet.

Index

Numbers